Great Power Intervention in the Middle East
(Pergamon Policy Studies-27)

Pergamon Titles of Related Interest

PERGAMON POLICY STUDIES ON INTERNATIONAL POLITICS

Great Power Intervention in the Middle East

Edited by
**Milton Leitenberg
Gabriel Sheffer**

Pergamon Press

NEW YORK • OXFORD • TORONTO • SYDNEY • FRANKFURT • PARIS

Pergamon Press Offices:

U.S.A.   Pergamon Press Inc., Maxwell House, Fairview Park,
                         Elmsford, New York 10523, U.S.A.

U.K.   Pergamon Press Ltd., Headington Hill Hall,
                         Oxford OX3 0BW, England

CANADA   Pergamon of Canada, Ltd., 150 Consumers Road,
                         Willowdale, Ontario M2J, 1P9, Canada

AUSTRALIA   Pergamon Press (Aust) Pty. Ltd., P O Box 544,
                         Potts Point, NSW 2011, Australia

FRANCE   Pergamon Press SARL, 24 rue des Ecoles,
                         75240 Paris, Cedex 05, France

FEDERAL REPUBLIC   Pergamon Press GmbH, 6242 Kronberg/Taunus,
OF GERMANY   Pferdstrasse 1, Federal Republic of Germany

Copyright © 1979 Pergamon Press Inc.

Library of Congress Cataloging in Publication Data
Main entry under title: 327.09
                                            G786
Great power intervention in the Middle East.

    (Pergamon policy studies)
    "Papers...prepared for a conference held by
the Cornell University Peace Studies Program in
April 1977."
    Includes index.
    1. Near East—Politics and government—
1945-   —Congresses. 2. Near East—Relations
(Military) with the United States—Congresses.
3. United States—Relations (Military) with the
Near East—Congresses. 4. Near East—Relations
(Military) with Europe—Congresses. 5. Europe—
Relations (Military) with the Near East—Congresses.
6. Near East—Defenses—Congresses.
I. Leitenberg, Milton. II. Sheffer, Gabriel.
III. Cornell University. Peace Studies Program.
DS63.1.G73   1979   327'.0956   79-341
ISBN 0-08-023867-X

Printed in the United States of America

Contents

Preface

The papers presented in this book were commissioned for a conference held by the Cornell University Peace Studies Program in April 1977. While most of the papers have been revised to varying degrees since then, no effort was made by the editors to bring any of the papers into line with a common view. The sole concern was to develop information and analysis concerning the differing forms of great power intervention in the Middle East, particularly those with some relevance to military activities. In addition, due to the very significant diplomatic developments that occurred in Middle East politics in late 1977 and in 1978, two additional papers were commissioned for the book to cover the events of this period.

The Cornell University Peace Studies Program is committed to research and teaching on the moderation or prevention of war. The Conference on "Great Power Intervention in the Middle East" was the third conference sponsored by the Program, having been preceded in previous years by conferences on nuclear proliferation and on problems on naval armaments.

The conference was supported by a grant from the Ford Foundation, to which we extend our appreciation. We should also like to indicate our particular thanks to the Cochairmen of the Peace Studies Program, Dr. Franklin Long and Dr. George Quester; the Program's secretary, Deborah Ostrander; and our editor who worked hardest and longest on the book, Nicole Ball.

Milton Leitenberg

Gabriel Sheffer

Introduction
Gabriel Sheffer
Milton Leitenberg

The purpose of this introduction is twofold. First, it attempts to put the question of intervention by the great powers in Middle Eastern affairs in proper perspective. It is argued here that this issue should be examined in the wider context of great-power involvement in less-developed countries (LDCs) after World War II. It is also suggested that the intervention of the great powers in the Middle East stems only in part from the existence and endurance of the Arab-Israeli conflict. The second purpose of this introduction is to outline the organization of the volume and the contents of its various chapters.

POST-WORLD WAR II DEVELOPMENTS AND THE ARAB-ISRAELI CONFLICT

Like other less-developed states established after World War II, most Middle Eastern countries face a multitude of severe problems. Both the poorer countries in the core Middle East (Lebanon, Syria, Jordan, Egypt, and Israel), and the richer countries on the region's peripheries (Iraq, Iran, Saudi Arabia, Libya, and Algeria) are still far from either achieving "the good society" or guaranteeing it for their citizens. Despite certain inevitable differences, all these countries face the tremendous cultural, social, economic, and political tensions that accompany the processes of belated modernization. In some of these Arab states, the process of modernization started a few decades ago, but has not yet ended; in others, it has started only recently and is the cause of great domestic political pressures and social unrest.

Paradoxically, the most serious modernization problems are the scarcity of natural and manpower resources, and the abundance of financial means. The majority of these countries lack modern infrastructure such as transportation, communications, trained manpower, and equipment. One of the most important results of this unstable and rapidly changing process has been the dependence of the regional states on extraregional powers. In addition, the tensions that these countries face are partly generated by a fundamental sociocultural factor which has far-reaching political ramifications. This factor is Arab and Islamic traditionalism. While traditionalism has contributed to a certain degree of cohesion, both within each of the Arab countries in the Middle East and among these countries, it also has exacerbated historical feuds and enhanced disagreement.

Although the Arab-Israeli conflict may not be the most profound issue either in regional politics or in the domestic affairs of most Middle Eastern countries, maximum attention has been given to it by those outside the region. There are several reasons why this has been so. First, the great powers have regarded this region as a sensitive spot, which can easily explode and probably trigger a comprehensive war involving the superpowers. Second, in the past, episodes of fighting have threatened the production and export of oil which has become vital to Western economies. These wars have also hampered free navigation of the Suez Canal. Third, since both sides to the conflict, the Arabs and the Israelis, have ethnically related population centers throughout the world, in certain cases their regional conflict has turned into an internal issue for the great powers. Most notably, this has been the case with the Jewish community in the United States and the Moslem minority in the Soviet Union. Finally, this regional conflict has acquired unique features which have served to differentiate it from other international conflicts in the period following World War II.

This uniqueness was maintained up to the 1973 War and stemmed from the way in which a number of factors combined and the intensity with which they did so. The Arab-Israeli confrontation has become the most enduring of modern conflicts. It has a large number of direct and indirect regional and international participants, and the issues involved have become multidimensional. Furthermore, the conflict's violent outbursts, i.e., the four Middle Eastern wars since the end of WWII, have exhibited certain recurring patterns.

The Endurance of the Conflict

The roots of the conflict were discernible at the turn of the last century. As recent research has shown, the conflict started with the simultaneous emergence of modern Jewish and Arab-Palestinian nationalism and the attendant appearance of organized political movements. The two embryonic national movements made initial progress in their struggle for political influence during the period when Turkey ruled Palestine. Each aimed at achieving Ottomon political support for its own movement. Britain's occupation of Palestine and its 1917 recognition of the right of the Jews to a national homeland there institutionalized the conflict. Until World War II, the conflict was largely confined to the boundaries of Palestine under the British mandate, but it continually intensified for various historical and political reasons, Arab Palestinians have participated only marginally in the main events since World War II. In the 1948, 1956, and 1967 wars, the main actors were the Arab states. Only in the wake of the 1967 War did the Palestinian Arab issue reemerge. Since then, the conflict has proceeded on two interconnected levels: Palestinian Arabs versus Israelis, and Israel versus the Arab states. These levels have become enmeshed beyond any easy separation.

Until now, the Arab-Israeli confrontation has been perceived by all participants as an endless conflict. Both the parties directly involved and outside observers have argued that the sheer duration of the conflict has contributed to the psychological difficulties involved in its solution. Only the 1977 visit of President Sadat to Jerusalem served to create some hope that a more stable and permanent solution could be found in the foreseeable future. This visit has created a new tempo in developments in the regional system.

Complexity

With the passage of time, new actors have been added to the Middle Eastern imbroglio, and others have lost either the interest or the capability to intervene in the conflict. This is true not only for regional actors, but particularly for international participants. It is interesting to note two facts in connection with the regional participants. The first is the growing interest of Arab countries on the peripheries of the conflict. Recently, countries like Morocco, Tunisia, Libya, Saudi Arabia, and Kuwait have intervened actively at various junctures. Secondly, the increased number of interested Arab states and the diversity of their attitudes toward the direct participants in the conflict have enhanced the importance of the coalition factor in regional developments isnce the end of World War II. This aspect was highlighted in the 1973 War when a prearranged coalition between Egypt and Syria, which had obtained the implicit blessing of Saudi Arabia, succeeded in launching a surprise attack on Israel. This coalition, however, encountered difficulties and disagreements in the wake of that war and experienced even more pronounced rifts in 1977.

The establishment and breakdown of coalitions, both in the Arab world and among Israel and its various historical partners, have acquired great importance in Israeli strategic calculations. Immediately after the establishment of Israel, the United States was its main supporter. In the 1950's and early 1960's, while Israel received some United States support, France became Israel's main patron. During the later stages of the conflict, and especially after the 1967 War when it became clear that France preferred to form a loose coalition with the Arabs and to grant them continuous political support, the United States once again became Israel's main friend. In the meantime, partly as a function of the endurance of the conflict and partly as a result of changing power ratios among Israel and the Arab states, other Western powers changed partners in the Middle Eastern minuet. During the early 1950s, for example, Great Britain, once the major power in the region, shifted its allegiance away from the Arabs and consequently, lost its influence. Recently, however, Great Britain has tended to support the Arab cause.

The Soviet presence and the fate of its alliances with regional powers is a further example of changes in the fortunes of superpowers in the Middle East. After elaborate and costly efforts to penetrate the region, in the 1960s the Soviet Union found itself in a close coalition with the larger Arab countries in the core area: Egypt, Syria, and Iraq. Gradually, the Soviet Union became the supreme patron of these states. However, since the late 1960s, the Soviet Union has lost much of its position in the area. Its influence has been eradicated in Egypt and has been considerably reduced in Syria and Iraq.

Multidimensionality of the Issues Involved in the Conflict

Both the endurance and the complexity of the conflict are connected to the multidimensionality of its main issues. Since its inception, when it was strictly confined to the Palestinian participants, the conflict has transcended such material interests as territory, water resources, borders, land and sea passages, markets, and competing labor forces. While there is no question that such material interests are important components of this conflict, other more abstract, but not less tangible, factors also profoundly affect the behavior of the various regional actors. These factors are cultural aspects and deep emotions. President Sadat, for example, stated during his November 1977 visit to Jerusalem that emotions and psychological factors have accounted for 70 percent of the conflict, while the remaining 30 percent were sheer material interests. This estimate is indicative of perceptions not only on the Arab but also on the Israeli side. There is no doubt that in order to terminate the conflict the two sides must overcome such emotions.

In addition, a cultural gap has existed between the two sides to the conflict. Israel can be characterized as a heterogeneous, rather industrially developed, secular, pro-Western society. The Arab societies can be characterized as relatively culturally homogeneous, agriculturally developing, traditional, and moderately pro-Western. These differences have intensified the conflict, added complexity to the issues involved, and increased the obstacles to its resolution.

Recurring Patterns of Behavior in the Conflict

The most obvious of these patterns is the inability to solve the conflict through peaceful means, which has let to the periodic outbreak of war. The four wars in the Middle East have shown that there is no possibility of a decisive military victory which would clearly determine the winners and losers for any relatively long period of time. This is so for two primary reasons. The first derives from the superpowers' potential and active intervention to terminate war when it reaches a critical stage. The second is that Israel, which until recently has had the upper hand from a military point of view, could not afford to enter the capitals of the Arab countries. Therefore, neither side could impose its conditions for peace, and Israel has been able to maintain the status quo for only brief periods.

The second recurring pattern has been the need for massive coalitions on both sides as a prerequisite for starting military campaigns and diplomatic moves toward a solution.

The third pattern has been the acute need of the regional powers for military resupply, which was evident during the last two wars of 1967 and 1973 and immediately thereafter. This need, of course, puts additional pressure on the decision makers in the region and enhanced the dependence of regional states on the supplying superpowers.

The fourth pattern has been that the actual decisions to launch the four Middle Eastern wars and the selection of their military and political targets were made by the regional powers independent of their superpower patrons. These wars have ended by cease fire agreements and temporary, partial solutions of one kind or another. Seldom, however, have these cease fire agreements been maintained for very long. Similarly, decisions to enter serious discussions concerning either partial solutions or more comprehensive peace negotiations have also been undertaken in Middle Eastern capitals rather than in any foreign center.

THE IMPACT OF THE 1973 WAR

Many of the seemingly stable structures of the Middle Eastern conflict system, as well as its main patterns of behavior, were drastically altered by the 1973 War. Three levels of interaction will be concentrated upon here: internal developments in the main participant states, developments at the regional level, and developments both in the relationships among the great powers themselves and among the great powers and the Middle Eastern states involved in the conflict.

Possibly for the first time in the post-1948 history of the Arab-Israeli conflict, the Arab states regained their military honor by initiating the war. Also, through their initial successes on the battlefield, Egypt and Syria fulfilled their main political goal, which was to create a political and diplomatic momentum after six years of stalemate in the region.

The 1973 War produced particularly devastating results for Israel's international relations. Not surprisingly, the war came at a period in which Israel found itself extremely isolated from its former Asian, African, and European friends. The fact that Israel had maintained close ties with the United States created the background for many American attempts at intervention. These interventions, planned and carried out by United States Secretary of State Henry Kissinger, contributed to the emergence of a new feature of the conflict, i.e. interim, partial agreements which were intended to transform the conflict and lead toward a more permanent solution.

The 1973 War created a new political situation within Israel. There is now no doubt that the consequences of the war, particularly the perception of Israeli debacles during the initial stages, contributed to the results of the 1977 general election. That election, in turn, brought about the end of 40 years of Labor movement hegemony in Israeli politics and established a new domestic coalition composed of traditionalist, rightist, nationalist, and liberal parties. This coalition controls a sizable majority in the Israeli Parliament and, therefore, displays considerable freedom of action, especially in economic and foreign affairs. Despite the fact that the 1977 election caused the formation of a stable government based on a large coalition, however, the main domestic issues are still far from resolved. Even when the country's attention was focused on the process initiated by President Sadat's 1977 visit to Israel, one could not escape the feeling that Israel had entered a period of domestic political instability.

On the other hand, in the Arab confrontation states the war served to strengthen the various regimes and the positions of their heads of state. This occurred because these leaders were regarded with novel esteem as the successful planners and implementors of the 1973 War and were credited with obtaining its main political and military objectives. At the same time, the war magnified some of the basic, chronic problems facing the Middle Eastern Arab countries. It emphasized their relative and absolute shortage of manpower, their inability to use initial military successes, and their strong dependence on financial and military aid granted either by richer Arab countries or by the great powers.

The cumulative changes that occurred in the domestic and international positions of the regional participants also caused some profound changes in the structure of the conflict system. These led to the separate negotiations which were conducted immediately after the 1973 War and which resulted in the 1974 Separation of Forces and the 1975 Interim Agreement. In turn, as President Sadat has stated, these interim agreements supplied the background for the 1977 peace initiatives.

The 1973 War also had far-reaching consequences for each of the superpowers, especially in their relations with their respective clients in the Middle East. Although both Israel and the main Arab states remained dependent on their patrons in the period following the 1973 War, there were many indications that they would try to enhance their autonomy. This was especially true as far as Egypt was concerned. Apparently, the simple but extremely important notion that war and peace should be and would be determined by the regional powers alone became clear to the leaders on both sides.

Consequently, even during the most difficult stages of the negotiations after the 1973 War, Egypt, Syria, and Israel demonstrated their resolution to shape their own fate. The various interim agreements were achieved as a result of a convergence of interests among Israel and its immediate neighbors. The superpowers' political role has been gradually reduced to that of brokers, sources for various kinds of aid, and as an ultimate recourse for military security when military operations turn out poorly.

An additional new and major factor, unrelated to the Middle East conflict but coincidentally occurring in the early and mid-1970s, was the growing dependence and interest of both the Soviet Union and the United States in oil, which resulted in a change in their relations with the rich Middle Eastern states. Oil and petrodollars have acquired a new dimension and have propelled new regional powers, such as Saudi Arabia and Kuwait, into positions of great importance both regionally and globally.

SOME ENDURING DILEMMAS

Despite the profound changes in the conflict which followed the 1973 War, there are still some dilemmas which must be confronted if a more permanent regional stability is to be attained. For the purposes of clarity, these persistent issues are presented here as three pairs.

The first pair of crucial issues facing the two sides is that of the formal recognition of Israel versus agreements to end belligerency. Israel has always claimed that in order to terminate the conflict the Arab countries should formally recognize its national rights, and that this recognition and subsequent normalization of relations should be included in the final peace treaties. The Arabs, however, have been ready to grant Israel only de facto recognition through a nonbelligerency agreement. In fact, this has been one of the main issues during the negotiations that began after Sadat's November 1977 visit to Israel.

The second pair of enduring issues also concerns attitudes held by the regional, i.e., their asymmetrical attitudes towards security and territories. After 1967, Israeli governments showed no intention of giving up territories that they had occupied in the 1967 War until the problem of security was solved to their complete satisfaction. However, the Arab states demanded a complete and unconditional Israeli withdrawal from these territories. The more extremist Arab countries and the Palestine Liberation Organization, PLO, called either for the disintegration of the Jewish state or for an Israeli withdrawal to the boundaries proposed in 1947. This pair of issues is not amenable to any easy solution.(1) Israeli government policy on the settlements in the occupied West Bank and Sinai after 1967 did not promise any intention of total withdrawal. The question of a Palestinian state and Palestinian self-determination depended on Israeli withdrawal from the occupied territories. Instead, Israel spoke of its security requirements, implying the need to expand its borders. The boundary revision which gave Israel the greatest sense of security in military and geographic terms was not one acceptable to Israel's neighbors, from which the territory would come. There seems little hope for peace of any sort for more than a few years at a time unless Israel withdraws from the greatest part of the occupied territories. Time and the passage of years will not work to Israel's advantage. It was necessary for Israel to demonstrate far more accommodation on these issues than it had ever done before. The Israeli government has shown a constant fear that the United States would apply pressure on these issues. At the moment of writing, the Camp David Summit of Presidents Carter and Sadat and Prime Minister Begin is taking place. It will test both the willingness of at least some of the parties to the conflict to come to an accommodation and the degree to which the United States is willing to apply pressure on one of the parties to do so.

The third pair of enduring dilemmas concerns the methods of reaching a stable solution. Here the choice is between piecemeal and comprehensive solutions. Until the 1973 War, both Israelis and Arabs talked only in terms of comprehensive solutions which generated great difficulties in finding even the proper formula for simply conducting the negotiations.   Among other things, the 1973 War created a new readiness on the part of both sides to accept interim and partial solutions which, it was hoped, could lead to a more comprehensive and lasting solution.   The 1974 Separation of Forces between Israel and Syria and Egypt, as well as the 1975 Interim Agreement with Egypt, clearly signified this change. It is still too early to determine whether these agreements have indeed paved the way to more comprehensive solutions or if they simply have enabled Israel to maintain more or less the status quo on the outstanding issues. Nevertheless, they did lead to Sadat's historic visit to Jerusalem and the ensuing Israeli-Arab negotiations.

Based on the history of step-by-step solutions and partial or interim agreements in post-World War II aims negotiations, the prognosis for these types of agreements is very poor. Each progressive step gets smaller and the basic issues are rarely touched. The critical question in a step-by-step process is whether <u>both</u> sides have the intention and the goal of making a major alteration in the situation towards the same end.

Related to the choice of methods for reaching an agreement is the question of whether the regional states have both the political readiness and the ability to reach more comprehensive solutions. The alternatives to these are the various kinds of pressure that can be applied by the superpowers jointly or separately. In this volume, this issue is referred to as the dilemma of an imposed solution versus solutions arrived at regionally. In essence, this issue is part of a much wider and more general set of questions, which are the prime concern of the present volume: the dependence of the regional powers on the superpowers, and the interests and mode of intervention and penetration of great powers into the Middle East. Even if the Arab-Israeli conflict were to be resolved, the great powers would very likely still be both interested and present in the area.

THE DEPENDENCE ON THE GREAT POWERS

For two main reasons, the superpowers have played an extremely important role in the history of the modern Middle East in general and in the Arab-Israeli conflict in particular. The first reason is historical. Since the nineteenth century, the region has been a constant target for the expansion of new European empires. The powers always regarded it as geostrategically and geopolitically important. Later, the great powers became interested in the oil which was discovered in significant quantities in the 1930s. Pre-World War II colonial traditions prepared the ground for the post-1945 intervention of the superpowers. After World War II, the superpowers were anxious not to leave a vacuum in any part of the globe, and, of course, particularly not in the Middle

East. Thus, when it became clear that Britain's hegemony in the region was approaching its end, the new superpowers were already competing for influence within the region.

In recent years, the presence of the superpowers in the region has been connected to a second factor, i.e., the need on the part of the regional states for various types of aid that only the superpowers can supply. The lack of an acceptable alternative source of aid stems from the fact that most of the resources needed for the processes of modernization in the regional states can only be acquired either directly from the superpowers or from other great powers with the approval of the superpowers. The recent moves made by the two sides to the Arab-Israeli conflict indicate that the leaders in the region are well aware of their dilemma. Their immediate problem is how to maintain their autonomy, yet obtain sufficient support from the superpowers.

The purpose of this volume is to elaborate on some of these issues. A reconsideration of these questions is particularly important on the eve of what seems to be a new epoch in the region and in the Arab-Israeli conflict. The special contribution of this volume is in its attempt to put these questions regarding the Middle East in a somewhat wider context.

THE ORGANIZATION OF THE VOLUME
AND THE NATURE OF ITS CHAPTERS

When commissioning the various papers for this volume, we felt that although the Arab-Israeli conflict and the role of the great powers in it have been the subject of many books and articles, there was, nevertheless, the need for a volume which would concentrate in a particular manner on certain issues which have not been sufficiently studied. We felt that the treatment of these issues should be analytical, comparative, and written from the perspective of the general phenomenon of great power intervention in developing countries. In addition, when commissioning the papers, we emphasized that they should be empirical rather than speculative.

We have limited the scope of the book to particular aspects of great power direct and indirect military intervention. The book opens with a discussion of the general problem of great power intervention in the Middle East in the post-World War II era. The second aspect treated is the export of nuclear power reactors to Middle Eastern nations and the possibility of the development of nuclear weapons by various states in the region. The third issue is the supply of conventional arms to Middle Eastern states by the great powers. A distinction is made between the policies of the patron, arms-supplier states and those of the recipients. The fourth issue involves the economic ramifications of weapons supplies, both for the great powers and for the regional states. An effort is then made to draw together and evaluate the impacts of these different factors. The final section assesses the possible roles of the great powers in an eventual settlement of the Middle Eastern conflict in view of the various forms which their involvement in the region has taken.

The opening paper by Yair Evron deals with great power intervention in the Middle East. His discussion is limited to military intervention in the domestic affairs or in the external behavior of Middle Eastern states between the end of World War II and 1973.

The second section of the book, which deals with the possibility of the "nuclearization" of the region, includes two papers. Steven Baker deals with great power nonproliferation policies toward the third world, with particular reference to the Middle East and the Persian Gulf. He argues that the goal of nonproliferation in these areas must be to keep some countries from acquiring nuclear weapons while preventing one country, Israel, from using them. The policies of the great powerss since the end of World War II have helped to create a difficult situation in this respect. The question is now whether the new policies of the great powers can prevent a bad situation from becoming even worse. The second paper, by Paul Jabber, highlights the possible acquisition of infrastructure and facilities by Arab states over the next dozen years, which would make the production of nuclear weapons possible. The major emphasis is on plutonium acquisition, and Jabber's projections are based exclusively on officially announced transactions, negotiations, and future plans.

The third section of the book, on conventional arms supplies, contains seven papers. Anne Cahn deals with United States arms supplies to the Middle East during the ten year period, 1967 through 1976. The main thesis of this paper is that the outpouring of military goods and services has in good measure been undertaken in pursuit of a myth, i.e., that military assistance is the most appropriate, efficient, or easiest way of implementing United States foreign policy objectives. Roger Pajak describes the Middle Eastern arms transfer policies of the major West European suppliers and of the Soviet Union. He briefly delineates the magnitude and direction of this trade, particularly over the past decade. He states that arms transfers to the Middle East and the Persian Gulf have far surpassed those to other developing areas of the world both in value and in quantity, with the notable exception of shipments to Southeast Asia during the Indochina War. Robert Harkavy discusses the development of overseas military basing systems and their relationship to arms transfers to LDCs. He sets the historical perspective for this phenomenon. The discussion is pursued on two levels. The first is that of the changing significance and mix of different types of strategic access. The second is broad, long-range structural and behavioral alterations in the international system. This paper attempts to weave these factors together to provide a context for analyzing the relationships between bases and arms transfers. James Foster discusses the potential effects of the introduction of advanced conventional munitions such as precision-guided munitions, both anti-tank and antiaircraft, into conflicts in third world areas. Such munitions have already made their appearance in the Middle East via arms transfers. The considerations dealt with in the paper concern the effects on battlefield interactions between two third-world nations, as well as between such a smaller nation and any one of the great powers.

This section continues with the economic effects of arms transfer on the great powers and on the regional participants to the conflict. Mary Kaldor writes about the short-term economic benefits from arms sales to the Middle East and the connection between arms exports, arms costs, and economic recession. The first part of her paper describes the various types of economic benefits conferred on Western suppliers by arms exports and how these have recently changed. The second part links changes in the West to certain developments in the Soviet Union. The last part of Kaldor's paper sketches some policy implications arising out of her analysis: the kind of military and economic planning that would need to accompany an agreement to restrain arms supplies to the Middle East. Fred Gottheil deals with the economic vulnerability of the Middle Eastern states. He elaborates upon the relationships between economic performance within these Middle Eastern economies and the nature of the various kinds of dependencies of these countries on extraregional powers. The mandate of Abraham Becker's comments was to link the discussion of great power intervention in and arms transfer to the Middle East with the concluding consideration of possible settlements for the Arab-Israeli conflict. The paper presents his reflections on the three major themes of the book: great power intervention, arms transfers, and settlement of the regional conflict.

The final section of the book concentrates on the political role of the superpowers in a possible resolution of the Arab-Israeli conflict and on the diplomatic events of 1977 and 1978. The first paper in this section is that by George Quester. He seeks to sort out and evaluate the military and strategic factors as opposed to the political and cultural aspects of the possibilities of an imposed solution. Walid Khalidi and Don Peretz comment on this paper and add their own views on the potential role of the great powers in the movement toward peace in the Middle East.

The papers in this volume were originally prepared in April 1977. The intervening period has been an exceedingly critical one in the history of the Middle Eastern conflict. We therefore commissioned two additional papers by Matityahu Peled and David Pollock to survey the political events between May 1977 and October 1978, when the manuscript went to the publisher. The two papers are written from substantially different viewpoints. One stresses events in Israel to a greater degree, and the other, events in Egypt. The two authors were asked only to interpret the events that had taken place in the 1977-78 period; they were not asked to provide such an interpretation particularly from the point of view of great power intervention. Nevertheless, the degree to which neither author is able to say very much about the mechanisms of United States and the Soviet Union influence — even in the period after Sadat's visit to Jerusalem and prior to the Summit negotiations in the United States — is noteworthy.

Finally, an epilogue was prepared to cover the events from September 1978 to the end of the year, the Camp David Summit of Prime Minister Begin and Presidents Carter and Sadat and its aftermath.

In treating great power intervention, we have not dealt with economic intervention nor with diplomatic pressure: what they are, how they operate, if there are any costs of resisting or rejecting them, or with threats to overcome such resistance. There is less in the book concerning France and the Great Britain, as compared to the United States and the Soviet Union, and little or nothing on China. We have restricted ourselves to aspects of direct and indirect military intervention. We are concerned with the degree to which actions of the great powers, including arms transfers, either produce, maintain, or exacerbate armed conflicts. When readers have completed the book, we hope that they will have a useful understanding of the role of arms transfers in particular, in both the process of military intervention and in its impact on the Middle East conflict.

NOTES AND REFERENCES

(1) A very short selection of recent sources on these issues are: E.L.M. Burns, "Peace in the Middle East," The Elusive Peace in the Middle East, ed. M.H. Kerr (Albany: State University of New York Press, 1975), pp. 311-47; W.E. Farrell, "What Went Wrong," The New York Times Magazine, (August 6, 1978): 28-34; G.W. Ball, "How to Save Israel in Spite of Herself," Foreign Affairs 55 (April 1977): 453-71; W. Khalidi, "Thinking the Unthinkable, A Sovereign Palestinian State," Foreign Affairs 56 (July 1978): 695-713; S. Avineri, "Peacemeal to Peace," Manchester Guardian Weekly, (July 23, 1978): 10; A.L. Atherton, "Middle East Peace Process: A status Report," Current Policy (US Department of State) no. 17 (April 1978): 1-7; N. Safran, Israel. The Embattled Ally (Cambridge: Belknap Press, 1978): S. Zion and U. Dan, "Untold Story of the Mideast Talks", Part I, New York Times Magazine (January 21, 1979): 20-22, 46-53, and Part II, New York Times Magazine (January 28, 1979): 32-41.

I

Strategic Concerns

1 Great Powers' Military Intervention in the Middle East*

Yair Evron

The subject of this paper is delineated both by area and by type of intervention. It will deal only with big power military intervention and its subcategory, "threats to intervene," in the domestic affairs or in the external behavior of the regional powers in the Middle East, from the end of the Second World War to 1973. The Middle Eastern countries comprise Egypt and Asian countries in this area, including Turkey and Iran. Intervention in this chapter is, therefore, one subcategory of the general phenomenon of intervention. It does not include the concept of arms transfer, although this sometimes borders on military intervention, since this will be covered in Chapters 4, 5, and 8. The discussion will focus first on the use of military force, or the specific threat to use military force, which is backed by military moves on the part of: (a) a big power, directed against (b) a regional Middle Eastern state, or (c) another big power. The objective of (a) is to coerce (b) to adopt, within the framework of its external behavior, a course of action which it otherwise would not follow, or to deter (b) or (c) from initiating or continuing a specific action. In the case of an intervention against (c), the objective is to affect (c)'s policy in the Middle East itself, not globally. A second focus will be the use of military force or the specific threat to use military force backed by military moves by (a) in order to affect the domestic political developments in (b).

It will be argued that intervention by big powers in the Middle East does <u>occasionally</u> serve as a regulatory measure and diminish instability by specifically reducing the frequency of war or limiting a war's duration or scope. The outstanding examples here are Soviet and American intervention to end the Wars of 1956, 1967 and 1973.(1) Other examples concern American behavior in the Lebanese crisis of 1958 and in the Jordanian crisis of 1957.

---

*I would like to thank Bruce Maddy for his important help in researching this article. I am grateful to Linda Miller, Joel Migdal, Mark Heller, and David Pollock for their helpful comments.

Some general comments on the concept of intervention may be useful in helping to clarify the definition of intervention used herein. Recently, there have been attempts to analyze the phenomenon of intervention systematically.(2) Both in these attempts and in the literature which preceded them, intervention is seen primarily as an involvement by one state in the internal affairs of another state through different means. The concept of intervention here, however, covers intervention both in external behavior and in the domestic affairs of other states.(3)

Although the emphasis has been on coercive measures in discussions of intervention, this phenomenon is increasingly associated with policies which utilize many means of both the "stick" and the "carrot" varieties: military involvement, arms transfers, foreign aid, and diplomatic and economic pressure. However, when dealing with attempts to influence the external behavior of another state, expanding the concept of intervention beyond the use of coercive means makes the concept too broad and, hence, meaningless.

An added aspect of interventionist or semi-interventionist actions is that some of them are aimed at affecting the whole set of interstate relations in a well-defined international subsystem. In that context, the Middle East serves as a good example of a well-defined and structured regional subsystem, with many patterned sets of interactions among the regional states in which big powers have intervened. These powers have attempted to affect not only the foreign-policy behavior of one state, but also sets of interactions among several states. A recent example of this taken from a different subsystem is the growing Soviet and Cuban involvement in West and South Africa.

One can ask if there are any behavioral characteristics which would serve to differentiate intervention from other phenomena. Rosenau has suggested two such features: convention breaking and power authority.(4) Both features, with some important qualifications, have relevance to the definition here. As for power authority, it should be noted parenthetically that on occasion even weak regional powers intervene in the domestic affairs of stronger ones, e.g., Libya in the affairs of Egypt. Thus, Rosenau's second characteristic is certainly relevant here but only in a limited way.

The notion of convention breaking needs some qualification. Since it resembles the definition of crisis, i.e., "situation which disrupts the system or subsystem."(5) If convention breaking covers ambiguous areas of states' interactions, such as the "rules of the game," then outside military intervention may not always be seen as convention breaking. Intervention may be a decisive diversion from the regular flow of interactions – one requiring extraordinary circumstances and taken only with great hesitation – but it may remain part of the rules of the game. In the Arab-Israeli region, for example, such an intervention is expected should one side in the regional conflict face complete defeat and collapse.

An important area is that of threats. A threat to intervene in order to affect an external policy of a target state could, in some cases, be construed as a very coercive measure and qualify as an intervention in itself.(6) However, it is impossible to include the whole range of threats in this group because of its wide variation. Intervention threats range from implied verbal statements, to more specific threats of diplomatic or economic sanctions, through explicit threats of military sanctions. A more definitive definition is thus required. It is suggested here that threats to intervene can be considered as acts of intervention if three conditions are met: it is a threat to intervene with military force; there is a specific, explicit threat which could, however, be signalled through explicit actions; and the threat is backed up by moves of troops either in the intervening country's territory or in the vicinity of the target state. All nuclear threats, or those which imply the use of nuclear weapons, should be included in this definition because nuclear weapons can be quickly and secretly targeted on the threatened country.

Because of the grave risks of escalation to a nuclear crisis attendant on superpower intervention in the Middle East and due to the whole structure of superpower relationships in that area, threats to intervene are more numerous than actual intervention and not less effective (see Table 1). Among other things, a threat to intervene allows for a brief "pause period" in which diplomatic contacts can be maintained and some compromise reached. These periods also allow for face-saving formulas.

Finally, while military intervention often takes place in a situation of crisis or causes a crisis, intervention is analytically and empirically different from that of crisis.(7) In the first place, intervention forms only one feature of a crisis situation. Second, crises can theoretically occur without military intervention or threats to intervene. Lastly, military interventions are not always carried out within a context characterized by the three usually accepted components of international crises: surprise, perceived threat to vital interests, and a short span of time for response to threats.(8) A fourth characteristic of crisis, high expectation of violence,(9) is sometimes suggested and, indeed, usually is associated with military intervention or threats to intervene.

A different definition of crisis, which brings it closer to the phenomenon of military intervention, has been suggested by Hazelwood et al.(10) This definition looks at crisis as an exercise in military management. However, even this definition focuses on some features, such as "conditions of rapid action," which are not a necessary part or component of military intervention. The growing body of theory concerning crisis behavior and management may, of course, serve as a reservoir of observations about patterns of behavior in situations of military intervention.

A BRIEF HISTORICAL BACKGROUND: TWO PERIODS OF GREAT POWER INTERVENTION IN THE MODERN MIDDLE EAST REGIONAL SUBSYSTEM

The modern state system of the eastern Middle East was formed after the Second World War. Although Britain was the dominant power in the area at the time, the local powers began to demonstrate independent foreign policies at the regional level. In these policies, one can discern both patterns of regional cooperation, competition, and conflict, as well as increasing resistance to British hegemony. With the 1948-49 Arab-Israeli war, the decline of British power in the region began. Indeed, Monroe termed the period of 1945-54 as "The Years of Impotence" in relation to Britain's role in the Middle East.(11)

Although British power in the Middle East was still seen as impressive in 1955 at the time of the establishment of the Baghdad Pact, it took only twenty-odd months until the British role as a major external power in this region was for all practical purposes finished with the Suez debacle. Yet, until this final scene in what Monroe called "Britain's moment in the Middle East," Britain, although under great constraints, was still active as a main external big power in the affairs of the region. Later on, it remained active in Aden and around the Persian Gulf.

Immediately after the Second World War, up to the end of the 1940s, the United States was willing to see Britain as the Western regulatory power in the Middle East, although not in its periphery. United States activity in the region centered upon deterring the Soviet Union in Turkey in 1945-46 and promoting of the Truman Doctrine – both actions outside the heart of the Middle East – and the American involvement in the Palestine problem beginning in 1946. From the early 1950s, however, American interest increased significantly. The United States was active in Iran and was the moving force in arranging the Tripartite Declaration of May 1950. Due to the "pactomania" which drove United States Secretary of state John Foster Dulles in 1953 and 1954, the United States sought to establish military alliances in the heart of the Middle East or along its "Northern Tier." To be sure, Britain was also seeking to establish military alliances in the region, in cooperation with the United States, but its main motivation was to maintain its erstwhile imperial position. The United States became more and more deeply involved in the region as a whole and was also instrumental in promoting the Egyptian position vis-a-vis Britain.

In the mid-1940s the Soviet Union, for its part, tried to maintain and increase its influence in Iran and to obtain concessions from Turkey. After that, it withdrew from active involvement. Soviet backing of the Zionist cause and of Israel in 1947-49 did not signify a significant change in that passive posture. Then, in 1955, the Soviet Union thrust itself into the affairs of the area. The Egyptian-"Czechoslovakian" arms deal is one of the major turning points in the modern history of the Middle East; this deal and the Soviet arms sales policy will be discussed in Chapter 5. From then onward, the two dominant external powers in the Middle East became the United States and the Soviet Union. Their competition in that area has been crucial to the interactions among states in the region.

The period since the end of the Second World war can thus be divided into two major parts: the final phase of colonialism, and controlled competition between two superpowers. During the final phase of colonialism, the power of the British and the French empires collapsed over a period of roughly ten years. The pattern of relations among the external powers and the regional ones was marked primarily by two struggles, one of independence, the other of big power attempts at intervention, the latter of which is discussed in cases 3-5 in the section on cases of intervention. The external powers were still, to a large degree, motivated by the desire to maintain imperial positions, albeit different from the old colonial systems of domination. A second motivation, primarily on the part of the United States, was to deny the Soviet Union access to the area. American involvement in the Arab-Israeli conflict resulted from an attempt to stabilize the region for its own sake, as well as out of a concern that instability there would eventually create opportunities for Soviet penetration.

The second part of the period since the end of World War II began after 1956 and can be characterized by controlled competition between the two superpowers. This part can be further divided into two stages: formative, and controlled competition. First came the formative stage leading up to 1967. Then came the actual stage of controlled competition. Despite variations in the superpowers' relative power positions and in their patterns of behavior, some mutual expectations about behavior, coupled with self-restraint, began to take shape gradually as Soviet power increased. The first major test of the new pattern was the 1967 crisis and War, when both the United States and the Soviet Union demonstrated through their actions that they took into account each other's expected initiatives and reactions. These modes served as the basis for the "rules of the game."

To be sure, during the late 1950s and early 1960s the Soviet Union was still in a weak position in the Middle East. The United States remained the major outside power in the region while the Soviet Union searched for ways to legitimize its presence there, if possible through American recognition of its new role. The 1967 War allowed the Soviet Union to increase its influence in the Middle east in a significant way. By championing the Arab position in the continuing Arab-Israeli crisis, considerably increasing the transfer of arms to the main Arab confrontation countries, and extending a de facto guarantee to defend the existence of some Arab regimes against a crushing military blow by Israel, the Soviet Union arrived at the height of its position. It suffered a considerable defeat in Egypt in 1972 but partly revived its position there until the October War of 1973.

During the final phase of colonialism, most great power military and diplomatic interventions were conducted in order to maintain or obtain — as in the case of initial Soviet interventions in Turkey and Iran a colonial or imperial role in the target state. The major intervention of this period was the Suez War. There, the main objective was really to reinstate old positions of influence and only secondarily, and far down on the scale of priorities, to enhance Western positions within the context of East-West relations.

Interventions during period of controlled competition were of a different kind. Most of them were conducted within the framework of global competition as projected into the Middle East. Some occurred in a direct way, e.g., the Lebanese intervention. Others took the form of attempts to affect regional developments so that regional allies and clients would be accommodated, but this was done as part of the general effort to increase one's own influence or to deny influence to the other superpower.

CONTROLLED COMPETITION

Controlled competition in the Middle East developed gradually, and it was fully evident only in 1967. After that point, it became useful as an analytical construct to explain the "when" and "how" of superpower military intervention. Controlled competition is an analytical construct in the sense that it only approximates reality and also in that it is not an explicit set of assumptions which serves as a guideline for decision makers. Rather, it can be gleaned from the actual behavior of the actors involved.

The pattern of controlled competition in the Middle East has emerged primarily as a result of three interacting factors. The first is the nuclear factor. It imposes on each superpower serious constraints and one overriding shared interest – to avoid escalation to nuclear war. The second factor is increased Soviet conventional military capability, coupled with important political inroads into the region. Finally, there is the rise and power of the regional states.

It is possible to offer at least a tentative definition of the main characteristics of this type of relationship,(12) although further research, in addition to the subsequent case studies, is required to draw final conclusions about the validity and comprehensiveness of these characteristics. To begin with, the superpowers explicitly or tacitly agree to accept each other's presence in the region. They also realize that each other's efforts to advance their own interests are unavoidable and should be strongly resisted only if these attempts threaten a brutal and rapid change in the region's balance of power. Second, the superpowers tacitly accept rules of behavior that circumscribe the means by which they might advance their unilateral interests. Third, the superpowers explicitly or tacitly agree to establish communication mechanisms in order to ensure a credible system of mutual expectations. Fourth, they explicitly or tacitly agree to maintain a system of tolerance thresholds, the crossing of which would reuslt in uncontrolled escalation. The actual thresholds are decided by a combination of factors: the relative power ratios between the superpowers at any given time, the extent to which threatened interests are vital to each superpower, and the perceptions held by each about the importance of these interests to the other side. Finally, the degree of control over United States-Soviet relations is greater than that over relations between local actors and the superpowers. At the same time, the degree of control over the latter is greater than the degree of control exerted by the superpowers over relations between and among the regional actors themselves.

This pattern of relationships suggests the following rules of behavior between the superpowers. The first formulation of points 1-4 was developed jointly with Dan Horowitz,(13) modified and enlarged here.

1. Each tries to increase its political and military influence.

2. Actions short of direct attempts at expelling the other are permissible. However, local actors may be encouraged to expel the other superpower from a position of influence within their own territory.

3. In crisis situations, each side's behavior is marked by a mixture of mutual deterrence and self-restraint to prevent loss or escalation. Direct military intervention occurs only in extreme cases. Threats to intervene are more frequent.

4. Local allies receive diplomatic and economic support and military aid, while superpowers try to maintain a measure of control and supervision over the behavior of local allies, which is not always successful.

5. In crisis situations involving domestic instability within a regional actor, the superpower allied with the legitimate regime is allowed greater freedom to maneuver and flexibility to intervene militarily than the other superpower. Its threats to intervene are also more credible.

6. Deterrence behavior, either by actions or threats, by a superpower against a military action by a regional actor whose objective is to defeat completely another regional actor or its regime will usually be effective. Counterthreats by the other superpower will be less credible.

One of the main results for these rules is that the complete expulsion of either superpower from the region is highly unlikely. Such expulsion may occur only if all the regional states agree on such a policy and that appears rather improbable.

FIFTEEN CASES OF INTERVENTION

Case 1: Soviet Pressure on Turkey 1945-46(14)

As World War II ended, the Soviet Union renewed a long-standing Czarist policy: greater control over the Turkish straits. Given Turkey's neutrality during the war and the general good will which still existed in the West for the Russian ally, the Soviet Union believed conditions to be favorable for this attempt. Thus, in June 1945, the Soviet Union requested from Ankara a naval base on the Dardanelles, as well as the retrocession of the Vilayets of Kors and Ardahan which had been Turkish since World War I. These demands, however, were not backed up by force or ultimatums.

In October and November 1945, the Red Army conducted large-scale military maneuvers on the Turkish-Bulgarian border. This aroused considerable concern within Turkey, and the Soviet Union quickly reassured the Turks of its peaceful intentions. Satisfied with encouraging favorable leftist trends within Turkey, the Soviet Union initiated no more overt actions.

In August 1946, as the renewal date of the Montreux Convention regulating the usage of the Straits came closer, the Soviet Union reiterated its demand for a naval base. This was accompanied by troop movements in the Caucasus and by fleet maneuvers in the Black Sea. The United States responded forcefully, informing the Soviet Union that Turkey would continue to be primarily responsible for the defense of the Straits.   the State Department reinforced American naval units in the area.

By autumn 1946, the crisis had eased. The Soviet Union never followed through on the legal procedures necessary to change the Montreux Convention. Apparently, it was not interested in provoking a military response. Soviet policy had the net effect of pushing Turkey more toward the west and of reinforcing the United States' determination to stand down the Russians when necessary. The American deterrent action was successful, and Soviet objectives were denied. In addition, the United States clearly established a tolerance threshold by emphasizing Turkey's primacy in the defense of the straits. By its restraint, the Soviet Union acknowledged that crossing this threshold might result in uncontrolled escalation of the dispute.

Case 2: Soviet Intervention in Iran 1946-47(15)

The end of World War II found the Soviet Union occupying much of northern Iran, while Britain was in control of the south. The Soviet Union delayed its required withdrawal in 1945 and 1946 to consolidate Soviet political power in Azerbaijan and Kurdistan and to press for an oil concession in northern Iran. On March 3, 1946, fresh Soviet troops poured into Iran and moved toward Teheran and the Turkish and Iraqui borders. United States Secretary of State Byrnes ordered the Soviet Union to withdraw or face an American response. In the meantime, Iranian Prime Minister Ghavam pursued an independent initiative and made significant concessions concerning oil rights in negotiations with the Soviet Union. These were included in the April 1946 agreement. Soviet troops were soon withdrawn from Iran, possibly because the Soviet Union achieved most of its goals in the 1946 agreement and was not interested in antagonizing the United States and Britain at the time.

The Iranian government delayed the ratification of the agreement. In spring 1947, the Soviet ambassador to Iran threatened Teheran. These threats were backed by a show of force. However, the Iranian government, with American diplomatic backing, succeeded in fending off this pressure. In October 1947, the Majlis rejected the 1946 agreement. In the end, the Soviet Union suffered a major political defeat. The American deterrence action coupled with flexible and imaginative Iranian diplomacy brought about this defeat. It appeared also that Stalin was absorbed at the time in consolidating Soviet gains in

Europe and that the Iranian affair, like the Turkish straits crisis, was of secondary interest to him.

Case 3: British Intervention Against Israel 1949-1946(16)

On January 7, 1949, at the end of the 1948 War, as Israeli troops advanced into the Sinai peninsula, the British government invoked the 1936 Anglo-Egyptian Treaty and threatened Israel with a military response if it did not withdraw from its captured Sinai positions. The Treaty was invoked notwithstanding the Egyptians' immediate repudiation of it for their own reasons. British Spitfires conducted overflights of the Israeli forces. Some were shot down by the Israeli Air Force on the initiative of the pilots involved.(17) It is unclear if the overflights were intended as a signal to Israel, but combined with United States diplomatic pressure, Israel did indeed withdraw from Sinai.

Case 4: British Threats Against Iran 1951-53(18)

Britain reacted to the 1951 Iranian nationalization of the Anglo-Iranian Oil Company (AIOC) by strong diplomatic pressure, backed by a show of force. However, Britain was in too weak a military, political, and economic position to enforce its will. In 1953, Iranian Prime Minister Mossadeq, who engineered the nationalization of the AIOC, was overthrown by army units loyal to the Shah, who himself had just been deposed, and covertly supported by the American CIA.

Case 5: The Suez War: British and French Intervention Against Egypt; Soviet and American Reactions, 1956(19)

The creation of the Baghdad Pact in February 1955, Israeli-Egyptian tension, and the Soviet-Egyptian arms deal of September 1955 had affected the political situation in the Middle East. Egyptian President Nasser responded to Dulles' cancellation of Aswan Dam funds in mid-1956 by the nationalization of the Suez Canal. The American government sought to resolve the crisis diplomatically but, at Sevres in October 1956, Britain, France, and Israel agreed to intervene militarily.

On October 29, 1956, the Israelis began the war. The next day, the British and French delivered a prearranged ultimatum to both Egypt and Israel to withdraw ten kilometers from the Canal. When the Egyptians refused, the British and French had their excuse to intervene, in order to protect the Suez Canal.

The United States confined its behavior during much of the crisis to diplomatic efforts to obtain a cease fire and an Allied withdrawal. At the same time, the United States Navy did close in on Suez. The Soviet Union also had no inclination towards intervention in the preliminary stages of the war. However, on November 5, as the Hungarian uprising seemed to be under control, the Soviet Union proposed that the United

States join it in military action to halt the fighting. Simultaneously, the Soviet Union sent identical letters to France and Britain implying a threat to use nuclear weapons against these countries. Another letter was sent to Israel, using very strong and rude language, threatening Israel's very existence. During that period, the Soviet Union also made several references to the possibility of sending volunteers to Egypt. On November 6, American military forces were placed on emergency alert. Soviet threats to intervene were of minimal credibility to the American government — although President Eisenhower found it necessary to call the alert — but of very high credibility to Israel and seemingly to France as well.(20) The United States however, used the Soviet threats to pressure Israel.

No actual movement of forces backed the Soviet threats. However, because nuclear threats were involved and since Soviet missiles are permanently targeted on Western Europe, the Soviet threats can be seen as a form of intervention. American behavior constituted diplomatic and economic intervention which was aimed at applying pressure on Britain, France, and Israel for a cease fire and withdrawal. The American reaction of an alert to the Soviet threats served as a deterrent threat against the Soviet Union. The pattern of controlled competition in the Middle East began to emerge only after the 1956 War, namely, only when Soviet political power in the Middle East became significant. The Eisenhower Doctrine can be seen in retrospect as an attempt to preempt the development of such a pattern of relationships, and its failure opened the way for the gradual emergence of controlled competition. In the 1956 War, there were already indications of what would later emerge as controlled competition: the Soviet threat and the subsequent United States alert established the tolerance thresholds which, if crossed, would have resulted in a major confrontation.

The main result of the war was that Britain and France were completely discredited in the region. Despite its action in favor of Egypt, the United States failed to reap the credit in the Arab world. In contrast, the Soviet Union with little effort or cost, was able to score important points in the region as the patron of Arab nationalism and to have some effect on American and Israeli behavior.

Case 6: American Intervention in Jordan 1957(21)

In April 1957, the United States aided King Hussein in his move against his own pro-Nasserite government. The Sixth Fleet undertook maneuvers in the eastern Mediterranean to warn the Soviet Union, Egypt, and Syria against intervention. Hussein's move was successful, and no threat or action came from these countries, which may have resulted from the American signals or from a unilateral decision not to act in the first place.

Case 7: American Intervention Against Syria and Soviet Counterintervention 1957(22)

By late summer of 1957, Syria was increasingly seen to be adopting a pro-Soviet orientation. It denounced the Eisenhower Doctrine, supported Nasser's proclaimed policy of positive neutralism, and signed a wide-ranging economic and technical agreement with the Soviet Union to complement previous Soviet military support. In addition, a number of key officers were purged in favor of suspected pro-Communists. A week later, three American diplomats were expelled from Damascus for apparently plotting to overthrow the regime. In Washington, the suspicion was strong that the Communists had taken control of the government. The United States quickly tried to recoup by invoking the Eisenhower Doctrine and by redefining the situation in terms of a Syrian threat of aggression against its neighbors. Encouraged by the United States, both Turkey and Iraq massed their troops on the Syrian frontiers, and the United States conducted naval maneuvers ₋in the eastern Mediterranean.

As countermeasures Egypt offered military support to the Syrian regime, and Bulganin warned Turkish Prime Minister Menderes in September that a war involving Turkey would not remain localized. Furthermore, Soviet forces conducted maneuvers near the Turkish border, and two Soviet Warships visited Latakia. The Soviet Union was satisfied with the outcome because Syria remained in the neutralist camp. The crisis demonstrated that the Eisenhower Doctrine was an unsatisfactory tool for conducting superpower competition in the Middle East.

The crisis involved two interventions by the superpowers, which reveal some features of the gradually emerging controlled competition. The United States tacitly accepted a rule of behavior, which circumscribed the means by which it might have advanced its unilateral goals. More specifically, the crisis demonstrated the greater flexibility accorded the superpower allied with the legitimate regime in a domestic dispute. Further, the superpower seeking to deter a regional actor from completely defeating the regime of another regional actor will usually be successful, while the other superpower's actions will be less credible (see page 40).

The Soviet Union was certainly banking on the natural opposition which could have been expected in the Arab world to an American-backed intervention against an independent Arab state. It was precisely this opposition which enabled the Soviet Union to deter American plans. At the same time, this interaction among superpowers and regional actors demonstrated the pattern of behavior suggested here.

Case 8: American Intervention in Lebanon 1958(23)

On July 15, 1958, over 14,000 American Marines began landing in Lebanon. One aim was to bolster the Chamoun regime against a perceived wave of radical Arab nationalism as exemplified by the overthrow of the Hashemite monarchy in Iraq. A nuclear threat was implied when the United States Strategic Air Command (SAC) was placed on an increased alert level. There were also signs of a possible military intervention in Iraq to reinstate to the ancien regime. In response, the Soviet Union conducted troop movements in the south of Russia and gave strong diplomatic support to the progressive camp in the Middle East. However, as documented by Heikal, Khrushchev stated clearly to Nasser that the Soviet Union would not have risked a confrontation with the United States even over the heartland of the Middle East, i.e., Iraq and by implication, Egypt.

Again, some elements of controlled competition can be discerned from the 1958 events in Lebanon. The tolerance threshold was set by the actual ratios of military capabilities in the region – the Soviet Union was militarily weak – and by the nature of the domestic instability – the United States was invited to act by the legitimate Lebanese regime.

Case 9: British Intervention in Jordon 1958(24)

In conjunction with American moves in Lebanon, British para-troopers landed in Jordan at King Hussein's request to forestall any possible radical rebellion there. The situation in Jordan remained stable throughout this period.

Case 10: British Intervention in Kuwait 1961(25)

The formal proclamation of Kuwait's independence in 1961 occasioned claims from Qasim's Iraq that Kuwait really belonged to the Iraqis.   Annexation was threatened. In response, Britain dispatched troops to Kuwait to forestall any annexation attempt. Later, Britain turned over its responsibilities to Arab League forces. In this case, British interests and those of the rest of the Arab world coincided neatly, thus rendering it easier for Britain to act.

Case 11: The 1967 War(26)

A new crisis broke out in the Middle East in mid-May 1967. Fearful of Israeli military action against Syria and mindful of his own waning prestige in the Arab world, President Nasser dispatched large segments of the Egyptian army deep into the Sinai to the Israeli frontier. This mobilization was followed up by the eviction of the United Nations Emergency Force (UNEF) and by the blockage of the Straits of Tiran. The United States maintained a fairly low profile militarily, concentrating on diplomacy to resolve the crisis and attempting to organize a multilateral flotilla which would reopen the Straits to Israeli shipping. The Sixth Fleet did move toward the eastern Mediterranean but kept well away from the coastline. Specifically, the aircraft carrier Intrepid which was passing through the Mediterranean to the Indian Ocean via the Suez Canal was deliberately kept apart from the Sixth Fleet to avoid the impression that the United States was reinforcing its forces in the area.

The war itself lasted only six days, at it was not until the fifth day, as the Israelis continued to rout the Syrian army, that the Soviet Union felt compelled to act more forcefully on behalf of its defeated Arab clients. At a two-day meeting of European Communist Party leaders on June 9 and 10, the Soviet Union warned both the West and Israel of dire consequences and hinted at sending Soviet volunteers if Israel proceeded to push on toward Damascus. President Johnson responded by moving the Sixth Fleet much closer to the eastern Mediterranean coastline and pressured Israel diplomatically to halt its advance.

All aspects of controlled competition were demonstrated by the behavior of the superpowers during the crisis. For the first time, the Washington-Moscow hotline was employed "to ensure a credible system of mutual expectations"(see page 22), thus reinforcing moderate superpower behavior. Each superpower openly recognized each other's presence in the region and the risks involved in challenging what were perceived by the other side as vital interests. This behavior was motivated by fear of an escalation to an uncontrolled nuclear crisis. By not intervening to prevent the collapse of Nasser's army, the Soviet Union circumscribed the means by which it might have advanced its interests: the strengthening and greater unification of the progressive wing of the Arab world. The Soviet Union's tolerance threshold, i.e., the preservation of the Damascus regime was clearly established on June 9-10. Because of the increased Soviet military power deployed in the eastern Mediterranean, the intensified involvement and links with Syria, and the Soviet defense of Syria against a potentially complete collapse, this Soviet threat was seen as very serious. Finally, the ability of the superpowers to control the behavior of their allies was found wanting. Nasser's bold strokes prior to the outbreak of fighting led him to positions far beyond what Moscow wished him to take or which Egypt could effectively manage. The United States was unable to restrain Israel from attacking the Arabs.

Case 12: Soviet Deterrence Posture Toward Israel by Means of a
Naval Presence in Egypt 1967-72(27)

Soviet warships were deployed in Alexandria and Port Said in late 1967. A specific objective was to deter Israel from military operations against these ports. A possible, more general objective was to signal the increased commitment of the Soviet Union to the integrity of Egypt and the survival of its regime. The Soviet Union thus strained onerule of behavior: there can be no direct military intervention which may involve one of the superpowers in actual military actions against one of the regional actors. However, this specific rule was not as yet breached since the Soviet deployment constituted a deterrent action in which the responsibility for a possible military confrontation was passed to the regional actor, Israel.

Case 13: Soviet Intervention in Egypt 1970(28)

1970 was a crucial year for the Middle East. Events led to a more explicit involvement of both superpowers than had existed before. The War of Attrition had left Egypt virtually defenseless against Israeli deep penetration raids. In January 1970, Nasser traveled to Moscow. The Soviet Union reluctantly agreed to augment its small advisory contingent of roughly 3,000 men to the level of 20,000 men, including advisers, technicians, air defense crews, and more dramatically, Soviet pilots to undertake combat missions in defense of Egypt's heartland. These missions started in the spring; soon after, Israel ceased the deep penetration raids. In July, Israeli pilots shot down five Russian piloted MIGs south of the Suez Canal. A cease fire was accepted eventually by both sides beginning in August. However, the Soviet Union actively encouraged the emplacement of surface-to-air missiles (SAMs) along the Canal, in open violation of the terms of the cease fire.

The main implication of Soviet behavior during this period was that the survival of the Egyptian regime, which was then perceived as doubtful due to the heavy losses suffered during the War of Attrition, had explicitly become part of the Soviet Union's vital interests. To ensure its survival, the Soviet Union demonstrated that it would take extraordinary measures, never before taken outside the Communist bloc. Thus, Moscow broke the rule of no direct military intervention in the Arab-Israeli conflict.

The United States, by not overtly challenging the presence of 20,000 Soviet advisors, tacitly recognized the importance of Soviet interests in Egypt and in the Middle East in general. For the first time the Russians were able to intervene militarily on a significant scale only because they were invited by the legitimate regime of the regional state, Egypt and because they limited themselves to deterrent and defensive measures. Thus, they established a rule of behavior which, in a sense, was already implicit in their 1967 threats concerning Israel's offensive against Syria: the superpower may intervene militarily in a deterrent or defensive mission in support of a legitimate regime of an ally and at its invitation.

Case 14: Jordan 1970(29)

The Civil War between King Hussein's forces and the Palestinian guerrillas escalated dramatically on September 18, 1970, as Syrian armored units crossed into northern Jordan to back up the guerrillas. Although Soviet advisers did not cross the frontier with their units, they were probably involved in planning the attack. American military moves began even earlier with an alert of American forces in the eastern Mediterranean following the hijackings which had triggered off the civil war.

Once the war started on September 17, units of the Sixth Fleet, including an aircraft carrier, approached the area. On September 19 after the Syrian invasion, a selective alert of American forces was put into effect, which included the 82nd Airborne Division and United States airborne units in West Germany. The Sixth Fleet's strength was augmented, and it sailed toward Lebanon and Israel, shadowed by Soviet naval units. On September 21 as fighting continued, King Hussein appeared to be in real danger of losing power. He requested, via the United States, Israeli intervention and then American and British help. Five United States' divisions in West Germany were put on alert, and the Sixth Fleet was increased from two to five carrier task forces. Later that night, Israel and the United States agreed that the former would intervene militarily to stop the Syrian tank thrusts and to save Hussein's regime. This agreement was made on the understanding that the United States would intervene militarily if Egypt or the Soviet Union responded in kind. The Israeli posture was, of course, motivated by Israeli interests and not dictated by American ones. The Soviet Union, after evaluating the seriousness of American determination to ensure Hussein's survival, counseled moderation to the Syrians and indicated to the Americans that they had done so. Even before that the Jordanian forces defeated the Syrians, who were deterred by the possibility of Israeli intervention from sending in more troops, especially their air force. The explicit United States-Israeli coordination stemming from their confluence of interests led to a new and deeper level of relations between them which lasted until October 1973.

All aspects of the controlled competition pattern were evident during the crisis. The Soviet Union prohibited its advisers from accompanying Syrian units into Jordan, despite Moscow's probable interest in a Syrian success. Communication mechanisms between the United States and the Soviet Union prohibited its advisers from accompanying Syrian units into Jordan, despite Moscow's probable interest in a Syrian success. Communication mechanisms between the United States and the Soviet Union were maintained throughout the crisis, primarily via the Soviet ambassador in Washington. The United States, by guaranteeing to intervene on Israel's side if Egypt or Russia reacted to Israel's planned military moves, explicitly established the tolerance threshold. The regional actors again played a decisive role in determining superpower behavior: the crisis was precipitated by the Palestinian guerrillas, and the Syrians certainly made their own decision to intervene. The Soviet Union could only react to its various clients' actions. Finally, it was the initial Jordanian military success, coupled with Israel's deterrence posture, which ultimately forced the Syrians to back down. It is not clear whether the United States would have intervened were the Syrians more successful and had Israel refused to act. Such an intervention seemed quite probable and would have fit into the rules of the game. The United States would have intervened were the Syrians more successful and had Israel refused to act. Such an intervention seemed quite probable and would have fit into the rules of the game. The United States would have been invited by the legitimate regime of Jordan, in response to a threat against that regime's very existence.

Case 15: October 1973(30)

As in the previous Middle East wars of 1956 and 1967, the threat of big power military intervention during the October 1973 War came near the end of the conflict when the Egyptian army was facing a major defeat. Before that, the superpowers had limited their activity to diplomatic moves and, more significantly, to the large-scale deliveries of arms via air and sealifts. The Soviet Union began its sealift on October 10, and Washington reacted in kind on October 12. Violations of the October 22 United Nations Cease-Fire by both sides were quickly taken advantage of by Israel, which strove to consolidate its military position and completely entrap the Egyptian Third Army. Fearing the Collapse of the Egyptian regime if Israel continued to attack, the Soviet Union acted.

On October 24, Secretary-General Brezhnev sent a blunt note to President Nixon, threatening unilateral action if Israel's cease fire violations were not halted. The Soviet Union was probably interested in some form of joint Soviet-American military intervention; short of that, it was sending signals about a possible unilateral intervention. Insisting on some form of mutually recognized military stalemate, the Soviet Union backed up its threat with a number of preparatory military moves, including troop movements. In addition, according to some sources, a Soviet ship supposedly carrying nuclear material passed through the Bosphorus. This event, if it actually took place, probably served as a deterrent signal. However, whether the ship actually carried nuclear warheads or just some nuclear material that the Russians were eager for Washington to detect remains a mystery. At the United Nations, also on October 24, Soviet Ambassador Malik reiterated his country's intervention threat, while qualifying it in two respects. The need for parallel, not unilateral, actions by Soviet and American forces was mentioned, and Malik spoke of contingents of forces, which probably can be distinguished from massive deployments. Thus, the possibility of Soviet intervention remained ambiguous, as Moscow most certainly intended it to be.

The American response to these Soviet moves was quickly to order a worldwide alert for all American military forces, including the nuclear strike forces. Diplomatically, the United States strongly rejected any Soviet idea of unilateral or joint big power action. At the same time, the United States applied pressure on Israel to desist in its military operations. Later on, it pressured Israel to allow supplies to pass through Israeli lines to the beleaguered Egyptian Third Army. The strong American reaction to the Soviet threat was justified in view of the alarming Soviet signals, such as troop movements, etc., and the precedent of Soviet intervention in 1970.   The result was that a second cease fire was declared on October 24. The fighting stopped by October 25. The Soviet Union abandoned its "go-it-alone" tactics, and a face-saving compromise on the composition of the United Nations force to be dispatched to patrol the cease fire lines was achieved.

Again, many aspects of controlled competition came into play. At first, Soviet behavior was perceived by United States Secretary of State

Henry Kissinger as a threat to detente. Eventually, however, the United States accepted this Soviet stance and reacted in kind. Soviet behavior may have been unexpected in terms of the American interpretation of detente, but it did fit into the pattern of controlled competition. There did exist, nonetheless, a clear line beyond which the Soviet Union would not act in the service of unilateral goals and interests; that was direct military intervention. However, this threshold was dangerously reduced when a complete collapse of the Egyptian regime was perceived as highly probable. Another rule of the game was again demonstrated: deterrence threats by a superpower against a regional power perceived to be intent on bringing about the total collapse of another regional power are highly credible and effective.

Regular diplomatic contacts were the main channel of communications utilized. The threats and counterthreats at the end of the war clearly established the tolerance threshold of each superpower. Finally, control over their respective clients again proved to be haphazard and fraught with obstacles. The Soviet Union was unable to restrain Egypt and Syria from launching the war, and Moscow acceded to Egypt's early demands not to press for an early cease fire. For the United States, the subsequent delay in obtaining Israel's compliance with the ceasefire resolution nearly precipitated a major Soviet-American confrontation.

CATEGORIZATION OF MILITARY INTERVENTIONS

The fifteen cases described above can be divided into three sets of categories: the nature of the intervening act, types of target states, and classification of policy objectives.

The nature of the intervening act include tacit threat, formal threats, transfer of military personnel, and direct limited intervention.

The types of target states encompass regional allies or clients; regional opponents, through alliance with other superpowers or through conflict with a regional ally; and another great power, primarily the other superpower.

The classification of policy objectives can include:

1. Intervening against a regional power because of imperial ambitions an intervention within the context of bilateral relations without reference to other regional powers.

2. Stabilizing a friendly regime domestically.

3. Intervening against a regional power within the context of global East-West relations.

4. Deterring a regional opponent of one's regional ally from initiating or continuing a course of action against the ally.

5. Compelling a regional opponent of one's own regional ally to reverse an action.

6. Applying pressure on the other superpower.

7. Increasing or creating influence with one's own and/or other regional allies, or potential allies.

8. Constraining one's own ally.

9. Signalling to the other superpower a commitment to one's own regional ally.

10. Strengthening a regional ally in political bargaining with a regional opponent.

Table 1.1 presents a summary of the fifteen cases of intervention discussed here in relation to policy objectives, reactions, and outcomes.

SOME OBSERVATIONS ON BEHAVIOR IN SITUATIONS OF INTERVENTION IN THE MIDDLE EAST

1. Two major periods of outside intervention in the region can be identified: 1945-58, and 1967 to the present. This sets the Middle East apart to some extent from the rest of the international system in terms of American intervention; since 1964-65, the level of intervention has decreased considerably excluding Southeast Asia.(31)

2. From 1965, the Arab-Israeli conflict is the primary issue that causes intervention. Moreover, the interventions with the greatest potential for escalation between the superpowers have occurred because of the Arab-Israeli conflict.

3. From 1958 until 1970, there was an increasing amount of evidence that because of the dangers of escalation to a nuclear crisis the two superpowers would avoid military intervention in the Middle East. Nonetheless, part of the Israeli decision-making group believed Soviet military intervention possible within the context of the Arab-Israeli conflict. This perception developed because of the famous Soviet ultimatum of 1956. To be sure, the ultimatum was hollow, and Washington immediately counteracted it. Later on, it was revealed that such a threat was, in fact, never meant to be operative and was carefully issued only after the United States had already intervened. However, the ultimatum left its mark. The expectation of direct Soviet intervention declined after 1967 when it was assumed that mutual superpower deterrence of direct intervention was a basic rule of the game. Following 1970, the perceived probability of Soviet intervention in some circumstances rose again.(32)

Similarly, the Egyptian leadership has always suspected that the United States would come to the aid of Israel if the Latter's existence were seriously placed in jeopardy. This explains the relief the Egyptians felt when they learned from the Soviet Union in May 1967 that Moscow would neutralize the United States and as Nasser indicated in his May 29 speech, the Soviet Union promised ". . . never (to) allow any state to intervene until things go back to what they were in 1956."(33) The

Table 1.1. Intervention: Typology of Policy Objectives, Reactions, and Outcomes

Cases	Intervention by				Reactions by			Outcome
	Soviet	American	British	French	Soviet	American	Regional Power	
1. Turkey 1945-46	1*					deterrence threats backed by military moves		successful deterrence
2. Iran 1946-47	1					deterrence threats	diplomatic concessions initially and then diplomatic rejection	successful reversal and deterrence
3. Israel 1949			4, 5, 7				countermilitary action and withdrawal	successfully compelled by intervention
4. Iran 1951-53			1					intervention unsuccessful
5. Suez War 1956			1, 3 (?)	1, 3 (?)	threats and diplomatic pressure	diplomatic pressure; deterrence action against Russia	military resistance by Egypt; diplomatic and other sanctions by other Arab states	intervention unsuccessful; major diplomatic defeat for interventionists

*Note: Numbers refer to typology of objectives, pages 63 and 64.

| Cases | Intervention by | | | | Reactions by | | Regional Power | Outcome |
	Soviet	American	British	French	Soviet	American		
6. Jordan 1957		2						intervention successful
7. Syria 1957		3			threats to regional powers			intervention unsuccessful
8. Lebanon 1958		2, 4 (?)			threats and troop movements		political protest in some Arab countries; Israel favorable	intervention successful but possibly redundant
9. Jordan 1958			2, 3, 7					intervention successful
10. Kuwait 1961			2, 4				other Arab states tacitly favorable	intervention successful
11. 1967 War	2, 3, 4, 6, 7					counter deterrence threats coupled with pressure on own ally, Israel, to stop action		intervention had some impact

(Table 1.1 Continued)

12. Soviet naval deterrence 1967-72	2, 3, 4, 7			not clear if intervention successful, as there may have been other reasons for Israel's self-restraint
13. Egypt 1970	2, 4, 6, 7		Israel backs down but tries to establish tacit understanding with Soviets on "red lines" (shooting down of MIGs)	intervention successful
14. Jordan 1970	1, 3, 4, 5, 6, 7	constraining activity vis-a-vis own ally	Israel deterrence posture in conjunction with American intervention	intervention successful
15. 1973 War	3, 4, 6, 7	deterrence threats and moves? pressure on ally to stop course of action		intervention successful

Egyptian perception was probably partly formed during the 1956 War when Egypt was attacked by two European powers.

4. It seems that from 1970 the rules of the game followed by the superpowers were modified to enable a blatant trespassing of some red lines to be halted. The superpower ally of the aggrieved regional power may intervene militarily in a limited way to stop the dangerous course of action taken by the regional opponent or to deter the regional opponent from some action. It is unlikely, however, that a superpower will intervene in order to reverse completely the course of action taken already. The red lines are defined primarily in political terms: the total collapse of the armed forces of a friendly regime and, consequently, of the regime itself resulting from a military action by a regional opponent. This point will be further elaborated below. Thus, a direct intervention may still be seen as convention breaking, but there is considerable expectation that it might occur.

It should, however, be added that the Soviet intervention which took place in 1970 may not have been a major shift from past policies. It can be argued, rather, that Soviet deterrent warnings and threats directed at Israel and the United States simply failed to achieve their objective. In the 1957 Syrian crisis, Soviet deterrent-oriented warnings, coupled with Arab reactions, were successful, while Soviet threats in 1967 to intervene militarily to defend Syria were not put to the test as Israel accepted the cease fire on June 12. It could be argued that had Israel pursued its offensive, some Soviet intervention would have materialized. In any case, the credibility of Soviet threats to intervene in a deterrence mode, and only in that mode has increased since 1970.

5. Intervention has a whole range of objectives and a whole range of target states. Moreover, some interventions may have multiple objectives, while objectives may vary according to target state. When the latter is an ally or client, the objectives will include the increase of influence and the reemphasis of credibility as a big-power ally. When the target state is a regional opponent, the objectives will be primarily the deterrence of military actions or the cessation of a military action already in progress. These are within the reach of the intervening power. Less achievable is the reversal of an outcome resulting from an action already taken. The last category is the attainment of objectives vis-a-vis another big power. Here, the interventions have always been directed by one superpower against the other, the only exception of which was the Soviet threat against Britain and France in 1956. Usually, the intervention served as a signal that more serious actions would follow if a certain activity did not stop. Alternatively, it indicated the depth of the commitment of the superpower to its regional ally in order to deter a certain possible future action by the other superpower against the regional ally. Examples of the latter case include American threats against the Soviet Union during the 1970 Civil War in Jordan and the movement of the Sixth Fleet to the eastern Mediterranean during the last part of the 1967 War. No intervention occurred which had the objective of actually compelling either the other superpower or an opposing regional power to take an action which it would otherwise not have chosen to adopt. The maximum that the intervening power hoped

to accomplish was the deterrence or the cessation of a certain course of action about to be or already taken by a target state.

6. The structure of the current international system diminishes the probability of actual military intervention in the Middle East because of the realization by all sides of the dangers involved. This, however, depends in the first place on the readiness of the regional powers to impose upon themselves some important restrictions, such as no trespassing of red lines. The superpowers, for their part, will pressure their respective regional allies to avoid crossing red lines. At the same time, each will continuously threaten, at least tacitly, the other superpower not to intervene in the area even if the client does cross the red lines. However, threats to intervene against a trespasser of red lines will be more credible than counterthreats. Threats to intervene have served and will probably continue to serve as an important instrument in the hands of the superpowers.

The concept of red lines is central and, therefore, requires some further elaboration. Basically, it refers to two situations. The first is the case of a violent internal threat to an established regime. If this involves a civil war with a high likelihood of victory for the opposition and the legitimate regime invites intervention, then the threat to intervene will be more credible than the other superpower's deterrent counterthreats. Second, and probably more likely, if an established regime is facing complete military collapse in a war with another regional actor, then again threats to intervene in order to deter the victor from further advances will be more credible than deterrent counterthreats by the other superpower. If no intermediate political action is taken to stop the trespass, some intervention is likely (see rules of behavior 5 and 6 on page 40).

The probability of threats to intervene or actual interventions depends on the depth of a superpower's commitment to regional actors. Only if it is clear that a superpower has vital interests involved in the survival of a regional actor or regime will its threats be credible. If these are not effective, intervention becomes more likely. Additionally, in order not to bring about a major confrontation with the other superpower, intervention must be seen as having only limited deterrent objectives. Finally, the intervening superpower must have the capability to transfer its forces to their destination or to act militarily in a threatening mode. In the 1957 Syrian crisis, the Soviet threats, coupled with Arab reactions, were effective because Soviet troops could be moved against Turkey. With the appearance of the Soviet squadron in the Mediterranean and the enhanced conventional strategic reach of the Soviet Union starting in the mid-1960s, Soviet threats in 1967 and in 1973 became much more credible. The United States has had similar capabilities in the Middle East and the eastern Mediterranean since the 1950s. The concern about intervention is such that in most cases the superpowers will confine themselves to threats and counterthreats, and these will be sufficient to stabilize the situation. When actual intervention takes place, it comes only after repeated threats and as a last resort.

7. The readiness to intervene by the two superpowers has changed

over the years. Up to 1967, the United States seemed readier to intervene. Although the 1958 intervention in Lebanon was perhaps redundant, it nevertheless demonstrated the predominance of United States power in the eastern Mediterranean and in the Middle East. The growing political power of the Soviet Union in the Middle East since then and the appearance of the Soviet naval squadron in the Mediterranean beginning in 1963-64 may have changed this situation even before 1967. The 1967 War itself served as a watershed in the political fortunes of the Soviet Union in the area. With it, the probability of Soviet intervention increased. The presence of Soviet naval units in Egyptian ports in order to deter Israel, coupled with the growing number of Soviet military advisers in the Egyptian and Syrian armies, gradually created a new pattern for Soviet intervention and also signaled Soviet commitment to the red lines. The fact that the Soviet Union has intervened more than the United States since 1967 is not the result of a greater Soviet propensity for intervention, but rather the fact that Israel's military victories continuously appeared to cross the red lines. However, growing Soviet involvement and increasing commitments may have created a situation in which Soviet intervention came to be seen as more likely than American intervention. This does not necessarily reflect the actual situation, as tough American behavior during the 1970 Jordanian crisis and in October 1973 demonstrated.

8. The pattern of superpower intervention in the future will depend primarily on the rules of the game. These, however, reflect a situation in which both superpowers are present in the area and both have recognized regional allies and clients. A change in that situation, such as the unilateral withdrawal of one, will change these rules. As mentioned, the military capabilities available to each superpower for quick deployment in the Middle East are added factors in assessing the credibility of threats to intervene.

It is a thankless task to predict the future, but it is safe to assume that if the Soviet Union maintains an important position in some Arab countries and its influence is not further eroded, then one may expect a continuation of the same set of rules of the game. What will happen with possible further erosion of Soviet influence is more difficult to predict. On one hand, if one considers the Arab-Israeli conflict, then it could be argued that the probability of Soviet intervention on the side of the Arabs in case the Israelis trespass some red lines will diminish. Intervention requires some preplanning, both political and military, on the part of both intervener and host country. In its absence, intervention becomes much more difficult. Moreover, the Soviet Union might suspect that whatever political fruits are to be reaped from intervention in the Arab world will be as transitory as the ones gained after 1967 and 1973. On the other hand, there may be some grave dangers involved in a situation in which the Soviet role eroded further and all sides did not expect a Soviet intervention. Israel might act without restraint. The United States might not be ready for a sudden change in Soviet behavior, and the Soviet threats might not be taken seriously. Most important, the Soviet Union might assume that an excellent opportunity for regaining influence presented itself, albeit accompanied by great risks, and might then pursue an interventionist course.

NOTES AND REFERENCES

(1) It has been argued, of course, that these interventions were not stabilizing since they stopped Israel from dictating peace conditions to the Arabs. This, however, is a highly debatable point, because it is very doubtful whether a more comprehensive Israeli military victory in any of these wars would have facilitated the sought-after peace. Indeed, one may argue that more instability would have ensued.

(2) An attempt to analyze the phenomenon of intervention systematically is contained in "Intervention and World Politics" (special issue). Journal of International Affairs 22:2 (1968).

(3) For definitions of intervention covering both aspects, see Max Beloff, "Reflections on Intervention," in ibid., pp. 198-207 and United Nations General Assembly, Resolution 2131 (xx) "Declaration on the inadmissibility of Intervention in the Domestic Affairs of States and the Protection of Their Independence and Sovereignty." Resolutions Adopted by the General Assembly During Its Twentieth Session, 21 September-22 December 1965. General Assembly. Official Records: Twentieth Session, Supplement no. 14 (A/6014). New York: United Nations, 1966, pp. 11-12.

(4) James Rosenau, "The Concept of Intervention", Journal of International Affairs, pp. 165-176.

(5) Raymond Tanter, "Crisis Management: A Critical Review of the Literature," The Jerusalem Journal of International Relations 1:1 (1975): 71. Tanter bases this system-level definition of crisis on Oran Young's observations regarding crisis. See Oran Young, The Politics of Force: Bargaining During International Crises (Princeton, New Jersey: Princeton University Press, 1968).

(6) A classical discussion of the role of threats in strategic bargaining situations is contained in Thomas Schelling, Arms and Influence (New Haven and London: Yale University Press, 1966), especially pp. 1-18. The concept of threats is, of course, central to modern strategy and has been discussed in many works, especially in those on deterrence. Bernard Brodie formulated the fundamentals of nuclear deterrence as long ago as 1945 in his The Atomic Bomb and American Security, Memorandum no. 18 (New Haven: Yale Institute of International Studies, 1945) and in the work he coauthored and edited The Absolute Weapon (New York: Harcourt, Brace, and Company, 1946).

(7) The body of literature on crisis behavior is extensive. Two basic approaches are identifiable: the system level and the individual or group decision-making level. For the first, see the pioneering works of Charles

A. McClelland et al., International Events Interaction Analysis (Beverly Hills, California: Sage Publications, 1972); as well as various other articles by McClelland; and of Oran Young (note 5 supra). For the second, see in the first instance C.F. Herman, ed., International Crises: Insights from Behavioral Research (New York: The Free Press, 1972). For a recent important volume addressing current developments in the field, which attempts to combine theoretical advances with policy relevance issues, see International Studies Quarterly 21 (March 1977). For an operational definition combining the system level with the decision-making approach, see Michael Brecher, "Toward a Theory of International Crisis Behavior: A Preliminary Report" in ibid., pp. 39-74.

(8) Herman, p. 13 (note 7 supra).

(9) Young, p. 15 (note 5 supra).

(10) Leo Hazelwood et al., "Planning for Problems in Crisis Management: An Analysis of Post-1945 Behavior in the U.S. Department of Defense," International Studies Quarterly, pp. 76-106 (note 7 supra).

(11) Elizabeth Monroe, Britain's Moment in the Middle East 1914-1956 (London: University Paperbacks/Methuen, 1965), especially Chapter 7.

(12) The first formulation of these was developed jointly with Dan Horowitz. See Yair Evron and Dan Horowitz, "Superpowers Involvement in the Middle East: Alternative Options" (manuscript, Jerusalem, 1974).

(13) Ibid.

(14) George Harris, "The Soviet Union and Turkey," The Soviet Union and the Middle East: The Post-World War II Era, eds., Ivo J. Lederer and Wayne S. Vucinich (Stanford, California: Hoover Institution Press, 1974), pp. 25-54; Yaacov Roi, From Encroachment to Involvement (New York: John Wiley & Sons, 1974), pp. 11-17; Adam B. Ulam, Expansion and Coexistence (New York: Praeger Publishers, 1968), pp. 389-90, 430-31.

(15) For sources, see Firuz Kazenzadeh, "Soviet-Iranian Relations: A Quarter Century of Freeze and Thaw" in The Soviet Union and the Middle East eds., pp. 55-77 (note 14 supra); Rouhollah K. Ramazani, Iran's Foreign Policy, 1941-1973 (Charlottesville: University Press of Virginia, 1975), pp. 109-53; Roi, pp. 17-21, 31-3 (note 14 supra); and George Lenczowski, Russia and the West in Iran, 1918-1948 (Ithaca, N.Y.: Cornell University Press, 1949), pp. 284-315.

(16) Michael Bar-Zohar, Ben Gurion, Vol. II (Tel Aviv: Am Oved, 1977), p. 862. (Hebrew text)

(17) Ezer Weizman, Lecha Shamaim, Lecha Aretz (Yours the Sky, Yours the Earth) (Tel Aviv: Ma 'ariv Publishing House, 1975), pp. 69-73.

(18) Ramazani, pp. 198-250 (note 15 supra).

(19) The literature on the Suez operation and the Sinai campaign is already extensive. Some of the sources used here are Hugh Thomas, The Suez Affair (New York: Harper & Row, 1969); Michael Brecher, Decisions in Israel's Foreign Policy (London: Oxford University Press, 1974), pp. 225-317; Moshe Dayan, Avnei Derech (Story of My Life) (Tel Aviv: Dvir Publishing House, 1976), pp. 192-342; Moshe Dayan, Yoman Ma' arechet Sinai (Sinai Campaign Diary) (Tel Aviv: Am Hassefer, 1967); J.C. Wylie, "The Sixth Fleet and American Diplomacy," Soviet-American Rivalry in the Middle East, ed. J.C. Hurewitz (New York: Praeger Publishers, 1969), pp. 55-60; Roi, pp. 182-98 (note 14 supra); Michael Bar-Zohar, Gesher 'Al Hayyam Hattikhon (Bridge Over the Mediterranean) (Tel Aviv: Am Hassefer, 1965).

(20) For the Israeli perception of the Soviet threat, see Brecher, pp. 289-93 (note 19 supra). For the American reaction, see Dwight David Eisenhower, Waging Peace, 1956-1961 (New York: Doubleday, 1965), pp. 89-99.

(21) Nadav Safran, From War to War (New York: Pegasus, 1969), p. 114.

(22) Patrick Seale, The Struggle for Syria (London: Oxford University Press, 1965); John Coert Campbell, Defense of the Middle East (New York: Harper, 1958), pp. 195-97; and Roi, pp. 234-46 (note 14 supra).

(23) Seale. (note 22 supra); Eisenhower, pp. 262-91 (note 20 supra); Roi, pp. 255-65 (note 14 supra); Council on Foreign Relations, The U.S. in World Affairs (New York: 1960), for the years 1957 and 1958; and Jack Shulimson, "Marines in Lebanon 1958," Marine Corps Historical Reference Pamphlet (Washington, D.C.: Historical Branch, G-3 Division Headquarters, US Marine Corps, 1966).

(24) Safran, p. 115 (note 21 supra).

(25) Benjamin Shwadran, "The Kuwait Incident," Middle Eastern Affairs 13 (January 1962): 2-13; and 13 (February 1962): 43-53.

(26) The number of sources on the 1967 crisis and war is extensive. For some of the various aspects of the crisis, see Walter Laqueur, The Road to War, 1967 (London: Weidenfeld and Nicolson, 1969); Safran (note 21 supra); Brecher, pp. 318-453 (note 19 supra); Benjamin Geist, "The Six Days War" (Ph.D. thesis, Jerusalem, 1974); and Alvin Z. Rubinstein, Red Star on the Nile (Princeton, New Jersey: Princeton University Press, 1977). For a discussion of the role of the superpowers as intermediaries or interventionists, see Oran Young, "Intermediaries and Interventionists: Third Parties in the Middle East Crisis," International Journal 23:1 (1967-68): 52-73.

(27) Rubinstein, pp. 46-7 (note 26 supra).

(28) Rubinstein, ibid., pp. 103-18; Yair Evron, The Middle East (London

and New York: Elek and Praeger Publishers, 1973), pp. 218-25; Lawrence Whetten, The Canal War (Cambridge, Mass.: The MIT Press, 1974), pp. 94-100, 107-22; Mohamed Heikal, The Road to Ramadan (London: Collins, 1975), pp. 160-64; Dan Margalit, Sheder Mehabait Halavan (A Dispatch from the White House) (Tel Aviv: Orpaz, 1971);Roi, pp. 528-536 (note 14 supra); Yaacov Roi and Ilana Diamant-Kass, The Soviet Military Involvement in Egypt, January 1970-July 1972 (Jerusalem: Hebrew University, 1974); and William B. Quandt, Decade of Decisions: American Policy Toward the Arab-Israeli Conflict 1967-1976 (Berkeley: University of California Press, 1977).

(29) Quandt, ibid.; Evron, pp. 159-61 (note 28 supra); Roi, pp. 536-40 (note 14 supra); Marvin Kalb and Bernard Kalb, Kissinger (Boston: Little, Brown, 1974), pp. 190-209; Henry Brandon, "Jordon: The Forgotten Crisis — Were We Masterful," Foreign Policy no. 10 (Spring 1973): 158-70; David Schoenbaum, "Jordon: The Forgotten Crisis (2) . . . or Lucky?" Foreign Policy no. 10 (Spring 1973): 171-81; Neville Brown, "Jordanian Civil War," The Military Review 11 (September 1971): 38-48.

(30) See inter alia Walter Laqueur, Confrontation (London: Abacus, 1974); Quandt, (note 28 supra); Jon D. Glassman, Arms for the Arabs (Baltimore: Johns Hopkins University Press, 1975); Rubinstein (note 26 supra); Whetten, pp. 242-300 (note 28 supra); William B. Quandt, Soviet Policy in the October 1973 War (Santa Monica: Rand Corporation, 1976); International Institute for Strategic Studies, Strategic Survey, 1973 (London: 1973); Chaim Herzog, The War of Atonement (London: Weidenfeld & Nicolson, 1975); Zeev Schiff, Reidat Adamah Be'October (Earthquake in October) (Tel Aviv: Zmora Bitan Modan, 1974); Dayan, Avnei Derech, pp. 569-676 (note 19 supra); and Kalb and Kalb, pp. 450-99 (note 29 supra).

(31) For the observation that American military intervention in the global international system has declined considerably since 1965, excluding Southeast Asia, see Barry M. Blechman and Stephen S. Kaplan, "Armed Forces as Political Instruments," Survival 19 (July-August 1977): 169-73. This article is based on their extended study of United States military interventions in 1946-75 and will be published soon. See also Hazelwood p. 81 (note 10 supra); and cf., David Gompert, "Constraints of Military Power: Lessons of the Past Decade," in Diffusion of Power: I. Proliferation of Force, Adelphi Papers no. 133 (London: International Institute for Strategic Studies, 1977): 1-13. See also Klaus Knorr, "On the International Uses of Military Force in the Contemporary World," Orbis 21 (Spring 1977): 5-27. Knorr points to the continued relevance of military power in the present international system and to the complex use of force and threats to intervene by the superpowers. His analysis of the balance of nuclear deterrence, on the one hand, and of the increasing strength of third world countries, on the other hand, leads him however to expect ". . . that the superpowers will have diminishing military influence in the Third World," p. 26.

(32) The Israeli leadership has been divided in its perceptions of the probability of Soviet intervention. As noted before, in 1956 Ben-Gurion considered Soviet military intervention very probable. In 1967, Dayan was again very concerned about a possible Soviet intervention, pp. 474, 485 (note 19 supra).

(33) Safran, pp. 294-96 (note 21 supra).

2 The Great Powers' Nonproliferation Policies toward the Third World with Particular Reference to the Middle East and Persian Gulf

Steven J. Baker

Nonproliferation policy in the Middle East and the Persian Gulf must seek to keep some countries from acquiring nuclear weapons while preventing one country from using the nuclear weapons it has already acquired. Past policies of the great powers have helped to create this difficult situation. It remains to be seen whether present and future nonproliferation policies can prevent a bad situation from becoming even worse.

GREAT POWERS AND NONPROLIFERATION

Since the end of World War II, the possession of nuclear weapons has been a significant dimension of great power status. Not surprisingly, the established great powers adopted nonproliferation policies designed to maintain their status and privileges relative to the rest of the countries of the world. No great power has given or sold nuclear weapons to other countries, although the United States and the Soviet Union did aid the nuclear weapons programs of their respective great power allies, Great Britain and China. The United States and the Soviet Union have also deployed their nuclear weapons in a dozen or more countries around the globe. Along with other advanced industrial countries, they compete in the worldwide export of peaceful nuclear energy technologies which could have weapons' applications. At the same time, they argue that they are opposed to the further proliferation of nuclear weapons.

This approach to nonproliferation is so riddled with ambiguities that it is questionable whether anything which can plausibly be described as a policy has been operative. At a high level of abstraction, it does seem possible to characterize the great powers as having pursued the goal of nonproliferation, but the priority accorded this goal has varied over time. The means used have not always been unambiguously related to the goal or to other means. Furthermore, the policy has differed among the three major types of great powers: the superpowers, the United

States and the Soviet Union; the second-rank powers which are nuclear weapons states, France, Great Britain, and China; and the non-nuclear weapons states which are great powers, West Germany and Japan.

Some have contrasted American and Soviet approaches to the problem of nuclear proliferation. While the United States has taken the universal approach, seeking to proscribe all further spread of nuclear weapons to any nation whatever, the Soviet Union has taken a more selective approach, concerned principally with preventing nations such as West Germany from going nuclear.(1) This generalization may be useful for the mid-1960s period when the Nuclear Nonproliferation Treaty (NPT) was being negotiated. It is less valid, however, for the broader sweep of nonproliferation policies of the superpowers. American nonproliferation policy has been, and to some extent continues to be, based on a case-by-case analysis of what the United States government has judged possible and/or desirable at the time. The United States government decided in the late 1950s to aid the British nuclear weapons program, but has generally discouraged the nuclear weapons aspirations of other European allies and those of Japan.(2) The United States chose not to protest the Indian nuclear test, but it applied heavy pressure on South Korea and Pakistan to cancel their proposed purchases of nuclear fuel reprocessing plants from France.

Soviet nonproliferation policy has been more restrictive and less ambiguous. Indeed, with the remarkable exception of nuclear aid to China, one might argue that Soviet practice has more closely approximated the universal nonproliferation model than has the United States practice. Until recently, Soviet foreign aid in peaceful nuclear technology has been very limited. Research reactors have been supplied to countries of the Soviet bloc, Yugoslavia, and a few countries in the third world — Egypt, Ghana, Iraq, and Indonesia.(3) No Soviet power reactors have been exported yet outside a small circle of nations, the Soviet bloc and Finland where the Soviet Union could expect to exercise the closest control. Nuclear aid to China is a significant exception. It seems clear that without Soviet help, especially in the design and construction of a gaseous diffusion uranium enrichment plant at Lanchow, China would not have been able to pursue its nuclear weapons program which resulted in the explosion of a nuclear device in 1964.(4) This aid goes far beyond American aid to the British weapons program, a fact which the Soviet Union likes to ignore when criticizing America's contribution to nuclear proliferation. This selective nuclear aid turned out to be a major policy error on the part of the Soviet Union.

Even if the Russians were primarily concerned with the identity of potential proliferants rather than the absolute number of additional nuclear states, their list of potentially worrisome countries has included most of the principal threshold nations, especially West Germany and Japan. Therefore, their selective concerns have been compatible with the United States' and other countries' more universal concerns. This provided for the kind of superpower consultation which led to the tabling of a Soviet-American joint draft NPT in 1967, concerted pressures to encourage adherence to the NPT, and cooperation in the context of the nuclear suppliers' talks which have taken place in London since spring of 1975.

It is significant that this superpower agreement emerged in the mid-1960s. This was the post-Cuba period in which the United States was actively engaged in its military "world-policeman" role and the Soviet Union was beginning its military build-up, the maturation of which in the late 1970s has given the Russians a global intervention capability. The spread of nuclear weapons would raise the potential costs of any future superpower military intervention around the world, thus introducing a whole new set of constraints on the exercise of the superpowers' global roles. Their cooperation on nonproliferation was, therefore, a logical result of a perceived need to make the world safe for superpower intervention.

The other great powers, which are also nuclear weapons states, have an objective interest in the persistence of an international nuclear weapons regime in which they have status and privileges which their rivals and other potential great powers do not have. This objective interest has not prevented these great power nuclear weapons states (NWS) from taking rather different positions on nonproliferation in general, and in particular on the nonproliferation regime as embodied in the NPT.

Dependent on the United States since the early 1960s for its major nuclear delivery systems, the British government has been generally inclined to follow the American lead on nonproliferation, including the imposition of the NPT regime, but it also sought to maintain an option for a European nuclear force should European political cooperation ever reach the point at which this would become feasible. Failing this, the British and other Europeans succeeded in winning from the United States a unilateral declaration to the effect that the future formation of a European nuclear force would not constitute proliferation.(5) Soviet opposition to the European clause is an example of its concern for the identity of nuclear powers rather than numbers. Even though a European nuclear force would reduce the number of its nuclear weapon adversaries the Soviet Union feared the creation of a more effective nuclear force and one over which West Germany might have some control.

Having chosen to persist in its nuclear weapons development at great cost and in the face of opposition from the United States, France rejected the NPT as one facet of an emerging Soviet-American condominium. But the French government also made it clear that it would act "as if" it were an NPT member and, therefore, would seek to maintain the nonproliferation regime. This put France in the enviable position of benefiting from Soviet and American exertions to gain maximum adherence to the NPT without having to make any politically costly exertions of its own.

Completely independent of Soviet technology and nuclear aid since 1960 and faced with growing ideological and territorial differences with the Soviet Union, China has rejected even the principle of an international nuclear regime. China has affirmed the right of nations to have nuclear weapons for their defense, but China has given no sign of seeking to aid other nations' weapons programs or even peaceful nuclear energy programs, which are in any case almost nonexistent in China.

Rather, in the nuclear field as in others, "self-reliance" is advanced as the policy maxim. This suggests that nuclear threshold countries can expect moral support from China but no more. It has been reported that the Chinese refused to sell Libya's Qaddafi a nuclear weapon which, if true, lends credence to the stated Chinese policy.(6)

Those great powers which are not nuclear weapons states (NNWS), Japan and West Germany, have been persuaded to support the existing nonproliferation regime even though it puts them at a political disadvantage vis-a-vis other great powers. This is a concommitant of their general dependence on the United States in international affairs in the postwar period. The security protection of the American nuclear deterrent was a precondition of their acceptance of the NPT; the promise of improved relations with the Soviet Union and other nations was held out as a reward for acceptance of the NPT. While not ignoring the sensitive question of political discrimination inherent in the nonproliferation regime, West Germany and Japan were particularly concerned about the impact of the NPT on commercial activities in the nuclear energy field. The possibility that the nuclear regime might inhibit the pursuit of commercial nuclear energy goals has become a reality with American opposition to the 1975 German-Brazilian nuclear energy deal. Bonn's apparent intransigence on the Brazilian issue is an example of the problems inherent in trying to maintain a nonprolifera-tion regime which no longer corresponds to the effective distribution of power in the world in the broadest sense: economic, political, and military power, with nuclear and nonnuclear dimensions.

What emerges from these observations is a general pattern of self-interested commitment to nonproliferation on the part of the great powers. But the emphases differ depending on the positions of each great power within the nuclear status hierarchy. The difficulty of maintaining this hierarchy is becoming increasingly evident as great powers jockey for position and new aspirants to great power status emerge.

NONPROLIFERATION AND THE THIRD WORLD

The proliferation of nuclear weapons to the third world was not a primary concern of the great powers until the 1974 Indian nuclear test. Great power nonproliferation policies have been tailored to developed nations such as Japan, West Germany, and a few others, since the prime threshold states have been defined as those which are threatened, particularly by an existing nuclear weapons state, and have a high level of technical capability. As late as 1973, the most frequently mentioned threshold countries in the third world were India and Argentina; Brazil appeared less frequently; and Taiwan, South Korea, and Iran were almost never mentioned. Nevertheless, a 1976 study sees the possibility of proliferation beginning in Asia and Latin America and only as a consequence, spreading to the industrialized threshold countries.(7)

Because of the high level of technical capacity, restricting the dissemination of nuclear technology was judged to be ineffective as a nonproliferation policy. It was also inimical to the economic interests of great powers seeking foreign markets for nuclear equipment.(8) Instead, the main tools of nonproliferation policy became political restraints on the uses to which technology might be put. Thus, intergovernmental, peaceful use agreements as well as bilateral and international inspection systems were sought. Spreading the technology was justified as a means of spreading these political restraints. The close complex ties between the great powers and the industrialized threshold countries made these kinds of political restraints a plausible part of an effective nonproliferation policy.

The same nonproliferation policies were extended to the third world where very different conditions prevailed. Nuclear aid and exports to the less-developed countries often created a technological capability where none had previously existed. The political commitments to restraint, which third world countries assumed, were often ambiguous. Peaceful use meant one thing to Canada and something else to the Indian government. Often, the complex web of collateral ties between great powers and third world countries was either lacking, or such ties as existed were negatively perceived by the third world governments. Many third world countries were caught up in regional rivalries unrelated to the great powers. The result was to introduce a new and destabilizing nuclear weapons potential into the third world. New nuclear threshold countries are emerging, which cannot be ignored by the great powers but which cannot be controlled by them either. This situation has given rise to demands for more stringent safeguards.

Under these shortsighted policies, the great powers' nuclear technology was widely disseminated in the third world from the mid-1950s. The economic development needs of the third world were used in part to provide a rationale for the American Atoms-for-Peace initiative of 1953 and for the subsequent nuclear energy development programs of the International Atomic Energy Agency (IAEA). Small research reactors were exported to several third world countries to stimulate an interest in nuclear energy, but the low level of much of the third world's economic development limited the relevance of nuclear-generated electric power throughout most of this period. Only six nuclear power reactors were exported to the third world between 1955 and 1969: four to India, and one each to Argentina and Pakistan. As the demand for nuclear energy began to grow in the late 1960s, additional developing countries placed orders for nuclear plants, including South Korea, Brazil, Mexico, and Taiwan. Following the 1973-74 oil crisis, there was a marked increase in interest in nuclear energy with major orders signed by Brazil and Iran. All of these exports took place pursuant to intergovernmental peaceful use agreements and involved international inspections.

While the 1973-74 rise in the price of oil made nuclear energy more economically attractive in the third world than it had been in the past, the perturbations of the world's economic system which accompanied the crisis made the financing of nuclear energy installations more difficult. Furthermore, while the great powers' higher oil import bills created a strong interest in nuclear exports, the 1974 Indian test sensitized governments and public opinion to the potential dangers inherent in nuclear exports. The result was to heighten the uncertainty regarding the economic viability and/or political wisdom of nuclear energy exports to the third world.

Some of these doubts were expressed in the 1975 report sponsored by the United States Energy Research and Development Administration (ERDA), which was particularly critical of the promotional activities of the International Atomic Energy Agency. It charged that the IAEA's methods consistently underestimated the costs of nuclear-generated electrical energy in the third world.(9) Certainly, the present rate of nuclear energy installation in less developed countries is considerably less than earlier IAEA projections.

Generally, capital-intensive nuclear energy seems to be a poor economic choice for most third world countries which are already staggering under a heavy burden of foreign debt. The nuclear exporter's financial subsidies, which reduce the initial cost of investment in nuclear energy, may simply aggravate the longer term financial problems of the third world. Since third world countries typically have large labor surpluses, their dependence on an energy source which requires small numbers of very highly skilled technicians is questionable. Oil and gas are more easily absorbed into the economies of developing countries than nuclear energy. They do not require the kind of investment in nuclear research centers and the training of technicians which distort the allocation of scarce economic resources in the third world. Nuclear energy exports contribute more to the balance of payments of the industrial countries than to the economic development of the third world. In addition to the economic and technical considerations, third world countries may have political reasons for not turning to nuclear energy. Nuclear exporters argue that exports work to the political advantage of the great powers by making the third world dependent upon them. If true, the result may be favorable to nonproliferation but negative in terms of the national interests of the third world countries in question. Since this is a central argument in nonproliferation policies, it is addressed separately below.

NONPROLIFERATION IN THE MIDDLE EAST AND PERSIAN GULF

Until 1974, none of the great powers considered the Middle East or the Persian Gulf as particularly attractive areas for major nuclear energy sales. Nor were they seen as areas where special caution had to be exercised in terms of nuclear research technology transfers and aid. These are not energy scarce areas, and existing safeguard systems were apparently judged adequate to cover the agreements under which research reactors were exported to Israel, Iran, Egypt, and Iraq.(see Table 2.1)

Power reactor exports to the Middle East were only proposed once before 1974, immediately following the 1967 War by a former United States official. Two reactors were to be built as joint Arab-Israeli projects, fostering peace, economic development, and a long-term

Table 2.1. Research Reactors in Major Middle East
and Persian Gulf Nations

Location	Designation	Type	MWth	Operating Date	Fuel	Theoretical Pu Production kg/yr
Egypt	WWR-C	Tank	2	7/61		
Iran	UTRR	Pool	5	11/67	Enr.U	
Iraq	WWR	Tank	2	1/63		
Israel	IRR-1	Pool	5	6/60	Enr.U	
	IRR-2	Tank, D^2O	26	12/63	Nat.U	2.3 tax

Most published sources give the Dimona reactor a plutonium production capacity of about one warhead equivalent per year, or five to six kilograms of plutonium, twice that indicated here. Estimates can be found for Dimona's plutonium production capacity as high as fifteen to twenty kilograms.

Source: David Rundquist, et al., Technology for Nuclear Weapons Capability (La Jolla, California: Science Applications, July 1975), p. 77.

American presence in the area. This proposal was apparently not taken seriously by the Johnson Administration.(10) In view of the 1974 reactor offers to Egypt and Israel, some members of the Nixon Administration seemingly felt that nuclear technology was still a useful foreign policy tool.

In retrospect, the most significant of the early nuclear transfers was the French shipment of a nuclear research reactor to Israel. Repeated reports in the last year and a half have reduced the ambiguity of Israel's nuclear status. Israel is now widely assumed to be an undemonstrated but militarily nuclear state; India, on the other hand, is a demonstrated but as yet nonmilitary nuclear state. Even those who require an official Israeli declaration or a nuclear test before conceding that Israel possesses nuclear weapons seem to agree that Israel is within a matter of hours of having weapons. Even if Israel had gone no farther than to manufacture components to be assembled in case of emergency, it would have to be considered a nuclear state. The nuclear threshold has become increasingly ambiguous as nations like Israel have approached it.(11) The plutonium produced by the Dimona reactor is presumably the basis for the ten to twenty nuclear weapons the Israelis are believed to have fabricated. The French have apparently exercised no inspection rights at all over this reactor.(12) In the early 1960s, the United States government was allowed to inspect the Dimona reactor. The results of any inspections under this arrangement have not been made public.

The French-Israeli case seems to be an exception to the terms under which nuclear technology has been transferred by great powers to the Middle East. As a rule, agreements for cooperation negotiated by the United States cover inspections of both the facilities transferred and the fuels. Where the safeguard function is superceded by a trilateral agreement between the supplier country, the recipient nation, and the IAEA, the Vienna agency carries out the actual inspections. The research reactor supplied to Iran is covered by this kind of agreement.(13) Future American-supplied power plants will also be covered in this manner. If the Iranian agreement with the IAEA ever were to cease, then the inspection rights would revert to the United States.

Until 1969, Soviet agreements for cooperation in nuclear energy did not include any provision for IAEA inspections.(14) In fact, they had few explicit safeguard procedures of any kind. Rather, the Soviet Union relied on the presence of its own personnel to monitor the activities of the exported facilities and fuels.(15) Research reactors were exported to Egypt and Iraq on these terms, but future Soviet transfers will presumably be consistent with the guidelines set down by the London Group discussed subsequently. Like the research reactor the United States supplied to Iran, the size and technical features of research reactors supplied by the Soviet Union to Egypt and Iraq suggest that they are incapable of producing appreciable quantities of plutonium. The contribution of these kinds of reactors to proliferation is, therefore, limited to the experience and technical competence gained by researchers working with these facilities.

This pattern of limited penetration of nuclear technology into these regions changed in 1974. In February, France and Iran announced an agreement through which as many as five power reactors would eventually be supplied to Iran, and as partial repayment, natural gas would be delivered to France. The total deal was estimated to be worth $4.5-5.0 billion, with the reactors valued at about $1 billion.(16) In 1975, Iran purchased a 12.5 percent share in the French, government-sponsored uranium enrichment consortium, Eurodif. For its share, Iran made a $1 billion loan to the French Atomic Energy Commission (CEA) on what were described as "very favorable terms." The total cost of the Eurodif plant has been estimated to be around $3 billion. Increased Iranian participation in a follow-on enrichment plant, Coredif, has been announced.(18) Apparently neither of these agreements involve the sharing of uranium enrichment technology between France and Iran, nor do present plans include the construction of an enrichment plant in Iran.

Pursuing its ambitious nuclear energy goal of 34,000 megawatt-electrical units to be installed by 1995, in the fall of 1974 the Iranian government announced an agreement with Germany's Kraftwerk Union (KWU) to supply an additional pair of 1,200 MWe pressurized water reactors (PWRs).(19) In March 1975, the biggest of these agreements was announced: the United States government would approve the sale to Iran of up to eight 1,000 MWe power reactors, the eventual value of which might well be in excess of $7 billion.(20) The implementation of this enormous agreement has become stalled in Washington, principally because of disagreement over eventual reprocessing of spent fuel. The United States government, as a matter of policy, will not export reprocessing capability as a precondition to implementation of the reactor deal.(21) Similarly, the draft of the American-Egyptian agreement for cooperation states that any eventual reprocessing shall be done outside the region.(22) With the advent of the Carter Administration, the policy, first enunciated for Iran, has been universalized.

Iran's development goals and oil revenues make it the principal market for nuclear technology in the Middle East and Persian Gulf regions. The size of the Iranian program dwarfs anything being considered by other states in the area, but since 1977 financial difficulties have slowed the Iranian push into nuclear energy . This provides a partial explanation of the patience of the Iranian government with the United States' hesitations in implementing the reactor supply agreement. Even more important, the domestic political upheaval in Iran during 1978-79 promises to produce a sharp curtailment in Iranian power reactor orders and construction. In addition, the Iranian program faces numerous other problems. Seismic activity and a dearth of interior rivers to provide cooling water are sources of siting difficulties. A general lack of material and industrial infrastructure, inadequate roads and port facilities, and a lack of trained local manpower make the Iranian nuclear program extraordinarily dependent on foreigners. These shortcomings have made the reactor programs into so-called "super-turnkey" projects in which everything must be supplied by the contractor.(23) The multiple uncertainties of constructing nuclear facilities under these circumstances make it doubtful that the Iranian program will be realized on schedule, even if financial and political difficulties prove to be transitory.

The proposed American sale of nuclear reactors to Egypt and Israel, announced in June 1974, were modest in comparison to the deals Iran was concluding.(24) But these offers had a major political impact in the United States, coming as they did only eight months after the most recent round in the Arab-Israeli war and one month after the Indian nuclear test. The offers took congressional and public opinion by surprise. President Nixon's entire Middle East tour was seen by many as a device to divert attention from his domestic political problems.

Unlike Iran, neither Egypt nor Israel has ratified the NPT; nor did the United States government make NPT adherence a precondition for receiving nuclear power plants and fuel supplies from it. Egypt has signed the NPT and has indicated its willingness to ratify if Israel does so. Israel has rejected the NPT because adherence would require IAEA inspection of all Israeli nuclear facilities, including the Dimona reactor. Congressional concern over these offers led to legislation ensuring that the entire Congress will be given an opportunity to approve any agreements of cooperation eventually concluded with Egypt and Israel.(25) Israeli objections to the supply of nuclear technology to Egypt and the resistance of both countries to the kinds of comprehensive controls that the United States government would like to impose on nuclear aid to the Middle East have blocked the implementation of this agreement, since the nuclear transfers to both countries have become a kind of package deal. Press reports have indicated that the Israeli government is proposing an alternative, joint, Egyptian-Israeli nuclear energy project in the Sinai.(26) Whether this is a serious proposal or merely an attempt to stall the implementation of the Egyptian agreement is unclear. The Carter Administration would probably prefer to allow these offers to languish, and it is not clear how any eventual reactor agreement will fare before Congress. In the meantime, Egypt has gone ahead and signed a letter of intent for a 600 MWe Westinghouse power reactor.(27)

In the wake of the initial check on the implementation of the American-Egyptian reactor deal, it was reported that the Soviet Union had concluded an agreement to supply Egypt with a reactor.(28) The status of the agreement remains unclear. The Soviet Union has apparently concluded an agreement with the government of Libya for the supply of a small nuclear power reactor.(29) The United States is said to have refused to supply such a reactor because of political objections to Colonel Qaddafi. Almost simultaneously, with the announcement of the Soviet Libyan deal, Libya ratified the NPT. This action suggests that adherence to the NPT may have been a political precondition demanded by the Soviet Union. An Iraqi purchase of a research reactor and power reactor from France has also been reported.(30)

Each of these technology transfers represents a form of great power intervention in the countries involved. While the predominate considerations are political and economic, there are military implications as well. Nuclear power reactors contribute to a nuclear weapons potential by producing plutonium. The creation of a large group of individuals trained in nuclear sciences and committed to put their skills to work may be one of the most important domestic political forces leading to a nuclear weapons option. While the interests of the great powers in these regions may be political and economic, the interests of the recipient countries may well be political and military. To increase the nuclear weapons potential in an area like the Middle East where nuclear proliferation has already occurred seems particularly dangerous. One possible Machiavellian explanation might be that the parallel American reactor and fuel transfers to Egypt and Israel disguise an attempt to reduce or redress the existing nuclear imbalance between Israel and Egypt. Americans might rationalize this policy as fostering the emergence of a stable nuclear deterrence relationship between Israel and Egypt,(31) but the uncertainties attendant on the emergence of a nuclear deterrence framework in the Middle East are so great that they transform any attempt at extreme subtlety into patent stupidity. Indeed, one might argue that the most stable situation is precisely that which exists now, stability based on imbalance rather than equality in nuclear capabilities.

The fact that these two areas, but particularly the Middle East, are prone to conflict is the principal reason for questioning the wisdom of nuclear transfers there. The persistence of conflict creates strong incentives for transforming nuclear energy technology into nuclear weapons. Nuclear facilities would become prime targets for attack during wars. Nuclear facilities and materials would be attractive targets for terrorist incidents, even though countries in these regions may be able to take physical security precautions beyond those possible in Western Europe and America. Past lapses into armed conflict suggest a high probability that nuclear weapons might be used should nuclear deterrence fail. Finally, to transfer nuclear technology to regions of the world with these troubling characteristics, which are also areas in which the interests of all the great powers are intimately involved seems to be imprudence bordering on madness. None of the great powers can hope to remain insulated from the effects of their shortsightedness.

The range of great power motivations for these nuclear transfers was most clearly articulated in response to American critics of the Egyptian-Israeli reactor offers. They may be summed up as follows: these transfers will increase our political leverage over countries dependent on our nuclear technology; exports benefit our economy; if we don't do it, someone else will.(32)

NUCLEAR EXPORTS TO THE MIDDLE EAST AND PERSIAN GULF

Nuclear Exports and Political Influence

A key argument advanced by the United States government in defense of its nuclear exports to the Middle East is that such exports are a means of extending its political influence within the area. This political influence would be used either to reduce the likelihood of armed conflict or to seek to control the course of such conflicts that do occur. In this sense, nuclear exports are one part of a web of dependence which binds the countries in these regions to the great powers and which is defended by the great powers as conflict-moderating.

In theory, countries dependent on the United States and other great powers for nuclear technology, fuels, facilities, and personnel will be inhibited from using these for the fabrication of nuclear weapons because of fear of great power opposition. None of the countries of the Middle East or Persian Gulf has an industrial base which would allow it to produce nuclear power facilities independently in the next decade or two. The companies of the advanced industrial countries, which are the source of the major components of nuclear power plants, all operate under close regulation by their home governments. They are often in part government owned and invariably government promoted. Nuclear power plants take from six to ten years to construct. Large numbers of foreign technicians are needed to build and operate a plant. Therefore, the dependence relationship is a prolonged one. The same can be said of nuclear fuel supplies. None of the nations in the Middle East has yet discovered appreciable quantities of uranium ore which could be processed into power reactor fuels, although prospecting continues.(33) Israel has successfully extracted small quantities of uranium from phosphate deposits in the Negev. These methods may be sufficient for small weapons programs but probably not for a major nuclear energy program. Israelis estimate that Israeli uranium deposits could supply three natural uranium-fueled reactors of the 400-600 MWe range,(34) but persistent reports that Israel has hijacked international uranium shipments, if true, suggest that Israel cannot supply even its present limited demands. The ready availability of natural uranium ores on the open market from nations other than the great powers might reduce fuel dependence. The ore, however, would have to be enriched for use in the types of power reactors now being ordered in these regions. As yet there are no plans for an indigenous enrichment capability in any of these countries apart from Israel, where laser isotope separation research is apparently far advanced.(35) Iran has secured a share of the French enrichment capability, which leaves open the remote possibility that enrichment technologies could in the future be imported from abroad as in the Brazilian example. Short of this, the nuclear energy programs of the area will be dependent on the nuclear suppliers for the fuels essential to produce weapons grade plutonium. Therefore, they will be open to the sanction of a fuel cut-off. Table 2 summarizes the nuclear power reactor exports committed to major Middle East and Persian Gulf nations.

Table 2.2. Nuclear Power Reactor Exports Committed
To Major Middle East and Persian Gulf Nations

	Size MWe	Supplier Country, Industry	Status of Agreement[a]	Eventual Pu Production Capacity[b] kg/yr
Egypt 1	600	United States, Westinghouse	1	97
Iran 1	1,200	West Germany, KWU	3	193
2	1,200	West Germany KWU	3	193
3	900	France, Framatome	2	145
4	900	France, Framatome	2	145
Israel 1	950	United States, unspecified	1	153
Iraq 1	600	France, Framatome	1	97

a (1) intergovernmental agreement in principle.
   (2) industrial contracts signed.
   (3) construction begun.

b Assumes inter alia a plant capacity factor of 75 percent.

The plutonium accumulated in spent fuel elements is the most troublesome aspect of nuclear exports to these regions. Nuclear suppliers are not only increasingly concerned that reprocessing of spent fuels be done outside the Middle East,(36) but they are also considering a range of possible restrictions on reprocessing plant exports. Recently, both France and West Germany have moved to prohibit reprocessing plant exports beyond those for which agreements already exist. Canada has imposed tighter standards on all nuclear exports. This includes the provision that the entire nuclear industry of a recipient country can be placed under international inspections, the so-called "poor man's NPT."(37) The Ford Administration proposed a three-year moratorium on all reprocessing plant exports.(38) Within the Carter Administration, there is renewed interest in guaranteeing fuel supplies to reduce the incentive for national facilities. Alternatively, spent fuel elements could be repurchased by the supplier before the plutonium is removed. In sum, the great powers are actively seeking a policy which fulfills their desire to exercise nonproliferation controls over fuel supplies and which simultaneously allows them to pursue their economic and political objectives in these areas.

Just how much political leverage is in practice afforded the great powers by the dependence of these countries on nuclear imports remains to be seen. The general assumption seems to be that the higher the degree of interchange between two nations, the more potential leverage exists. However, the case for supplier leverage based on experiences with conventional weapons transfers is ambiguous. Nuclear exports to these regions would seem to complicate the tasks of controlling the course of conflicts while increasing enormously the destructive consequences of failing to control them.

More specifically, the argument that nuclear exports give leverage over the future uses of nuclear technology is unconvincing. For example, nuclear industry spokesmen argue that large nuclear power programs are less likely to lead to nuclear weapons than small, semiclandestine nuclear programs.(39) By implication, for nonproliferation purposes, heavy dependence on nuclear energy is preferable to small nuclear power programs. If this reasoning is sound, then few countries in the Middle East or Persian Gulf should be receiving nuclear technology since few can usefully adopt nuclear energy on a large scale, certainly not Libya or Iraq and probably not Israel or Egypt. Assuming a 600 MWe cut-off point, the IAEA projects no more than two power plants for Egypt and none for the others before 1990.(40) Industries, however, have shown no reluctance to export to these countries. Iran alone has the population and development potential which would appear to justify a substantial nuclear energy program. Even in Iran, the size, number, and sittings of nuclear plants seem more a political than an economic or a technical issue.

The argument that a large nuclear program will be more susceptible to political manipulation is open to serious question. It ignores the reciprocal, interdependent nature of the supplier-consumer relationship in what is increasingly a buyer's market in nuclear technology. If a move toward nuclear weapons were to halt a small nuclear program by suspension of construction on a single reactor or interruption in fuel supplies for one or two small plants, the cost would be relatively small to the supplier. The limited costs of sanctions imposed on a small program would make the imposition of sanctions more likely. But if a move toward a nuclear weapons option were to halt work on two, four, or six reactors and/or involve suspension of fuel deliveries for several reactors, it could well mean financial ruin for the industrial suppliers in question. To protect its own economic interests, the home government of a nuclear industry would be under intense domestic pressure to prevent nuclear related sanctions from being imposed on a large nuclear program.

If the specific nation in question were Iran, the prospects for using nuclear related sanctions in the event of some move toward the acquisition of nuclear weapons are very dim indeed. The Iranian nuclear program to date is based on different versions of the same PWR reactor type. It might not be too difficult for an alternative supplier to finish a nuclear plant begun by someone else or to step in to supply fuels for a reactor constructed by someone else. Diversifying suppliers of a product which is substantially the same gives the consumer greater leverage than any one of the individual suppliers. Only the cooperation of all suppliers would allow them to exercise effective leverage in such a case. The reluctance of nuclear exporters to impose nuclear sanctions on Iran would be particularly great given Iran's role as an oil supplier and major force in OPEC. A nuclear energy embargo would almost certainly be followed by an Iranian oil embargo. Some nuclear suppliers would certainly be tempted, or indeed compelled, to break ranks and refuse to honor the nuclear energy sanctions in return for uninterrupted oil supplies. Neither the general features of large nuclear programs nor the particular features of the Iranian nuclear energy program give much cause for optimistic assumptions concerning the nonproliferation leverage afforded by nuclear exports. In the future, Iran must be assumed to be essentially free to use the technologies acquired as the Iranian government sees fit.

There are levers which might have a positive nonproliferation impact, but it is questionable how important nuclear technology per se is in that pattern of political influence. It is argued that in order to have any influence over what nations do with nuclear technology, the United States or other great powers must be "a factor in the market." Some formulations seem to equate the degree of influence with the share of the market held by a supplier. Limited experience to date suggests that nuclear technology per se is not an effective source of political leverage. In 1976, the United States government successfully persuaded the South Korean government to cancel its order for a spent-fuel reprocessing plant from France. South Korea is dependent on the United States for the completion of its Westinghouse power reactors and for the fuel elements for those reactors. However, there is little evidence that threatened nuclear plant construction halts or fuel supply interruptions were either necessary or sufficient to the success of American pressure on Korea. Rather, the stakes included the withdrawal of American troops stationed in South Korea and the possible withdrawal of United States tactical nuclear weapons. At the same time, past American nuclear technology transfers have increased the credibility of Korea's threats to acquire nuclear weapons in the event of a precipitate United States withdrawal. With the announcement by the Carter Administration that proposed troop withdrawals will be slowed, it is not clear who has more leverage over whom. To the extent that moves toward a nuclear weapons option are motivated by security concerns, nuclear energy-related economic sanctions are not likely to be very successful tools of a nonproliferation policy. If nuclear technology transfers are irrelevant as tools of the nonproliferation policy, there does not seem to be much political justification for them at all.

The South Korean example is exceptional both in the range of levers at the disposal of the nuclear supplier government and in that government's apparent willingness to use those levers. Quite the opposite occurred following the Indian detonation. United States legal experts pointed out that India had not broken any international agreements, and, therefore, there was no pretext for nuclear-related sanctions. Even the subsequent discovery that American heavy water was apparently used to produce the plutonium for the Indian detonation did not trigger a direct American response. The ensuing administrative review of Indian fuel supply deliveries was primarily imposed by lawsuits initiated by American environmentalists. In May 1974, the United States might have cut off nuclear fuel supplies or sought to shut down American supplied reactors; it did not do so. Even where nuclear energy leverage existed, the United States government was unwilling to exercise it. Far more important, the United States government was unwilling to exercise other-than-nuclear forms of leverage available to it to protest the Indian test. While not as dependent on the United States as South Korea, India could have been subjected to diplomatic and economic sanctions. The aim would have been less to alter Indian policy than to show other threshold countries that going nuclear involves real costs. Not only were diplomatic and economic pressures not applied, but the United States soon moved to improve relations with India, thus setting a very unfortunate precedent. However limited, leverage of any kind is only as good as the willingness to use it. To date, political will has been lacking in nonproliferation policies more than political leverage.

United States political leverage apparently has not prevented Israel from producing nuclear weapons. Yet the United States government proposes to provide Israel with American nuclear reactors and fuels. Israel is being rewarded either in spite of or because of its nuclear "bombs in the basement." The lesson will not be lost on Egypt, Iran, and other nations around the globe.

The burden of proof rests on those who argue that nuclear exports contribute to the great powers' political leverage in the Middle East and Persian Gulf. They must establish that the leverage gained is sufficient for nonproliferation purposes and that it is likely to be exercised. Unless these conditions can be met, there should be a very strong presumption against nuclear exports to these areas.

The Economics of Nuclear Exports

The past and present involvement of great powers in the Middle East and the Persian Gulf has largely been a function of their pursuit of national economic interests. Most recently this has taken the form of securing access to the oil and gas resources of these areas. American policy since 1967 represents a deviant case in which political commitments to Israel have grown at the same time as America's economic dependence on Arab oil has grown. The other great powers have tried to avoid the kinds of internal and international stresses resulting from such incongruities.

Nuclear energy exports to these regions have increased as a result of the oil price rise after 1973-74. With more money to spend, these countries can afford imported, energy-intensive development programs and life styles. As these imports increase in cost, the price of oil increases to pay for them. For the great powers, nuclear energy exports to the Middle East and Persian Gulf represent one way of recycling petrodollars; the other way is through massive arms sales.

The principal economic interest of nuclear suppliers is in reactor sales. Up to now, the nuclear suppliers have simply exported their excess capacity. The uncertainty of the international nuclear energy market has created little incentive to maintain production lines geared exclusively to the needs of foreign customers.

The size of economically viable nuclear plants in the industrial countries has continued to increase to the point where 600 MWe is the smallest nuclear plant being produced by nuclear industries. The 1,000 MWe plant is becoming the standard size. The market for nuclear energy in the Middle East and Persian Gulf is thus very limited. IAEA projections suggest that only Egypt and Iran will be able to absorb 600 MWe plants in the period 1980-90.(41) But according to the same IAEA projections, the availability of smaller nuclear plants would considerably expand the market for nuclear exports in these regions. Given the 1974 oil price rise, nuclear plants as small as 150 MWe would be economically competitive with fossil fuel plants. Saudi Arabia, Syria, Kuwait, Lebanon, and Iraq would be possible markets for one or more small-sized power reactors. A few European industries have shown an interest in producing reactors especially for this market.(43) However, no such orders have yet been placed. It is possible that at some future point India might join the ranks of reactor exporters since its national reactor type is a copy of a Canadian 200 MWe pressurized heavy water reactor (PHWR). Its size and technical characteristics would make it very attractive to other third world countries.

Nuclear suppliers, e.g., Germany,(44) seek to penetrate the Middle East-Persian Gulf market at least in part because of a slump in domestic nuclear energy demand which creates an increased interest in exports – exports which governments are eager to support. American firms like Westinghouse have bigger domestic markets, but must now also look to foreign business to keep their nuclear divisions going.(45)

The principal form of export subsidy for power reactors has been trade credits and long-term loans guaranteed by the nuclear supplier governments. Indeed, competition in financing terms has been one of the most significant aspects of the nuclear trade.(46) But differences in the terms of loans and financing have equalized over time and have helped to narrow the competitive advantage of American nuclear reactor exporters.(47) The American share of the world reactor market has dropped from 85 percent before 1972 to its present 42 percent.(48) The commercial value of nuclear fuel supply contracts is subject to many uncertainties. The value of uranium ores has followed the rising price of oil, tripling between July 1974 and July 1975.(49) A fear of growing uranium ore scarcity may drive the ore prices up even if oil prices stabilize.(50) More likely still, both may continue to rise. Commercial enrichment charges have also continued to climb, in part because enrichment processes are energy intensive and, therefore, reflect increases in the price of oil. Iran has moved to secure its enrichment needs through Eurodif and the follow-on Coredif plant. Eventual Egyptian and Israeli power reactors will presumably be supplied with fuels by the United States government. Therefore, unless large numbers of small reactors are installed, the nuclear fuel supply market in the Middle East and Persian Gulf is a limited one which is essentially closed for the foreseeable future.

None of these nuclear energy programs is sufficiently large to warrant national fuel facilities, either reprocessing or enrichment, on purely economic grounds. It is not clear whether reprocessing fuel for recovery and recycling of uranium and plutonium on any scale will ever be economically justified. Preliminary studies seem to agree that commercial reprocessing will not be economically justified for fewer than about 30 reactors of around 1,000 MWe each.(51) By this standard, even the Iranian program would not justify a reprocessing capability on economic grounds alone much before the year 2000.

On the other hand, a small reprocessing plant is quite inexpensive compared to the cost of nuclear power reactors. While a 1,000 MWe reactor is projected to cost around $1 billion in the United States today, a small reprocessing facility might run between $50-150 million with a capacity to service one or more reactors of the 1,000 MWe size.(52) If reprocessing on any scale is a marginal activity economically, then noneconomic considerations might well tip the balance in favor of reprocessing. The technology could be mastered now for eventual large-scale application, perhaps in a fast breeder reactor program. A national reprocessing capability provides a future nuclear weapons option. Even nations which have committed themselves not to produce nuclear weapons may be legitimately interested in providing themselves with an option to meet contingencies for which the NPT allows. Countries are allowed to withdraw from the treaty if extreme interests are jeopardized by extraordinary events. This kind of nuclear weapons option is all the more attractive because it is relatively cheap.

As noted above, the United States-Iranian agreement on the supply of nuclear reactors is being held in abeyance. This is an example of an extraordinary sacrifice of economic interest to political priorities. The reactor contracts are potentially worth several billion dollars to economically hard pressed American industries. That the implementation of the agreement should be jeopardized by disagreement over ancillary facilities valued at a few tens of millions of dollars is almost without precedent. Certainly, the German government has not shown a similar willingness to jeopardize its multibillion dollar nuclear deal with Brazil to respond to objections to the fuel-cycle facilities which are a small part of the package. But agreements involving reactors and fuel facilities are only part of the problem. There may well be a market for reprocessing facilities alone, a market which only France and West Germany have sought to exploit. The fact, however, that the value of such a market is small relative to the broader nuclear market suggests that it may be easier for the nuclear suppliers to agree to restrict fuel-cycle exports than it would be for them to agree to restrictions on reactor exports.

None of these figures suggests an overwhelming great power economic stake in nuclear power exports to these regions. These nuclear exports are only one part of the economic exchanges between the great powers and the nations of these regions. Yet, even though a small part of the total, such exports are perceived by the nuclear supplier nations as being a favorable contribution to their balances of trade and payments. ERDA estimates nuclear exports will account for 2.4-2.7 percent of total United States exports in 1985 and will increase to 3.2-4.0 percent by the year 2000.(53) Also important is the differential interest of some suppliers as opposed to others. The Europeans are relatively more dependent on nuclear exports than is the United States. Some companies within each supplier are more export-dependent than others; for example, Germany's KWU is more export-oriented than France's Framatome. These differential interests in the nuclear trade help to explain varying degrees of willingness to cooperate to restrict trade in the pursuit of noneconomic priorities like nonproliferation.

Competition, Exports, and Nonproliferation

Competition among great powers for nuclear exports to the Middle East and the Persian Gulf is, of course, one dimension of the pursuit of the political and economic interests outlined above. Competition has affected the diffusion of nuclear weapons potential in this area by influencing the type and rate of nuclear technology transfers and the terms of export.

Competition in the nuclear energy field has had the kind of stimulative impact that economic theory supposes it will have. Indeed, if the profit picture is as bleak as industry sources maintain, one might argue that only government subsidized competition has kept the nuclear energy industry going.(54) International competition has been particularly important. American-British competition stimulated United States nuclear energy exports to Western Europe in the late 1950s, even though the economic prospects for nuclear energy in that period were to prove disappointing. Soviet-American competition in the same period led to the sharing of nuclear technology and to the export of small research reactors to nations of the third world. Competition among the United

States, Canada, France, West Germany and the Soviet Union in the sale of nuclear generating equipment and fuels has created a situation in which there are several alternative sources for obtaining nuclear technology. Countries like Japan, Italy, Sweden, and Switzerland are emerging as major nuclear power component suppliers.

This competition among suppliers was one of the rationales advanced by American defenders of nuclear exports to the Middle East: if we don't do it, someone else will. This is an important argument which recurs in conventional arms sales as well. It suggests that competition among suppliers could work to the detriment of political controls which might otherwise be imposed on nuclear transfers. Indeed, one United States government spokesman maintained that the "someone else" who would sell reactors to Egypt might be "far less concerned with nonproliferation goals" than the United States.

It is true that some governments have been more interested in placing antiproliferation controls on past exports than other governments. The "someone else" in the Egyptian case was said to be France, not the Soviet Union; i.e., competition seemed to have more commercial than political overtones. But, it is not clear that France would have been willing to impose less rigid controls than the United States in this case. The French-Israeli precedent occurred more than a decade ago and has not been repeated elsewhere. Furthermore, if French controls promised to be significantly less than those demanded by the United States, it is not clear why Egypt chose to deal with the United States instead. On the surface, at least, it appears that the United States proposed to supply a reactor to Egypt with little emphasis on the question of controls. The need to exact greater than usual safeguards arose only afterwards, in response to American Congressional criticism of the deal. Just as some governments are more interested in controls than other governments, at the domestic level Congress was more interested in imposing controls than was the administration.

Nuclear transfers to all of the countries of these regions, except Egypt and Israel, will be subject to the same international standards since all are parties to the NPT and, therefore, subject to the inspection system of the IAEA. Up to the mid-1970s, there was a general assumption that ratifying the NPT and demonstrating compliance through submitting to inspection was sufficient to qualify a nation for any nuclear imports which it could afford. Indeed, Article IV of the NPT seems to establish this as a kind of commitment on the part of the nuclear weapons states. But the commercialization of nuclear energy coincided with increased concern about proliferation. In the United States, it was feared that competition among suppliers could drive the level of safeguards down to that of the lowest common denominator, just as financing terms had been competitively reduced.

There were those in the United States government who argued that America could not afford to impose more stringent conditions on its nuclear exports than other suppliers were willing to impose lest United States Industries simply lose markets to competitors.(56) This meant that the United States could not unilaterally make NPT adherence a precondition for receiving nuclear exports, nor could the United States indefinitely refuse to supply reprocessing and/or enrichment technology to nations that wanted it. But domestic and international concern over proliferation since 1974 increased to the point where additional guarantees began to be sought by suppliers. Proposed French and German reprocessing plant sales were covered by trilateral agreements even more stringent in most regards than the NPT required.(57) The United States insistence that Iran forego a national reprocessing capability is another example of tightening standards. In other words, a period of increasing competition in nuclear exports has been accompanied by an increased readiness to impose controls on those exports, rather than the decreased willingness which might have been expected. An exercise of political initiative has helped to transform a deteriorating situation into a more positive one.

The possibility of imposing more stringent controls on nuclear exports is a result of a series of bilateral and multilateral negotiations among nuclear supplier nations . These were largely instigated by the United States Arms Control and Disarmament Agency (ACDA). Bilateral consultations led to the series of meetings oʻ the so-called "London Group"(58) which since spring 1975, has met intermittently to discuss nuclear export policy. Bilateral consultations have not been superseded by the Group's formation. Indeed, as the Group has doubled from the original seven members, the role of bilateral consultations may have increased in importance as many specific issues are more productively handled by the parties directly concerned, e.g. the United States and West Germany.

The achievements of the London Group to date are modest. Essentially, the group has agreed on standard terms of nuclear transfers which will be followed by all suppliers. These terms include international safeguards. It has stopped short of requiring NPT adherence as a precondition. This decision was made partly out of deference to the non-NPT member, France. It was also agreed upon in order not to compromise Germany's interest in exports to nonparty Brazil and to accommodate the United States interest in exports to nonparties, Egypt and Israel. What is important is that within the group, discussion has proceeded beyond the terms of transfer to the possibility of proscribing certain kinds of transfers altogether, especially fuel-cycle plants. If recent policy changes announced by the French and German governments mean what they appear to – that in the future, no reprocessing plants will be exported – these changes may be assumed to be examples of the kind of concerted policy the London Group has fostered.

The London Group talks set a precedent for future agreements. While not yet a nuclear cartel, the group does aim at coordinating policies.(59) This should have the effect of making it difficult for any nuclear customer to play off one supplier against the others, especially where safeguards, reprocessing facilities, and enrichment technology are concerned. By narrowing the range of competition among suppliers to those dimensions of nuclear commerce farthest from weapons potential, these suppliers' talks have been a valuable nonproliferation device.

The relevance for the Middle East and the Persian Gulf is clear. Reducing competition among suppliers may reduce the stimulative spread of nuclear technology in these regions. Certainly it will help to impose uniform controls and hopefully keep potentially dangerous fuel-cycle facilities out of the area. The London Group is based on the suppliers' conception of common interest in both political and economic terms. This perception of common interest transcends both the East-West divide and other divisions among the great powers like nuclear weapon state versus nonnuclear weapon state. The principle affirmed, which is generally relevant to conventional arms supplies as well, is that limited cooperation in politically sensitive fields like nuclear exports can meet the economic and political interests of several supplier countries better than unrestricted competition among them. The willingness of the great powers to cooperate in this is perhaps directly proportional to their inability to escape the consequences of a failure to cooperate. Since the Middle East and the Persian Gulf are so important to the political and economic aims of the great powers and since they are all necessarily affected by the course of any conflict there – as opposed to Latin America, for example – the high degree of great power intervention in these regions may in the end have a positive nonproliferation impact by inducing supplier restraint.

While outside intervention may prove to be positive, the form that intervention takes is crucial. It is sometimes argued, for example, that the great powers must continue to supply arms to client states lest cut offs increase the incentives for these clients to go nuclear.(60) The threat of nuclear proliferation is used to legitimize conventional arms sales. While there may be specific instances in which this is plausible, the proposition should not be accepted as a general rule, nor be applied specifically in regard to the Middle East. It seems more convincing to argue that in general, conventional arms build ups whet the appetite for nuclear weapons. Arms sales help create large, effective military establishments with a dominant claim on the resources of the nation. Trained in the military dogmas of the great powers, these military establishments are likely to see nuclear weapons as a complement to the nuclear-capable delivery systems increasingly being imported. This kind of military establishment is also likely to take over governments where they have not already done so, calling into question the political commitments of the regimes they replace. This would, of course, include nonproliferation commitments. Intervention in the form of arms shipments will generally stimulate proliferation.

Indeed, the contradictions inherent in the proposition that conventional arms sales should be seen as a substitute for nuclear weapons are manifest in present policies towards Israel. If the United States government really believed in nuclear deterrence, it should reduce arms shipments to Israel, trusting to the Israeli nuclear capability and the present conventional capabilities to maintain the peace. But the opposite appears to be true. The United States government seems to be acting on the premise that Israel must be supplied with more conventional arms lest in any future conflict the Israelis be forced to use the nuclear weapons they have acquired. While skepticism about the viability of nuclear deterrence in the Middle East, which this policy betrays, seems justified, the proper lesson of the Israeli example for American arms supply policies has not been drawn.

Past arms shipments have failed to convince the Israelis that nuclear weapons are unnecessary for their national security. Faced with a nuclear-armed Israel, it will be increasingly difficult to convince the Egyptians and Syrians that any level of conventional armaments will be sufficient to assure their national security. To the extent that they consider conventional arms a contribution to security, the lesson of the Israeli example is that a few bombs in the basement is the best way to guarantee a steady supply of conventional arms from the great powers. Far from being a substitute for conventional arms in the Middle East, the possession of nuclear weapons or a technically advanced nuclear option may be a means of assuring conventional arms supplies. Great power intervention in the form of conventional arms shipments to regions where proliferation has already occurred has a negative impact. It reinforces the incentives to proliferate as well as rewards the proliferants.

Past competition among the great powers for political influence and economic gain in the Middle East and the Persian Gulf has resulted in proliferation and increased both the potential and the incentives for additional countries to go nuclear. At best, nonproliferation policies can only slow a process that probably cannot be reversed. The competitive policies of the great powers in the past have been negative in effect, accelerating the process of proliferation in the Middle East. It will require the collective ingenuity and cooperation of the great powers to reverse these policies and slow their effects.

NOTES AND REFERENCES

(1) For treatments of the superpowers' nonproliferation policies, see William Bader, The United States and the Spread of Nuclear Weapons (New York: Pegasus, 1968); and Toby Trister Gatti, Soviet Perspectives on Nuclear Proliferation, no. 66 (Santa Monica: California Seminar on Arms Control and Foreign Policy, November 1975).

(2) Bader, ibid., Chapter 1.

(3) Arnold Kramish, The Peaceful Atom in Foreign Policy (New York: Harper and Row, 1963).

(4) Jonathon D. Pollack, "China as a Nuclear Power," Asia's Nuclear Future, ed. William H. Overhold (Boulder, Colorado: Westview Press, 1977); and Walter C. Clemons, Jr., The Arms Race and Sino-Soviet Relations (Stanford, California Standord University Press, 1968).

(5) Ian Smart, Future Conditional: The Prospect for Anglo-French Nuclear Cooperation, Adelphi Papers no. 78 (London: International Institute for Strategic Studies, August 1971), pp. 29-32; and William

Epstein, The Last Chance; Nuclear Proliferation and Arms Control
(New York: Free Press, 1976), pp. 87-8.

(6) Pollack (note 4 supra).

(7) Lewis A. Dunn and Herman Kahn, Trends in nuclear proliferation,
1975-1995, 2336-rr/3 (Croton-on-Hudson, New York: Hudson Institute,
May 15, 1976).

(8) Steven J. Baker, Commercial Nuclear Power and Nuclear Proliferation, Peace Studies Program Occasional Paper no. 5 (Ithaca, New York:
Center for International Studies, Cornell University, May 1975).

(9) Barber Associates, LDC Nuclear Power Prospects, 1975-1990:
Commercial, Economic, and Security Implications, ERDA-52, UC-2
(Washington, D.C.: ERDA, 1975). (Hereafter referred to as the Barber
report).

(10) C. L. Sulzberger, "Atoms for Peace in the Middle East," New York
Times, June 26, 1974: 39.

(11) For some of the implications of these new nuclear statuses, see
Steven J. Baker, "The International Political Economy of Proliferation,"
Arms Control and Technological Innovation, eds. David Carlton and
Carlo Schaerf (London: Croom, Helm, 1977).

(12) Fuad Jabber, Israel's Nuclear Option and US Arms Control Policies
(Santa Monica: California Seminar on Arms Control and Foreign Policy,
February 1972), p.22.

(13) US Library of Congress, Congressional Research Service, United
States Agreements for Cooperation in Atomic Energy, Prepared for the
Committee on Government Operations, United States Senate (Washing-
ton, D.C.: January 1976).

(14) American Bar Association, Task Force on Nuclear Technology
Transfer, "International Instruments for the Transfer of Nuclear
Technology," prepared for presentation to the Conference on Nuclear
Technology Transfer, April 3-7 1977, Shiraz, Iran), Chapter VIII.

(15) Kramish, pp. 64-5 (note 3 supra).

(16) Le Monde (February 11, 1974).

(17) New York Times (January 4, 1975).

(18) Le Monde Hebdomadaire (September 16-22, 1976): 9.

(19) Anne Hessing Cahn, "Determinants of the Nuclear Option: The
Case of Iran," Nuclear Proliferation and the Near Nuclear Countries,

eds. Onkar Marwah and Ann Schulz (Cambridge: Ballinger Publishing Co., 1975), pp. 190-1.

(20) New York Times, March 5, 1975: 1.

(21) Leslie Gelb, New York Times (March 8, 1975).

(22) Nuclear Industry 23 (August 1976): 11.

(23) Cahn, p. 191 (note 19 supra).

(24) On the proposed sales to Egypt and Israel, see New York Times (June 15,1974): 1; and New York Times (June 18, 1974): 1.

(25) For the text of Public Law 93-485 (88 STAT. 1460) see US Congress, Senate, Committee on Government Operations, Peaceful Nuclear Exports and Weapons Proliferation: A Compendium (Washington, D.C.: April 1975), p. 318.

(26) Newsweek (December 27, 1976): 11.

(27) Nuclear Engineering International 22 (March 1977): 34.

(28) New York Times (December 3, 1974): 11.

(29) Washington Post (June 3, 1975): 3.

(30) Nuclear News 18 (October 1975): 88.

(31) For a treatment of some of the problems involved, see Steven J. Rosen, "Nuclearization and Stability in the Middle East," in Marwah and Schulz (note 19 supra).

(32) US Department of State, Bureau of Public Affairs, The Export of Nuclear Technology; Special Report No. 9 (Washington, D.C.: October 1974). See especially the remarks by Undersecretary of State, Joseph Sisco, pp. 11-14, and Chapter 4 in this book for a discussion of rationales as applied to US conventional arms transfers.

(33) Achille Albonetti, L'Economie Energetique et la Politique Nucleaire Europeenne (Paris: Institut Atlantique, March 1972), Table 30;   and David Rundquist et al., Technology for Nuclear Weapons Capability (La Jolla, California: Science Applications, July 1975), Table 3.

(34) S. Flapan, "Israel's Attitude Towards the NPT," Nuclear Proliferation Problems, Stockholm International Peace Research Institute (Stockholm: Almquist and Wiksell), P. 273.

(35) Robert Gillette, "Uranium Enrichment: Rumors of Israeli Progress with Lasers," Science (March 22, 1974): 1172-4.

(36) Cahn p. 191 (note 19 supra) discusses the Iranian case.

(37) Nuclear Industry (January 1977): 32.

(38) For an analysis, see John Gorham Palfrey, "Nonproliferation and US Nuclear Export Policy, A Positive First Step," Arms Control Today 6 (November 1976): 1-4.

(39) Carl Walske, "Proliferation and Electric Power," International Security no. 3 (Winter 1976): 99-100.

(40) Barber Report, Figure II-19 (note 9 supra), from this study for not being a developing country. For Israeli maximum projections of ten 400-600 MWe reactors by 2000, see Flapan (note 34 supra).

(41) Barber Report, Figure II-19 (note 9 supra).

(42) Ibid., Figure II-17.

(43) J. Baujat and J. P. Raul, "Small Reactors Extend the Market for Nuclear Power," Nuclear Engineering International 21 (December 1976): 65-9.

(44) Richard Masters, "Standardization and Quality are Priorities at Kraftwerk Union," Nuclear Engineering International 21 (August 1976): 41.

(45) Tom Stevenson, "Gloom on the Monongahela," Saturday Review, (January 22, 1977): 8.

(46) Nuclear News 19 (July 1976): 58.

(47) Barber Report pp. IV 38-45 (note 9 supra); and Development Agency, US Nuclear Power Export Activities, Final Environmental Impact Statement, Vol. 1 ERDA-1542 (Washington, D.C.: April 1976), pp. 3-156 to 3-164.

(48) Walske, p. 103 (note 39 supra).

(49) Nuclear News 19 (July 1976): 52-4

(50) On uranium ore scarcity, see, "Is There Enough Uranium?" OECD Observer no. 79 (January-February 1976): 33-6.

(51) The IAEA multinational regional reprocessing facility study takes 750/MT/U/yr capacity as the smallest feasible plant. Assuming a 1000 LWR throughput of about 26 MT/U/yr, such a plant could service about 30 reactors. IAEA Bulletin 18 (February 1976): 22-3

(52) The cost for the reactor would be less in Western Europe and more

on a turnkey basis in the third world. Estimates place the cost of a 30 MT/U/yr processing plant at $50 million; Runquist, p. 55 (note 33 supra) the proposed French plant for Pakistan is said to have a $150 million price tag, New York Times (October 13, 1976).

(53) Barber Report, pp. 4-15 (note 9 supra).

(54) On the question of nuclear equipment manufacturers' profits, see Stevenson, pp. 7-8 (note 45 supra); and US Congress, Senate, Committee on Government Operations, Hearings, The Export Reorganization Act of 1976, 94th Cong., 2nd Sess., January 19, 20, 29, 30 and March 9, 1976, p. 515.

(55) US Department of State, Bureau of Public Affairs, p. 12 (note 32 supra).

(56) Tom Alexander, "Our Costly, Losing Battle Against Nuclear Proliferation," Fortune (December 1975): 143-150.

(57) William W. Lowrance, "Nuclear Futures for Sale: To Brazil from West Germany, 1975," International Security 1 (Fall 1976): 155-6.

(58) The original seven were the United States, the Soviet Union, Britain, France, West Germany, Canada, and Japan. They have been joined by Belgium, the Netherlands, Italy, East Germany, Sweden, Poland, Czechoslovakia, and Switzerland.

(59) Michael Mandelbaum, "A Nuclear Exporters Cartel?" Bulletin of Atomic Scientist 33 (January 1977): 42-50.

(60) Richard K. Betts, "Paranoids, Pygmies, Pariahs, and Nonproliferation," Foreign Policy no. 26 (Spring 1977): 157-3.

3 A Nuclear Middle East: Infrastructure, Likely Military Postures, and Prospects for Strategic Stability
Paul Jabber

Analysis of the problem of nuclear weapons proliferation into the Middle East region to date has focused mainly on two issues. The first is whether, when, and in what circumstances Israel – as the only regional power with a nuclear threshold capability – will develop these weapons. The second area of concern is whether an eventual Arab-Israeli "balance of terror" will be stable. This derives from the assumption that calculations of strategic stability will be a determining factor in governmental decisions to go nuclear. The current status of the Arab-Israeli relationship; in both its diplomatic and strategic dimensions, and as affected principally by the results of the 1967 and 1973 Wars, provides the situational context for the bulk of discussion on these matters.(1)

SHORTCOMINGS OF THE CURRENT APPROACH

The terms of the contemporary debate were appropriate at an earlier stage, but have now become too narrow and inadequate in several respects. To begin with, there is insufficient recognition of the degree to which regional nuclear capabilities that are being gradually built up in a number of countries, as well as on the region's periphery, will inevitably interact with each other. The result of such an interaction would be to create a strategic environment more complex and unpredictable than the dyadic Israeli-Egyptian relationship commonly envisaged. As the subsequent country-by-country analysis will indicate, within a decade at least six Middle Eastern countries may be producing weapon-grade fissile material. Any calculus that seeks to integrate threats, interests, and perceptions into a reasoned analysis of nuclear stability, or even forecast the likely chain of proliferation, must take this into account. This paper is a first step in that direction.

Another misleading deficiency in the logic of much current analysis is the fixation observers continue to have with divining the physical status of the Israeli option and the circumstances in which a weapons arsenal may be <u>disclosed</u>. This, unfortunately, distracts attention from what is by now much more significant and instructive for any prognosis of the future of proliferation in the area: the elucidation of the actual meaning and policy implications of Israel's <u>announced</u> posture, as these must be perceived by the principal presumptive targets of an Israeli nuclear capability, the Arab opponents.

Jerusalem's posture rests on three pillars. The first is a public avowal at the highest political levels of an advanced capability to build nuclear devices. The second is an ambiguous pledge not to be the first to introduce nuclear weapons into the region, coupled with a proviso that the first such introduction by others will be immediately matched by Israel. Finally, Israel possesses a nuclear establishment with sufficient plant, scientific manpower, and technological skills to endow both the avowal and the proviso with high credibility. The ambiguity has been defended by Israelis on grounds that it maximizes freedom of action, provides bargaining leverage with the United States for conventional arms and political support, does the least damage to Israel's international image, and is sufficient to deter the Arabs from undertaking extreme hostile acts, such as attacks on population centers in wartime. Furthermore, it is expected to discourage the Arab governments from actively seeking a nuclear capability of their own. Presumably, it will fulfill this latter function by fostering hopes that nuclear weaponry may not be needed after all, or by convincing Arab governments that the initiative is theirs and nuclearization can be avoided as long as they deny themselves such weapons.(2)

A moment's reflection will show that there is obvious tension, if not outright contradiction, between the first set of objectives and the second. The first set is predicated on the assumption that Israel possesses the independent ability to build and deploy nuclear weapons at short notice or that it may have already done so in secret. The second set, as well as the hopes of all those who believe that Middle East proliferation can yet be avoided, rests on the premise that Israel possesses neither ready weapons nor their political equivalent, a threshold or "last-screw" option. This latter premise, while probably correct at the outset of the 1970s, can no longer be maintained against the weight of contrary evidence and persuasive inference. More important, the Arabs themselves believe it is incorrect, and their highest officials credit the Israelis with an advanced nuclear status. The notion that Israel can go on indefinitely cashing in on the deterrence and bargaining advantages of an undeclared nuclear status without triggering a compensatory Arab effort may be psychologically comfortable, but is also unrealistic and dangerously self-deluding.

Predictably, such compensatory efforts on the part of several Arab governments have not been lacking in the past.(3) They have been mainly of the "quick-fix" variety, aimed at importing the finished product rather than developing indigenous nuclear weaponry. On the face of it, these endeavors have failed to provide the Arab side with an autonomous deterrent; on the other hand, they may have succeeded in procuring a conditional Soviet pledge of nuclear supply in response to

Israeli deployment.(4) The apparent shipment of Soviet nuclear war-heads to Egypt during the latter stages of the October 1973 War remains shrouded in mystery and subject to varied interpretations. Even so, it may be viewed as a precautionary implementation of Soviet pledges of nuclear protection and/or a signal to Israel that injection by the latter of nuclear weaponry into the confrontation – both during the hostilities in progress or in the future – would be met with a firm Soviet response. It should be remembered that this Soviet move on October 22-25 followed Israeli strategic bombing of Syrian cities, industrial and military installations, and other rear area targets beginning on the 9th and a warning by Sadat on the 16th that in-depth attacks on Egypt would be answered in kind. It also coincided with Egypt's first use of Scud surface-to-surface missiles (SSMs) against Israeli forces on the 22nd. There was a clear possibility that Egyptian and Israeli population centers might become involved in the fighting, which might in turn have triggered an Israeli decision to bring the nuclear deterrent more into the open. The future, therefore, portends a much more determined attempt by several Arab states to develop domestic nuclear programs for civilian purposes which, by the middle of the next decade, will open up significant military options.

This leads to a third, related misconception in the proliferation literature. Despite much gloomy talk about the horrors that would be visited on a nuclearized Middle East, there remains a residue of optimism in much of the discussion that such a state of affairs may after all be avoided or postponed into an indefinite future. Alas, such optimism is groundless. It flies in the face of both reason and contrary evidence. From a political-psychological-deterrent perspective, nuclear weapons in effect <u>have already been introduced</u> into the area by a local party, Israel. Israel's foes <u>perceive</u> that this has been done, and the Arab bloc must be fully expected to marshal its efforts into a determined bid to obtain a similar arsenal of its own. In turn, this will trigger a predictably similar response on the part of Iran, if by then an Iranian decision has not already been dictated by a Pakistani bomb or other nuclear spread in Asia.(5)

In thus postulating the near certainty of widespread regional nuclearization within the next ten to fifteen years, there is no implied policy prescription that the United States and other exporters of nuclear fuel-cycle components should soft-pedal antiproliferation strategies. Though economically and politically costly, such strategies may prove extremely beneficial if they help delay overt nuclearization until after a substantial settlement of Arab-Israeli differences has been achieved. Codes of nondestabilizing military behavior in a context of nuclear deterrence will stand a better chance of developing with a minimum of crises and alarums if Egypt and Syria are in a position to work toward a relationhip of long-term military stability with Israel. Such a relationship would be keyed to maintenance and defense of the territorial and political status quo rather than its revision.

Of course, the argument made here bypasses the whole debate on whether unilateral nuclearization or an eventual nuclear balance would or would not enhance Israeli security, deter different levels of hostile

Arab action, stabilize the regional arms race, aid in conflict resolution, and so on. Such a debate becomes largely irrelevant as a factor in the shaping of decisions to "go nuclear" or as an analytical predictor of state intentions once a party to the conflict has, for whatever reasons, attained the capability to do so. Distinctions usually made between a technological option and a political decision are meaningful for states not involved in ongoing military confrontations or active political disputes. Governments that are thus involved will invariably tend to see in adversary capabilities a true measure of intentions and will react accordingly.

Historically, weapons innovations have been induced by technological feasibility rather than by reasoned calculations of strategic advantage. Once the physical ability to procure a weapons system is obtained, and if a modicum of security incentives exists, a strategic rationale for its procurement will follow sooner or later. This technological imperative is particularly insidious in the nuclear realm, where "a more determined political act may be required not to produce nuclear weapons than to do so."(6) Unless an overwhelming consensus of opinion exists against the strategic and/or political advisability of a particular weapon that is within technical reach, a "worst-case" analysis of threat contingencies will assert itself and pressures for procurement will prevail. No such consensus exists in Israel regarding production of nuclear armament, whether among analysts or the political elite. Judging from the results of a recent opinion poll, even the public has apparently accepted with surprising equanimity and practically no debate the notion that Israel already may be a nuclear power. The Tel Aviv daily Ha-Aretz reported on March 25, 1976, that 77 percent of Israelis questioned thought Israel should have nuclear weapons and that 62.3 percent thought Israel already had them. Only 4.3 percent were certain it did not.(7)

On the Arab side, an additional imperative with an equally rich record will almost inevitably assert itself, viz., what one might call the imperative of "deterrent emulation" of a feared adversary. As pointed out in a classical piece on military competition, "in most instances in history, arms races have involved similar forces rather than complementary forces ... usually that type of military force with which (opponents) are best able to harm each other."(8) Regardless of any qualms some Arab strategists might have about the potential instability of a regional nuclear face-off, the overwhelming balance of pressures – bureaucratic, psychological, and political – will favor deterring the opponent's nuclear force with nuclear force.(9)

PRESENT/PLANNED NUCLEAR INFRASTRUCTURE
AND WEAPONS POTENTIAL

The following analysis will highlight the acquisition of facilities over the next twelve to fifteen years by Middle Eastern states capable of providing them with the fissile materials needed for weapons production; Chapter 2 contains additional information. The major emphasis will be on plutonium acquisition, and projections will be based exclusively on officially announced transactions, negotiations, and future plans. The availability of adequate weapons-delivery capabilities for regional missions is generally assumed to exist and will not be examined, except briefly in the context of the final discussion of likely military postures.

Iran

If current plans for expansion of nuclear-generated power production are carried out, by the 1990s Iran will have the world's fourth largest nuclear program, although the political upheavals of 1978-79 have put these plans in some doubt. Since 1975, when only a small 5 megawatt-thermal (MWth) research reactor was operational, the Iranian government has commissioned the construction of two atomic power plants with a total capacity of 2400 megawatt-electrical (MWe) and has nearly completed negotiations for two 900 MWe units with France. It is seeking several additional reactors in France and the United States to supply another 8000 MWe. The first two 1200 MWe reactors under construction by Kraftwerk Union (KWU) of Germany at Bushire on the Gulf coast will come on line in 1980-81. The two French 900 MWe Framatome units are expected to become operational by 1984.(10) All four are pressurized water reactors (PWR), fueled with slightly enriched uranium and using light water as both moderator and coolant. France will also build a nuclear research center at Isfahan and provide training for scientists and technicians.(11)

Where the fuel-cycle is concerned, maximum feasible independence is clearly an Iranian priority objective and one which the Shah has pursued with French cooperation. Large cash loans to France in 1975 enabled Iran to gain partnership in two French-based European uranium enrichment plant projects which will use the gaseous diffusion method. The Eurodif plant, in which Iran has a 12.5 percent stake, will begin operating in 1979. The Coredif facility, scheduled to be ready by 1983, is 25 percent Iranian. Negotiations are at an advanced stage for the purchase of a chemical fuel reprocessing plant from France as well. This could be of much more immediate military significance, though the safeguards issued and strong United States opposition to the sale loom as potential obstacles to completion of this transaction.(12)

Active exploration for uranium is under way, and significant finds in the Kirman area have been rumored.(13) Iran has already concluded uranium purchase agreements with a number of countries and in 1975 was negotiating a deal for some $700 million worth of ore from South Africa.(14) Several agreements for nuclear cooperation and training have been signed, notably with Great Britain for general servicing of the Iranian program, and most recently with India in February 1977. The Indian agreement was sought to reduce Iran's dependence on Western sources of scientfic information and expertise, according to Atomic Energy Organization chairman, Etemad.(15)

Israel

Existing facilities include two research reactors: a small American-supplied 6 MWth unit fueled with highly enriched uranium at Nahal Soreq, and a French-built, 26 MWth plant at Dimona in the northern Negev that burns natural uranium. Since the mid-1960s, the Dimona reactor has produced the unsafeguarded plutonium by product which forms the basis for Israel's presumed status as a nuclear weapons country. Uranium ore is extracted locally as a by product of the phosphates industry and is also imported from abroad. Professor Shimon Yiftah, a prominent Israeli nuclear scientist and former director of the Nahal Soreq Research Center, stated in 1975 that Israel possessed up to 60,000 tons of uranium and could extract 60 tons per year at the Arad chemical works for use in nuclear reactors.(16) Fuel-element fabrication and heavy-water production are also available domestically. A clandestine capability to reprocess chemically the irradiated output of the Dimona reactor on a very small scale almost certainly exists within the Negev nuclear complex.

Projects calling for construction of large nuclear power plants, both for electricity production and water desalting, have existed since the early 1960s. New impetus was provided in 1974 by President Nixon's offer of American reactors to Israel and Egypt, and Israel is currently negotiating the purchase of two 950 MWe light-water reactors. The first plant, to be located at Nitzanim on the Mediterranean coast south of Tel Aviv, is scheduled for completion in 1985, with the second unit – plans for which are more tentative – to follow eighteen months later.(17) Since Israel is not a signatory of the Nonproliferation Treaty (NPT), the supply of American reactors has been made conditional on Israeli acceptance of "the most stringent safeguards of any agreement" for transfer of United States nuclear technology concluded to date.(18) At the time of writing the executive and legislative branches were hammering out these safeguards, though Israeli acquiescence and even the availability of adequate funding – cost is estimated at $2,500 million – are in doubt.

An alternative to reactor-produced plutonium as a source of weapon-grade fissile material is reportedly being successfully pursued by Israeli scientists working for the defense establishment. This would involve uranium enrichment through laser isotope separation. This method is cheaper, less power-intensive, and more efficient than other enrichment techniques now in use.(19) If published Israeli claims of the method's efficiency are correct, Israel should be able to build a small number of uranium fission bombs by the mid-1980s.

Egypt

As in the Iranian case, Egypt's plans for expansion of energy-production capacity to meet expected demand over the next quarter of a century rely heavily on nuclear power. Construction of about a dozen nuclear units by 2000 is envisaged. These would have a total capacity of

9200 MWe which would double current power production. Although the aid agreement of June 1974 with the United States provides for the Amercans to supply of two 600 MWe reactors, letters of intent have been signed with Westinghouse for only one 600 MWe PWR unit, to be located at Sidi Kreir, west of Alexandria. Implementation of the deal remains, as in the Israeli case, dependent on agreement regarding safeguards and financing. Talks were also conducted in 1976 with the Soviet Union, West Germany, and France for the supply of additional power stations, and Cairo has evinced interest in Canadian CANDU reactors.(20)

For the foreseeable future, the only way in which Egypt can acquire a domestic capability for nuclear-weapons manufacture is through the establishment of a civilian power program that would yield plutonium byproducts while building up local scientific and technical expertise in handling nuclear materials. The existing 2 MWth research reactor, at Inshass near Cairo, has no military value. The number of Egyptian scientific personnel working in the nuclear field is still very small. In 1971, it was reported that Egypt had fifty scientists engaged in nuclear research, most of them employed by the Atomic Energy Organisation. They were said to be involved primarily in work on desalination, and "the use of atomic blasts in engineering and petroleum projects." The latter aspect has obvious military implications.(21) Egypt remains at least six to eight years away from an indigenous nuclear option but Egyptian nuclear scientists are currently being trained at the Trombay facilities, where, perhaps significantly, India's small chemical reprocessing facility for plutonium extraction from reactor wastes is located. Close cooperation with India, which builds on a tradition of joint research and development efforts in the field of conventional armaments, could provide Egypt with quick access to a wealth of vital information and expertise, particularly with regard to plutonium reprocessing, that might otherwise need to be acquired at great cost in time and resources.

Iraq

As a party to the NPT, Iraq has placed its small, Soviet-supplied 2 MWth research reactor under International Atomic Energy Agency (IAEA) supervision. It is currently negotiating with France for the supply of two reactors. One is a large 70 MWth research unit, reportedly of the Osiris type, to become the nucleus of a research center at Baghdad.(23) This reactor would be fueled with highly enriched uranium and would, therefore, produce negligible amounts of plutonium. However, the uranium fuel itself is of weapons-grade, and if diverted and treated chemically, could provide the fissile cores for several bombs per reactor loading. The other is a 600 MWe PWR plant, similar in design to those being sold in Iran. Iraqi negotiations for a Canadian CANDU reactor have also been reported.(24)

Libya

The Qaddafi regime has rather openly sought to acquire nuclear weaponry over the past few years, through purchase rather than fabrication given the total absence of domestic nuclear infrastructure. Though Libya's reported approaches to China and France were quickly rebuffed, they are clear indicators of the government's thinking.(25) Early concurrent efforts were made after the regime came to power in 1969 to begin training substantial numbers of university graduates in the nuclear sciences, both in the United States and France. Some are now presumably being trained in the Soviet Union, which has agreed to supply a 440 MWe nuclear dual-purpose plant for power production and desalination. After a year of negotiations and an exchange of visits by nuclear experts, the Soviet Union and Libya signed a final agreement during Qaddafi's visit to Moscow in December 1976.(26) This transaction marks only the second time Russia has supplied power reactors outside the Soviet bloc; the other recipient was Finland. No details have been published about deadlines, cost, or safeguard arrangement. Regarding the latter, however, it should be noted that Libya ratified the NPT in late 1975 after a seven-year delay following signature in 1968, only a short time before serious talks with the Soviet Union began.

A second power reactor is being sought from France. The two countries signed an initial agreement in March 1976 for construction of a 600 MWe pressurized light water reactor, supplementing a 1974 accord on uranium prospecting and manpower training.(27)

Others

The accelerating regional interest in nuclear power has recently extended to several additional Arab states. In the Arabian peninsula, only Kuwait has announced definite plans. Initial steps include the setting up of a nuclear research and training center built around a small 40-50 MWe reactor and attached desalting plant. These activities are to be followed by the progressive acquisition of four to six 600 MWe dual-purpose units by 2000, starting in the late 1980s.(28) Germany's KWU and Alsthom/Technicatome of France, as well as a British consortium, have been asked for bids on the initial training facility. According to Kuwait's Minister of Electricity and Water, this facility would "ensure that the introduction of nuclear power plants to the country will not be on a black-box basis." The Kuwaitis have laid heavy stress on the need for training Arab manpower in the nuclear field through regional cooperation and have endorsed the notion of regional fuel-cycle centers to secure enrichment and reprocessing services for their program.(29)

Syria established an Atomic Energy Commission attached to the Prime Minister's Office in March 1976, a few weeks after it was announced that significant uranium deposit finds in phosphate rock would be exploited. In some areas, uranium concentrations in the range of 200-300 grams per ton of phosphates were found.(30) Syrian phosphate resources are estimated at 100 million tons. In May 1976, the government announced that a large triple superphosphate fertilizer plant would be built at Deir Ez-Zor in eastern Syria, using Rumanian technology and Iranian financing, with uranium extraction as part of the process. Plans are already being laid for purchase of a nuclear power plant in the next decade.(31)

Morocco, another large Arab phosphate producer, has announced plans to build a French-supplied nuclear power reactor which will be fueled by domestically obtained uranium. The uranium reportedly is to be extracted with Soviet assistance.(32) Algeria, which has an estimated 28,000 tons of uranium recoverable at low prices $15/lb, is planning to begin mining by 1980. It recently awarded a contract for preliminary work to a French consortium.(33)

Table 3.1 summarizes available information on projected reactor construction in the Middle East to 1990, with IAEA estimates to 2000, and shows estimated accumulations of separable fissile plutonium stockpiles. These estimates are based on the assumption that all power reactors will be of the pressurized light water variety, which use 2-3 percent enriched uranium as fuel. When operated under normal conditions for power production, such reactors produce about .237 kilograms of plutonium power MWe per year, if a 75 percent load factor is assumed.(34)

Given long irradiation times, the quality of the plutonium would not be optimal for weapons use, since there owuld be a substantial percentage of the unstable Pu-240 and Pu-242 isotopes present. Nonetheless, while obtainable explosive yields will be lower and less dependable for bombs built with this material, such drawbacks become significant only in weapons designed for tactical use in the battlefield or for the destruction of hardened point targets, such as missile silos or some command and control centers. In all other cases, any grade of reactor-produced plutonium available would produce a nuclear explosion of sufficient yields to fulfill its strategic objectives.(35) This would be the case in a nuclearized Middle East, at least during the first several years. Besides, yields can be increased by improving the implosion techniques used to trigger the nuclear burst.(36) Of course, if purer plutonium is desired, burn up time in the reactor could be reduced. This would, however, be uneconomical and might create suspicions of military intent in internationally safeguarded programs that are ostensibly of a civilian character.

From Plutonium to Weaponry

The simple acquisition of fissile material in an unseparated state certainly does not amount to a weapons option. Nevertheless, it is a giant step that puts even a safeguarded nuclear program in a position to build the weapons virtually with a few months, if not weeks, of a political go-ahead decision, provided necessary reprocessing and weapons construction facilities and research have been readied in advance. Availability of the plutonium is the sine qua non. The remaining steps, given currently available technical data and hardware in the public and

Table 3.1. Projections of Nuclear Reactor Capacity and Stockpiles
of Separable Plutonium-239 in the Middle East

Country	Current Capacity MWT	Estimated Capacity MWe		IAEA Forecast MWe		Kg. Accumulations of Separable Pu	
		1985	1990	1990	2000	1985	1990
Iran	5	4200[b]	15000[b]	10000	28000	3128	12324
Israel	32	960	1910	3900[c]	15300[c]	385	2450
Egypt	2	600	4200	5000	12600	142	2985
Libya	–	1040	1040	–	–	350	1580
Iraq	2	623	623	1100	2600	142	859
Kuwait		50	1250	1300	3200	36	1090
Syria			600	500	1900		472
Saudi Arabia			600	200	1400		188
Morocco			600	400	1600		280
Tunisia			200	200	1600		94
Lebanon					1000		
Sudan					800		

a The lower estimate for reactor capacity was used in case.
b My estimate is based on 50 percent implementation of current plans.
c Estimates for Israel are from Atomic Industrial Forum, INFO News Release (May 19, 1975).

commercial domains, no longer present any major difficulties.(37) One may assume with confidence that, by the mid-1980s, Middle Eastern countries determined to acquire a nuclear weapons capability and having access to plutonium will encounter no physical or technological barriers.

It is not clear, however, if they will indeed have access to the plutonium byproducts of their nuclear plants. All units that have been sold or are in the process of negotiation will be subject to some form of international supervision. This will be effected through the NPT safeguards system managed by the IAEA, as in the case of Iran and Iraq, or through a combination of bilateral and IAEA safeguards, as is probable in the event of United States supply of nuclear stations to Israel and Egypt. In either case, however, safeguards will be effective only for as long as the subject country itself chooses to forego a declared military capability. It is well known that the IAEA's safeguards system provides a mere warning mechanism and is not an adequate preventive mechanism.(38) Even this limited warning purpose can be thwarted in at least two ways: through undetectable diversion, and by minimizing the time lag between diversion and weapons manufacture.

Substantial leeway for undetectable diversion to a clandestine weapons program is provided by the fact that IAEA bookkeeping practices used for nuclear materials control cannot, with present-day technology, account for more than 92-98 percent of all such material in the cycle.(39) However, limits of error in material unaccounted for (MUF) are subject to controversy. According to Wohlstetter, 99 percent reliability can be obtained; other sources mention limits of error in the 2-3 percent range. Material unaccounted for may thus serve as a camouflage for engaging in a surreptitious weapons program without formal breaching of a safeguards agreement. If it is assumed that some eight kilograms of commercial reactor-grade plutonium are required to produce a critical mass for a fifteen to twenty kiloton bomb(40) and that an average MUF discrepancy of 3 percent will go unchallenged, Table 3.2 shows the number of bombs that several Middle Eastern states hypothetically could build in 1985 and 1990 despite international inspection if concealment were maintained and nuclear reactor wastes were stored locally.

Obviously, the number of devices that most Middle Eastern countries, other than Iran, could obtain by following the MUF diversion route over the next decade would be very small, even in the most favorable conditions, and the weapons would not be very reliable. A more likely course of action would be a sudden de facto denunciation of safeguard undertakings through large-scale diversion to military purposes at a well-prepared and timely juncture, such as immediately after completion of an IAEA inspection visit. The time interval between large-scale diversion of separable plutonium and completion of the bombs could be narrowed to a few weeks. This could be accomplished by erecting in advance the small unsophisticated reprocessing plant that would be needed to extract the plutonium from reactor wastes and carrying out the requisite research on conventional high explosives for the nuclear trigger and bomb design. IAEA procedures, in practice, cannot give timely warning to the international community of a militarily significant breach of safeguards unless the violator is inept or indifferent.(41) The effectiveness of the IAEA thus very much depends on the level of cooperation by the safeguarded state. If the latter wishes to subvert the system, it can easily do so for long enough to produce the weapons and face the world with a _fait accompli_ before the IAEA alarm can go off.

Awareness of these weaknesses has led to the current American insistence on supplementing IAEA safeguards with bilateral United States-Egyptian and United States-Israeli safeguard arrangements to govern the sale of power reactors to these two countries. These additional precautionary measures, which would be symmetrically applied to both, would include: (a) reprocessing, fabrication, and storage of nuclear materials only in facilities acceptable to the United States

Table 3.2. Maximum Number of Nuclear Weapons Middle Eastern States May Build from Locally Produced Plutonium, 1985 and 1990

Country	Kg stockpiles of separable Pu[a]		No. Pu bombs 15-20 kt		No. Pu bombs 3% MUF	
	1985	1990	1985	1990	1985	1990
Iran	3128	12324	391	1541	11	46
Israel	385	2450	68[b]	320[b]	40[b]	58[b]
Egypt	142	2985	17	373	—	11
Libya	350	1580	43	197	1	6
Iraq	142	859	17	107		3
Kuwait	36	1090	4	136		4
Syria		472		59		1
Saudi Arabia		188		26		
Morocco		280		35		
Tunisia		94		11		

[a]Figures from Table 3.1, p. 151.
[b]Israel would have approximately 160 kilograms in 1985 and 200 kilograms in 1990 of unsafeguarded plutonium with a purity of 90+ percent of the Pu-239 isotope obtained from the Dimona research reactor. Only four kilograms of this weapons-grade plutonium would be required per bomb.

and located outside the recipient countries; (b) an American buy-back option on plutonium byproducts; (c) implementation of physical security measures to prevent terrorist theft, sabotage, or attack; (d) recipient undertakings not to use the facilities or materials produced in them to construct nuclear explosives, even for peaceful purposes.(42) Moreover, Washington initially pressed the two Middle Eastern governments to accede to the NPT as another condition of the reactor sale in order to open up their entire nuclear programs to inspection. The United States dropped this demand after Israel not surprisingly rejected it. If the final agreements covering the United States reactor sales do include such safeguards, they would clearly inhibit any Egyptian effort to build weapons through surreptitious long-term diversion of plutonium wastes. Simultaneously, they would leave Israel's capability, which is based on Dimona's output, essentially unaffected. However, the Egyptians one day could shut down the reactor and appropriate the irradiated fuel rods. If the operation were well-timed, the rods would contain weapons-grade plutonium with minimal Pu-240 contamination. The Egyptians could then move through quick reprocessing and weapons assembly into possession of four to six bombs before any hostile action could make itself felt.

Alternatives to Exclusively Domestic Plutonium-Based Weapons Programs

A quick glance at Table 3.2 shows that the Arab states, because of a shortage of separable fissile material and barring early denunciation of safeguard undertakings, will be at a substantial disadvantage vis-a-vis both Iran and Israel in their ability to move quickly to meaningful nuclear status well into the late 1980s. Another medium-term weakness, which Iran shares, is the lack of sufficiently experienced manpower and ancillary capabilities for research into and handling of nuclear materials. Indigenous developmental efforts will not be exclusively relied upon, especially if regional levels of international conflict remain as high as they have been over the past several decades. They will be supplemented with attempts to proceed along some or all of the following paths, on which limitations of space allow only brief comments:

– Strong regional cooperation within the Arab block could emerge. It might include pooling scientific and financial resources, erecting jointly owned and operated facilities, and sharing Arab-produced uranium. Eventually it might even extend to pooling fissile materials for weapons production. The degree of integration will, of course, hinge on the state of inter-Arab relations and the urgency of the perceived threat. Efforts in this direction were begun over the past several years and include the formation of a Joint Scientific Arab Board for the use of nuclear energy, following the conclusion in November 1970 of an Arab Cooperation Agreement for the Use of Nuclear Energy for Peaceful Purposes.(43)

– Unsafeguarded fissile material might be imported from nonmembers of the NPT. This is a less provocative and more realistic variation on the by now familiar scenario in which India, for instance, sells nuclear weapons to the Arabs in exchange for five billion petrodollars. The Indians reportedly have already been made, and have refused, an offer along these lines.(44) Nonetheless, a likely development in the next decade will be the increasing willingness on the part of India and other countries outside the NPT, which possess growing stockpiles of reprocessed plutonium and uranium enrichment capabilities, to sell such materials discretely at steep prices for ostensibly peaceful purposes – perhaps including peaceful nuclear explosions to Middle Eastern states with expanding nuclear establishments. The onus of later diversions to military purposes would be on the recipients, not on the suppliers. One should note in this connection that by the early 1980s the entire structure of safeguards painstakingly erected around the IAEA and the NPT over the previous two decades will become easy to circumvent by nuclear aspirants due to the emergence of essentially complete fuel-cycle services in the non-NPT world.(45)

  – The emphasis on plutonium as an explosive should not obscure the fact that uranium bombs may become a feasible option in the 1980s for both Israel and Iran, as well as perhaps other regional powers. Perfection of laser enrichment would provide Israel with an alternative, fully indigenous route to nuclear weaponry. The slightly enriched uranium that Iran's nuclear power plants, as well as those of other Middle Eastern states, will use as fuel will have already undergone more than half the enrichment work required to obtain weapons-grade material. If the construction of small enrichment plants using the centrifuge, the Becker nozzle, or other relatively less demanding processes by Iran, Egypt, or Saudi Arabia becomes technologically and economically feasible, as is likely to be the case within a decade, U-235 in militarily significant quantities may become available to these Middle Eastern states. Over the medium-term future, however, this remains an unlikely prospect.

  – The geographic continuity of adversaries, the short distances involved, and the vulnerability of all regional states to very serious national damage as a result of even one well-placed nuclear burst give strategic significance to the possible acquisition by some regional party – national government, transnational movement, or fringe terrorist group – of a nominal nuclear capability. Such capability might be obtained through government-to-government transfer, theft, blackmarket purchase, impounding, or other acquisition of one or two nuclear bombs. The resulting situation would be extremely unstable, and it would be likely to trigger and legitimate large-scale proliferation in the region and beyond. It is hard to conceive of a purposeful coherent political or military strategy that could be served by such a move. Nevertheless, while such behavior is unlikely at the state level, it is not altogether improbable in desperate situations where one side might feel backed into a corner by a nuclear-armed adversary. As for irresponsible, small groups coming into possession of these weapons, probabilities depend on the thoroughness of security measures enforced to protect nuclear materials, devices, and installations.

  – A final option often mentioned is that of obtaining an advanced nuclear deterrent from one of the great powers for local emplacement, either under a two-key control system or under full control and manning by the donor. The only likely candidate for nuclear succor to Arab countries remains the Soviet Union, which may in the event be extremely reluctant to extend it. This would be a very consequential step, entailing direct Soviet participation in the Arab-Israeli conflict. The Israelis would be put at a disadvantage in numbers and sophistication of weapons involved. The United States might feel compelled to intervene on the Israeli side, with all the consequent risks attendant on a superpower nuclear confrontation under volatile and potentially uncontrollable conditions. This is a contingency the likes of which both Moscow and Washington have always tried very hard to avoid in the Middle East and elsewhere.(46)

LIKELY NUCLEAR POSTURES AND PROSPECTS FOR STABILITY

The actual sequence of events and the particular circumstances that will in each case trigger "go nuclear" decisions are difficult to foresee with confidence. Nonetheless, the next ten to fifteen years will very probably witness the acquisition of an overt nuclear weapons capability by several Middle Eastern states: Israel; Iran; and an Arab coalition probably composed of some combination of Egypt, Iraq, Syria, Libya, and Saudi Arabia. The strategic environment that will emerge in a nuclear Middle East and which will determine military postures, targeting doctrines, weapon deployment modes, delivery system procurement, and other elements – the specification of which is necessary for any detailed discussion of potential military outcomes – will be shaped by several important variables. The effects of these variables are themselves wrapped in ambiguity and subject to the vagaries of change and circumstance. Principal among these parameters are: the time frame, the status of the Arab-Israeli conflict, and the impact of the Iranian factor. Only a cursory treatment of these variegated elements can be attempted here, in order to sketch out in a general and preliminary fashion – that is suggestive rather than conclusive – the broad elements of the strategic environment in a proliferated Middle East at the end of the next decade.

The Time Frame

The fact that the introduction of nuclear weapons might be substantially asynchronous may have important implications for the strategic situation. Current domestic capabilities, as have been shown, are not symmetrical. If Israel were, for whatever reasons, compelled to declare a nuclear posture in 1979, the ensuing situation might be drastically different from that which would be created by such an Israeli decision in 1985.

Over the next five to seven years, only two immediate nuclear responses would be open to the Arabs. One would be to trust in superpower guarantees that might be extended to them, but which would ultimately be of limited political reliability and in any case not very credible. The alternative would be to use their influence and financial leverage to procure a few explosive devices from India or fissile material for one or two bombs form some other willing source to serve as a basis for a minimal deterrent until they could build their own weapons. That bombs or plutonium may be available for purchase at any price within the next few years is in itself rather doubtful but, assuming the Arabs were successful, the ensuing balance could be very unstable. The Israelis, as the initiators, presumably would have deployed a nuclear force that was substantial in number. If all of Dimona's output were reprocessed, they might have twenty-five to twenty-eight twenty-kiloton warheads in 1979 and thirty-five to thirty-eight in 1983. In any case, they would not have less than ten to twelve. This force would be composed of bombs that are dependable and of delivery systems –

principally missiles, but also supersonic strike aircraft – that could be relied upon to penetrate enemy defenses and that would have an excellent chance of survivability for an adequate retaliatory second strike. The Arab side would have a much less secure and dependable force. Their bombs are likely to be based on commercial reactor grade plutonium. They would, therefore, be bulky and of uncertain yield, with weight and size specifications that would probably limit Arab delivery means to the use of vulnerable medium-range bombers, such as the Tu-16.(47) These weapons would be very few in number and of dubious survivability in the event of an Israeli surgical preventive strike, even on restricted to conventional weapons. Thus, for several years, any major crisis or war situation might generate powerful pressures on Israel to attempt to destroy the Arab nuclear force on the ground, and on the Arabs to launch their nuclear weapons at the slightest indication of a possible Israeli disarming attack. The more primitive and vulnerable the Arab force were, the higher the chances that misperception, accident, or faulty intelligence might trigger a devastating nuclear exchange.

If the shift from conventional to nuclear defense postures did not happen until the second half of the 1980s or later, chances would be much improved for the emergence of a more stable deterrent relationship.(48) Both sides would be in a position to equip themselves with sufficient quantities of bombs and adequate delivery capabilities to create a strong presumption of survival for retaliatory forces able to inflict unacceptable damage on the adversary. The accurate dimensions of such mutually assured destruction capability are difficult to specify a decade in advance, but the concentrations of population centers and other value targets in the main Arab-Israel confrontation states are such that only a small percentage, 10-15 percent, of deployed weapons need survive to deliver intolerable retaliation.

Skeptics of the prospects for stability of an Arab-Israeli nuclear balance, who argue that temptations to resort to nuclear strikes will be numerous and relatively easy to succumb to because ". . . a 'damage-limiting' pre-emptive blow will at one time or another appear as the most viable way out of a tense situation,"(49) labor under a misconception derived from the Soviet-American strategic model that they themselves usually dismiss as irrelevant to the Middle East situation. This misconception lies in the very notion that damage limitation through preemptive nulcear strike is a viable policy option for states that stand to lose a very substantial proportion of their human and material resources if they are hit with only one or two Hiroshima-type nuclear weapons. Unless a political leadership has a very high degree of confidence bordering on certainty that it can carry out a disarming first strike with 100 percent success, any such damage-limiting strategies will be dismissed as suicidal. Such 100 percent success is most improbable, with the possible exception of a diversified Israeli force facing an improvised minimal Arab deterrent up to the mid-1980s.

Threats to nuclear stability of a different nature would indeed exist, just as they do in the central superpower balance. Risks of unauthorized seizure and use by fanatic, disaffected, or mentally deranged military personnel; catalytic third-party behavior; accidental launches; and the like are significant in any nuclear environment regardless of locale. Their existence would provide strong incentives for the institution of direct communication channels between Jerusalem and Arab capitals to deal with potential incidents. This should be done even if ten years hence there has been no breakthrough toward normalization of Arab-Israeli relations.

Status of the Arab-Israeli conflict

Obviously, the degree of stability accruing to any Arab-Israeli nuclear balance would be sensitive to the contemporary state of the overall political relationship between the two sides. Maximal instability would ensue if an asymmetric balance emerged over the medium-term, in the absence of steady movement toward a settlement of the current conflict and in conditions of acute diplomatic and military confrontation.

Paradoxically, these are the conditions most likely to bring forth an Israeli decision to go nulcear. Such a decision might be taken in a no-war context in order to: supplement the conventional deterrent in the face of a threatened large-scale Arab attack; keep defense expenditures necessitated by a continuing arms race within tolerable limits; or signal determination, stiffen public morale, and strengthen the Israeli bargaining posture against a perceived impending imposition of an unacceptable political settlement. In a wartime situation, nuclear weapons might be introduced: in a counterforce mode, to stem a successful Egyptian conventional breakthrough that threatened to extend across the pre-June 1967 borders; also in a counterforce role, to decimate large Egyptian attacking forces in Sinai that could be defeated conventionally, but only at great costs in casualties and equipment or at the expense of retreats on other fronts; or a countervalue threatening mode, to deter large-scale Arab strikes against Israeli cities in conditions of escalating reciprocal rear area bombing. Clearly, such an Israeli move under any of the conditions listed would be viewed by the Arabs as extremely provocative and would prompt drastic efforts to obtain a countervailing deterrent.

Progress toward a negotiated settlement of outstanding issues would both decrease the incentives for nuclearization and create the conditions for a more stable political and military environment that would, in turn, enhance the chances for stability of an eventual nuclear balance. Much would depend, however, on the nature of further diplomatic progress. Several possible outcomes of a future political negotiation may be envisaged.

– There could be further limited step-by-step type agreements between Syria and Israel and/or Egypt and Israel. These would create a modus vivendi that could last several more years, perhaps to 1982, with moderate instability. The Palestinian factor would remain unresolved and would serve to perpetuate the basic dispute.

– In the wake of a drastic weakening of the PLO as a result of events in Lebanon, an agreement between Israel and Jordan would return the bulk of the West Bank to Jordanian jurisdiction. This would implement something akin to the Allon plan.(50)

– A further Israel-Egypt agreement might return most of Sinai to Egypt in what would amount, in practice, to a separate peace. This would, however, be couched in a formula that made Egypt's position tenable within the inter-Arab context.

All these potential outcomes have one crucial negative element in common: some principals to the conflict continue to have unrequited grievances. As a result, destabilizing revisionist claims would remain active, and the quest for military superiority would not abate. The arms race would continue at high levels, and a relapse into acute military confrontation would remain a likely prospect.

– An overall settlement, involving all principal parties, might be concluded. It would define final borders, terminate all national claims, end all acts of belligerency, and establish a modicum of normal diplomatic relations between the two sides. Despite the comprehensiveness of such a solution, it is likely that a significantly high level of tension, military readiness, and cautious expectancy would remain for a number of years, given the historical record of animosity and mistrust among the parties. Nonetheless, a basically stable situation would have been created. The parties would be enabled to favor policies that would promote relaxations of tension and arms control objectives: defensive military postures, stability of mutual deterrence, and reduction of defense burdens.

If a comprehensive settlement could be achieved within the next three to five years, it is conceivable that overt nuclearization by either side might be postponed until the 1990s. Such a postponement might occur because of the complex of international guarantees, the local presence of large peacekeeping forces, and the arms control arrangements that would inevitably form part of any overall solution. Additional impetus would be provided by the attenuation of security concerns that would accompany a formal end to the conflict. Prospects for such restraint are very slim, however, both because the Arab leadership believes that Israel's nuclear capability is, for all practical purposes, already in being and because Arab-Israeli nuclearization may come about in response to proliferation elsewhere in the region.

The Iranian Factor

Despite the large dimensions of the nuclear program Iran has launched, the Shah's views and intentions regarding the military uses of atomic energy are not at all clear, though perhaps the most significant fact remains his explicit statement, later retracted, that he would indeed seek a nuclear bomb and sooner than people think.(51) Although Iran is an NPT member and has completed a safeguards agreement with the IAEA covering all the country's nuclear installations and material, what transpires from the welter of Iranian pronouncements on the subject is a clear determination to build nuclear weapons if any other

Middle Eastern country does so. While Teheran so far apparently accepts Israel's official nonnuclear status at face value, this could change quickly if Israel's capability became more visible. It could also change if the Iranians decided for their own reasons that they wanted to withdraw from the NPT and needed a handy excuse to legitimize their actions. In any case, no domestically produced plutonium for an Iranian bomb will become available before the early 1980s. Furthermore, if the Shah is unable to return to Iran following the domestic upheavals in 1978-79, successor governments may follow different policies relative to potential nuclear weapons production.

Assuming that no urgent nuclear threats to Iran's security that could drive it to seek to purchase ready-made atomic bombs from the "grey market" are likely to materialize before 1982, there are several incentives other than Israeli or Arab proliferation that might encourage Iran to embark on a weapons development program once fissile material becomes available. Deterrence of Soviet invasion and deterrence of further Indian dismemberment of Pakistan are the two security-related roles most often mentioned. The utility of nuclear weapons for such purposes, particularly the discouragement of Soviet interest, may be highly debatable; yet, similar arguments were made, in vain, against a force de frappe for France. An additional incentive, which may in the event prove determinative and also played a large role in the mix of motives that produced a nuclear France, is that of prestige. Since the oil price revolution of 1973 which he spearheaded, the Shah has repeatedly expressed his determination to bring Iran to advanced global status before the end of the century. Moreover, he has proved by his actions that he means what he says. Accelerated industrialization that is overtaxing the country's absorptive capacity and one of the largest conventional arms buildups in the world attest to this. In addition to great power standing, a drive for uncontested regional preeminence in the area between the Levant and the Indian subcontinent clearly animates Iranian planning for the future. In light of such ambitions, it would be surprising if a move by Pakistan, or even by more distant South Korea or Brazil, to acquire nuclear explosives does not in short order bring about an Iranian political decision to do so as well. Even a step by already-nuclear India away from the fiction of peaceful nuclear explosives toward avowed weapons deployment could trigger an Iranian decision. Since circumspection would be desirable, however, to avoid strong superpower pressures or preventive action by a worried Soviet neighbor across the border, the Iranians are likely to proceed quietly. An Iranian nuclear capability is not likely to become a regional factor until announced toward the late 1980s. Clearly, however, all of the foregoing prestige estimates and comparisons depend on the Shah being in power far more than the prestige considerations for France depended on de Gaulle's presence as the decisive policy maker on nuclear weapons questions. With the Shah gone, unless he were replaced by a military junta, his vision of Iran's role in the Persian Gulf and the world would be gone, along with the expectation of Iran as an imminent nuclear weapon state.

It is worth considering the effects that a nuclear armed Iran would have on the rest of the Middle East. Of all possible conjectural scenarios for regional nuclear warfare anywhere on the globe, that which envisages a nuclear exchange in the Persian Gulf among the local parties is perhaps the least plausible. Nonetheless, an Iranian bomb might elicit strong interest in a similar acquisition by Saudi Arabia and certainly by Iraq. Again, the immediate motive here is less likely to be the deterrence of nuclear attack than a counterbalancing of the aura of Iranian military power to discourage the Shah from throwing his weight around in regional political disputes. Not to match the Iranians would amount to conceding to them the role of protector of the Gulf, its hinterland, and ocean reaches, and ultimate arbiter of the area's political destinies. This is a role local Arab powers historically have strongly resisted bestowing on Teheran. Besides, the last few decades have witnessed much discord, including at times substantial armed clashes, between Iran and Iraq on grounds that extend beyond recently resolved border issues to intangibles of ideology, racial-national antipathy, and competition for regional influence.

An Iraqi effort to obtain the bomb may be carried out individually, relying on domestic resources, or in cooperation with other Arab states. Iraq's first planned nuclear power station is not likely to be operational before 1985, and any Iraqi nuclear posture would inevitably become part of the Arab-Israeli equation. Thus, close cooperation with Egypt and possibly Libya in the scientific and technological aspects of the effort, with substantial Saudi funding if required, is the more likely alternative. An integrated Arab effort would shorten the time required for weapons development. It would also help lay the basis for coordinated nuclear planning following their acquisition. While secrecy may be difficult if not impossible to maintain in a multinational project of this nature, it may be no longer necessary in the early or mid-1980s. This would be particularly true for a bloc of countries facing nuclear neighbors or adversaries and possessing, in their control of oil resources, a strong bargaining counter and dissuasive tool with which to deter international measures aimed at crippling their weapons program. Regardless of whether Iraq proceeds alone or in tandem with other Arabs toward developing nuclear weaponry in response to an Iranian initiative, such a development would quickly bring Israel's nuclear posture into the open, with predictable effects on Egyptian and Syrian calculations.

This underscores an important consideration. In the nuclear arena, unlike the conventional arms field, Israel will perceive every weapon in Arab hands as aimed exclusively at itself, and all Arab governments will, in turn, expect that every Arab warhead will be available for use against Israel were it to employ nuclear weapons against any one of them. Furthermore, the fact that initially, and for a number of years, Israel would possess a more sophisticated and diversified nuclear force than the other side, would place a heavy premium on optimizing Arab capabilities. Hence, regardless of whether the proliferation sequence in the Middle East region begins with Israel or Iran, one is led to postulate that there is likely to be substantial integration of Arab bomb development efforts, joint nuclear planning, and coordinated deployment across international boundaries to maximize survival chances of retaliatory forces. In addition, one can expect centralization of mechanisms for quick decision making on nuclear weapons use in time of conventional war or in case of surprise attack. While this may be a very bold prognosis in view of traditional inter-Arab rivalries and ideological differences, the alternative of multiple Arab centers of decision in a proliferated nuclear environment almost certainly would be prohibitively unstable. It would make it extremely difficult for the Arab side to implement the carefully modulated and precisely managed strategies that render nuclear deterrence workable. It would place the balance of terror at the mercy of the vagaries of domestic politics in several countries with a recent history of political instability and military interventionism.   It also would multiply exponentially the chances of an accidental or catalytic nuclear war that, given the dynamics of the Arab-Israeli conflict, would be likely to engulf the entire region.

A MIDDLE EAST NUCLEAR FUTURIBLE

In The Art of Conjecture, Bertrand de Jouvenel defines a futurible as "a futurum that appears to the mind as a possible descendant from the present state of affairs."(52) A very probable 1990 descendant of the current Middle Eastern situation in the nuclear realm is the following:
— There will be a deployed Israeli nuclear force with a minimum of 30-40 devices of various kiloton yields atop mobile short-range ballistic missiles (SRBMs), supersonic fighter bombers, and possibly cruise missiles and remotely piloted vehicles (RPVs).
— There will likewise be an Arab nuclear force of ten to fifteen devices in the twenty-kiloton range, deployed in Egypt, Syria, and Iraq. It will be deliverable by mobile Scaleboard SRBMs and medium-range bombers, with or without air launched cruise missiles, and will be subject to centralized command and control.
— Iran will possess a nuclear force of twenty to thirty weapons in the twenty-kiloton range carried by supersonic fighter bombers.
— Though Iranian proliferation may be induced by weapons programs in the Arab-Israeli theater, Iranian planning and deployments are likely to be primarily directed toward the Indian subcontinent and the Soviet Union, and only collaterally toward the Persian Gulf countries. The strategic linkages between the Iranian-Iraqi-Saudi relationship, on the one hand, and the Arab-Israeli nuclear context, on the other hand, will be tenuous and purposely deemphasized by Iran, which would have no interest in becoming involved in an Arab-Israeli nuclear exchange.
— Counterforce doctrines will be entertained for possible use in a last resort interdiction role during conventional war, particularly by Israel. The prevailing targeting strategy, however, will be counter city. The main Israeli objective will be to deter an Arab resort to large-scale conventional war through the threat of escalation; the Arab purpose will be to deter an Israeli disarming first strike.
— After an initial stage of strongly asymmetric capabilities providing

strong incentives for an Israeli preventive strike – which in all probability will be prevented by a host of political considerations – the Arab-Israeli nuclear balance will become basically stable. The stability will grow out of the recognition that unacceptable damage can be inflicted on either side by even a minimal countervalue retaliation of one or two twenty-kiloton bursts. Rather than a race to get in the first punch, we are likely to see in crisis situations a prudent crawl up the ladder of escalation to its highest rungs. Each side will shift onto the other's shoulders the burden of a fateful decision that would likely spell reciprocal annihilation.

   – This degree of stability implies that the presence of nuclear weaponry will not by itself deter all levels of hostile military action. While all-out conventional war, on the 1967 or 1973 model, as a deliberate policy choice will have become too risky, guerrilla warfare, frontier clashes, and across-the-border operations – with all the inherent potential for uncontrolled escalation – might occur. The crucial variable in determining the incidence and intensity of such destabilizing activities will be the political status of the Arab-Israeli dispute. If, a decade hence, that much sought-after final settlement still eludes the peacemakers, perhaps the sobering prospects of unintended escalation into the horrors of nuclear war will provide the requisite stimulant for an honorable negotiated solution.

NOTES AND REFERENCES

(1) Compare, for instance, Paul Jabber, Israel and Nuclear Weapons: Present Option and Future Strategies (London: Chatto and Windus, 1971); Yair Evron, "Israel and the Atom: The Uses and Misuses of Ambiguity, 1957-1967," Orbis 17 (Winter 1974): 1326-43; Avigdor Haselkorn, "Israel: From an Option to a Bomb in the Basement?" in Nuclear Proliferation, Phase II, eds. Robert M. Lawrence and Joel Larus (Lawrence: University Press of Kansas, 1974); Lawrence Freedman, "Israel's Nuclear Policy," Survival 17 (May-June 1975): 114-20; Robert Tucker, "Israel and the United States: From Dependence to Nuclear Weapons?" Commentary 60 (November 1975): 29-43; Steven J. Rosen, "Nuclearization and Stability in the Middle East," Jerusalem Journal of International Relations 1 (Spring 1976): 1-32; and Alan Dowty, "Israel and Nuclear Weapons," Midstream 22 (November 1976): 7-22.

(2) For a further description see Evron, ibid., and Dowty, ibid., pp. 12-13.

(3) Mohamed H. Heikal lists Egyptian and Libyan attempts to obtain nuclear weapons abroad in his lead article in Al Ahram (November, 23, 1973), and further discusses Libyan efforts in The Road to Ramadan (London: Collins, 1975), pp. 76-7.

(4) "Soviet Said to Give Arabs Atom Pledge," New York Times (May 12, 1974). For analyses of the "Soviet nuclear shipment" incident, see

William B. Quandt, Soviet Policy in the October 1973 War (Santa Monica, California: The Rand Corporation, May 1976), pp. 30-1; Jon D. Glassman, Arms for the Arabs: The Soviet Union and War in the Middle East (Baltimore and London: Johns Hopkins University Press, 1975), p. 163; and Alvin Z. Rubinstein, Red Star on the Nile: The Soviet-Egyptian Influence Relationship since the June War (Princeton, N.J.: Princeton University Press, 1977), pp. 271, 275-76.

(5) For alternative proliferation chains and scenarios, see Lewis A. Dunn and Herman Kahn, Trends in Nuclear Proliferation, 1975-1995, A Hudson Institute Report prepared for the US Arms Control and Disarmament Agency (Croton-on-Hudson, New York: Hudson Institute, May 1976), pp. 23-75.

(6) William Van Cleave, "Nuclear Technology and Weapons," Lawrence and Larus, p. 59 (note 1 supra).

(7) Jerusalem Post (January 8, 1971).

(8) Samuel P. Huntington, "Arms Races: Prerequisites and Results," The Use of Force, eds., Robert J. Art and Kenneth N. Waltz (Boston: Little, Brown and Co., 1971), p. 374.

(9) See Al Ahram (note 3 supra); the Ismail Fahmi statement in Arab Report and Record (April 16-30, 1976); and the Ali Fahmi statement in Foreign Broadcast Information Service (Egypt), (February 24, 1975).

(10) Nuclear Engineering International (March 1977): 31-3.

(11) Ibid.; and Washington Post (October 7, 1976).

(12) Editorial, "Who will Horse-Trade Nucler Plant for Oil?" Nuclear Engineering International (March 1977): 3-4.

(13) Ibid., p. 32.

(14) Nuclear News (December 1975): 14.

(15) Middle East Economic Digest (March 4, 1977): 20.

(16) Los Angeles Times (October 9, 1975).

(17) Nuclear Engineering International (March 1977).

(18) Statement by State Department spokesman, Frederick Z. Brown, quoted in ibid. (September 1976): 9.

(19) Robert Gillette, "Uranium Enrichment: Rumors of Israeli Progress with Lasers," Science (March 22, 1974): 1172-74.

(20) For a recent report on Egyptian nuclear energy plans, see Nuclear Engineering International (March 1977): 34-35; and Nuclear News (December 1975): 61.

(21) Al-Ahram (July 31, 1971).

(22) Washington Post (May 30, 1975).

(23) International Herald Tribune (October 29, 1976); Nuclear Engineering International (January 1976): 9.

(24) Ibid.

(25) Heikal, Al-Ahram (note 3 supra), and Heikal, The Road to Ramadan (note 3 supra).

(26) Arab Report and Record (February 1-14, 15-29 and December 1-15, 1976).

(27) Nuclear News (April 1976): 15; Nuclear Engineering International (April-May 1976): 13.

(28) Nuclear Engineering International (March 1977): 35-7.

(29) Ibid. (February 1977): 11; and Middle East Economic Digest (March 25, 1977): 20-1.

(30) Arab Report and Record (March 16-31, 1976).

(31) Arab Report and Record (February 1-14 and May 1-15, 1976).

(32) Nuclear Engineering International (January 1976): 10; and Arab Report and Record (December 1-15, 1976).

(33) Nuclear Engineering International, (note 29 supra); and Nuclear News (March 1977): 52.

(34) The United States Atomic Energy Commission figures are cited in Albert Wohlstetter et al., Moving Toward Life in a Nuclear Armed Crowd?, A Report prepared for the US Arms Control and Disarmament Agency (Los Angeles, California: Pan Heuristics, April 1976), p. 35. Plutonium output is not very sensitive to reactor type. Boiling water reactors would produce .23 kg/MWe/year; pressurized heavy water reactors, .29; gas cooled reactors, .25.

(35) On the inaccuracy of earlier beliefs that commercial grade plutonium was unfit for weapons use, see Van Cleave (note 6 supra) and works cited therein.

(36) Ibid., p. 43.

(37) United States Congress, House, Committee on International Relations, Subcommittee on International Security and Scientific Affairs, Testimony by Dr. Theodore Taylor, Hearings: Nuclear Proliferation: Future U.S. Foreign Policy Implications, 94th Cong., 1st Sess., October-December 1975, p. 82.

(38) For an appreciation of how truly limited the safeguard functions of IAEA are, see the testimony of United States ambassador to IAEA, Gerald Tape, ibid., especially pp. 178-84. A good discussion is found in Ryiukichi Imai, Nuclear Safeguards, Adelphi Paper no. 86 (London: International Institute of Strategic Studies, March 1972).

(39) Imai, ibid., p. 12. Wohlstetter figures from Wohlstetter et al., p. 66 (note 34 supra). A descriptive breakdown of the numerous sources of potential error or material losses is found in Imai, ibid., pp. 32-34.

(40) Given the multiplicity of sources of possible error or material losses and the potential political repercussions of an IAEA finding that diversion may have taken place, which will tend to produce extreme caution on the part of the inspectorate, a 3 percent tolerance for MUF is in practice likely and will be assumed in this paper. It may be significant that, to this day, the IAEA has not lodged a single accusation of potential diversion against any state party to a safeguards agreement.
　　With a good implosion design, four kilograms of Pu-239, and probably less, would suffice for a critical mass. Pu-240 contamination in the 10-20 percent range, typical of commercial reactor-grade byproducts, increases the size of the critical mass to about eight kilograms.
　　P.L. Olgaard, "On the Possible Military Significance of the Superheavy Elements," in Impact of New Technologies of the Arms Race, B.T. Feld et al. (Cambridge: The MIT Press, 1971), p. 120; and Mason Willrich and Theodore B. Taylor, Nuclear Theft: Risks and Safeguards (Cambridge: Ballinger, 1974), pp. 13, 20.

(41) Daniel Yergin, "The Terrifying Prospect: Atomic Bombs Everywhere," The Atlantic Monthly (April 1977): 60.

(42) United States Congress, House, Committee on Foreign Affairs, Subcommittee on International Organizations and Movements and the Near East and South Asia, Testimony by United States Under-Secretary of State Joseph J. Sisco, Hearings: U.S. Foreign Policy and the Export of Nuclear Technology to the Middle East, 93rd Cong., 2nd Sess., June-September 1974, pp. 237, 239.

(43) Text published in the Lebanese Official Gazette (June 1972); English translation in the Economic Review of the Arab World (September 1972): 51-64; and Heikal, Al-Ahram (note 3 supra).

(44) Yergin (note 41 supra).

(45) For a fuller discussion of these points see Lewis A. Dunn, "Nuclear 'Gray Marketeering.'" International Security 1(Winter 1976-77): 107-18.

(46) For a more detailed discussion of Soviet and American reactions and possible roles of other nuclear great powers, see my article, "Israel's Nuclear Options," Journal of Palestine Studies 1 (Autumn 1971): 21-38; and Rosen (note 1 supra).

(47) A good description of nuclear delivery systems currently available to the Arabs and Israel is in Robert J. Pranger and Dale R. Tahtinen, Nuclear Threat in the Middle East (Washington, D.C.: American Enterprise Institute for Public Policy Research, 1975), Chapter 3.

(48) Jabber, pp. 141-144 (note 1 supra); and Rosen (note 1 supra).

(49) Alan Dowty, "Nuclear Proliferation: The Israeli Case" (mimeographed), p. 25.

(50) For a description of this plan see Yigal Allon, "Israel: The Case for Defensible Borders," Foreign Affairs 55 (October 1976): 38-53.

(51) Quoted in George Quester, "The Shah and the Bomb," Policy Sciences (March 1977): 21-32. This is a good analysis of Iran's nuclear option.

(52) Bertrand de Jouvenel, The Art of Conjecture. Trans. by Nikita Lary. New York: Basic Books, 1967.

II
Aspects of
Arms Transfer

4 United States Arms to the Middle East 1967-76: A Critical Examination*

Anne Hessing Cahn

During the decade 1966-75, the United States physically transferred, as opposed to signed orders or contracts, over $7 billion in arms, ancillary support equipment, spare parts and services to the Middle East-Persian Gulf (MEPG) region, as indicated in Table 4.1. The following countries are included in MEPG in this paper: Egypt, Iran, Iraq, Israel, Jordan, Kuwait, Lebanon, Oman, Saudi Arabia, Syria, and Yemen. The following countries are excluded because the United States has transferred no arms or negligible amounts of arms since 1966: Aden, Behrain, Qatar, and the United Arab Emirates. Military assistance programs and foreign military sales orders for MEPG totalled $398.8 million in 1967 and ten years later had increased fourteen-fold to $5.7 billion, as indicated in tables 4.6-4.9. At the beginning of the decade, MEPG accounted for 13 percent of all American military assistance programs; by 1976, 60.7 percent of all United States military assistance programs and sales orders came from MEPG countries.

The data need to be disaggregated into several categories: United States grants and sales to Israel vis-a-vis American grants and sales to the other MEPG countries, to Iran vis-a-vis Arab states, and to Iran vis-a-vis Saudi Arabia. Tables 4.2 and 4.3 show that of total American sales and grant aid to MEPG in the twenty-year period 1950-70, Israel received just about one-tenth the amount received by its Arab and Moslem neighbors. Since 1971, Israeli Foreign Military Sales (FMS) orders and commercial deliveries have totalled $5.6 billion while the other MEPG nations have accounted for $22 billion.

---

*This paper was prepared for the conference on Great Power Intervention in the Middle East held at Cornell University in April 1977, prior to my joining the United States Arms Control and Disarmament Agency (ACDA). The views expressed are solely those of the author and do not represent the views of ACDA or any other executive Branch, Department or Agency.

Table 4.1. Comparison of ACDA and DSAA Data for US Arms Transfers to the Middle East, 1966-1975
(million current dollars)

Country[a]	ACDA Data Total Imported	Imported from US %	(% total)	DSAA Data Imported from US
Egypt	2,780	–	–	1.4
Iran	3,877	2,702	(70)	2,814.0[b]
Iraq	1,721	2	(0)	13.3
Israel	4,031	3,856	(96)	3,007.3[b]
Jordan	538	400	(74)	370.0[b]
Kuwait	97	14	(14)	.7
Lebanon	126	21	(17)	19.8
Oman	67	3	(5)	2.8
Saudi Arabia	1,038	473	(46)	1,026.6[b]
Syria	1,905	3	(9)	1.9
Yemen	65	1	(2)	2.6
Totals: Near East	16,245	7,475	(46)	7,260.4[b]

[a]Aden, Bahrain, Cyprus, Qatar, and United Arab Emirates are included in ACDA's Near East Region, but are not included in this paper since the US has transferred no arms or negligible amounts of arms to each since 1966.

[b]Whenever inconsistent Defense Security Assistance Agency (DSAA) data exist, the figures used in this table are based on the mean.

Looking at total United States grant aid and sales to MEPG exclusive of Israel, Iran received 30 percent during 1950-70 and has received 49 percent since then. Since 1950, Iran has received more than twice the amount of grant aid and total sales acquired by Israel, i.e. $13.9 billion to $6.3 billion. Of the total United States military package to Saudi Arabia since 1972, 80 percent has been for construction and services, while in Iran the situation is reversed with hardware accounting for 80 percent and support and services for 20 percent.

Expressed as hardware rather than dollars, during the last ten years, the United States supplied MEPG with more than 1,300 tanks, 1,750 armored personnel carriers, 1,350 jeeps, 85 C-130 cargo planes, 235 F-

Table 4.2. US Arms Transfers to Israel 1950-76*
(thousand current dollars)

	Total 1950-70	1971	1972	1973	1974	1975	1976	Total 1950-76
Foreign Military Sales Orders	580,905	413,492	409,230	181,740	2,455,205	864,052	923,245[a]	5,904,274
Commercial Deliveries	72,897	26,526	63,068	21,555	50,118	46,746	137,570[b]	200,910
Total Sales	653,802	440,018	472,298	203,295	2,505,323[c]	910,798[d]	1,060,815	6,322,754

*Except as noted below, Israel received no grants during the years covered.

[a]$750,000 payments waived,
[b]Supplied by Office of Munitions Control.
[c]$1,500,000 payments waived.
[d]$100,000 payments waived.

Source: Department of Defense Security Assistance Agency, Foreign Military Sales and Military Assistance Facts (Washington, D.C.: December 1976), pp. 8, 12, 16.

103

Table 4.3. US Arms Transfers to MEPG Excluding Israel 1950-76
(thousand current dollars)

Country	FY 1950-70	1971	1972	1973	1974	1975	1976	1950-76[a]
Iran								
Grants[b]	892,521	2,080	888	339	2	–	–	895,830
Sales[c]	903,101	423,900	556,085	2,176,776	4,408,547	3,070,389	1,472,284	13,011,082
Total:	1,795,622	425,980	556,973	2,177,115	4,408,549	3,070,389	1,472,284	13,906,912
Jordan								
Grants	65,867	29,798	46,265	55,471	45,896	71,009	55,785	370,091
Sales	149,713	17,594	19,023	6,113	61,543	77,612	456,060	787,658
Total:	215,580	47,392	65,288	61,584	107,439	148,621	511,845	1,157,749
Saudi Arabia								
Grants	36,670	632	429	179	169	37	–	38,116
Sales	3,899,777	23,181	465,766	1,999,271	1,924,732	1,408,424	2,585,307	12,306,458
Total:	3,936,447	23,813	466,195	1,999,450	1,924,901	1,408,461	2,585,307	12,344,574

Other Arab States[d]

Grants	59,684	4,480	—	695	171	174	350	65,554
Sales	29,320	1,170	371	8,402	45,167	381,442	331,736	797,608
Total:	89,004	5,650	371	9,097	45,338	381,616	332,086	863,162

TOTALS

Grants	1,054,742	36,990	47,582	56,684	46,238	71,220	56,135	1,369,591
Sales	4,981,911	465,845	1,041,245	4,190,562	6,439,989	4,937,867	4,845,387	26,902,806
Total:	6,036,653	502,835	1,088,827	4,247,246	6,486,227	5,009,087	4,901,522	28,272,397

Source: Department of Defense Security Assistance Agency, Foreign Military Sales and Military Assistance Facts (Washington: D.C.: December 1976), pp. 12, 13, 16-19, 22, 23, 26, 27.

[a]Includes Transitional Quarter (FY 1977).
[b]Includes Military Assistance Program, Excess Defense Articles Program-Acquisition Cost, and International Military Education and Training Program.
[c]Includes Foreign Military Sales agreements 1950-76 and Commercial Exports 1960-76.
[d]Egypt, Iraq, Lebanon, Oman, Syria, and Yemen.

5E fighters, 190 Skyhawks, 370 Phantom F-4s, 4,500 TOW antitank missiles, 2,500 Sparrow III missiles, 2,700 Maverick air-to-surface missiles and 250 gunship helicopters. Other items included training planes, sophisticated electronics surveillance systems, patrol boats, and so on. Under its foreign military sales program, the United States has also established and managed logistics systems; built and supported military hospitals, schools, barracks, military headquarters, and family housing; dredged harbors; built roads and cement plants; and provided training for more than 4,500 Middle Eastern military personnel in the last ten years.

The thesis of this paper is that this outpouring of military goods and services has in good measure been undertaken in pursuit of a myth. That myth is that military assistance is the most appropriate, efficient, or easiest way to implement the foreign policy objectives of the United States in MEPG. In the past, American arms transfers to MEPG have often been executed without a clear understanding of their regional implications. Nor have there been adequate analyses of long-term risks, in addition to short-term benefits, or an adequate exploration of alternate means to achieve foreign policy goals. Finally, the effectiveness of the "open arms" policy has never been sufficiently evaluated.

Most past academic efforts at evaluating United States arms sales have tried to construct quantifiable indices of political influence and/or control and economic penetration or benefit to the supplier. Almost without exception, the influence assumed to flow from arms transfers cannot be substantiated empirically. Conclusions reached are:

Arms do not result in influence (and may in fact have the opposite effect).(1)

The U.S. (and France) realized few political benefits from their arms transfers.(2)

The data show a strong negative correlation, reflecting the fact that a decrease in arms transfers results in increased trade and vice-versa.(3)

Looking at the results as a whole . . . lend(s) support to the main premise of this study — that arms transfers are at best of dubious utility as an instrument of major power influence.(4)

Despite the lack of evidence indicating a positive relationship between arms supplies and influence, the strongly rooted belief that such is the case persists. This paper attempts to analyze the issue more qualitatively, examining the rationales most often cited by the United States in the past for its arms transfers to MEPG.

On May 19, 1977, President Carter announced a new conventional arms transfer policy stating that "the United States will henceforth view arms transfers as an exceptional foreign policy implement, to be used only in instances where it can be clearly demonstrated that the transfer contributes to our national security interests."(5) The policy establishes the following controls, applicable to all countries except NATO, Japan, Australia, and New Zealand:

— The dollar value (in constant FY 1976 dollars) of orders for FY 1978 shall be less than the FY 1977 total. (Services and commercial sales are excluded.)

— The United States will not be the first to introduce into a region newly developed, advanced weapons systems which could create a new or significantly higher combat capability.

— Advanced weapons cannot be developed or significantly modified solely for export.

— Coproduction agreements for significant weapons, equipment, and major components are prohibited.

— The United States may stipulate that no requests for retransfers of certain weapons will be considered.

— All actions by agents of the United States or private manufacturers, which might promote the sale of arms abroad, require policy level authorization by the State Department.

The effectiveness of the new arms trade policy will depend, as that of all policies, on the implementation process. At the time this paper was written in July 1977, it was too early to make a judgment concerning the new arms trade policy. This paper, of necessity, deals with past rather than present United States arms transfers policies in the Middle East. It examines the political, economic, and military-strategic rationales used to promote and justify American arms transfer policies.

POLITICAL RATIONALES

The most frequently cited, but least examined, rationale for United States arms sales is to derive political influence from the transaction. It is useful to distinguish among the amount, form, scope, and temporal aspects, as well as the direction of the influence flow.

Amount of Influence

The amount of influence flowing from arms transfers is alleged to be great, with the implicit assumption of a positive linear correlation between the quantity of weapons transferred and the quantity of influence derived. It is open to question if the relationship between arms and influence really is that simple.

In 1978, the 95th Congress and President Carter acceded to the widely predicted requests of President Anwar Sadat for sizable United States arms sales to Egypt. Surely the first $25 or $50 million sales to Egypt will carry a great deal more influence than a comparable $25-50 million added to Israel's already sizable arms acquisition from the United States. It may well be that, for the supplier, garnering the first contract for arms sales from a new client brings a large payoff in terms of influence. Supplying additional arms by providing, for example, 20-70

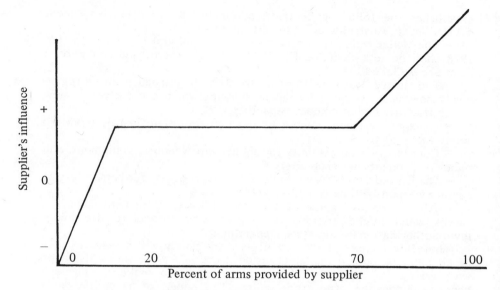

Figure 4.1. Zero-sum influence game.

percent of a nation's arms, may carry a negligible amount of further leverage over the recipient, as illustrated in figure 4.1.

However, becoming the sole source of arms may bring a large additional gain on the influence curve. Nonetheless, even sole source arms suppliers cannot always exercise the influence they are assumed to possess. Although Israel receives some military equipment from Britain and France, it is for all practical purposes completely dependent upon the United States for those arms it does not produce indigenously. Even so, Israel often pursues policies counter to expressed American views. The issue of United States influence over Israel is complicated by the countervailing influence which Israel exerts in the United States through the Jewish community and sympathetic members of Congress.

Being a sole source of arms can also pose dilemmas for the supplier. If the supplier is so conspicuously committed to the recipient that it fears disengagement, it may become the captive of a recalcitrant recipient, e.g., the United States-South Vietnam relationship illustrated in figure 4.2. It should be recognized that sole source-supply relationships may carry unanticipated costs which far outweigh the expected political and economic benefits.(6)

Figure 4.3 depicts multiple supplier-recipient relations. If the competition to supply arms is between alliance partners, say France and Britain, the recipient may or may not be able to play off one against the other. If the alternative sources of supply cut across the traditional alliance bloc lines, the leverage of the recipient is greatly enhanced.

The Shah of Iran is adept at using this to his advantage. In the summer of 1966, he let it be known that he was considering the purchase of Soviet surface-to-air missiles (SAM). The Shah was

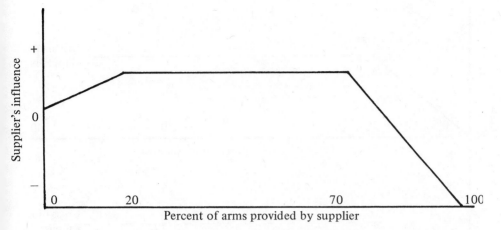

Figure 4.2. United States-South Vietnam.

persuaded to buy the American Hawk missile instead, but only on the condition that the United States would look favorably on his next request – to buy the supersonic F-4 fighter aircraft. Permission was speedily granted, and the only surprise was that less than five months after signing the letter of offer for the first squadron of F-4s, the Shah concluded an arms barter agreement with the Soviet Union as well.(7) More recently, the Shah wanted to purchase the American Redeye, a portable shoulder-fired SAM. Faced with American reticence, Iran turned to Moscow.(8) From the timing of the arrival of Soviet mobile SA-7 missiles in Iran, it is reasonable to conclude that Iran started negotiations with the Soviet Union before it got a definite answer from the United States.

To assess the amount of influence derivable from a given arms transaction, consider the matrix Table 4.4.

The matrix is presented for heuristic purposes only. The variables are not presented in rank order, nor are they mutually exclusive; indeed several are interrelated. The pariah state syndrome – the diplomatic isolation of Israel, as well as Rhodesia, South Africa, South Korea, and Taiwan – is intimately intertwined with the nonavailability of alternate sources of supply, be it for arms or for nuclear reactors. The diplomatic isolation of the recipient and a perceived threat to natonal survival are probably the most important determinants of the arms supply-influence nexus. United States influence over Israeli foreign policy is a good example.

The pressure to produce arms indigenously will be heightened by facing a real national security threat, by lacking alternate sources of supply, or by perceiving oneself to be a pariah state. The power of the purse is illustrated by comparing the frank, if tactless, remark of General George Brown that Israel is more of a burden than an asset to the United States, with the statement of an American military official in Jiddia, Saudi Arabia, "I do not know of anything that is non-nuclear

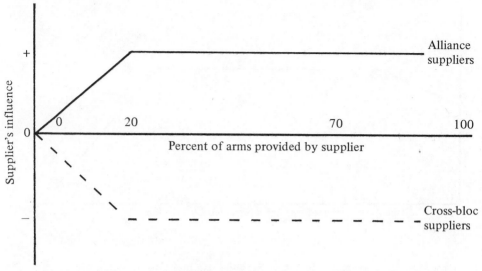

Figure 4.3. Multiple Supply Sources

that we would not give the Saudis. We want to sell and they want to buy the best."(9) Nearly all past Congressional attempts to legislate restrictions on arms transfers for human rights of other considerations have been addressed to grant aid or credit sales, not cash sales.

From the recipient's point of view, obtaining arms from a certain supplier or obtaining certain kinds of weapons from that supplier may become a matter of prestige. Such seemed to be the case with President Sadat's initial request to buy six C-130s from the United States, as well as his predicted requests for other American arms.

Based on these variables, Israel is the most susceptible to supplier influence attempts, followed by Jordan and Egypt. Israel has had no alternate supply source since 1967. It is unable to pay for all its arms purchases and is dependent on the United States for critical components of indigenously produced weapons, e.g., turbine blades for the Kfir engines. In addition, Israel faces a real threat to its national survival and does not possess oil or other scarce high-demand resources in appreciable quantities.

As long as Jordan is dependent upon Saudi Arabia financing its arms purchases, it may be constrained in its ability to turn to non-Western sources of supply. Snider asserts that Iraq is least susceptible to manipulation by arms transfers. It is able to pay for its arms acquisitions, and despite its left-wing ideological orientation, it has purchased aircraft and armored fighting vehicles from France.(10)

Snider places Iran, Saudi Arabia, and Syria "somewhere between Egypt and Iraq in their susceptibility to be influenced by arms." Iran and Saudi Arabia can pay for and choose among Western suppliers. However, according to Snider, they are precluded from turning to Soviet-bloc countries as an alternate source of supply by their

Table 4.4. Influence Derived From Arms Transactions

Supplier's influence is maximized when the recipient:	Recipient's influence is maximized when the recipient:
• has no alternate sources of supply	• has multiple sources of supply, especially cross-bloc
• cannot pay for the arms	• has the ability to pay
• is a "pariah" state within the international community	• has the multiple diplomatic and cultural relations within the international community
• has no indigenous weapons-production capability	• has an indigenous weapons-production capability
• does not occupy a strategic geographic position	• occupies a strategic geographic position
• has a small storage capacity for spare parts	• has ample storage capacity for spare parts
• perceives a real threat to its national survival	• does not perceive a real threat to its national survival
• does not possess scarce unsubstitutable raw materials	• possesses scarce unsubstitutable raw materials
• requires supplier personnel for weapons maintenance and training	• has sufficient technically trained indigenous personnel
• perceives that receiving arms from supplier is particularly prestigious	• perceives that the seller's prestige is "on the line"
• has such a strong ideological orientation that switching suppliers is suppliers is precluded	• is ideologically unhindered in switching suppliers

conservative orientation. Moreover, Snider states, "these two monarchies are, or have been, highly dependent upon the US for political support against domestic and foreign adversaries alike."(11) Dependence upon United States military advisers to operate much of the sophisticated American-furnished arms may further vitiate some of these two countries' other advantages vis-a-vis their arms suppliers; statistics on American personnel in Iran and Saudi Arabia are contained on pages 208-217.

It is the strongly held American belief that the supply of arms carries with it significant, if unspecified, amounts of influence that give rise to the preemptive rationale for arms transfers to deny influence to other supplier states.(12) This argument does not address the question of how the national interest of the United States is weakened if the arms come from other sources, especially from American allies.

Forms of Influence

Influence accruing from arms transactions can be tacit or overt and is likely to be perceived differently by the recipients and the suppliers. The intangible psychological aspect of the arms-influence relationship was expressed by Julius Nyerere, when he led the opposition to the British government's proposal to resume arms shipments to South Africa in 1970:

> The selling of arms is something which a country does only when it wants to support and strengthen the regime or the group to whom the sale is made. . . . You can trade with people you dislike; you can have diplomatic relations with government you disapprove of; you can sit in conference with those nations whose policies you abhor. But you do not sell arms without saying, in effect: "In the light of the receiving country's known policies, friends, and enemies, we anticipate that, in the last resort, we will be on their side in the case of any conflict. We shall want them to defeat their enemies."(13)

In the early 1950s when American arms were primarily given as grant aid and not sold, the expected influence, or "tit for tat," was overt and acknowledged. Recipients of United States aid were to "contribute to the defensive strength of the Free World" (Mutual Security Act of 1951) and to control their trade with Communist countries (Mutual Defense Assistance Control Act of 1944). Legislation also required recipients of grant aid to accept a Military Assistance Advisory Group (MAAG), which would provide training, coordinate arms procurement, and monitor compliance with end-use and retransfer provisions.

To the degree that influence is perceived as zero-sum, recipients either deny that influence accompanies arms — which is easier to do if the influence is tacit, rather than overt — or strive to avoid becoming the subject of influence. Egyptian President Gamal Nasser emphatically refused to allow a MAAG mission in Egypt, telling the United States that "he might be accused of selling his country to another big power before the British even got out of the place."(14) After Nasser refused the initial United States offer of a MAAG mission of 500 instructors and technicians, the Americans offered not only to reduce the number greatly but even "to send the mission in civilian clothes and to quarter them at the US embassy as 'assistant military attaches'."(15) Nasser still demurred, and after he signed an arms agreement with the Soviet Union in 1955, the United States dropped most of the strings it had previously attached to its aid programs to all nations.

Scope

The scope of influence alleged to stem from arms transfers is widespread and often seems unlimited. United States arms sales are proclaimed to influence behavior, attitudes, and external as well as internal policies of recipients.(16) For example, former Under Secretary of State Joseph Sisco justified the sale of six C-130 transport planes to Egypt as a means of demonstrating United States support of Egyptian domestic policies.(17)

The predominant behavior desired by the United States – to prevent war – does not have. a good track record in the Middle East. A second goal – to reduce the tendency to go to war – is currently translated into the argument that United States arms sales to Egypt would enhance the chance for peaceful resolution of the Arab-Israeli conflict. The argument is made that when the United States acts as the "honest broker" between Israel and Egypt, management or even resolution of the conflict appears more feasible. It is claimed that arms sales increase Egyptian confidence and trust in the United States, thus enhancing the United States' role of honest broker in the Israeli-Egyptian dialogue.(18)

The evidence for supplier leverage is, however, complex and contradictory. The Jordanian army, for example, armed primarily with American weapons, began hostilities against Israel on the first day of the 1967 War, although this was against the wishes of the United States. It seems that when vital interests of even a small and dependent state such as Jordan are at stake, the supplier finds it very difficult to prevent the outbreak of war.

The ability of the United States to dissuade Egypt from initiating a war against Israel varies. The most important variable affecting Egyptian behavior is the intensity of the conflict with Israel. If, for example, there is not further movement toward conflict resolution and the status quo continues, a Saudi-Egyptian alliance might decide to renew war with Israel in cooperation with Syria and Jordan. It is unlikely that the United States would then be able to deter Egypt, even by threatening to cut off resupplies.

Arms sales to the Persian Gulf area allegedly "encourage indigenous regional cooperative efforts" to insure the security of the area.(19) It is debatable whether arms are the best or the only way to achieve regional cooperation. Massive transfers of high technology weapons may very well create suspicions and heighten tensions in an historically volatile region. We should ask why economic or technical assistance could not be the means of achieving the desired ends of security and stability. We might also ponder why it is that Soviet arms are always said to contribute to instability while American arms are claimed to be stabilizing.

Temporal Aspects of Influence

There are several components to the temporal aspects of the arms-influence link. Influence derived from supplying arms may occur before the outbreak of hostilities, during a crisis, at the end of the conflict, or as a reward for actions previously undertaken. Schelling has commented:

> Compared with efforts to compel action . . . encouraging inaction tends to be easier and quieter. Deterrent threats often go without saying. When they succeed they go untested. They do not involve deadlines . . . There is no need for overt submission by the deterred party. Deterrence can be reciprocal . . .(20)

The United States succeeded in using its arms supply relationships to prevent or deter hostilities between Greece and Turkey in 1967. One could argue that if the United States were to supply arms to Egypt it could deter Egypt from initiating hostilities with Israel. This argument has three facets. First, the implicit threat of halting deliveries during a war could deter Egypt from initiating hostilities. Second, if the United States became Egypt's main arms supplier but practiced restraint in supplying Egypt with large stocks of ammunition and spare parts during peacetime, this could increase Egypt's dependence in case of war and thus also serve to deter war. Finally, by supplying arms to Egypt, the United States could help bring both sides to the negotiating table, thereby lessening tensions and making the outbreak of war less likely.(21) The well-known phenomenon of "anticipated reactions" may be operative. The hypothesis is that Egypt moved toward moderation in 1974-75 because it anticipated that Western arms supplies would be forthcoming.(22)

The Egyptian-Soviet arms supply relationship illustrates the complexities and the shifting nature over time of the arms supply-leverage linkage. Through the period 1955-67, the Soviet Union used the supply of arms first to establish a presence in Egypt and then to increase its penetration into Egyptian affairs. The relationship oscillated; despite intermittant periods of cool or even hostile relations, Egypt tended to maintain its political freedom of maneuver, and the Soviet Union generally supplied large amounts of arms. After 1967, Egyptian dependence on the Soviet Union increased considerably, and the Soviet Union was able to demand political and strategic advantages. The naval facilities in Alexandria were used extensively by the Soviet squadron in the Mediterranean. Following the increasing role of Soviet personnel in the defense of Egypt in 1970, six Egyptian air fields became exclusive Soviet bases.

Notwithstanding the great dependence of Egypt on the Soviet Union for its arms supplies, the training of military personnel, and most important, on the tacit Soviet guarantee against another Israeli victory, Sadat reacted strongly against growing Soviet influence on three occasions. The first was when he purged the pro-Soviet group led by Ali Sabri in spring 1971 and the second, and more dramatic, when he expelled Soviet advisors in July 1972. Lastly, Sadat completely changed the course of Egyptian foreign policy after the 1973 War and established a posture much closer to American policy, which will be discussed on pages 277 and 279. In the first two instances, Sadat was ready to threaten the relations with his main arms supplier while no alternative source of arms was available, and the prospects for war with Israel were very great. The most recent change in direction also was taken before Sadat was sure of securing alternative sources of arms.

This brief historical review indicates that the ability of the supplier to extend influence over the recipient is limited, at best, and at crucial points, can cease to exist altogether. It also illustrates the shifting nature of the arms supply-leverage linkages over time. The supplier's leverage during a conflict depends on various factors. When consumption or attrition rates are high, or spare parts stocks are depleted and no alternate suppliers appear, then arms suppliers can end an ongoing conflict as Britain and the United States did in the Indo-Pakistan War in 1965. Even during hostilities, the leverage point can be the carrot or stick of _future_ rather than present deliveries. This was the case with the United States and Israel in the closing days of the 1973 Yom Kippur War.

Arms sales are also touted as rewards for past actions. The United States' sale of six C-130 transport planes to Egypt was defended by Kissinger as a reward to Sadat for his moderate behavior. "If Congress should reject the sale," Kissinger stated, "the capacity of the United States to respond to governments that adopt policies we favor would be called into further question by countries who have long been skeptical on this score."(23)

Arms supplies can be justified as a reward to one country for affecting the policies of another. The billion dollar sale of improved Hawk missiles to Saudi Arabia was explained in a briefing session to selected Senators, Congressmen, and their staff in June 1976 as a reward to Saudia Arabia for having pressured the Jordanians not to buy arms from the Soviet Union. This rationalization ran counter to testimony by former United States ambassador to Saudia Arabia James Akins, who thought that the Saudi government would finance a Jordanian purchase of a Soviet missile system. He pointed out that the Saudis gave considerable economic assistance to Syria "and what Syria does with this money is Syria's business."(24) Syria has been a major recipient of Soviet arms.

A basic assumption of this paper is that suppliers manipulate their arms transfers to maximize the influence they can derive. Transactions such as credit sales, which stretch over several years, provide multiple leverage points. In contrast, cash payment for delivery of a gross of submachine guns is a "one-shot" affair. Arms which require continuing supplier maintenance or spare parts deliveries also provide long-term access points. With some current arms deals, which require large numbers of supplier personnel to be associated with the transferred weapons, it no longer is clear who is influencing whom.

Direction of Influence

A recent report of the United States Senate Foreign Relations Committee describes the symbiotic relations which flow from some contemporary arms supply contracts. The United States is currently selling some weapons to Iran which are among the most sophisticated in the American inventory, the F-14 fighter and the spruance class destroyer.(25) Iran lacks the technical, managerial, and industrial manpower to operate such systems and has to rely on increasing numbers of American personnel to go to Iran in a support capacity. In July 1976, there were 24,000 such Americans in Iran; prior to the political ciris of 1978-79 that number has been estimated to reach 50,000-60,000 or higher by 1980.(26)

In theory, the United States has the ability to immobilize the Iranian armed forces by cutting off spares, resupplies, and maintenance support. In practice, however, the study concludes that the direction of influence may in fact flow from the Iranians to the Americans. The study suggests that in times of crises, the United States personnel in Iran could become hostages. This would be particularly true to the extent that the performance of the supplied weapons reflects upon the reputation of the United States as a superpower. The dilemma is that if the United States attempts to limit the use of American-supplied weapons it may lead to a break in United States-Iranian relations. If it fails to restrain the Iranians in situations where armed conflict may not be in the best United States interests, it provides implicit approval of Iran's actions and would almost certainly, according to the Senate study, lead to the use of United States personnel in a support capacity.(27)

In conclusion, the supply of weapons naturally creates a tie of sorts between the supplier and the recipient. The amount of influence, the form it takes, its scope or range, and its length of duration remain difficult to measure and are sufficiently variable to defy easy generalizations.

ECONOMIC RATIONALES

From the suppliers' side, domestic economic rationalizations for arms sales stem from two main concerns: the overall health of the national economy, e.g. employment, and the overall health of defense industries. On the international level, the two major benefits attributed to arms sales are improving balance-of-payments and linkages with other commercial transactions, both of which are also discussed in Chapter 8.

Domestic Benefits

On the level of the defense industries, a number of economic benefits are ascribed to arms exports. They include lengthening production lines and increasing learning curve benefits, thereby reducing per unit costs. They help to recoup research and development costs, to increase domestric employment, and to develop and maintain technological expertise in weapons production. Arms exports also encourage the maintenance of a viable domestic arms industry and aid in the disposal of surplus or obsolete equipment at better than scrap material prices.

Studies by the Congressional Budget Office indicate that, based on the current mix of sales of weapons, services, and construction, each year foreign military sales in the United States generate approximately 7 percent in savings for the United States.(28) However, longer production runs may not reduce unit costs, depending on when in the production run the foreign unit order occurs. Since the Yom Kippur War, the M-60 tank has increased 60 percent in cost. The M-113 is also 60 percent more expensive, and the UH-1 helicopter cost 52 percent more. These increases are all far above the national inflation rate.(29)

There are at least three explanations for such increased costs, all stemming from the fact that foreign orders may delay American procurement. First, when this occurs, United States forces are temporarily denied a needed resource and must "expend additional maintenance on the systems to be replaced."(30) Second, delayed American purchases can mean higher budgetary costs due to inflation; these, however, may be offset by increases in the absolute amount of tax receipts.   Third, foreign orders may require costly production readjustments.   According to the Congressional Budget Office study, the Iranian order of eighty F-14s initially saved the Navy $60 million in production expenses.   Additional costs, however, associated with closing the order, while continuing slightly slower procurement for American orders, totaled $120 million.(31)

Individual industries, particularly aerospace, are becoming heavily dependent upon arms exports. About 30 percent of United States aerospace production is exported. Figures for individual American firms' dependence on foreign military sales are Bell Hilicopter, 42 percent; Northrop, 34 percent; and Grumman, 25 percent.(32)

Estimates based on Bureau of Labor statistics indicate that arms sales of $9 billion a year generate about 400,000 jobs in the United States, approximately 0.5 percent of total employment. According to a 1975 Bureau of Labor Statistics study, $1 billion spent on defense creates 51,000 jobs, while that same $1 billion would create 60,000 jobs if spent on public housing, 88,000 jobs if spent on Veterans Administration health care, and 136,000 jobs if spent on manpower training.(33) To be sure, arms sales contribute to domestic employment, but since defense industries are capital, not labor-intensive, exports of more labor-intensive productions would better answer employment needs.

International Benefits

Table 4.5 shows the relationships between total exports and military exports of the major supplier nations. The United States remains the number one arms exporter, although its share of the total market has declined from 53 percent to 50 percent.

For the United States, total exports of defense articles and services during fiscal 1975 constituted about 0.2 percent of the American gross national product, 4 percent of all exports, and about 5 percent of manufactured goods exports.(34) Thus, arms exports have relatively little impact on aggregate economic output.

It is useful to distinguish short and long-term balance-of-payments effects. Short-term advantages accruing from increasing military sales to countries with foreign exchange constraints may be partially offset by reductions in purchases of capital equipment and other nonmilitary imports by these countries. If the United States limited arms sales to the Persian Gulf area, countries like Iran "would probably spend less in total on arms imports, because other suppliers would not be able to sell either as much or as sophisticated equipment as Iran is obtaining from the United States." Iran might spend more on nonmilitary imports, of which a portion would be civilian American products. These increased civilian sales "would partially offset US economic losses from the reduction of its arms exports."(35) These considerations, of course, would not apply to countries like Saudi Arabia which have no foreign exchange constraints.

In the longer term, increases in American arms sales or any exports bring about an appreciation of the exchange rate. The strengthened United States dollar would eventually cause exports of nonmilitary goods to decline, a condition which might cause lower employment in nondefense industries. With a fully recovered economy, total American employment would be approximately the same with or without the increased arms sales, but the relative positions of specific firms and of the military and civilian industries would be different.

Balance-of-payments justifications for arms sales are pernicious for several reasons. First, arms constitute only a minor component of United States exports. Second, they provide open-ended rationales since they can be used to justify any arms sales. Lastly, sales of civilian goods produce the same balance-of-trade benefits as military exports.

MILITARY-STRATEGIC RATIONALES

Historically, the most enduring rationales for arms trade have been military and strategic factors. Strengthening one's allies to enable them to repel internal or external foes, obtaining military rights in exchange for arms supplies, and having a client or ally battle test one's new weapons are supplier's rationales with long historical roots.

Strengthening Allies

In the 1950s the bulk of United States arms transfers went to Western European allies and nations on the perimeters of the Soviet Union and China. There was a clear congruence between the primary

Table 4.5. Comparison of Four Major Military Exporters

	Total Exports (billion current $)	Exports as % of GNP	Military Exports (billion current $)	Military Exports as % of Total Exports	Military Exports as % of World Military Exports
1972					
United States	49.8	4.2	4.1	8.2	41.5
Great Britain	24.4	14.0	0.471	2.0	4.8
France	26.5	10.8	0.726	2.7	7.4
Soviet Union	15.4	2.4	2.84	18.4	28.8
1973					
United States	71.3	5.4	5.0	7.0	38.4
Great Britain	30.7	15.8	0.583	1.9	4.5
France	36.7	13.4	0.863	2.4	6.6
Soviet Union	21.3	2.9	5.04	23.6	38.5
1974					
United States	98.5	6.9	4.16	4.3	36.7
Great Britain	38.9	18.0	0.544	1.4	4.8
France	46.3	14.7	0.695	1.5	6.1
Soviet Union	27.4	3.3	4.18	15.3	36.8

Table 4.5. Comparison of Four Major Military Exporters (cont'd.)

	Total Exports (billion current $)	Exports as % of GNP	Military Exports (billion current $)	Military Exports as % of Total Exports	Military Exports as % of World Military Exports
1975					
United States	108.0	7.1	4.8	4.4	40.4
Great Britain	44.1	19.3	0.501	1.1	4.2
France	53.1	15.8	0.654	1.2	5.5
Soviet Union	33.3	3.0	3.78	11.4	31.5
1976					
United States	115.0	6.8	5.2	4.5	38.8
Great Britain	46.3	19.2	0.638	1.4	4.8
France	57.2	15.3	0.840	1.5	6.3
Soviet Union	37.1	3.6	3.74	10.0	28.0

Source: US Arms Control and Disarmament Agency, World Military Expenditures and Arms Transfers, 1967-1976 (Washington, D.C.: June 1978).

foreign policy goal, rebuilding American allies' capacities to defend themselves against Communism, and the means for attaining those ends, providing the necessary arms. Much of the bipartisan foreign policy consensus of that era was based on that congruence of ends and means.

By the mid-1950s, both the Soviet Union and the United States were supplying arms to nations other than their military alliance partners. In response to the Soviet Union's increased arms supply activities, the "if we don't, someone else will" argument for arms transfers gained currency in the United States. The alleged influence accruing to an arms supplier was unchallenged, and soon the United States argued that, at the very least, its arms deals denied influence to other, possibly less benevolent, suppliers.

In the early 1960s, the Kennedy Administration added the concept of counterinsurgency to the repertory of military-strategic rationales for arms transactions. The voguish counterinsurgency phase of the 1960s has been supplanted by internal stability in the 1970s. The major impetus, however, remains unchanged: to maintain the status quo, and to quell threats from separatists or guerrillas.

By 1970, the major military-strategic rationale for arms sales was embodied in the Nixon Doctrine: reduced United States presence overseas required large-scale arms transfers to enable American allies to defend themselves and aid the "common defense."(36) But arms sales did not always become a substitute for direct United States involvement, and indeed, in some instances seemed more a vehicle, intended or unintended, for the American presence overseas. By 1976, more than 17,000 United States personnel were in Iran and 12,000 in Saudi Arabia to oversee the sale, maintenance, and repair of American-supplied military equipment.

More recently, balance-of-power considerations have come to be emphasized as arms sales justifications.(37) The primary rationale for supplying American arms to Israel is based on maintaining a military balance-of-power which enables Israel to deter or defeat an Arab attack. This balance is predicated not on the quantity of Israel's arms as compared to all the Arab countries, or even the "confrontation" countries by themselves, but on the quality of the systems coupled with such intangibles as morale, military organization, leadership, and general military acumen.

Military Rights

Another rationale frequently advanced for foreign military assistance is the need to buy military rights in other countries; the competition for military bases and access rights, particularly between the United States and the Soviet Union, is dealt with in Chapter 6. In emergencies, bases are not always useful. During the Yom Kippur War resupply effort, United States planes were denied landing rights at all its bases in Europe except the Azores. A recent Congressional study has raised serious questions about the value of bases in relation to their long-term costs and uncertainties concerning their utilization in times of crises. The study proposes that the development of a self-sufficient American airlift be considered.(38)

Weapons Testing

Lastly, supplier nations may gain military advantages by having their new weapons battle tested. The Vietnam War, where according to one analyst fifty-four new military items were battlefield tested,(39) and the Yom Kippur War, with massive use of precision guided missiles, are recent examples of supplier nations eagerly assessing the effectiveness of their inventories under battlefield conditions.

Laurance has pointed out that even without actual combat conditions, advantages may accrue to the supplying nation. The experience gained "about how weapons perform in an increasing variety of climates and terrain" can serve to modify and improve the equipment before it is supplied to the United States armed services. For example, Laurance postulates that if the DD-963 destroyer ordered by Iran proved to be noisy, it might "be perfectly adequate for Iran's requirements in the Arabian Sea, yet unacceptable for US anti-submarine missions against more sophisticated equipment." He concludes that the quieting modifications "could be tested on Iran's DD-963s, causing no decline in Iran's capability and yet resulting in a better DD-963 for US purposes."(40)

Counter Arguments

From the supplier's point of view, there are at least two possible military objections to arms transfers. First, massive transfers of arms to other countries can reduce the supplier's own military readiness. The massive and rapid resupply of Israeli military forces after the 1973 Yom Kippur War so depleted American stockpiles and reserve inventories that they will not be fully replaced until 1981. The resupply of Israel after the 1973 War was an unusual occurrence. Yet, if future wars consume military equipment at an even faster pace than they have in the past, resupply of dependent allies may compromise the preparedness of military forces in the supplier nation.

A second concern is of much less significance, and is limited to a few producer nations. Many arms transfers involve training of local military forces; indeed, most American arms deals entail greater expenditures on infrastructure items than on actual combat equipment. This training component of arms transfers requires a substantial number of military personnel from the supplier state. The United States, which places much greater emphasis on training than do some other suppliers, found a significant number of its military forces involved in such activities in the mid-1970s. As the size of the American military establishment declines and as military pay continues to increase, the cost of diverting such manpower will be drawn into increasing question over the next few years.

A third concern might be that the transfer of sophisticated, high technology weapons to other nations increases the possibility that these items will fall into the hands of hostile nations. The proposed sale of AWACs to Iran has raised this concern in the minds of some who fear the possibility of a crew defecting to the Soviet Union.

In conclusion, two aspects of contemporary international relations are at variance with most of the military-strategic rationales advanced for arms transactions. These are the transitory nature of most international alliances, enmities or friendships, and the fact that relations between neighbors, not superpower or north-south considerations, are paramount determinants of most nations' foreign policies.

APPENDIX INCONSISTENCIES IN US DEFENSE DEPARTMENT DATA ON ARMS TRANSFERS

All data should be thought of as approximations. United States government data are inconsistent from one year to the next, both interdepartmental — Department of Defense (DOD) versus Arms Control and Disarmament Agency (ACDA) — and intradepartmental.

DOD data come from the Defense Security Assistance Agency (DSAA), which publishes Foreign Military Sales and Military Assistance Facts each year. The data include material and military equipment, services, and training under the following programs: Foreign Military Sales, Military Assistance Program Grant Aid, Military Assistance Service Funded, International Military Education and Training, and Excess Defense Articles. The data in Table 1 in the text are for fiscal years and are based on deliveries, not orders or agreements.

ACDA data prior to 1974 were compiled under contract for ACDA by the United States Department of Commerce. Since 1974, ACDA uses "official trade statistics on arms transfers compiled by the US Bureau of the Census and information provided by the US Department of Defense." The data are for calendar years and are based on "goods actually delivered during the reference years."(41)

ACDA data include weapons and ammunition, support equipment and spare parts but exclude training, services, consumables, and construction, all of which are included in the DSAA data. During the period FY 1960-75, such training, services, and construction accounted for 24 percent of total American military exports. ACDA data include some categories of dual civil-military use equipment, such as trucks that are not included in the DSAA data. These are estimated to account for less than 1 percent of the total.

From these explanatory notes one could expect that ACDA data would be about 23 percent less than DSAA data, but from Table 4.1 it can be seen that ACDA figures are 3 percent higher than DSAA figures for the Middle East.

Appendix Tables 4.6-4.9 are all based on the DSAA annual

publication, <u>Foreign Military Sales and Assistance Facts</u>. All the data are based on deliveries, not orders or programs. For Iran, as indicated in Table 4.6, the largest discrepancy concerns Foreign Military Sales (FMS) delivered in 1972: the figure given in 1975 is $66.3 million less than was given in 1973.

For Israel, as indicated in Table 4.7, the most discrepant year is 1971. The 1973 publication states that $397 million of FMS was delivered.   In the 1974 publication, that figure dropped to $323.8 million. By 1975, it has been further reduced to $315.1 million, nearly $82 million less than the earliest figure.

The data for Jordan, indicated in Table 4.8, are the most consistent. They vary from a low of $13.9 million FMS delivered for 1971 in the 1974 book to a high of $21.7 million for 1971 deliveries in the 1973 publication.

The largest variance occurs in the data on Saudi Arabia, shown in Table 4.9. Estimates for FMS delivered in 1967 range from $27.6 to $68.9 million. Estimates for 1969 deliveries range from $5 to $59 million. The figure given for 1970 deliveries in 1974 is less than one-tenth the figure presented one year later.

Table 4.6. DSAA Inconsistencies: Iran
(million current dollars)

	1966	1967	1968	1969	1970	1971	1972	1973	1974	1975
Military Assistance Program (MAP) Deliveries	41.1[a]	41.1[a] / 37.1[e]	38.7[a] / 34[e]	50.9[a] / 45.3[e]	15.2[a] / 12.8[e]	6.6[b] / 4.3[e]	6.3[b]	2.3[c] / 2.6[d]	*[d]	*[d]
Excess Defense Articles Delivered	0.3[f] / 0.9[h]	0.1[f]	1.2[f] / 3.6[h]	*[f]	0.4[f] / 1.1[h]	0.1[g] / 0.3[h]	— / —	—	—	—
Foreign Military Sales Delivered	52.1[i]	38.9[i]	56.7[i]	99.2[i] / 94.9[k]	189.7[i] / 127.8[k]	79.4[j]	263.5[j] / 200.7[k] / 197.2[m] / 214.8[n]	234.3[k] / 238.6[n]	509.8[m] / 510.3[n]	944.7[n] / 956.4[n]
International Military Education & Training Delivered[p]		3.9	4.7	3.2	2.4	2.3	0.9	—	—	—
Commercial Sales Delivered[r]	5.1	2.0	5.1	10.1	9.8	27.1	37.0	19.4	35.3	49.4

Table 4.6. DSAA Inconsistencies: Iran (cont'd.)

		1966	1967	1968	1969	1970	1971	1972	1973	1974	1975
TOTALS:	Average	99.0	84.0	105.3	158.5	185.7	114.5	263.3	258.3	545.4	1,000.0
	High	99.9	86.0	108.8	163.4	218.2	115.7	307.7	260.6	545.6	1,005.8
	Low	98.7	82.0	101.7	153.5	153.2	113.2	241.4	256.0	545.1	994.1

*Less than $50,000

Sources:
aUS Department of Defense, Military Assistance and Foreign Military Sales Facts (Washington, D.C.: March 1971), p. 10.
bUS Department of Defense Security Assistance Agency, Military Assistance and Foreign Military Sales Facts (Washington, D.C.: May 1973), p. 8.
cUS Department of Defense Security Assistance Agency, Foreign Military Sales and Military Assistance Facts (Washington, D.C.: April 1974), pp. 18-19.
dIbid., (November 1975): 26-27.
eIbid., (December 1976): 20-21, excluding training.
fMarch 1971, p. 12.
gMay 1973, p. 10.
hNovember 1975, pp. 30-31.
iMarch 1971, p. 22
jMay 1973, p. 20.
kApril 1974, pp. 16-17.
mNovember 1975, pp. 16-17.
nDecember 1976, pp. 14-15.
pDecember 1976, pp. 28-29.
rDecember 1976, pp. 16-17.

Table 4.7. DSAA Inconsistencies: Israel+
(million current dollars)

	1966	1967	1968	1969	1970	1971	1972	1973	1974	1975
Military Assistance Program (MAP) Deliveries										
Excess Defense Articles Delivered										
Foreign Military Sales Delivered	20.6[k] 20.1[m]	14.5[j] 14.1[m]	29.4[j] 28.6[m]	80.4[j] 61.9[k] 60.3[m] 72.5[n]	221.8[j] 215.9[m]	397.0[j] 323.8[k] 315.1[m]	207.6[j] 201.1[m] 192.5[n]	189.7[m] 189.9[n]	958.5[m] 978.1[n]	686.5[m] 667.7[n]
Commercial Sales Delivered[r]	1.3	4.6	10.5	11.7	37.2	26.5	63.1	21.6	50.1	46.7
TOTALS: Average	21.7	18.9	39.5	80.5	256.1	371.8	263.5	213.1	1,018.4	723.8
High	21.9	19.1	39.9	92.1	259.0	423.5	270.7	216.5	1,028.2	733.2
Low	21.4	18.7	39.1	72.0	253.1	341.6	255.6	211.3	1,008.6	714.4

+See source notes for Table 4.6.

Table 4.8. DSAA Inconsistencies: Jordan+
(million current dollars)

	1966	1967	1968	1969	1970	1971	1972	1973	1974	1975
Military Assistance Program Deliveries	2.8[a]	11.9[a] 11.8[e]	2.1[a] 1.8[e]	1.8[a] 1.6[e]	1.0[a] 1.3[e]	15.4[b] 15.2[e]	22.6[b] 21.6[e]	21.0[c] 24.3[d] 23.4[e]	31.0[d] 30.2[e]	14.2[e]
Excess Defense Articles Delivered	0.1[f] 0.3[h]	1.2[f] 3.7[h]	0.1[f] 0.4[h]	– –	0.2[f] 0.5[h]	0.3[g] 0.9[h]	0.7[g] 2.2[h]	10.6[h]	12.7[h]	4.8[h]
Foreign Military Sales Delivered	25.3[k] 25.0[m]	11.4[j] 11.1[m]	12.4[j] 12.0[m]	24.8[j] 24.0[m] 24.2[n]	56.5[j] 54.7[m] 53.1[n]	21.7[j] 14.3[k] 13.9[m] 14.4[n]	11.6[j] 11.3[m] 10.6[n]	17.9[k] 17.3[m] 15.2[n]	12.7[m] 14.8[n]	19.9[m] 16.7[n]
International Military Education and Training Program Deliveries[p]	0.1	0.1	0.3	0.2	0.2	0.2	0.5	0.7	0.5	1.0
Commercial Sales	0.1	0.5	0.2	0.2	1.1	1.6	0.05	*	0.09	0.2
TOTALS: Average	28.3	26.3	15.0	26.4	57.7	33.8	35.3	51.0	57.7	38.5
High	28.5	27.6	15.4	27.0	59.6	39.8	37.0	53.5	59.6	40.1
Low	28.0	24.7	14.4	26.0	55.6	31.2	33.5	47.5	56.2	36.9

+See source notes for Table 4.6.

Table 4.9. DSAA Inconsistencies: Saudi Arabia+
(million current dollars)

	1966	1967	1968	1969	1970	1971	1972	1973	1974	1975
Military Assistance Program (MAP) Deliveries	1.5[a] 1.3[c]	0.8[a] *e	1.0[a]	0.6[a] 0.5[d]	0.5[a]	0.6[b]	0.4[b] 0.7[c] 0.4[d]	0.2[c]	0.2[d]	*d —
Excess Defense Articles Delivered[f]	*	*	—	—	—	*	—			
Foreign Military Sales Delivered	9.2[k] 12.2[m]	68.9[j] 38.9[k] 48.9[m] 27.6[n]	43.4[j] 23.4[k] 36.9[m] 36.9[n]	59.7[j] 5.6[k] 32.1[m] 32.1[n]	11.9[j] 4.9[k] 51.9[m] 51.9[n]	11.2[j] 18.8[k] 63.8[m] 63.8[n]	14.4[j] 14.4[k] 49.9[m] 65.6[n]	91.0[k] 108.0[m] 86.2[n]	216.5[m] 226.5[n]	316.1[m] 300.4[n]
International Military Education and Training Program Deliveries[p]		0.8	1.1	0.6	0.6	0.6	0.4	0.2	0.2	*
Commercial Sales Delivered[r]	14.9	33.6	35.5	6.3	12.7	8.2	6.4	5.6	18.0	20.1

Table 4.9. DSAA Inconsistencies: Saudi Arabia+ (cont'd.)

		1966	1967	1968	1969	1970	1971	1972	1973	1974	1975
TOTALS:	Average	27.0	81.3	72.8	39.9	44.0	48.8	43.4	101.1	239.9	328.4
	High	28.6	104.1	81.0	67.2	65.7	73.2	73.1	114.0	244.9	336.2
	Low	25.4	62.8	74.5	13.0	18.7	20.6	21.6	92.2	234.9	320.5

+See Source notes for Table 4.8.

NOTES AND REFERENCES

(1) David J. Sylvan, "Influence and Control: Concepts and Models in the Case of Arms Transfers," (Paper delivered at the Annual Meeting of the International Studies Association, St. Louis, Missouri, March 1977), p. 23.

(2) Edward J. Laurance, "Arms Transfers and Influence in Latin America: 1961-1973," (Paper delivered at Annual Meeting of the International Studies Association, Toronto, February 1976), p. 16.

(3) Ibid., p. 21.

(4) Lewis W. Snider, "From Arms to Influence: A Reassessment of the Effectiveness of Arms Transfers as a Policy Instrument in the Middle East" (Paper, Claremont Graduate School, Claremont, California, 1976), p. 35.

(5) US Department of State, Munitions Control Newsletter, no. 37 (May 19, 1977).

(6) See comments by Congressman Pierre DuPont in US Congress, House, Committee on International Relations, United States Arms Sales to the Persian Gulf, Report of a Study Mission to Iran, Kuwait and Saudi Arabia, 94th Cong., 1st Sess. May 22-31, 1975, p. 20.

(7) US Congress, Senate, Committee on Foreign Relations, Subcommittee on Near Eastern and South Asian Affairs, Hearings: Arms Sales to Near East and South Asian Countries, 90th Cong., 1st Sess., March, June 1967, p. 100.

(8) "Iran: More Procurement from USSR?" (Report on Strategic Middle Eastern Affairs), Defense/Foreign Affairs Weekly 2 (15 December 1976): 1-2.

(9) General Brown quoted in "Pentagon Hears Army Chief Call Army of Israel a Burden to US," New York Times (October 18, 1976): 6. US official in Saudi Arabia quoted in Juan de Onis, "US Role Grows in Arming Saudis," New York Times (September 11, 1974).

(10) Snider, p. 33 (note 4 supra).

(11) Ibid.

(12) Statement by Secretary of State Henry Kissinger, Department of State Bulletin 72 (February 17, 1975): 214.

(13) Julius Nyerere, "The Devil's Flunkey," Far Eastern Economic Review (January 30, 1971): 25.

(14) Testimony of Assistant Secretary of State Henry Byroade, "The President's Proposal on the Middle East," November 5, 1954, cited in Fuad Jabber, "The Politics of Arms Transfer and Control: The Case of the Middle East" (Ph.D. thesis, University of California, Los Angeles, 1974), p. 225.

(15) Ibid. pp. 225-26.

(16) See comments by former Secretary of Defense James R. Schlesinger in US Congress, House, Committee on Appropriations, Subcommittee on Foreign Operations and Related Agencies' Appropriations, Hearings: Foreign Assistance and Related Programs, FY 1974, Parts I and II, 93rd Cong., 1st Sess., April, May, June, July, 1973, p. 1295.

(17) US Congress, House, Committee on International Relations, Subcommittee on International Political and Military Affairs, Hearing: Proposed Sale to Egypt of C-130 Aircraft, 94th Cong., 2nd Sess., April 6, 1976, p. 13.

(18) See Anne H. Cahn and Yair Evron, "The Politics of Arms Transfers: US Arms Sales to Egypt" (Manuscript, Harvard University, December 1976), for fuller exposition of this argument.

(19) US Congress, House, Committee on International Relations, Special Subcommittee on Investigations, Hearings: The Persian Gulf, 1975: The Continuing Debate on Arms Sales, 94th Cong., 1st Sess., June, July 1975, p. 3.

(20) Thomas C. Schelling, "Who Will Have the Bomb?" International Security 1 (Summer 1976): 85.

(21) Cf. Cahn and Evron (note 18 supra).

(22) William B. Quandt, "Influence Through Arms Supply. The American Experience in the Middle East," (Paper prepared for the conference on The Military Build-up in Non-Industrial states, The Fletcher School of Law and Diplomacy, Medford, Mass., May 1976), p. 4.

(23) Department of State Bulletin 74 (April 19, 1976): 507.

(24) US Congress, p. 206 (note 19 supra).

(25) US Congress, Senate, Committee on Foreign Relations, Subcommittee on Foreign Assistance, staff Report: U.S. Military Sales to Iran, 94th Cong., 2nd Sess. July 1976, p. viii.

(26) Ibid., p. vii.

(27) Ibid., p. x.

(28) US Congress, Congressional Budget Office, Foreign Military Sales and U.S. Weapon Costs, Staff Working Paper (Washington, D.C.: May 1976).

(29) John F. Lehman, Keynote Address, 1976 Senior Conference, United States Military Academy, West Point, N.Y., p. 11.

(30) US Congress, p. 9 (note 28 supra).

(31) Ibid.

(32) US Congress, Senate, Committee on Foreign Relations, Subcommittee on Foreign Assistance, Hearings: Foreign Assistance Authorization: Arms Sales Issues, 94th Cong., 1st Sess., June, November, December 1975, p. 276.

(33) Paul Lewis, "Defense Costs and the Economy," New York Times (December 19, 1976).

(34) US Arms Control and Disarmament Agency, World Military Expenditures and Arms Transfers, 1967-1976 (Washington, D.C.: June 1978).

(35) Edward R. Fried, "The Economics of Arms Transfers" (Paper, Washington, D.C., June 1976), p. 13.

(36) US Congress, House, Committee on Appropriations, Hearings: Foreign Assistance and Related Agencies' Appropriations, 91st Cong., 2nd Sess., 1970, p. 307.

(37) US Congress p. 83 (note 19 supra).

(38) US Congress, House, Committee on International Relations, Subcommittee on Europe and the Middle East, Report: The United States' Military Installations and Objectives in the Mediterranean, 95th Cong., 1st Sess., April 1977.

(39) Milton Leitenberg, cited in Ulrich Albrecht, "Arms Trade with the Third World and Domestic Arms Production," Instant Research on Peace and Violence (Oslo) (January-February 1976): 58.

(40) Edward J. Laurance, "The Changing Nature of Conventional Arms Transfers: Implications for U.S. National Security Planning and Policy Research," 1976 Senior Conference, United States Military Academy, West Point, N.Y., p. 100.

(41) US Arms Control and Disarmament Agency, World Military Expenditures and Arms Transfers 1966-1975 (Washington, D.C.: 1976), p. 8.

5 West European and Soviet Arms Transfer Policies in the Middle East *

Roger F. Pajak

Arms transfers to the Middle East and Persian Gulf regions in recent years have far surpassed those to other developing areas of the world both in value and in quantity, with the notable exception of shipments to Southeast Asia during the recent Indochina War. This paper characterizes the arms transfer policies of the Soviet Union and the major West European suppliers: France, the United Kingdom, and West Germany (the FRG). The paper focuses largely on the Middle East and briefly delineates the magnitude and direction of the arms trade, particularly over the past decade.

For the purposes of this paper, the various "developing" areas of the world are treated as geographic entities. Thus, the Middle East here includes Israel — even though, by most standards, this country is regarded as "developed" — and the Persian Gulf countries.

Arms "transfers" in this paper are synonymous with "deliveries" or "exports" and represent the actual shipment of military equipment under grant, credit, or cash sales terms. This is in contrast to sales, orders, agreements, or contracts, which may result in a future transfer of goods.

The following graphs should help to place the Middle East share of the worldwide arms trade in perspective. Figure 5.1 depicts total arms transfers to developing countries in five geographic areas.

Figures 5.2 and 5.3 indicate the percentage shares of worldwide and Middle East arms transfers, respectively, accounted for by each of the major suppliers. While the United States share of total arms transfers to the Middle East is slightly lower than the its worldwide share, the Soviet Union's percentage of shipments to the area is substantially higher than its worldwide share. Another notable trend is a reversal of

---

*The views expressed in this paper are the author's and do not necessarily reflect the views of the United States Government or any of its Agencies or Departments.

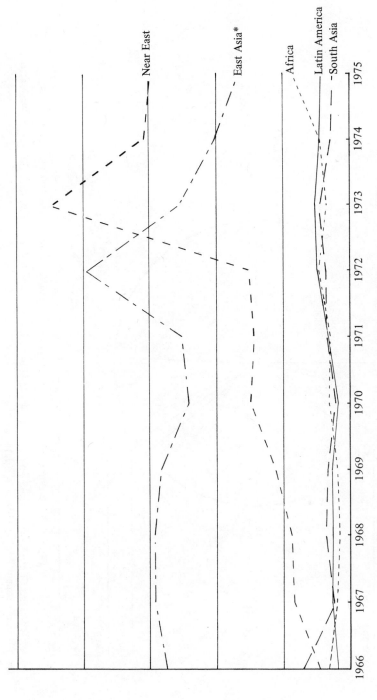

Figure 5.1. Arms Transfers to Developing Regions (billion constant 1974 dollars)

*Includes Southeast Asia

Source: US Arms Control and Disarmament Agency, World Military Expenditures and Arms Transfers 1966-1975 (Washington, D.C.: US Government Printing Office, 1976), pp. 56-57.

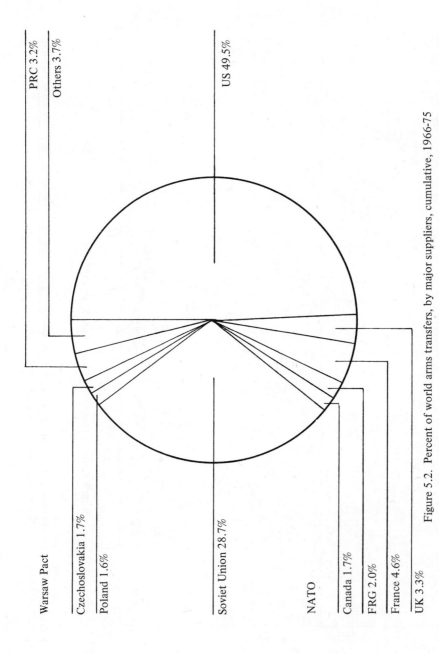

Figure 5.2. Percent of world arms transfers, by major suppliers, cumulative, 1966-75

Source: US Arms Control and Disarmament Agency, World Military Expenditures and Arms Transfers 1966-1975 (Washington, D.C.: US Government Printing Office, 1976), pp. 78-80.

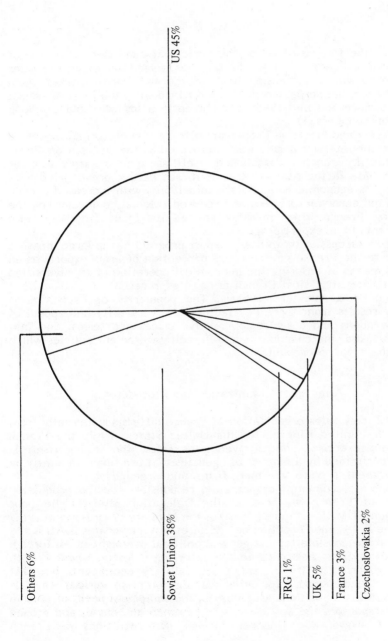

Figure 5.3. Percent of arms transfers to the Middle East, by major suppliers, cumulative, 1966-1975

US 45%

Soviet Union 38%

Others 6%

FRG 1%

UK 5%

France 3%

Czechoslovakia 2%

Source: US Arms Control and Disarmament Agency, World Military Expenditures and Arms Transfers 1966-1975 (Washington, D.C.: US Government Printing Office, 1976), p. 78

the rankings of France and the United Kingdom in terms of their shares of the Middle East market, in comparison with their shares of worldwide arms exports.

FRANCE

One of the few countries in the world that can offer a full line of weapons of indigenous design, France has waged an extensive sales campaign to win an increasing share of the world arms market. As a result, France, has surpassed the United Kingdom in the level of annual deliveries since the mid-1960s and currently holds third place among world arms suppliers.(1)

The lively and lucrative French arms trade that ensued during World War I and the interwar period was interrupted by the Occupation during World War II. France reestablished itself as a major arms supplier relatively late in the postwar era, as it was earlier preoccupied with rebuilding its economic base. By the mid-1950s, with increased French military and economic prowess and reduced colonial commitments, the burgeoning French arms industry shifted its focus from domestic requirements to an export program.

France's success in its military export program has in large measure been due to the French government's perception of arms exports as an efficient means of ensuring the economical operation of its diversified armaments industry. Most French arms sales in recent years have been transacted on a commercial basis. The popularity of French arms evidently results from three key factors: the versatility and appeal of French weapons and designs; competitive prices and terms, and "no-questions-asked" merchandizing; and French government policies which support the export program.(2)

Arms Sales Organization and Procedures

The military sales organization of France differs substantially from that of the United Kingdom or the United States. While the French government exercises control over arms sales, the selling itself is actually performed by a number of agencies that are financed jointly by the government, private armament firms, and large banks.

The key governmental organization responsible for the production and sale of French weapons is the Delegation Ministerielle pour L'Armement (DMA), established within the Ministry of Defense in 1961. Within the DMA, the Direction des Affaires Internationales (DAI) is the department responsible for the general political oversight of all foreign arms sales and for assistance to the exporting industry. Under French law the government itself cannot sell military equipment, but DAI provides critical support for arms manufacturers in various ways. It organizes military missions which assess the equipment needs of foreign countries; sponsors the world-renowned French air, naval, and ground equipment shows; and finances foreign demonstrations of French weapons.(3) DAI also advances funds to manufacturers seeking to design equipment uniquely for export.(4) Under the overall policy guidance of DAI, several quasi-government agencies provide a vital link between the government and the manufacturers and relieve the private companies of much of the effort and expense of promoting foreign sales.(5)

In the important aerospace field, the Office Francais d'Exportation de Materiel Aeronautique (OFEMA) is responsible for sales in Western and allied countries, while the Office General de l'Air (OGA) handles sales in more politically sensitive areas, such as the Middle East. Both agencies perform such functions as conducting sales negotiations, preparing contracts, and arranging postcontractual service. They differ mainly in the degree of government financial control. OFEMA is 70 percent government financed through nationalized industries, while OGA is financed entirely by private companies. OGA's activities, however, are fully supported by the French government, which occasionally finds it extremely useful for transacting sales arrangements with "the more difficult countries" with which the government does not officially wish to be associated.(6) Thus, the government assures that potential combatants are at least negotiating with different sales teams, even if the same type of equipment is under discussion. Accordingly, OFEMA has dealt with India and Israel, while OGA has negotiated with the Arab countries.(7) Similar organizations for the promotion of exports exist for the navy and the army: La Societe Francaise d'Exportation des Armements (SOFREXAN), and La Societe Francaise Materiels d'Armement (SOFMA), respectively.(8)

This unique system of sales organizations significantly benefits the arms manufacturers by avoiding the overhead expense of maintaining an extensive export sales force. The foreign representatives of OFEMA and OGA, working with French embassy staffs, serve to make the initial contacts with interested governments. After the contractual negotiations are set up, OFEMA and OGA then become directly involved. French government support has been of crucial assistance in placing French manufacturers in a more competitive position in the international arms market.(9)

The relatively liberal financial terms offered for French arms provide added inducement for the foreign buyer. Credit of up to eight years can be negotiated through the facilities of the Compagnie Francaise d'Assurance pour le Commerce Exterieur (COFACE).(10) Interest rates vary from 3 to 7 percent, with the latter being the norm.(11) Besides offering attractive credit terms, the French have been willing to grant a special concession to foreign buyers: a specified share of the cost of military equipment is offset by the purchase of local goods and services.(12) One interesting commercial arrangement was the 1964 French arms deal with South Africa, where the supply of South African uranium was involved.(13) It is not surprising that the supplier states most likely to consider such negotiating inducements would be those like France with favorable balance-of-payments postures, not those with unfavorable foreign trade balances, such as the United Kingdom in recent years.

In addition to a governmental requirement for export licenses for private firms, the sales agencies require governmental authorization for any export promotion activities or discussions. On occasion, exporting firms are required to post a percentage of a contract's value as a deposit, pending certification of arrival of the equipment at the authorized destination.(14)

Military Sales Policy

The French arms sales policy has been keyed to the goal of enhancing France's image as a major power. By providing an alternative, nonsuperpower, source of military equipment, foreign arms sales also have had the equally important economic objectives of improving France's balance-of-payments posture and assuring the viable operation of a modern large-scale armaments industry by improving production efficiency and lowering unit costs, promoting domestic economic development, and obtaining economic concessions abroad.(15) The scale and diversity of the French arms export program have enabled France to offer an alternative source of arms and influence to the developing states.(16)

In addition, given the relatively narrow limitations imposed by its self-applied political restrictions, France has taken advantage of the embargoes and export restraints of other arms suppliers and has successfully penetrated markets traditionally supplied by them. Notable examples here are Pakistan, South Africa, and Latin America. France has thus been able to capitalize on the proclivities of certain customers for French equipment and on the attractiveness of such transactions as devoid of any ideological stigma, otherwise attached to purchases from the United States or the Soviet Union.

With respect to the Middle East, arms exports have served as an effective instrument of policy with the complementary purposes of gaining economic concessions and ensuring access to oil supplies. Until the June 1967 War, France was a major supplier of arms to Israel. At the outbreak of that conflict, the Israeli air force was almost totally equipped with French aircraft. As a consequence of the war, however, France placed an embargo on the shipment of additional aircraft and other major weapons to Middle East battlefield countries. The embargo caused a serious strain in French-Israeli relations, primarily over the disposition of fifty undelivered Mirage V jets for which Israel had previously paid. Not until 1972 did Israel finally agree to accept reimbursement of the amount paid, plus interest.(17)

The relationship with Israel points up the adroitness with which the French government has operated to derive maximum political advantage from its sale or denial of arms. When France's close relationship with Israel was perceived as no longer in the French interest after the 1967 War, the French arms embargo, which primarily affected Israel, assisted France in regaining prestige in the Arab world. France thus escaped Arab castigation after the June War, despite the crucial role played by French built aircraft in Israel's stunning victory. The French sale of 110 Mirage fighters to Libya in 1970 underscored the pragmatic nature of

French arms sales policy. France no doubt desired to ensure continuing access to oil concessions in Libya. At the same time, the Mirage contract probably reflected the French perception that the Libyans at that time welcomed an independent Western source of arms as an alternative to a Soviet deal and as a counterweight to Egyptian influence.

The aftermath of the October 1973 Middle East war seemed to promise France even more room in which to maneuver diplomatically and to gain from its arms export program. After conducting a review of its arms supply policy, France lifted its embargo on military sales to the battlefield countries in August 1974. This relieved Paris of the necessity of taking any embarrassing action in response to Libya's unauthorized transfer of Mirages to Egypt during the October War.(18) It also cleared the way for Paris to negotiate unrestricted arms sales with all of the Middle East states, thereby helping to ensure continuing supplies of Arab oil and domestic benefits to the French economy.

The post-October War situation in the Middle East did not immediately result in a sudden upsurge in French arms sales to the area. It has, however, allowed the Arab states to purchase selected categories of weapons which, for one reason or another, have not been available from other suppliers. The Libyan case notwithstanding, French arms sales policy does not appear to have been excessively burdened by end-use restrictions, and this has given France a competitive edge over other suppliers. For pressing political reasons, however, restrictions still are applied in selective cases. One recent example was the French demurral over the sale of ten missile patrol boats to Libya on the grounds that the crafts might be regarded as threatening the security of Egypt.(19)

At the same time, France has already concluded or is in the final stages of negotiating substantial new arms sales in the Middle East. Numerous reports indicate that French companies and the Egyptian government have held extensive discussions on the sale and subsequent coproduction in Egypt of Mirage F-1 fighter aircraft, Alphajet trainer light attack aircraft, and various other types of equipment. Involved questions of Arab priorities and financing remain to be worked out.(20) Meanwhile, a French firm has reportedly agreed to produce badly needed components to keep Egypt's inventory of Soviet built, surface-to-air missiles (SAM) in operation.(21) Elsewhere in the Middle East, France and Iraq finally agreed in mid-1977 on the sale of a reported seventy-two Mirage F-1s, as well as helicopters and other equipment. Valued at $1.4 billion, this is one of the largest such deals transacted by France with a Middle Eastern country.(22) France currently appears to be exerting a maximum effort to replace the Soviets as a source of weapons for the Arab countries and to acquire a share of the existing United States arms market.

Arms Trade Pattern

The annual level of French worldwide military exports doubled from

Table 5.1. French Arms Deliveries
(million current dollars)

Year	Value
1966	215
1967	86
1968	181
1969	216
1970	198
1971	154
1972	534
1973	564
1974	561
1975	504

Source: US Arms Control and Disarmament Agency, World Military Expenditures and Arms Transfers 1966-1975 (Washington, D.C.: US Government Printing Office, 1976), p. 63.

$100 million in 1961 to about $200 million by the end of the decade.(23) Since 1972, annual deliveries have exceeded the $500 million level, as shown in Table 5.1. By 1968, weapons and other military equipment amounted to 22 percent of total French capital goods exports, with some sixty-five countries importing French military products.(24)

An efficient and well-organized export program, supported by ample credit resources and a well-regarded product line, has enabled France to develop lucrative markets throughout most of the third world. Paris has been particularly successful in expanding exports to all major developing areas, except East Asia, as indicated in Table 5.2.

The rapid growth in French worldwide arms sales since the mid-1960s is indicated in Table 5.3.

Most of the deliveries resulting from contracts signed in the last several years will not be completed for some years hence; the $7.5 billion in foreign military equipment orders outstanding in July 1975 will probably maintain overall defense production at current levels for at least the next two or three years.(25) Sales activity in 1976 was maintained at about the same level as for the previous year. For example, in 1976 aerospace export orders amounted to $1.94 billion; $1.85 billion were registered in 1975.(26) Moreover, indications of substantial new foreign arms orders in 1977, as evidenced by the recent agreement with Iraq, may have made 1977 a near record year for French military sales.

The special popularity and appeal of French aircraft and missiles have enabled the aerospace sector to account for the lion's share of military exports. The value of total aerospace production has accordingly tripled in the last decade and one-half, with the share of exports in such production increasing from 25 percent in 1960 to over 70

Table 5.2. French Arms Deliveries, by Area of Destination in Developing
Regions, Cumulative 1966-75
(million current dollars)

Region	Value	Percent of Total French Arms Exports to Developing Areas
Africa	741	35
Middle East	544	26
Latin America	502	24
South Asia	260	13
East Asia	45	2
Total	2,092	100

Source: US Arms Control and Disarmament Agency, World Military Expenditures and Arms Trade 1966-1975 (Washington, D.C.: US Government Printing Office, 1976), pp. 77-80.

percent in recent years.(27) The primary reason for France's booming aerospace exports is the widespread appeal of the Mirage aircraft line produced by the world renowned, designer builder, Marcel Dassault.(28) Because of its price and performance characteristics, the basic Mirage III interceptor was particularly popular in the export market during the 1960s. In consonance with the French predilection for designing equipment with foreign customers in mind, Dassault subsequently developed the Mirage V basically as an export version of the Mirage III. Characterized by a less complicated avionics system, the Mirage V is much simpler for inexperienced foreign pilots to fly.(29) About 1,500 of various models of the Mirage have been produced or were on order for seventeen countries as of early 1974, as indicated in Table 5.4, with some additional sales having been made then.

Helicopters have been another widely selling item abroad with some 4,400, including 2,800 of the Alouette family, having been sold to eighty-five countries as of mid-1975.(30) France is also the only country, apart from the United States and the Soviet Union, to have developed missiles in all categories. French missiles have proven extremely popular among foreign customers, as indicated in Table 5.5. The excellent international reputation of French military equipment will likely remain a vital factor in the French foreign arms sales program.

THE UNITED KINGDOM

The United Kingdom, currently the fourth largest of the world's arms suppliers, was a major exporter of military equipment before World War II. The variations in British arms export policy over the past

Table 5.3. French Arms Sales
(million current dollars)

Year	Value
1965	570
1966	650
1967	530
1968	825
1969	490
1970	1,300
1971	1,300
1972	950
1973	2,200
1974	4,500
1975	4,500

Sources:

For 1965-70: John Stanley and Maurice Pearton, The International Trade in Arms (New York: Praeger, 1972), p. 127.

For 1971: Le Monde (January 26, 1974).

For 1972: Jean Klein, "Arms Trade and Policy: France, A Case in Point," (Paper delivered to the Eighth Congress of International Relations, Quebec, September 30-October 3, 1976), p. 1.

For 1973-74: Jean Klein, "Ventes d'Armes et d'Equipements Nucleaires," Politique Etrangere, no. 6 (1975), p. 614.

For 1975: Armies and Weapons (Geneva) no. 27 (September 15, 1976), p. 27.

several decades reflect the changes in the international role of the United Kingdom. In the late 1940s and early 1950s, the United Kingdom was second only to the United States as the largest exporter of arms in the world. Due to the United Kingdom's extensive military commitments during that period, many countries were dependent on British military equipment, while arms exports underscored its overseas interests.(31)

As the United Kingdom withdrew from its colonial territories, British military exports began to decline. This was due to increasing competition from other suppliers, particularly the United States, the Soviet Union, and France, as well as the British failure to produce the types of equipment, especially aircraft, most appropriate for export. Ironically, British arms sales began to decline precipitously just as the increasing sophistication of British equipment made it imperative to export in order to recoup some of the increasing costs of military procurement.(32)

Table 5.4. Dassault Mirage Series Customers as of March 1, 1974

Buyer	Mirage: IIIA	IIIB	IIIC	IIID	IIIE	IIIO	IIIR	IIIS	5A/E	5D	5R	F-1	G-8	Totals
Abu Dhabi	–	–	–	–	–	–	–	–	2(10)	1(1)	–	–	–	14
Argentina	–	–	–	2	10	–	–	–	–	–	–	–	–	12
Australia	–	–	–	16	–	100	–	–	–	–	–	–	–	116
Belgium	–	–	–	–	–	–	–	–	63	16	27	–	–	106
Brazil	–	–	–	4	12	–	–	–	–	–	–	–	–	16
Columbia	–	–	–	–	–	–	–	–	15	3	–	–	–	18
France	10	45	95	–	200	–	75	–	50	–	–	23(82)	2	582
Israel	–	3	72	–	–	–	–	–	–	–	–	–	–	75
Lebanon	–	2	12	–	–	–	–	–	–	–	–	–	–	14[b]
Libya	–	–	–	–	–	–	–	–	32	48(20)	(10)	–	–	110[c]
Pakistan	–	–	–	3	18	–	3	–	28(30	2	–	–	–	84
Peru	–	2	–	–	–	–	–	–	12(8)	2	–	–	–	24
Saudi Arabia	–	–	–	(4)	(34)	–	–	–	–	–	–	–	–	38
South Africa	–	3	16	3	35	–	4	–	–	–	–	(48)	–	109[d]
Spain	–	4	–	–	26	–	–	–	–	–	–	(21)	–	51[e]

Table 5.4. Dassault Mirage Series Customers as of March 1, 1974 (cont'd.)

Buyer	Mirage: IIIA	IIIB	IIIC	IIID	IIIE	IIIO	IIIR	IIIS	5A/E	5D	5R	F-1	G-8	Totals
Switzerland	–	2	1	–	–	–	18	37	–	–	–	–	–	58
Venezuela	–	–	–	2	3(10)	–	–	–	–	–	–	–	–	15
Subtotals														
Delivered	10	61	196	30	304	100	100	37	202	72	27	23	2	1,164
In Order	–	–	–	(4)	(44)	–	–	–	(48)	(21)	(10)	(151)	–	(278)
TOTALS	10	61	196	34	348	100	100	37	250	93	37	174	2	1,442

Note: Figures in parentheses indicate the number of aircraft yet to be delivered.

[a]Order for eighteen Mirage IIIEs believed pending.
[b]Eleven aircraft remaining in inventory are up for sale.
[c]Deliveries planned to be completed in 1974.
[d]Licensed production planned for Mirage F-1s.
[e]Spain has also optioned an additional eighteen Mirage F-1s.

Source: Defense Marketing Service, Monthly Intelligence Report, March 1974, p. 2 [Used by permission].

Table 5.5. Selected Types of French Missiles Sold Abroad,
as of Mid-1975

Type of Missile	Number of Units Sold	Number of Foreign Purchasing Countries
ENTAC antitank missile	140,000	13
SS-11 antitank and AS-11 air-to-surface missiles	160,000	32
SS-12 antitank and AS-12 air-to-surface missiles	6,000	21
HOT antitank missile	4,300	4
MILAN antitank missile	18,000	10
Exocet antiship	710	12
AS-20 air-to-surface missile	5,700	4
AS-30 air-to-surface missile	3,900	6
R-530 air-to-air missile	2,600	15
MAGIC air-to-air missile	3,300	10

Source: Military Aviation News (June 1975): 9.

Arms Sales Organization and Procedures

In an attempt to revitalize its sagging arms export program, the United Kingdom reorganized its military sales apparatus in 1966. A Defense Sales Organization was created within the Ministry of Defense to centralize and systematize sales efforts. The new head of Defense Sales, Sir Raymond Brown, was instructed to "insure, within the limits of government policy, that as much military equipment is sold overseas as possible and also to develop research to stimulate the interests of future buyers."(33) Besides being charged with promotional efforts to be carried out by a special sales staff and designated British embassy personnel, the Defense Sales Organization, with a staff of nearly 300 persons, was made responsible for the incorporation of foreign requirements in British designed and built weapon systems.(34) The government also began distribution of an annual catalog entitled British Military Equipment. This includes the gamut of conventional military gear from supersonic fighter aircraft and hydrofoil vessels to sleeping bags and fire extinguishers. As part of its sales promotion efforts, the United

Kingdom began to offer medium-term (five-to-seven year) credits in lieu of strictly cash sales. The facilities of the export Credit Guarantee Department (ECGD) were made available to foreign buyers to provide credit guarantees, another vital means by which the British government facilitated arms exports. The ECGD was to see that:

> ... British exporters are able to offer the same length of credit as their foreign competitors can do with official support, but not generally to take the initiative in offering longer terms than normal in a particular field.(35)

Other sales terms offered by the UK were similar to those offered by France but apparently did not include the special concessions, such as barter or offset agreements, sometimes granted by the French.

The Defense Sales Organization at first was basically a new collective term for the army and navy sales divisions of the Ministry of Defense and the exports and International Relations Division of the Ministry of Technology. The latter was responsible for aircraft, missile, and electronic equipment sales. What changed significantly with the establishment of the Defense Sales office was not simply the organization of the governmental sales apparatus, but the momentum behind the sales promotion campaign resulting from Sir Raymond Brown's commercial expertise and personal exuberance. British arms sales rose accordingly, from $360 million in 1967 to an estimated $520 million in 1971.(36)

Sir Raymond's successor, Lester Suffield, introduced further organizational changes in an effort to achieve still greater sales professionalism. The separate army and navy sales divisions were replaced by single organizations responsible for both ground and naval equipment in specified geographic areas. Two support groups were also set up. One was responsible for presales activities, "market research, publicity, demonstrations, and coordination with British military attaches overseas," and the other was concerned with the delivery of equipment and post delivery service.(37) Each proposed foreign arms sale is reviewed by an interministerial committee composed of representatives of the Foreign Office, the Ministry of Defense, the Ministry of Technology, and the Board of Trade.(38) Politically sensitive sales, such as those for South Africa, go to the Cabinet-level Strategic Exports Ministerial Committee for decision.(39)

While all private arms exports require a license issued by the Board of Trade, British licensing procedures are generally simpler than those in effect for some other suppliers. There is no legal provision, for example, for stipulating end-use of an item. The government may negotiate a separate agreement prohibiting retransfer of equipment, but it is not included as a matter of course. Similarly, licensing is not required for any defense coproduction arrangement entered into abroad, as it apparently is assumed that governmental control will be extended through the sale of associated parts and material. While true to some extent, the absence of a licensing requirement for the transfer of technology does represent a loophold as far as third country sales are concerned.(40)

Military Sales Policy

British arms sales policy is determined on an ad hoc basis. Prospective sales are weighed in terms of their effect on British policy interests and on their impact on the recipient area. In addition, London generally avoids arms sales to areas of conflict or tension, although this consideration has on a number of occasions been overridden for political reasons, as in the cases of Jordan or Nigeria. On the other hand, political considerations have caused the British government to impose arms embargoes or to limit the types of arms provided to particular clients, even at substantial economic cost to the United Kingdom.(41)

The Middle East has been more of an arms-sales dilemma for Britain. Beginning with the October 1973 War, the United Kingdom placed an embargo on major arms shipments to all battlefield countries. While theoretically applied to both sides evently, the ban on shipments was regarded by some British members of Parliament as affecting Israel more than the Arab states. The objective was to avoid antagonizing the latter, with which London was maintained longstanding political and economic ties.(42)

In June 1974, the British government announced that it would thereafter consider the sale of weapons to the Middle East "that did not threaten a lasting settlement in the region." Despite this relaxation of restraints, however, London refused to sell Jaguar fighters, Chieftain tanks, and submarines to Libya during negotiations for a $1.4 billion arms package in early 1975. While the British were willing to sell other equipment, including transport aircraft, frigates, and tank transporters, the Libyans, desiring an all or nothing package deal, broke off negotiations. At about the same time, London lost another potential Middle East order for Jaguars when Saudi Arabia refused to provide assurances that the aircraft under negotiation would not be transferred to Egypt.(43)

To maintain its dependability as a supplier, the British government has apparently strived to adhere to two additional policy tenets: to avoid unilaterally modifying existing contracts, and to avoid interfering with the supply of spare parts for previously sold equipment.(44)

The basic motive for British arms sales is economic, although strategic and political motives also play important roles. The latter are particularly important in sales to former colonies or present members of the Commonwealth. Arms exports are sought in order to lower unit production costs, to recover some research and development expenditures, to maintain "warm" production lines in defense industries, to dispose of surplus equipment, and, perhaps most important, to contribute to a favorable balance-of-payments.

Arms Trade Pattern

Although British arms sales to NATO and other European countries have decreased substantially in the past decade, the United Kingdom's arms export drive in the third world has been relatively successful.

Total foreign military sales increased from about $400 million in 1969 to nearly $1 billion annually by 1973. They accounted for about one-third of total British defense production.(45)

Because of the normal lag between sales agreements and deliveries, the actual volume of exports has increased less dramatically. Table 5.6 indicates annual British worldwide arms deliveries during the period

Table 5.6. UK Arms Deliveries
(million current dollars)

Year	Value
1966	147
1967	97
1968	159
1969	197
1970	83
1971	178
1972	312
1973	333
1974	463
1975	378

Source: US Arms Control and Disarmament Agency, World Military Expenditures and Arms Transfers 1966-1975 (Washington, D.C.: US Government Printing Office, 1976), p. 74.

1966-75. Definitive data on annual British exports to the Middle East are not available, but for the ten-year period as a whole, the United Kingdom transferred about $775 million in arms to that area. This amount represented about 33 percent of total British worldwide arms exports during the period and 5 percent of total arms transfers by all suppliers to the area.(46)

The Middle East, particularly Saudi Arabia, Iran, Jordan, and Kuwait, has been Britain's best third world market, accounting for half of its total arms shipments to developing areas over the past decade, as indicated in Table 5.7.

Naval craft, including destroyers, patrol boats, hovercraft, and submarines, have accounted for a substantial share of Britain's arms exports. The mainstays of British aircraft sales have been somewhat older models, such as the 1950 vintage supersonic Lightning and the subsonic Hawker Hunter. At the same time, the modern Jaguar, thus far ordered by Oman and Ecuador, has considerable promise as an export item.(47) The Jet Provost and Strikemaster trainer light strike aircraft have also been popular export items, having been purchased by at least twelve countries. In addition, the United Kingdom has provided a full line of other military equipment, ranging from surface-to-air missiles to tanks and infantry weapons. Over 3,000 Centurion tanks have been sold to at least fourteen countries, while Iran has purchased 800 late model Chieftain tanks and a variety of other equipment.(48) The Rapier SAM system is another popular item that has so far been ordered by Iran, Abu Daabi, and Oman, among Middle East countries.(49)

Table 5.7. UK Arms Deliveries, by Area of Destination in
Developing Regions, Cumulative 1966-75
(million current dollars)

Region	Value	Percent of Total British Arms Exports to Developing Areas
Middle East	775	50
Latin America	328	21
Africa	219	14
East Asia	134	9
South Asia	96	6
Total	1,552	100

Source: US Arms Control and Disarmament Agency, World Military Expenditures and Arms Transfers 1966-1975 (Washington, D.C.: US Government Printing Office, 1976), pp. 77-80.

In addition to equipment sales, Britain has been extensively involved in providing military technical assistance to a number of countries, most notably Saudi Arabia. in early 1977, London was reportedly in the final stages of negotiations with the Saudis for renewal of a technical support agreement for the Royal Saudi Air force. The value of the contract, which would continue existing arrangements for operating an air academy and various maintenance, training, and construction programs over a four-year period, is estimated to range from $1.3 billion to $1.7 billion. The present 2,000-man British technical support contingent for the Saudi air force is accordingly expected to increase to 8,000 men.(50)

The United Kingdom, like other major arms exporters, also has concluded contracts for the partial assembly of British equipment in the recipient country. Moreover, British firms have entered into licensing arrangements, particularly with India, under which the recipient country is permitted to produce British designed equipment, including fighter aircraft and tanks.

Egypt remains potentially the most lucrative British market for major arms sales, as well as for a variety of coproduction or licensing ventures. Since the May 1975 agreement to establish the Arab Military Industrial Organization (AMIO) in Egypt, with the financial support of Saudi Arabia and several Persian Gulf states, the United Kingdom has been involved in intensive discussions with Egypt over the sale and subsequent coproduction of Hawk light strike aircraft, Lynx helicopters, and antitank missiles, as well as electronic and other equipment. The discussions have so far proven extraordinarily complex because of the many political and economic issues to be resolved. On the economic side, for example, Cairo was having difficulty in considering its many options because, as a British aerospace official put it, "the Middle East is up to its ears in quotes."(51) While it will undoubtedly require some years after arrangements are finalized to attain a substantial output, the planned production facilities would eventually serve as the nucleus of Egypt's modernized arms industry.(52)

FEDERAL REPUBLIC OF GERMANY

Since resuming arms production in the mid-1950s, West Germany has maintained a relatively restrictive policy for foreign arms sales. The bulk of West German exports have been earmarked for NATO and other European countries. West Germany ranks after France and the United Kingdom among West European suppliers.(53) At the same time, its small share of the world arms market is reflected in the fact that military exports in recent years have comprised less than 0.3 percent of total German exports.(54) Even so, between 1966 and 1975, the annual level of West German arms shipments abroad nearly quadrupled, as indicated in Table 8.

Table 5.8. Federal Republic of Germany Arms Deliveries
(million current dollars)

Year	Value
1966	68
1967	58
1968	98
1969	101
1970	189
1971	130
1972	226
1973	26
1974	223
1975	257

Source: US Arms Control and Disarmament Agency, World Military Expenditures and Arms Transfers 1966-1975 (Washington, D.C.: US Government Printing Office, 1976), p. 63.

Table 5.9 indicates that, of the developing regions, the Middle East has ranked first among recipient areas for German arms shipments in the same period.

International treaty requirements, coupled with a strong desire to avoid association with countries in conflict, have impelled the Germans

Table 5.9. Federal Republic of Germany Arms Deliveries, by Area of
Destination in Developing Regions, Cumulative 1966-75
(million current dollars)

Region	Value	Percent of Total West German Arms Exports to Developing Areas
Middle East	224	38
Latin America	199	34
Africa	109	19
South Asia	29	5
East Asia	26	4
Total	587	100

Source: US Arms Control and Disarmament Agency, World Military Expenditures and Arms Transfers 1966-1975 (Washington, D.C.: US Government Printing Office, 1976), pp. 78-80.

to adhere closely to a policy of not exporting military equipment to non-Nato countries and to areas of tension. In addition to production restraints imposed by Protocol III of the Brussels Treaty of 1959, the Bonn government has applied strict legislative restrictions on exports of military equipment through the War Materiel Control Act and the Foreign Trade Act. Under the terms of this legislation, the government is empowered to refuse permission to export. In particular, export licenses will not be granted when there is a risk that arms will be used in a conflict situation or for domestic political purposes, or when the license applicant is considered unreliable.(55) West German law, moreover, requires the maintenance of a War Materiel List, indicating embargoed military equipment by category. Such types of equipment require special approval before they can be exported.(56) Besides commercial sales by private arms dealers, the West German government provides military equipment to a small number of countries under military assistance agreements. The latter types of assistance to non-NATO countries comprise such items as transportation, communications, and support type equipment, but generally exclude weapons.

A longstanding embargo on arms shipments has applied to both sides in the Arab-Israeli conflict, but some transfers of equipment have occurred. In late 1973, a quantity of radios was sold to Syria and Libya causing some international controversy about possible embargo violations. However, the West German Foreign Office asserted that since the radios were for civilian use, they did not violate the embargo, despite the fact that some of the radios were equipped with adapters for use on tanks.(57)

By and large, however, West Germany has continued to observe a restrictive export policy. In 1974, a potentially lucrative order for 800 Leopard tanks to Iran was lost, reportedly because the Shah could not obtain West German assurances that Germany would not suspend its shipment of tanks and parts in wartime.(58) Bonn similarly decided against a $600 million sale for 800 armored personnel carriers to Saudi Arabia that had been under consideration for some time.(59)

By 1975, however, because of the worsening economic slump and growing unemployment in West Germany, the government came under increasing internal political pressure by industry and labor to relax restrictions on arms sales to the developing countries. Additional pressure has been generated by Germany's NATO partners in several collaborative weapons development projects with export prospects. These latter include the Alphajet trainer light strike aircraft, developed jointly with France; the Anglo-German-Italian MRCA fighter aircraft; and the HOT and MILAN antitank missiles, also developed with France.(60)

A change in arms export policy has been viewed as particularly difficult for the West German Social Democratic government in view of the party's image as the "antiwar representative of the working class." Chancellor Helmut Schmidt, moreover, reportedly has been concerned with the potential expansion of the West German arms industry, lest it become overly dependent on exports. At the same time, the Bonn government is expected to continue to approve sufficient export sales to maintain military equipment production at a roughly constant level in order to prevent further significant unemployment.(61)

Chancellor Schmidt has continued to delay reconsideration of his government's restrictive arms sales policy, apparently in the hope that an improving economic situation would dissipate some of the pressure by arms manufacturers to enlarge their markets. Meanwhile, although government spokesmen have denied that there has been any change in overall policy, they have begun to emphasize the government's flexibility and case-by-case review of arms requests.(62) Several significant exceptions to existing West German arms export policy were granted in early 1977. In February, for example, the West German government approved the sale of two submarines to Indonesia, with a guarantee of repayment to the German manufacturing firm. This was the first time that this sort of government credit was extended to a non-NATO country such as Indonesia.(63) While Indonesia was declared to be an area "free of tension," as required by West German law, the cabinet reportedly was heavily influenced by the existing shortage of orders in West German shipyards. The sale of six submarines to Iran in early 1978 presumably also fell within the same guidelines that applied to Indonesia.(64)

While criticizing such sales as contrary to the spirit of the law, an editorial in the influential West German financial newspaper, Handels-blatt, suggested that the legislation itself is outmoded in the present era of "cooperative international arms production."(65) With German made weapons highly appealing to the world and with mounting economic pressure buffeting the Bonn government, the recently granted exceptions to its arms export policy may be more than vagrant straws in the wind.

SOVIET UNION

In the Soviet drive to acquire influence and weaken the position of the West in the nonaligned developing areas, arms aid has emerged as perhaps the most effective instrument in Moscow's diplomatic repertoire. The priority accorded the Middle East in Soviet foreign policy calculations is reflected in the share of total Soviet arms aid allocated to the area; between 1955 and 1976, Middle East states received about $14 billion of an estimated $21 billion in sales.(66)

Arms Sales Organization and Procedures

The key organization involved in administering the Soviet arms export program is the Chief Engineering Directorate (GIU), which is subordinate to the State Committee for Foreign Economic Relations (GKES). The GIU negotiates with the client country and acts as the supplier in military assistance contracts.The GIU works closely with the external Relations Directorate of the General Staff and with the Ministry of Defense in determining the types and amounts of weapons and equipment, as well as technical assistance to be provided. If a client state requests advanced weapons systems, the request must be approved by the Soviet Minister of Defense or the Premier himself. After an agreement is signed by both parties, the GIU arranges for delivery fo the equipment with the Ministry of Foreign Trade and Ministry of Maritime Fleet.(67)

The Soviet Union has generally sold its arms to third world countries at heavily subsidized, bargain basement prices and on terms generous to the recipient. The latter have typically comprised repayment periods of eight to ten years, following a grace period of one to three years, at interest rates of 2 to 2.5 percent. The loans have sometimes been repayable in commodities or soft currency, and on occasion the Soviet Union has granted moratoria on payments when clients have been unable to meet annual installments.(68)

In most Soviet arms sales contracts with developing countries, an estimated 40 percent of the value of the equipment is written off as grants. Even without the discounts, the list price of most types of Soviet weapons have been substantially below those charged for comparable Western equipment; tanks and fighter aircraft, for example, have been 40-50 percent lower.(69) Although the size of the discount probably reflects Moscow's assessment of a client's ability to pay, political favoritism undoubtedly enters the equation as well.

As in the case of the arms sales contracts of some Western countries, Soviet sales agreements contain restrictive and end-use clauses. The Soviet Union customarily prohibits a recipient state from transferring military equipment to another country without Soviet approval, but Moscow has permitted some retransfers when Soviet policy objectives were served.(70)

Arms Transfer Policy

The Soviet Union is a relative newcomer to the postwar international arms trade, not entering the field until 1955. In deciding to become an arms supplier, Russia was probably motivated by: the general success of its postwar economic recovery; the plentiful stocks of surplus conventional arms made available as a consequence of military manpower reductions and changes in military doctrine during the 1950s; and the failure of local Communist elements to make appreciable political gains in the newly emerging, developing countries.

Following the death of Stalin, Soviet foreign policy dramatically shifted away from the then prevailing, highly polarized two-camp concept toward a more flexible view of the world embodied in the doctrine of peaceful coexistence. That flexibility was aptly demonstrated in the September 1955 conclusion of a military assistance accord between Egypt and Czechoslovakia (which acted as a Soviet proxy); it was the first such transaction between a Communist and a nonaligned country.(71)

The Soviet Union has used its arms aid program as a vital tool of policy to increase its influence and decrease that of the West in selected areas and to gain acceptance by its adversaries as a global power. On a number of occasions, the arms aid program has served as an entree into countries which otherwise might have been less susceptible to Soviet approaches. It has assisted in aligning progressive forces with Soviet foreign policy and in maintaining regimes in power favorable to the Soviet Union. Moscow also has used its arms aid to pursue the additional objective of preventing the Chinese from extending their influence. In pursuit of such goals, the Soviet Union has demonstrated that it can move rapidly and easily to exploit new opportunities.

The fact that Soviet arms offers have been tendered in diverse areas at different time suggests that Moscow's arms transfer policy is not designed to implement a predetermined plan but to respond to opportunities to establish influence wherever possible. The opportunities that initially drew the Soviet Union into the Middle East in the mid-1950s, for example, can be viewed in the light of traditional Russian strategic interests. During that period, Moscow was concerned about the western military presence, via the Baghdad Pact, being established on the Soviet Union's southern periphery. The Russians sought to counter those developments by means of the arms aid tool.

Through the use of arms transfers as one of its major tools of diplomacy, Moscow has recognized that in many developing states the military establishment is either the actual or potential locus of power. The Soviet Union has generally sought to encourage contact and rapport with military leaders. These efforts have been facilitated by the presence of Russian technical advisers, by the training of the client state's military personnel in the Soviet Union, and by periodic exchange visits of high ranking military delegations.

Soviet arms aid policy in the Middle East has been supportive of all of the above goals. In addition, while the primary motives of Soviet arms sales policy have been political and strategic, rather than commercial, Russia has not been averse to reaping the increasing economic benefits derived from friendly relations with the Middle East countries, particularly those with oil, e.g., Iraq, or other important raw material resources, e.g., natural gas in the case of Iran.

Arms Trade Pattern

In the early days of the Soviet arms aid program, Moscow was able to keep the net cost of its military assistance program relatively low by supplying obsolete equipment made available by its own modernization program. As these stocks were depleted, the Soviet Union was forced to shift increasingly to the export of more modern equipment. Because of Soviet political priorities, some developing recipient states eventually were provided with the same types of air defense and other equipment being distributed to the Soviet Union's own forces, even before the Warsaw Pact states in some cases. Besides being the first non-Communist nation to acquire the new SA-3 surface-to-air missile system, Egypt, for example, in 1970 received such late model equipment as the ZSU-23-4 radar controlled, mobile antiaircraft gun. This weapon was regarded as the most effective Soviet weapon against low flying aircraft and, until then, was known to be deployed only in the Soviet Union and Poland.(72)

In the period 1955-76, the Soviet Union concluded military assistance and sales agreements totaling an estimated $21 billion with at least 37 nonaligned countries, as indicated in Table 5.10.(73)

Table 5.10. Soviet Arms Aid Agreements with Developing Countries, 1955-74 (million current dollars)

Year	Value
1955-66	4,500
1967	525
1968	500
1969	350
1970	1,150
1971	1,600
1972	1,500
1973	2,800
1974	3,500
1975	2,000
1976	2,450
Total	20,875

Source: US Central Intelligence Agency, Communist Aid to the Less Developed Countries of the Free World, 1976 (Washington, D.C.: 1977), p. 3.

Because the Soviet arms aid program is partly a response to available opportunities and is partly influenced by the absorptive capacity of the recipients, the annual magnitude and direction of arms exports, as Table 5.10 indicates, have been highly variable. During the late 1950s, the first Soviet agreements were concluded largely with Middle East countries. In the early 1960s, sizable annual commitments were influenced principally by Indonesia's dispute with the Netherlands and confrontation with Malaysia, Sino-Indian tensions, and the civil war and Egyptian involvement in Yemen. Most of the activity in the late 1960s and early 1970s reflected continuing arms buildups and modernization in the Arab countries in the aftermath of the 1967 and 1973 Wars and significant new commitments to India, Iran, and Libya.(74) Table 5.11 indicates that during the period 1966-75, the Middle East accounted for nearly 70 percent of total Soviet deliveries to the developing regions, excluding China, North Vietnam, North Korea, and Cuba.

Table 5.11. Soviet Arms Deliveries, by Area of Destination in Developing
Regions, Cumulative 1966-75
(million current dollars)

Region	Value	Percent of Total Soviet Arms Exports to Developing Areas
Middle East	6,300	68
South Asia	1,749	19
Africa	1,086	12
Latin America	84	1
East Asia	15	negligible
Total	9,234	100

Source: US Arms Control and Disarmament Agency, World Military Expenditures and Arms Transfers 1966-1975 (Washington, D.C.: U.S. Government Printing Office, 1976), pp. 77-80.

Of the nonaligned developing countries, Egypt has received the largest share, approximately 25 percent, of Soviet arms deliveries to the developing regions during the 1966-75 period.(75) Although vast quantities of Soviet equipment were lost in the last three wars with Israel, the Egyptian forces have been repeatedly resupplied, with some exceptions following the October 1973 War.

Longstanding strains in the Soviet-Egyptian relationship were exacerbated by new frictions which arose during the October conflict. The worsening state of the relationship was reflected in President Sadat's watershed speech of April 18, 1974, in which the Egyptian leader announced that Egypt would end its exclusive reliance on the Soviet

Union for arms and would seek its weapons elsewhere.(76) In the wake of Sadat's announcement, all shipments of Soviet arms and spare parts temporarily came to a halt.

Following the impetus provided by Sadat's January 1975 arms shopping visit to Paris, some Soviet deliveries of MIG-23 fighters and other equipment ordered under earlier contracts took place in the first several months of 1975. The arrival of about twenty-four MIG-23s finally raised overall Egyptian air force strength to nearly the pre-October War level.(77) After mid-1975, however, Soviet deliveries of major military equipment to Egypt ceased once again. Egypt's relations with Moscow became increasingly strained following the Sinai II disengagement agreement signed between Israel and Egypt in September 1975, and was reflected by the withdrawal later in the month of four Soviet manned Foxbat reconnaissance aircraft from Egypt.(78)

While few facets in Soviet-Egyptian relations remained unaffected by this progressive deterioration, Sadat moved even further in his anti-Soviet policies in early 1976. On March 15, he surprisingly called for the abrogation of the 1971 Soviet-Egyptian Treaty of Friendship and Cooperation and ordered the Soviet navy to abandon the use of its base at Alexandria by the following month. In his speech, Sadat charged that the Soviet Union was trying to exert military and economic pressure on Egypt "in order to make us kneel before her. I kneel only before God," he declared.(79) The virtual cessation of the Soviet military aid relationship with Egypt is reported to have seriously affected the operational capabilities of the Egyptian armed forces.(80) This situation has impelled a maximum Egyptian effort to obtain arms from the West.(81)

The sizable Soviet military aid extensions to Syria and Iraq reflect Moscow's important political-strategic interests in these countries. For the most part, Moscow has maintained a relatively close relationship with the two Arab states. Soviet resupply during and after the October War has built up Syrian and Iraqi major arms inventories to a point well above prewar levels. Because of the current frigid state of Soviet relations with Egypt, Syria and Iraq have undoubtedly become all the more crucial in Soviet policy calculations.(82)

While Syrian involvement in the Lebanese civil war during 1976 caused serious strain and some acrimony in the Soviet-Syrian relationship, neither side has appeared willing to push the other to the point of an irreparable break. Consequently, early 1977 reports indicating that Syria had requested the Soviet navy to discontinue use of Syrian port facilities were subsequently demonstrated to be false.(83) In a similar vein, given the Soviet interest in retaining close relations with Iraq, reinforced by Moscow's interest in Iraqi oil and access to the Persian Gulf, one can expect a sustained commitment on the part of the Soviet Union in military aid and other support for Iraq. This was demonstrated in the signing of a new $1.1 billion arms agreement recently reported in the press.(84)

OTHER SUPPLIERS

Western

The remaining West European arms suppliers of any significance, Belgium, Italy, Sweden, and Switzerland, can offer a certain range of weapons and equipment to selected countries in effective competition with the major suppliers. The smaller exporting countries' products, such as small arms, ground forces equipment, missiles, jet fighters, and trainers, have special appeal to states that prefer not to be aligned too closely with a major power. Even those countries that are so aligned occasionally find it to their advantage to cultivate secondary sources of supply, despite the resulting adverse effect on standardization of equipment. Some of the recipient countries have learned from experience the consequences of relying on only one or two suppliers since any cutoff of supplies affects a recipient's ability to act independently.

The sales procedures of the smaller supplier countries generally follow the model of France or the United Kingdom. Their objective is to maximize arms sales with the minimum of delay. All of these countries operate quite effectively along commercial lines and give indications of continuing to seek a share of the market.

Warsaw Pact

Czechoslovakia and Poland, each with its own well-developed armaments industry, have been substantial military equipment suppliers over the past two decades. The bulk of their arms transfers, primarily specialized ground forces equipment, jet trainers, and naval landing craft, has been earmarked for the Soviet Union and other Warsaw Pact states. However, a significant share of Czechoslovak transfers has gone to the Middle East.

In their exports to developing countries, both suppliers have basically abandoned their former roles as intermediaries for the Soviet Union. Czechoslovakia and Poland have for some years commercially exploited available opportunities for the sale of selected military equipment. With an emphasis on economic considerations in the sale of their equipment, Czechoslovak and Polish credit terms have been more businesslike, commercial interest rates, shorter repayment periods, and payments in convertible currency, than those offered by the Soviet Union.(85)

NOTES AND REFERENCES

(1) US Arms Control and Disarmament Agency (ACDA), The International Transfer of Conventional Arms (Washington, D.C.: US Government Printing Office, 1974), p. A-3.

(2) Robert D. Heinl, Jr., "French Armaments Industry Now World's Third Largest," Armed Forces Journal 109 (November 1971).

(3) John Stanley and Maurice Pearton, The International Trade in Arms (New York: Praeger, 1972), p. 94.

(4) Pierre Rocheron, "Arms and the Frenchman," Defense and Foreign Affairs 10 (1975): 7.

(5) Stanley and Pearton, p. 94 (note 3 supra).

(6) Charles Latour, "Armament Sales," NATO's Fifteen Nations 18 (April-May 1973): 77.

(7) Stanley and Pearton, p. 95 (note 3 supra).

(8) Latour,p. 77 (note 6 supra).

(9) Stanley and Pearton, p. 95 (note 3 supra).

(10) ACDA, p. 33 (note 1 supra).

(11) Stockholm International Peace Research Institute (SIPRI), The Arms Trade with the Third World, rev. ed. (New York: Holmes and Meier, 1975), pp. 128-9.

(12) Stanley and Pearton, pp. 120-121 (note 3 supra) discusses a Franco-Brazilian offset deal.

(13) SIPRI, p. 129 (note 11 supra).

(14) ACDA, p. 33 (note 1 supra).

(15) Regarding domestic employment, see comments by Robert Galley in Le Monde (January 26, 1974).

(16)

(17)

(18) New York Times (August 28, 1974).

(19) Baltimore Sun (December 30, 1976).

(20) "Airscene," Air International 12 (March 1977): 106.

(21) The Boston Globe (March 16, 1977).

(22) Le Monde (July 8, 1977) cited in Foreign Broadcast Information Service, Middle East, Daily Report (July 21, 1977).

(23) ACDA, p. A-3 (note 1 supra).

(24) Pierre Gallois, "French Military Aeronautics Make Bid for World Markets," NATO's Fifteen Nations 15 (August-September 1970): 28.

(25) New York Times (July 28, 1975).

(26) "French Aerospace Exports Rise Slightly," Aviation Week and Space Technoloy 106 (March 7, 1977): 50-51.

(27) SIRPRI, p. 129 (note 11 supra).

(28) Defense Marketing Services, Market Intelligence Report, March 1974, p. 4.

(29) Stanley and Pearton, p. 99 (note 3 supra).

(30) Military Aviation News 14 (June 1975): 8.

(31) SIPRI, p. 100 (note 11 supra).

(32) Ibid.

(33) ACDA, p. 33 (note 1 supra).

(34) Stanley and Pearton, p. 93 (note 3 supra).

(35) Ibid., pp. 112-113.

(36) Ibid., p. 93.

(37) Ibid.

(38) SIPRI, p. 108 (note 11 supra).

(39) "Defense Policy and Arms Sales," Journal of the Royal United Services Institution (December 1976): 65-66.

(40) See, for example, SIPRI, p. 108 (note 11 supra).

(41) See, for example Stanley and Pearton, pp. 173-4 (note 3 supra).

(42) New York Times (October 16, 1973).

(43) Washington Post (April 12, 1975).

(44) "Defense Policy and Arms Sales," p. 66 (note 39 supra).

(45) "Arms Across the Channel," Armed Forces Journal International 110 (May 1973): 58.

(46) ACDA, World Military Expenditures and Arms Transfers, 1966-1975

(Washington, D.C.: US Government Printing Office, 1976), p. 78.

(47) "Britain's Aerospace Industry," Flight International (London) 108 (October 2, 1975): 483.

(48) "Arms Across the Channel," p. 57 (note 45 supra).

(49) "New Missile Research Funds Lacking," Aviation Week and Space Technology 105 (September 6, 1976): 82.

(50) Military Aviation News 16 (February 1977): 19.

(51) "Westland Looks to Product Improvement," Aviation Week and Space Technology 105 (September 6, 1976): 121.

(52) For further discussion of this subject, see Roger F. Pajak, Soviet Arms Aid in the Middle East (Washington, D.C.: Georgetown Center for Strategic and International Studies, 1976).

(53) ACDA, p. 77 (note 46 supra).

(54) Military Aviation News 14 (September 1975): 9.

(55) ACDA, p. 34 (note 1 supra).

(56) Washington Post (January 26, 1974).

(57) Washington Post (February 10, 1974).

(58) Washington Post (October 6, 1975).

(59) Baltimore Sun (January 23, 1976); Washington Post (January 21, 1976).

(60) Military Aviation News 14 (September 1975): 9.

(61) Baltimore Sun (September 21, 1975); Washington Post (October 6, 1975).

(62) Baltimore Sun (January 23, 1976).

(63) Baltimore Sun (February 5, 1977).

(64) Washington Post (March 6, 1978).

(65) Quoted in the Baltimore Sun (Feburary 5, 1977).

(66) Based on data in US Central Intelligence Agency, Communist Aid to the Less Developed Countries of the Free World, 1976 (Washington, D.C.: 1977), p. 3; and projections from US Department of State,

Communist States and Developing Countries: Aid and Trade in 1974 (Washington, D.C.: January 1976), p. 30.

(67) ACDA, p. 37 (note 1 supra).

(68) Ibid., p. 27.

(69) Ibid., p. 37.

(70) Ibid.

(71) Ibid., p. 35.

(72) For further information on the pattern of Soviet arms deliveries to Egypt, see Roger F. Pajak, "Soviet Arms and Egypt," Survival 17 (July-August 1975): 168.

(73) US Central Intelligence Agency, pp. 3 and 6 (note 66 supra), and US Department of State, p. 30 (note 66 supra).

(74) Based on data contained in SIPRI, pp. 81-4 (note 11 supra).

(75) ACDA, pp. 77-80 (note 46 supra).

(76) New York Times (April 19, 1974).

(77) Washington Post (June 13, 1975).

(78) Baltimore Sun (November 23, 1975).

(79) "Egypt Begins Search for Arms Supply," Aviation Week and Space Technology 104 (March 22, 1976): 21.

(80) New York Times (November 10, 1975).

(81) For a comprehensive discussion of the background and recent developments in the Soviet-Egyptian arms aid relationship, see Pajak (note 52 supra).

(82) Also see, ibid.

(83) "Syria: Strategic Ties with USSR are Unbroken," Weekly Report on Strategic Middle Eastern Affairs 3 (March 30, 1977): 1.

(84) Washington Post (April 6, 1977).

(85) ACDA, p. 38 (note 1 supra).

6 Strategic Access, Bases, and Arms Transfers: The Major Powers' Evolving Geopolitical Competition in the Middle East

Robert Harkavy

OVERVIEW

The competition among the major powers in the Middle East for general diplomatic influence, for access to and control over resources, particularly petroleum, and for overall economic advantage has been extensively examined. A somewhat muted and overlooked theme, however, has been the ongoing traditional geopolitical competition for strategic access and for denial of such access to rivals. The ultimate meaning of this competition, in the Middle East and elsewhere, is much disputed. There is little agreement on its contribution to the overall big power military balance, its implications for resource control, or the subtle and subjective perceptions by others of national status and power. On the one hand, some may be inclined to shrug at what often appears a mindless race for proliferating colored dots and symbols on the map. At the opposite pole, others conjur up images of blocked chokepoints (Bab El Mandeb, Molucca Straits), interdicted sea lanes (Cape of Good Hope), and outflanked alliance and defensive positions (NATO and Mediterranean).

For much of the postwar period, the staple concerns of traditional geopolitics, i.e., control of space and lines of communication and transport, and spatial configurations of global conflict, were somewhat ignored, at least in a general, conceptual sense. Several factors contributed to this disinterest in traditional political geography. These included the centrality of the strategic nuclear balance, the role of ideology as a locus of world political conflict, and questionable assumptions about the declining military importance of distance factors (power over distance gradients). Also important here was the hitherto inability of the Soviet Union to project power over great distances.

Just very recently, however, there appears to have been a sudden, surprising increase in attention to geostrategic questions, and specifically, to the basing phenomenon evidenced in scholarly journals and also in the public political domain.(1) To a great extent, this no doubt has been merely a reflection of the spotlighting of some crucial recent events. The Azores Islands played an important role in the United States arms resupply of Israel in 1973. The Soviet Union utilized a lengthy staging network to supply its Angolan clients. There have been diplomacy and propaganda battles surrounding Berbera and Diego Garcia, as well as the United States-Turkey imbroglio over bases amidst the Cyprus crisis. There have been Arab attempts to buy the West out of bases in the Azores and Malta, and Soviet basing problems in Egypt, Syria, and Libya. Finally, Israel's use of Kenyan staging facilities on the way home from Entebbe dramatically helped focus attention on this issue.

Concurrently, the United States' postwar basing network is obviously contracting amid an overall withdrawal of power. The United States has been engaged in negotiations over renewal, acquisition, or disgorging of facilities in a number of dispersed areas: Spain, Greece, Thailand, the Philippines, Morocco, and Ethiopia, among others. In what is becoming a rapidly less permissive environment for American overseas bases, previously obscure placenames like Ramasun, Incirlik, Kagnew, Rota, and Sigonella have become daily fare on the nation's front pages.

Meanwhile, ongoing developments in military technology, as well as altered military requirements, have created needs for new types of overseas facilities, as well as changing the importance of traditional ones. Both superpowers, and some others as well, continue to maintain forward garrisons involving the stationing of army units, aircraft, and naval vessels. Such deployments may be for either offensive or defensive purposes in relation to general war contingencies, and they are often used to provide credibility for the deterrence of attacks on weaker client states or alliance partners. Otherwise, there are many traditional uses of facilities. These include training, often where uncongested space or certain kinds of terrain or weather are available; staging of arms, personnel, aircraft, and spare parts; refueling of aircraft; and naval repair, replenishment, refueling, and shore leave. Also important here are forward contingency positioning of war materiel and petroleum, oil, and lubricants (POL); antisubmarine (ASW) monitoring and other reconnaissance operations; and port visits which allow for "showing the flag," maintaining a presence, and demonstrating resolve.(2)

On a less visible and hence less sensitive level, there is the matter of aircraft overflight privileges, involving a range of practices and traditions. Some nations allow others more or less full unhindered and continuous overflight rights. In other cases, ad hoc formal applications for permission to overfly must be made well ahead of time; approval may or may not be granted depending upon the purpose and situation. Turkey and Yugoslavia, for instance, granted the Soviet Union over-flight rights during the 1973 airlift to the Arabs, while some NATO allies of America did not grant similar access to the United States on behalf of Israel.(3)

In addition to the traditional uses of basing and staging facilities, a variety of mostly new technical functions have come to require strategic access to the territory of others, varying in their applicability to strictly military purposes. These facilities for the most part can be broken down into function relating to intelligence, surveillance, and communications.   Among the numerous activities included here – utilizing terminology specific to the United States, but duplicated elsewhere – are communications (COMINT), signal (SIGINT), and electronic (ELINT) intelligence; naval and presidential or executive communications networks; LORAN and OMEGA navigational aid systems; satellite tracking networks; deep space surveillance; oceanographic research; nuclear test detection (seismographic and air sample collections); and underwater submarine detection. There are also a variety of esoteric facilities involved in monitoring both strategic and tactical missile tests. Many of these activities, while periodically cited and briefly discussed in the press, are shrouded in considerable secrecy and mystery and are thus technically obscure to the layman. Also in similarity to many staging bases, the functioning and importance of these facilities can often only be gauged in terms of global or regional networks, involving matters of complementarity and redundancy again usually beyond the view of casual scholarly observers.

Some overseas facilities may fall into a grey area between civilian and military use. The Soviet Union, for instance, has developed an extensive network of access for its large fleets of fishing vessels, some of which may have less benign than advertised roles. Stations for tracking satellites with predominantly civilian utility may also involve functions blurring into the military domain.

Another phenomenon of increasing importance is the growing nexus between base acquisitions and other types of international transactions. Most notable is the use of arms transfers as a quid pro quo, explicit or merely implied. This can be traced historically through three distinct phases describing changes in international basing systems: those of the interwar, early postwar, and recent postwar periods.(4)

Throughout the period between World War I and the early 1960s, the major powers, with the exceptions of Germany and the Soviet Union, were easily, almost automatically, availed or far-flung basing systems through colonial possessions or obvious tight spheres of influence.(5) Britain, of course, had the most highly developed global network. It stretched around the world through Gibraltar, Malta, Cyprus, Suez, Aden, Simonstown, Freetown, Mombasa, the Seychelles, Ascension, Ceylon, India, Burma, Singapore, and many, many other places.(6) France's smaller but still significant system included outposts in Vietnam, Djibouti, Reunion, Dakar, Bizerte, and Martinique. Even the United States, late getting into the race for imperial possessions, had facilities in the Philippines, Cuba, and elsewhere even before World War II.(7) During the early postwar years, intact colonial remnants and the permissive basing environment corresponding to the far-flung Western alliances and security commitments around the then Sino-Soviet periphery allowed Western strategists to take their strategic geographic assets almost for granted. The Soviet Union, although initially boxed in within its own continental empire, slowly expanded its basing facilities, most importantly in the Middle East and Cuba during the late 1950s and early 1960s.

In the past decade or so, however, basing rights have increasingly become items of exchange. As a result, arms transfers have entered the picture in a far more significant way. Before World War II, the arms trade was essentially a free wheeling bailiwick of private manufacturers and traders; only after 1945 was the sale of arms to become a really purposive instrument of diplomacy.(8) Even in the early postwar period, with its close correlation between military aid and basing rights, there was little tension between the two domains. Recipients welcomed both, assuming them additive and necessary to their own security; indeed, bases on a dependent nation's soil were thought to underpin the credibility of its protector's security commitments.

In recent years, particularly for the West, alliances and security commitments have become weaker and more tenuous. As many dependent nations have reoriented their foreign policies, the security formerly thought to derive from a foreign base presence has perhaps receded in importance. Many third world countries have now come to acquire arms from both Western and Soviet-bloc suppliers, often simultaneously, utilizing the leverage inherent in the availability of competing sources. Arms competition between the Soviet Union and the Western powers has become fully enmeshed in basing diplomacy. The former's revisionist drives now are underpinned by a more aggressive arms selling policy which, in turn, hinges upon a massive arms production base.

With specific reference to the Middle East, one major set of generalizations must be stated at the outset. On the one hand, the central crucial location of the region as a cockpit of superpower competition is difficult to gainsay. This position is derived from its overriding importance as a source of oil as well as its location at the juncture of three continents with its narrow chokepoints at Suez, the Bab El Mandeb, and the Straits of Hormuz. On the other hand, in relation to arms transfer policies, it is clear that economic rationales (oil supplies and related large export markets and balances-of-payments) predominate in the Middle East. This situation contrasts, to some extent, with that in other regions, particularly sub-Saharan Africa.

Some 70 percent of American arms transfers are now accounted for by the Near East; similar proportions exist for Britain and France. For the Soviet Union, the need for Western currency to finance technology imports acts to propel arms sales to oil-rich nations such as Libya, Kuwait, Iran, Iraq, and Algeria. This occurs in a manner perhaps transcending geopolitical rationales, though that is at least arguable. By contrast, relatively insignificant Soviet arms sales to sub-Saharan Africa, spread over some twenty client states, have achieved numerous points of strategic access in a very cost effective manner. Even here, however, economic rationales, such as access to resources and their denial to the West, are by no means absent. Of course, the now latent relationship between military access and oil supplies in the Middle East could one day become manifest.

DEFINING THE MIDDLE EASTERN REGION IN TERMS OF
STRATEGIC ACCESS AND GEOPOLITICAL STRATEGIES

In a static sense, the Middle East is generally not difficult to define in terms of boundaries. There are, however, some grey areas, and some peripheral regions may or may not be included from various perspectives. Surrounding the core areas of the Arab-Israeli confrontation, the Persian Gulf, and the Arabian peninsula, there are the peripheries of the Mahgreb; Turkey, Malta, Crete, and Cyprus; Sudan and the Horn of Africa; Afghanistan; and perhaps Pakistan.

However, it ought to be stressed that the strategic assets directly relevant to the Middle East are not confined to the region itself. Likewise, some assets located within the region (American intelligence bases in Turkey and Iran, for instance) are primarily important in terms of big power military calculations. These are essentially extrinsic to Middle Eastern politics and to the big powers' involvement in them. Some examples may serve to illustrate the point.

During the competitive, respective American and Soviet arms resupplying of Israel and the Arabs in 1973, the provision and denial of staging facilities and overflight rights outside the immediate Middle Eastern area were crucially important. Denied the use of facilities and air space all over Western Europe and along the Mediterranean littoral under the pressure of the Arab oil embargo, the United States and Israel were vitally dependent on the Portuguese Azores Islands. The Soviet Union, meanwhile, was allowed access to ports and airfields in Yugoslavia. It is not clear what mix of Soviet pressure and Yugoslavian sympathy for the Arab cause led to this important concession. In addition, the Soviet Union was allowed to overfly Turkey, a NATO ally of the United States which was also bound by Muslim solidarity.(9)

Haselkorn, among others, has pointed to an elaborate and structured Soviet security network stretching across the Middle East and South Asia. This network involves an interlocking system of bases and staging facilities unable for ferrying prepositioned military equipment to points of conflict.(10) It enabled Soviet aircraft to be quickly moved from Egypt, Syria, and Iraq to India during the most recent Indo-Pakistani War. More recently, the rapid Soviet arms buildup in Ethiopia has been expedited through arms caches in South Yemen and Libya. This provides a further manifestation of the linkage of forward positioning between the Middle East and places further afield.

The Soviet Union has, of course, made extensive use of Middle Eastern staging points for ferrying arms and advisors to Angola and Mozambique. Algeria and Libya were initial staging points en route to Angola, with facilities in Mali, Equatorial Guinea, Guinea, and the Congo utilized further along the route. A similar long-range network running through Libya, Iraq, South Yemen, and Tanzania has been used to supply Mozambique for war against Rhodesia. Soviet aspirations to add the Seychelles and Comoros Islands to this network are now becoming apparent.

The United States has also utilized overflight privileges from some moderate Arab states in the Middle East for supplying arms to Kenya

and Ethiopia, up to the recent sundering of the latter client relation-
ship. This has been particularly useful as overflying or staging through
Israel is considered too sensitive or provocative in sub-Saharan Africa.
Sudan and Zaire may together now provide the United States with a long
absent overflight corridor across the center of the African continent.
This may later have relevance to the Middle Eastern equation.

Soviet facilities in Aden and Socotra, and perhaps others now to be
added in Ethiopia, are most certainly a part of the central Middle
Eastern equation. They might be used in the event of a future anti-
Israel blockade at the entrance to the Red Sea and its exits. The Soviet
Union retains this capability even after the loss of its naval base at
Berbera in Somalia.

There are still other examples of the manner in which strategic
access outside the Middle East can feed back into its central conflict.
One is the Israeli use of the Nairobi airport after the Entebbe raid. The
American base at Diego Garcia may have some later importance for
staging or intervention activities related to Arab-Israeli or Persian Gulf
conflicts. On the periphery, there is the American P-3 Orion aircraft
surveillance network around the Indian Ocean, hinged on Mombasa,
Masirah, and Bandar Abbas. It is part of the war of nerves with the
Soviet Union in the Indian Ocean and affects others' perceptions of
evolving power equations in the area.

In short, strategic access into or out of the Middle East involves a
far-flung, complex, and often subtle set of factors. These are intimately
connected to the overall strategic nuclear balance and to symbolic
naval and airposturing over a wide expanse of territory.

Both of the superpowers utilize facilities in the Middle East across
the full spectrum previously outlined. There are, however, some
important differences between their requirements and uses. These
differences are primarily a function of the region's asymmetric
proximity to the Soviet heartland and its corresponding distance from
the United States. Also relevant are variations in force structure,
mixes of deployed military technology, and the extent and nature of
alliances and access in the region.

The United States, for instance, has a crucial interest in access
along the northern rim of the Middle East, particularly in Turkey and
Iran. It seeks access for intelligence listening posts, telemetry monitoring facilities in conjunction with Soviet missile tests, and perhaps
other technical functions. Earlier, it had based U-2 reconnaissance
aircraft in Turkey and Pakistan. Cuba, of course, now avails the Soviet
Union of offshore access for comparable purposes. The United States
also uses Middle Eastern bases in Turkey for its forward based, nuclear
armed aircraft as part of its strategic deterrent scheme vis-a-vis the
Soviet Union; obviously there is no Soviet equivalent.

The Soviet Union, despite considerable access to Mediterranean, Red
Sea, and Indian Ocean ports, still maintains an extensive system of
offshore anchorages.(11) The American use of some nuclear ships
reduces somewhat its requirements for access to naval refueling
facilities.

Whereas both powers prepare for a range of contingencies involving possible military interventions and seek access accordingly, here too there are some differences. Ability to stage military supplies to Israel in a crisis is a primary American consideration. Access is very precarious, particulary if the Azores will no longer be available for such a purpose. This is mitigated by the now bolstered American long-range transport capacity with aerial refueling. Soviet staging of supplies to the Arabs is a simpler matter, but overflight privileges in Turkey and Yugoslavia still remain a perhaps somewhat contingent matter in specific situations.

In the Persian Gulf and Indian Ocean, where the Soviet Union may contemplate interdicting Western oil supplies, the West thinks obversely in terms of protecting its lifelines. The Soviet Union, meanwhile, may be able to move large numbers of troops more easily and quickly to the Middle East than can the United States. Again, this is in part based on better access to staging facilities.

Both superpowers, of course, count on alliances and ideological affinities to provide access, either permanent or on an ad hoc basis during crises. However, whereas the Soviet Union seems to have assured access in almost any contingency in staunch radical bastions such as South Yemen, Iraq, Libya, and perhaps now Ethiopia, the United States must rely increasingly on ad hoc convergences of interest, given its weakened alliances and the often cross-purposes of their memberships. The 1973 War provided a graphic demonstration of that.

Concerning staging networks, the two major powers make perhaps asymmetric use of axes in different directions. The United States is primarily concerned with an east-west axis running from Gibraltar, across the Mediterranean to Israel, and for some contingencies, beyond that to Iran and Pakistan. For the eastern part of the Near East, routing supplies across the Pacific and Indian Oceans through Diego Garcia may offer an alternative. The Soviet Union, particularly in view of its expanded arms sales policy in Africa, makes greater use of a north-south network of staging points. American staging and overflight needs to supply clients in East Africa may be met either across central Africa, or perhaps via the Suez-Red Sea route. Some situations may, of course, allow for supply by sea, providing less onerous or at least less time-dependent requirements on both sides.

THE DEVELOPMENT OF SOVIET OVERSEAS BASING FACILITIES: ARMS TRANSFERS AND STRATEGIC ACCESS IN THE MIDDLE EAST

During the first decade of the cold war, up to the mid-1950s, the Soviet Union was almost totally lacking in overseas facilities, leaving aside the forward deployment of a massive land army in eastern Europe. In addition, it had a weak navy and little long-range air transport capability. Its only significant facilities outside of the Warsaw Pact were the navy bases at Porkalla, Finland, and Port Arthur in Chinese-controlled Manchuria. Both were returned to indigenous control during the 1950s. Later, from 1958-61, some use was made of submarine bases in Albania, which ended with the Sino-Soviet and Albania-Soviet breaks around 1961. The Soviet Union was essentially constrained, in terms of strategic access and overall geopolitical strategy, within the interior lines of a heartland empire. Some submarines were, however, deployed early in both major oceans.

Also, prior to 1955-56, Soviet arms transfers were limited primarily to the Warsaw Pact and China, i.e., within the then aptly designated Sino-Soviet bloc. The still relatively weak Soviet arms production base was almost entirely occupied with equipping Soviet-bloc forces. The United States and the United Kingdom controlled most of the arms markets in the developing world.

Beginning in the mid and late 1950s, however, the Soviet Union became a weightier factor in the arms markets of the developing world. Arms deals with Egypt and Syria in 1955 were harbingers. They were followed by the initiation of arms client relationships with North Yemen (1957), Indonesia (1958), Guinea (1959), India (1961), and indirectly, the Algerian rebels in the late 1950s.(12) Soviet arms supplies tended during this period to be large and concentrated in a few key client states, which served as initial wedges in cracking the iron ring of alliances around the Soviet Union set up by United States Secretary of State John Foster Dulles. The penetrations were based primarily on ideological affinity, even if that sometimes only entailed left-leaning neutralism on the part of recipients. Still, these initial arms client relationships did not immediately translate into overseas basing facilities for the Soviet Union.

A watershed was reached around 1964, in the wake of the Cuban missile crisis. The humiliated Soviet military leadership began, under Admiral Gorschkov's leadership, to attempt to rectify its exposed naval shortcomings, as well as to close the overall strategic nuclear gap.(13) It began its naval expansion with a limited deployment of submarines and surface ships to the Mediterranean, at a time when Soviet access to port facilities was restricted.(14) Mostly, its small Mediterranean fleet plied back and forth for limited periods from the Black Sea. Use was made of auxiliary ships for fuel, water, and other stores, as well as for routine maintenance.

After the 1967 War, during which the United States held clear naval superiority in the Mediterranean, the Soviet Union expanded its Mediterranean deployments. It began to make greater use of foreign ports and offshore anchorages, mainly in Egypt, but also in Syria, Yugoslavia, Algeria, and Morocco, all of which were primarily reliant on Soviet arms supplies at that point. In 1968, in a further step, there was a formal agreement with Egypt providing access for Soviet naval forces in Alexandria, Port Said, and Mersa Matruh. The agreement also allowed the use of Egyptian airfields by Soviet reconnaissance aircraft monitoring the eastern Mediterranean. The agreement corresponded with the massive Soviet arms shipments to Egypt between 1967 and 1972. In 1972, however, President Sadat expelled most Soviet personnel and curtailed access to the facilities. In 1975, Soviet access was completely terminated, but not without some pushing and shoving over the offshore anchorage at Sollum. Simultaneously, Soviet arms supplies to Egypt dropped off sharply, leaving the Egyptians to scrounge about for spare parts through third party transfers in India, North Korea, Yugoslavia, and some other Eastern European countries. In early 1976, Egypt apparently ended all Soviet access rights to Alexandria.(15)

As access to Egyptian facilities was curtailed after 1972, the Soviet Union attempted to compensate with expanded access to those in Syria. This involved regular use of the ports at Tartus and Latakia after the 1973 War. Ships used as floating repair and maintenance bases were transferred from Egypt to Syria. During the period between the 1973 War and the Lebanese crisis in 1976, the Soviet Union poured massive quantities of weapons into Syria: MIG-23 Flogger and SU-20 fighters; Scud missiles; SAM 3, 6, and 7; T-62 tanks; modern artillery and armored personnel carriers (APCs). Among Soviet motives was to signal clients of the benefits derived from providing the Soviet Union with desired strategic access.

Then in 1976 during the Lebanese crisis, the Egyptian pattern was partially repeated in Syria. When Soviet arms supplies were curtailed, the Syrians began to limit access to the Soviet navy.(16) The Soviet Union then began to concentrate its Middle Eastern arms supplies in Iraq. In addition to all of the usually supplied modern systems, the Russians provided Scud missiles; Tu-22B Blinder bombers, otherwise sold only to Libya in the Middle East; and MIG-25 Foxbats. They also concluded an agreement with Iraq which apparently allowed full Soviet access to Iraqi air and naval bases.(17) Simultaneously, greatly increased Soviet arms shipments and the sale of some nuclear technology to Libya seemed aimed at achieving naval and/or air facilities further west in the Mediterranean. These sales were well beyond the country's absorptive capacity and were supplemented by considerable amounts of French, Italian, and British arms. By early 1977, however, full access to Tobruk and Benghazi had not yet been granted. Parallel Soviet aims at acquiring substantial Western currency were, however, satisfied.(18)

Still further west in the Mediterranean, Soviet arms supplies to Algeria and Morocco had also achieved some strategic access. Algeria had long been primarily reliant on Soviet arms and received increased shipments in 1976-77 as tensions with Morocco over Spanish Sahara mounted. Some Soviet access to Algerian ports has been granted, though not full use of the large ex-French base at Mers El Kebir. The Soviet Union has also apparently used Algerian as well as Libyan airfields for staging military supplies to Angola and Mozambique. Morocco, an important Soviet arms client in the early 1960s, which presently still receives some Soviet arms while relying primarily on the United States and France, has allowed Soviet port visits. Spain has as well. Meanwhile, the Soviet Union has made extensive use of offshore anchorages throughout the Mediterranean, near both its own arms clients and NATO countries such as Greece.(19)

All around the vast Indian Ocean littoral, and particularly in areas related to the Middle East, the Soviet Union has also judiciously utilized arms transfers as an opening wedge leading to grants of strategic access.(20) The Soviet naval presence in the Indian Ocean, negligible up to 1968, has grown steadily in the interim. For the most part, arms client relationships have preceded the granting of strategic access. India, Indonesia, Pakistan, Iraq, both Yemens, Sudan, and Tanzania were significant recipients of Soviet arms during the early and mid-1960s, before the deployment of a Soviet Indian Ocean naval force. Arms transfer relationships can thus, in some cases, be perceived as chips which were later to be cashed in gradually for strategic access.

The Soviet Union now has some degree of strategic access in a number of Indian Ocean locales; the major naval base facilities are in South Yemen and Iraq. Somalia, of course, earlier provided the Soviet Union with its major air and naval facilities in the region, after long having received massive — for the region — Soviet arms shipments. These began with transfers of MIGs in 1963, and tanks and APCs in 1965. They were then extended to a wide range of weaponry which continues to menace regional rivals in Kenya and Ethiopia. Port facilities at Berbera and Chisimaio and an airfield in Hargeisa provided the Soviet Union with POL, maintenance, shore leave, a floating drydock, landing fields for Tu-95 Bear D reconnaissance aircraft, and communications facilities. There was also apparently a facility for handling Styx ship-to-ship missiles.(21)

The further of Soviet access in the Horn area, and hence continued Soviet presence at the entrance to the Red Sea, has recently been enmeshed in a complicated and rapidly changing diplomatic situation. Now-radicalized Ethiopia is engaged in a massive arms buildup with Soviet equipment, while Sudan has moved into the western arms orbit. Somalia, while still pledging fealty to the "world Socialist movement," has moved out of the Soviet orbit and is trying to obtain Western arms with Saudi financing. Generally, a contest for control over the Red Sea and Bab El Mandebhas developed, which pits the Soviet Union and its radical friends against a Saudi-led coalition of moderate Arab states. The former French base at Djibouti is now up for grabs following its independence. It is at least possible that a Soviet-backed Ethiopia — particularly if it should lose Assab and Massawa to the Eritrean independence movement — will attempt to take it over by way of compensation.

Otherwise, South Yemen has received Soviet arms since 1967, acquiring its first tanks in that year and then MIGs in 1969. It began to allow the Soviet navy to use strategically located Aden in 1968. Later, refueling facilities for Soviet naval aircraft as well as some use of the island of Socotra were provided.(22)

Iraq has been an important Soviet arms client since 1958. It has recently escalated its purchases, but also has utilized its oil wealth to diversify by making considerable purchases of French arms. The new agreement with the Soviet Union apparently allows the Russians to use naval facilities on the Persian Gulf at Umm Quasr and Basra, as well as several inland air bases.(23)

On balance, the Soviet Union has experienced mixed fortunes in its drive to achieve dominant strategic access in the Middle East and on its perimeters. It has, however, exhibited considerable flexibility and opportunism. It moves quickly and decisively to cut losses and to open still other gates when rebuffed, always with prompt and massive doses of military assistance. Setbacks in Egypt and, to a lesser degree, in Syria were partly offset in Libya and Iraq; access in Ethiopia has been traded off for access in Somalia and Sudan. Ideological imperatives involving competition both with the United States and China, as well as the complexities of strategies to deal with the more moderate Arab states, have acted to complicate and balance off military requirements for strategic access.

Keeping in mind the perceived necessity of preparing for virtually all contingencies and for redundant access to hedge against loss of some facilities, the evolving Soviet strategy involving bases and access, underpinned by arms supplies, appears to involve the following elements.

– The Soviet Union seeks staging facilities, forward positioning of war materiel, and emplacement of small fire brigade forces to deal with the possibility of direct military intervention or the threat of same to provide deterrence. Intervention might be envisaged for another Arab-Israeli conflict, either in Sinai or Syria or both; on behalf of Libya vis-a-vis Egypt and Sudan; or on behalf of Ethiopia vis-a-vis Somalia or Sudan. The Soviets might also intervene on behalf of South Yemen versus Iran; Oman or Saudi Arabia; or to counter a hypothetical American attempt at taking over Persian Gulf oilfields. Crucial in all of these contingencies are naval port facilities, airfields for use of Soviet tactical aircraft, overflight privileges, and access to airfields for staging of troops and material. Also crucial is the proximity of Soviet facilities to the key regional chokepoints: Gibraltar, Suez, Bab El Mandeb, and the Straits of Hormuz.

– The Soviet Union seeks staging facilities and overflight rights for the movement of arms and personnel to potential areas of conflict all over sub-Saharan Africa and to Indian Ocean islands such as the Seychelles and Mauritius, as well as for movement of material along an east-west axis stretching from North Africa across to South Asia.

– Soviet access is necessary to provide intelligence and surveillance of the American fleets in the Mediterranean and Indian Ocean, particularly when using long-range naval reconnaissance aircraft.

– Soviet bases and access offer visual evidence of a Soviet presence, and are intended to impress others with Russia's growing strength (showing the flag).

– The strategy is designed to intimidate pro-Western regimes, and intended to force them into a more accommodating posture vis-a-vis Moscow.

– It is also meant to strengthen relations between Soviet client states such as Iraq, Syria, Libya, South Yemen, and India. They will be drawn into an at least implicit security network involving the movement of materiel, advisers, and so on.

As part of a continuing policy to weaken Western Europe and drive it towards "Finlandization," the strategy provides Western Europe with a pessimistic cognitive map involving the outflanking of Southern Europe and the realization of Soviet influence over Middle Eastern oil supplies. This policy also presumably is directed, in a psychological sense, at bolstering the growing tide of Euro-Communism in Italy, Spain, Portugal, and France and at putting further pressure on Yugoslavia, Greece, and Malta.

The Soviet Union must, of course, worry that an expanding overseas presence will engender anxieties about a new imperialism and about infringements of sovereignty in nations still hypersensitive to such considerations in a post colonial context. Soviet experiences in Egypt and Sudan have borne this out. The Soviet Union has also had access limited for these very reasons even where, as in Libya and Algeria, a rather strong ideological affinity and convergence of policies exist. Thus, strivings for continuous expansion of influence are somewhat tempered. Overall Soviet strategy now appears one of flexible movement, opportunism, taking advantage of subregional conflicts and tensions to tilt in one direction or another, and acquisition of facilities in the process as a quid pro quo.

One other key point bears mention here. Concerning economy and concentration of effort, it is rather clear that Russia's vast expansion of basing assets has been achieved at relatively low cost. For, although data on the mix of Soviet arms trade and aid in various places are not easy to come by, it is clear that many bases have been acquired merely through extensive cash arms sales; Chapter 5 discusses the Soviet Arms trade policy. Often, bases have been acquired where the Soviet Union has provided clients access to weapons sufficiently sophisticated in the regional context so that qualitative advantages over rivals have been achieved. This has been most evident through africa, where in the face of some Western efforts to control qualitative levels of arming, the Soviet Union has usually introduced supersonic jets and tanks to its clients first.

Of course, the strategic value of a given nation to a major power may not, and normally will not, bear any relationship to the size of its arms markets. That is determined by location (access to the sea, control over key chokepoints) and land area. The Soviet Union has thus been able to acquire some major strategic assets, for instance, in Somalia, South Yemen, and Mali, in exchange for arms sales at a very modest level relative to those in some of the world's more heavily armed hot spots, such as in the central Middle Eastern area and South Asia. Soviet arms sales to some key major basing hosts in the decade 1965-74 were: South Yemen ($114 million), Guinea ($42 million), Mali ($12 million), and Somalia ($134 million). Egypt – where Soviet access has now been curtailed – and Syria accounted for $2,465 million and $1,758 million, respectively, during the same period. Again, these were mostly arms sales, not aid.(24) Comparisons will be made subsequently between these costs and those now being demanded of the United States for the renting of bases by some of its erstwhile clients.

US ARMS TRANSFERS AND STRATEGIC ACCESS

The previous postwar and current development of the relationship between American basing facilities and arms transfers has, of course, been very distinct from the Soviet experience in the Middle East and elsewhere. In the immediate wake of World War II and at the onset of the cold war, the United States and its allies were provided with a very extensive global basing system by colonial remnants, through alliances, by economic and military aid relationships, and generally, as a consequence of the force deployments emerging from World War II. The Soviet Union gradually built a global basing system mostly through new arms client relationships, and this process accelerated after 1960. The West, on the other hand, has experienced a gradual degradation of its strategic assets. It has been forced to assume considerable and increasing economic and political costs in order to cling to some still very extensive and dispersed positions.(25)

The United States now maintains or controls most of the useable Western basing facilities. The following is a brief review of the American global basing network. It is examined both in the context of arms transfer relationships and as applied to an extended definition of the Middle Eastern strategic milieu.

The United States has, of course, numerous facilities in Western Europe and in the Atlantic area through its NATO alliance. Some of these, however, may not be available for purposes not directly connected with NATO's primary ostensible mission, defending against Soviet aggression. This possibility was indicated during the 1973 War. The Turkey-Greece imbroglio over Cyprus has also indicated the overall precariousness of some American base facilities. This certainly holds true to the extent that their continued use depends heavily on a continuing flow of arms supplies to the host countries.

The United States is also still able to make use of some facilities in areas outside of Europe controlled by NATO allies. In some cases these are applicable to Middle Eastern contingencies. The large base in the Portuguese-owned Azores, Diego Garcia in the Indian Ocean, and perhaps in some cases, the British air base at Akotiri on Cyprus, which has been used to stage U-2 flights over the Middle East, are the most important. It is not clear whether Lajes could now be used for another American resupply of Israel during a war. Improvements in American long-range air transport capability (extended ranges and enhanced aerial refueling capability) will by now have mitigated the problem somewhat, albeit with tradeoffs in terms of higher transport costs and lower load efficiency.(26) The United States has been attempting, in conjunction with other NATO powers, to bolster the Portuguese military and to keep it within NATO. This is done partly to extend American access to the Azores bases, which are useful for antisubmarine warfare and surveillance activities as well as for staging.

Around the Mediterranean, American strategic access has been dwindling as Soviet assets have been enhanced. Many of the bases used by American forces now would not be available for Middle Eastern operations on behalf of Israel. Still, important bases are maintained in Europe and the Near East. In Spain, there are strategic and tactical air bases and facilities for aerial refueling and submarine maintenance. In Italy, United States Sixth Fleet has its homeport plus numerous other facilities on the mainland and in Sicily and Sardinia. In Greece, there are airfields and communications and intelligence facilities, on the mainland and on Crete. Turkey tentatively provides airfields, communications, intelligence, and so on.(27) The nexus between access and arms transfers is most obvious in the latter two cases. Maintained or increased arms supplies, for forces now partially deployed against each other, have become a regional price for continued access to vital facilities.

The United States navy also visits Moroccan and Tunisian ports and maintains a naval communications facility in Morocco. Both of the moderate North African states now rely primarily on American arms to balance massive Soviet shipments to rivals in Libya and Algeria. Morocco also receives weapons from France and the Soviet Union; Tunisia from France and Italy. Continued access is a primary American rationale for continued supply. Both nations have been requesting escalated qualitative levels of weaponry (modern aircraft, missiles, helicopters, and air defense systems) to match those possessed by their rivals. The American interest in impeding escalated arms races conflicts here with its interest in continuing strategic access.

Around the Indian Ocean, American arms transfers have been used to maintain scattered enclaves of strategic access to match the expanding Soviet basing network, most notably in Iran, Oman, Kenya, Ethiopia, and Singapore. Iran, in conjunction with massive American arms shipments including an impressive array of modern sophisticated systems such as the F-14 fighter, Spruance-class warships, and TOW antitank missiles, has allowed the United States access to crucial communications and intelligence facilities. These would become all the more critical as backups if use of Turkish bases were lost or restricted.

On the southern arc of the Middle East in the Horn of Africa, the formerly important American arms supply relationship with Ethiopia has been sundered. With it has gone American use of the Kagnew communications complex which had, at any rate, become superfluous because of the introduction of new surrogate satellite technology as well as backup facilities in Iran, although the 1978-79 crisis in Iran has placed the continued functioning of American bases there in some doubt. A growing arms supply relationship with heretofore moderate and threatened Kenya, beginning with sales of F-5E aircraft, has allowed continued American naval visits to Mombasa and the possible use of Kenyan airfields for staging P-3 Orion surveillance flights over the Indian Ocean.(28) It remains to be seen whether American displacement of Soviet influence in Sudan, and perhaps also Somalia will result in corresponding American strategic assets. Increased United States navy use of Port Sudan and overflight rights in Sudan and across Zaire are possibly involved in calculations of whether or not to initiate a major arms supply relationship.

Oman, now a significant recipient of American arms and also closely tied to Iran, allows staging of P-3 Orion flights from Masirah Island in the wake of the British departure from a long held base.(29) Diego Garcia, meanwhile, will provide an important strategic outpost in the middle of the Indian Ocean. It will be used by naval and air units as well as, presumably, for a variety of other functions. This use would apparently be subject to an ad hoc British veto in specific situations. The veto would most likely apply to situations involving assistance to Israel, particularly if home bases in the United Kingdom were similarly rendered off-limits to the United States.(30)

Overall, the picture provided is one of a still extensive though dwindling American basing network broadly encompassing the Middle Eastern Region. The maintenance of strategic assets is crucially dependent on continued arms supplies and also on continuing security commitments. There is not, of course, always a one-to-one correspondence between arms supply and strategic access. Both the United States and Soviet Union have numerous arms clients where weapons have not been translated into access. This has even occurred in some places where their arms predominate. Sensitivity to sovereignty, low supplier leverage, resentment of supplier support of rivals, and even the lack of a supplier's desire for bases are the main reasons for the lack of one-to-one correspondence.

American arms supplies have not resulted in significant basing rights in Jordan, Israel, Kuwait, or Saudi Arabia. However, Israel and perhaps Jordan might be used for staging activities on an ad hoc basis in some foreseeable contingencies. Some scenarios earlier bruited the use of Israeli air bases for a hypothetical American invasion of the Persian Gulf oilfields. This possibility is now a perhaps more fanciful scenario in light of the apparently increasing pro-Arab tilt of American policies. Likewise, Soviet arms have not produced comprehensive or even significant basing facilities in Algeria, Libya, and Sudan, though some access has been granted for overflights, port visits, minor technical facilities, and routine refueling.

The most significant aspect of current American basing problems involves the vastly increased economic and political costs demanded by formerly willing hosts. Some of them no longer perceive their security problems as altogether congruent with American interests, and they may also be under considerable domestic political pressure to reduce the visible American profile. Needless to say, the United States defeat in Vietnam has contributed to this process in reducing its prestige and credibility. It has also emboldened indigenous radical political forces to push for American withdrawal.

During the recent past, the United States has been involved in strenuous negotiations and political struggles over key basing facilities in Spain, Greece, Turkey, and in particular, the Philippines. A Treaty of Friendship and Cooperation was signed in 1976 with Spain. This extended the use of most critical American facilities with the exception of the Rota submarine base which will be phased out in 1979.(31) The price for the United States was somewhat above $1 billion in military and economic aid plus additional Eximbank loan commitments to be delivered over a five-year period. There were also commitments to modernize Spanish forces with advanced weapons systems such as the F-16 fighter. Similar negotiations were in progress with Greece and were emeshed in some serious status of forces issues. The United States seemed willing to provide a military aid package in the neighborhood of $700 million to extend the use of its numerous facilities.(32)

Overall, American interests in maintaining forward access in and around the Middle East can be summarized according to the following set of criteria, paralleling and in counterpoise to the aforementioned Soviet strategy:

– The United States seeks to maintain at least essential equivalence in naval and air combat capability with the Soviet Union in the Mediterranean, for a variety of subnuclear and even all-out nuclear contingencies.

– The United States wants to ensure the adequate staging of weapons to Israel, and to other American allies or dependencies in the Middle East, in the case of open hostilities.

– The United States seeks to provide a presence in support of Greece, Turkey, and Yugoslavia, for purposes of deterrence, demonstrations of strength, and overall diplomatic support.

– Intelligence and surveillance networks around the southern rim of the Soviet Union and Warsaw Pact are sought for monitoring nuclear tests, telemetry monitoring of missile tests, communications intercepts, and the like.

– Staging facilities are required to move arms either from the United States or Western Europe to clients in the Middle East, South Asia, and Africa. This involves countries such as Saudi Arabia, Kuwait, Iran, Pakistan, Sudan, Kenya, Israel, and Zaire.

– The United States wants to support a permanent naval presence in the Mediterranean, Red Sea, Indian Ocean, Persian Gulf aimed among other things at keeping the sea lanes open for the transport of oil.

– Finally, forward access is sought to provide air bases from which to mount surveillance patrols over Soviet ship movements throughout the area.

To some extent, of course, the primary aim of maintaining the capability to resupply Israel with arms contradicts some of the others. American support of Israel has rendered its bases in places like Bahrain and Masirah precarious. This is particularly true since the radical, rejectionist Arab states have had a propaganda field day in castigating their more moderate brethren for availing the United States of facilities which might be used on Israel's behalf, even if it is obvious that such use would not be allowed in a crisis. Likewise, American efforts to retain access both in Greece and Turkey – both of which cases are linked to demands for arms – have come into conflict, and the attempt to mollify each may have served to alienate both. There are parallels here with the recent Soviet dilemma involving Ethiopia and Somalia.

It has been indicated that the global competition for basing rights, largely acquired as quid pro quo for arms transfer relationships, has pretty much been a two nation game. This state of affairs reflects the fact that only the United States and the Soviet Union now have global security interests and responsibilities in addition to a global military reach. For the other major powers, the arms trade has primarily been a commercial matter. Arms sales have been useful for rectifying payments imbalances, maintaining domestic employment, and assuring continued viable indigenous arms production bases; Chapter 5 discusses

Western European arms sales both in general and with specific reference to the Middle East.

Other Western Suppliers

France, as the world's third largest arms supplier, but without a really global navy or long-range intervention capability, has not often, if at all, used its arms supplies as a wedge for gaining strategic access. Many or all of its major arms clients — Saudi Arabia, South Africa, Iraq, Libya, Brazil, and Pakistan — provide it with no bases. France's current major overseas basing problem seems to be that of finding a new home for its small Indian Ocean fleet now that Djibouti is independent. Some very recent reports do, however, point to French aspirations for access on both African coasts. French Jaguar aircraft based at Dakar reportedly have been used in Spanish Sahara.(33)

Britain, too, no longer sells or gives away arms to maintain strategic access. Like France, it sales rationales are primarily economic. Its now constricted basing system, with Malta, Mauritius, and Masirah being phased out and Cyprus precarious, is essentially divorced from its arms transfer policy.

COMPETITIVE BASE DENIAL STRATEGIES AND ACTIVITIES

The geopolitical strategies of each of the superpowers, and of some others as well, have been directed not only at obtaining and hanging on to bases. They have equally been aimed at nudging rivals out of bases or at preventing opponents from acquiring them. A variety of instruments have been used to that end: economic and security inducements, threats, propaganda, and preemptive base acquisition.

The Soviet Union, in particular, has long mounted a strenuous propaganda effort, much of it through foreign language broadcasts aimed at creating political pressures on the United States and other Western bases. This propaganda effort always escalates during American bilateral base negotiations. It is focused on the allegedly unequal status of forces agreements, the menace of American bases to neighboring countries, and generally, the symbolic dependency issue.

Recently, the Soviet Union has placed considerable emphasis on exposing what it perceives, correctly or not, to be the development of new American basing networks and strategies. The manner in which this is done often reveals Moscow's global cognitive map. In the Middle East, Oman and Bahrain have been prominent recent targets of Soviet propaganda. The United States as well has often used both carrots and sticks in an attempt to block the expansion of the Soviet basing network. Still limited American arms supplies and economic aid have helped pry Egyptian bases from Soviet control. A similar pattern may be in the initial stages in Syria.

Oil rich OPEC nations have also now become factors in the base-denial game. Arab financial leverage has been used to jeopardize

American use of the Azores as well as to deny the West further use of Malta.(34) Saudi money has been used to turn Sudan from its prior Soviet arms client status although access was also at stake. A similar attempt may now be made to convert North Yemen and Somalia. All this is part of a Saudi strategy to turn the Red Sea into a Soviet-free Arab lake that is menacing to Israel. India's laments to the United States with respect to Diego Garcia and other Indian Ocean bases constitute a further common example of base-denial activities.

SOME CONCLUDING GENERALIZATIONS
ON BASES AND ARMS TRANSFERS

Amid the welter of detail describing the nexus between big power strategic access and arms transfers in the Middle East, a number of broad generalizations are suggested. Among them are those dealing with:

— the correlation between various types of arms transfer acquisition patterns and degrees of access provided the major powers;

— interpretations of basing strategies along the traditional lines of overall status quo and revisionist foreign policy orientations;

— big power spatial strategies and related cognitive maps, corresponding to the gradual ongoing shift from a mutual heartland-rimland confrontation to a much more diffuse, dispersed, and less ideological competition; and

— the conflict, for the United States at least, between geopolitical strategies and arms control goals.

Concerning the first of these, the preceding analysis has demonstrated the obvious truism that there is a high correlation between arms transfer acquisition patterns and the granting of strategic access. Of course, given the current importance of arms transfers as an instrument of diplomacy, they may clearly be described as an intervening variable measuring overall association. As such they are underpinned by ideological affinity and by the facts of alliances and other kinds of security arrangements.

Most basing arrangements seem to occur where a recipient acquires all or most of its arms from one supplier.(35) Conversely, multiple-source acquisition of arms more often than not occurs where no major power has significant strategic access. This is particularly true if the recipient obtains both Western and Soviet-block arms simultaneously. Multiple-source acquisition indicates a degree of neutrality or ideological even-handedness.

Virtually all the dependent nations in the Middle East and on its peripheries which have granted the Soviet Union major basing facilities receive most of their arms from Russia. This is true of Syria, South

Yemen, Iraq, and until recently Somalia. Iraq has, however, now begun to acquire some French materiel, including Mirage F-1 fighters, while vastly increasing its acquisitions from Russia. It is also noteworthy that those major and primarily Soviet clients which have maintained diversified arms sources across the blocs have also demonstrated some reluctance to grant the Soviet Union major facilities. This category includes Libya and to some extent, Algeria. This may in some cases have less to do with lack of complete ideological affinity than with the recipient's diplomatic leverage, based on size and wealth, as it translates into the availability of alternative sources of arms. The contrast between Libya and India versus Somalia and Angola may be instructive. At the same time, the impact of a Soviet presence in deterring external threats may also play a role here. In no case does the Soviet Union have major basing facilities where American or other western arms predominate.

The same generalizations hold for the hosts to major American bases. Greece, Turkey, Spain, and Portugal have all relied primarily on American arms. There are only a few cases where American and other Western basing rights coexist with some Soviet arms supplies to the host. Iran and Morocco are the most notable cases, along with the complicated and anomalous one of Cyprus. What earlier could have been described as a competition for strategic access fitting the heartland-rimland paradigm has now become a much more complex and less easily defined game as both sides seek crucial, dispersed points of access all around the globe.

Both superpowers now have at least some naval and air points of access in virtually every area of the globe. The vast and dispersed proliferation of Marxist regimes, most of which are Soviet arms clients, has long since shattered the old United States containment policy. In Africa, for instance, there are now around twenty regimes which have become Soviet-bloc arms clients. These include: Libya, Algeria, Sudan, Ethiopia, Tanzania, Uganda, Burundi, Mozambique, Zambia, Angola, Equirotial Guinea, Congo-Brazzaville, Nigeria, Togo, Benin, Chad, the Central African Republic, Mali, Guinea, Guinea-Bissau, and Madagascar. Peru, Cuba, and perhaps also Guyana and Jamaica have cracked the American latter-day Monroe Doctrine policy in Latin America. Above all, of course, the shift in focus from east-west to north-south issues, and from political-military to economic issues in an age of resource shortages has lent a new meaning to geopolitical strategies on both sides. These questions are thus superimposed upon the traditional bipolar American-Soviet nuclear strategic competition.

The Soviet counterpart of the containment doctrine, from the Soviet perspective, was long tied to the perception of "capitalist encircle-ment," implying a weak and defensive posture and a corresponding global strategy. The Soviet strategic breakout, as measured by the development of a global basing system, is one aspect of an obviously altered perception toward a new "objective correlation of forces." Soviet rhetoric now often implies an overall offensive strategy. Containment has long since been leapfrogged, and Western economies, their overall strengths notwithstanding, are now subject to precarious overseas resource dependence.(36)

NOTES AND REFERENCES

(1) A good analysis of the postwar lack of attention to traditional geopolitical modes of analysis is in Geoffrey Kemp, "The New strategic Map: Geography, Arms Diffusion and the Southern Seas" (Paper delivered at the Fletcher School's conference on the "Implications of the Military Build-Up in Non-Industrial States," Boston, May 6-8, 1976). See also Robert E. Walters, The Nuclear Trap (Baltimore: Penguin, 1974); and Colin Gray, The Geopolitics of the Nuclear Era (New York: Crane, Russak, 1977) for lengthier expositions of some of the same themes.

(2) For general material on the breakdown of various types of facilities and associated defnitions, see Herbert G. Hagerty, Forward Deployment in the 1970's and 1980's, National Security Affairs Monograph 77-2 (Washington, D.C.: National Defense University, 1977); Richard B. Foster et al., Implications of the Nixon Doctrine for the Defense Planning Process (Menlo Park, California: Stanford Research Institute, 1972), prepared for Office, Chief of Research and Development, US Army, Part IV D; and B.M. Blechman and R.G. Weinland, "Why Coaling Stations are Necessary in the Nuclear Age," International Security 2 (Summer 1977): 88-99.

(3) On Yugoslav policy during the 1973 War, see Laurence Silberman, "Yugoslavia's 'Old' Communism," Foreign Policy no. 26 (Spring 1977): 3-27; and Avigdor Haselkorn, "The Soviet Collective Security System," Orbis 19 (Spring 1975): 231-54.

(4) Among the various attempts at describing and theorizing in terms of epochal international systems, see Morton A. Kaplan, System and Process in International Politics (New York: Wiley, 1957); Richard Rosecrance, Action and Reaction in World Politics (Boston: Little, Brown, as is according to National Union Catalogue, 1963); Kenneth J. Holsti, International Politics (Englewood Cliffs, New Jersey: Prentice-Hall, 1967), especially Chapters 2, 3; and Robert E. Harkavy, The Arms Trade and International Systems (Cambridge; Ballinger, 1975).

(5) For data and general analyses of interwar basing systems, see George Weller, Bases Overseas (New York: Harcourt, Brace, and Company 1944); and R. Ernest Dupuy, World in Arms (Harrisburg, Pennsylvania: The Military Service Publishing Co., 1939).

(6) See D.H. Cole, Imperial Military Geography (London: Sifton Praed and Co., 1950); Paul M. Kennedy, The Rise and Fall of British Naval Mastery (London: Allen Lane, 1976); and Gerald S. Graham, The Politics of Naval Supremacy (London: Cambridge University Press, 1965).

(7) On American bases prior to World War II, see Weller (note 5 supra), and Buel W. Patch, "American Naval and Air Bases," Editorial Research Report (Washington, D.C.) 1 (February 1939).

(8) See Harkavy especially Chapter 2 (note 4 supra).

(9) On Yugoslavian policy during the 1973 War, see Silberman (note 3 supra); Haselkorn (note 3 supra); and "Yugoslavs Report that Tito Rebuffed Brezhnev on Air and Naval Rights and Role in the Warsaw Pact," New York Times (January 9, 1977): 8.

(10) Haselkorn (note 3 supra).

(11) for information on Soviet offshore anchorages in the Mediterranean, see "Instability in NATO Examined," Washington Post (April 18, 1976): A17-A18.

(12) The dates of initiation of Soviet arms client relationships can be pinpointed in the Stockholm International Peace Research Institute (SIPRI), Arms Trade Registers (Cambridge, Mass.: MIT Press, 1974) and broken down by recipients and by armed services: army, navy, and air equipment.

(13) On Soviet naval expansion aims, see Sergei G. Gorschkov, Red Star Rising at Sea, trans. T.A. Neely, Jr. (Annapolis: US Naval Institute, 1974). See particularly the final chapter entitled "Some Problems in Mastering the World Ocean."

(14) See C. Joynt and O.M. Smolansky, Soviet Naval Policy in the Mediterranean, Research Monograph no. 3 (Bethlehem, Pennsylvania: Lehigh University, Department of International Relations, 1972); and the chapters by Alvin Z. Rubinstein et al., Soviet Naval Policy, eds. M. MccGwire, Ken Booth, and John McDonnell (New York: Praeger, 1975).

(15) See Robert O. Freedman, "The Soviet Union and Sadat's Egypt" Chapter 12 in MccGwire, ibid.

(16) See "Syria-USSR: Soviets Asked to Leave Syrian Naval Port," Defense and Foreign Affairs Daily (January 14, 1977).

(17) See "Iraq: Defense Protocol with USSR," Defense and Foreign Affairs Daily (October 13, 1976).

(18) See "Libya: Soviets Building up Tobruk," Defense and Foreign Affairs Daily (August 25, 1976).

(19) For information on Soviet offshore anchorages in the Mediterranean, see Washington Post (note 11 supra).

(20) See, inter alia, MccGwire (note 14 supra); Geoffrey Jukes, The Indian Ocean in Soviet Naval Policy, Adelphi Paper no. 57 (London: International Institute for Strategic Studies, 1969); W. Adie, Oil, Politics and Seapower: The Indian Ocean Vortex (New York: Crane, Russak, 1975); and George E. Hudson, "Soviet Naval Doctrine and Soviet

Politics, 1953-1975," World Politics 29 (October 1976): 90-113.

(21) Among numerous articles on Soviet facilities in Somalia, see "Somalia-USSR: Major Naval Complex Nearly Ready," Defense and Foreign Affairs Daily (January 7, 1977); and J. Bowyer Bell, "Strategic Implications of the Soviet Presence in Somalia," Orbis 19 (Summer 1975): 402-14.

(22) Note of Soviet use of an intelligence facility on Socotra is made in "USSR: Intelligence Ship Deployment: Naval Deployment in Mozambique," Defense and Foreign Affairs Daily (August 3, 1976).

(23) See (note 17 supra).

(24) These data are drawn from the US Arms Control and Disarmament Agency, World Military Expenditures and Arms Transfers (Washington, D.C.: US Government Printing Office, 1976), an annual publication. It should be noted, however, that Soviet transfers to some of these African countries have accelerated since 1974.

(25) For a somewhat pessimistic analysis of the decline of American basing assets, see Alvin J. Cottrell and Thomas H. Moorer, U.S. Overseas Bases: Problems of Projecting American Military Power Abroad, The Washington Papers, no. 47 (Washington, D.C.: Georgetown Center for Strategic and International Studies, 1977).

(26) See "High Stakes in the Azores," The Nation Magazine (November 8, 1975); and "In-Flight Refueling in Aid C-5 Wing Life," Aviation Week and Space Technology 105 (12 July 1976): 32-34.

(27) On US Spanish bases see, inter alia, Stephen S. Kaplan, "The Utility of U.S. Military Bases in Spain and Portugal" (Paper, Brookings Institution, 1976); "Spain Pact Has Plusses for Both Sides," Washington Star (March 4, 1976): A4; "Secret U.S.-Spain Airlift Accord Told," Washington Post (October 11, 1976): A24; and "No Secret Pact on Bases, Spain Says," Washington Post (October 14, 1976): A25. On American bases in Greece, see "Rising Hatred of U.S. in Greece is Imperiling a Vital Defense Flank," Wall Street Journal (January 6, 1976); and "U.S., Greece Initial Pact on Military Bases and Aid," New York Times (April 16, 1976): 3. On American bases in Turkey, see "The Turkish Bases: A Turning Point in Ties with U.S.," New York Times (July 31, 1976): 9; "Turks Expect to Close U.S. Bases if Congress Rejects Military Aid," New York Times (September 28, 1976): 12; and "U.S., Turkey, Renew Talks on Bases," Washington Post (March 25, 1976): A14. See also US Library of Congress, Congressional Research Service, Foreign Affairs and National Defense Division, United States Military Installations and Objectives in the Mediterranean, prepared for the Committee on International Relations, Subcommittee on Europe and the Middle East (Washington, D.C.: US Government Printing Office, 1977).

(28) "Kenya Offers New Flexibility to U.S. Indian Ocean P-3 Patrols," Baltimore Sun (July 30, 1976), reprinted in U.S. Naval Institute Proceedings 102 (October 1976): 143-5.

(29) On US base activities in Masirah, see "Oman: UK to leave Masirah by March 1977," Defense and Foreign Affairs Daily (July 21, 1976); and "Masirah: Oman Denies Possibility of U.S. Presence." In the same issue, see also "Bahrain: NATO Warships Welcome in the Gulf" See also "UK Keeps Persian Gulf Fleet Small as Nations in Region Build Strength," New York Times (July 17, 1976).

(30) See "Diego Garcia's Role Grows," Washington Star (July 14, 1976).

(31) See "U.S., Spain Agree to Sign Full Treaty," Washington Post (January 23, 1976): A18; "Spanish Treaty Contains Terms for F-16 Sales," Aviation Week and Space Technology 105 (July 5, 1976): 69-70; and Center for Defense Information, "The Spanish Connection: A Wider Commitment in the Making," The Defense Monitor 5 (February 1976).

(32) See "U.S., Greece Initial Pact on Military Bases and Aid," New York Times (April 16, 1976): 3.

(33) For analysis of French aims at finding a new home for its Indian Ocean fleet to replace Djibouti, see "France: Moves into Indian Ocean to be Backed by Bases," Defense and Foreign Affairs Daily (April 1, 1976).

(34) See "Mintoff Appears Headed for a Slim Victory in Malta," New York Times (September 20, 1976): 2, for a discussion of Libyan attempts to deny the West use of Malta.

(35) For a pathbreaking typology of donor-recipient arms acquisition styles, see Amelia C. Leiss et al., Arms Transfers to Less Developed Countries, C/70-1 (Cambridge: MIT Center for Internatoinal Studies, 1970).

(36) See Peter H. Vigor, "Soviet Understanding of Command of the Sea," in MccGwire, Chapter 32 (note 14 supra); Haselkorn (note 3 supra); and Edward N. Luttwak, "Defense Reconsidered," Commentary 63 (march 1977): 51-8. According to the latter, "Russian imperial strategy has already emerged fully formed in the classic mode."

7 The "Revolution" in Conventional Arms: Implications for Great Powers, Middle Powers, and Others

James L. Foster

The 1973 Middle East War was the catalyst in creating the conditions and raising the issues that this chapter will attempt to evaluate. First, the military and economic consequences of the war established conditions for a major increase in arms transfers to the Middle East, including substantial quantities of the most modern, sophisticated, and expensive weapons systems. Second, the war served to focus public attention on the implications of new conventional weapons technology both as it affects the balance of forces among the great powers and as it may affect political-military conditions in the third world. The purposes of this chapter are to review and critique the arguments that have been raised in the debate on these issues, and in doing so, to formulate a set of propositions covering the broad range of possible military implications of the development and diffusion of advanced conventional weaponry.

THE ISSUES

The debate over the implications of current technological advances in weaponry, while revealing significant differences of opinion about specific policy measures, indicates an apparent widespread acceptance of a number of general propositions. Those propositions suggest a dramatic change in the balance of forces in favor of the United States and its allies:

— Developments in conventional weapons technology portend a revolution in conventional warfare capabilities. This characterization refers to expectations of rapid changes in the effectiveness of a given force size and of fundamental changes in the nature of conventional warfare.

— New weapons technologies threaten to make obsolete those weapons which have been the core elements of conventional forces, especially armored vehicles and tactical aircraft.

188

- New weapons technologies favor the "defense" and, therefore, favor the United States and its NATO allies in the great power competition, enhancing deterrence in Europe and yielding greater stability in the European balance of power.

- Improved conventional weaponry may raise the nuclear threshold by reducing reliance on nuclear weapons as a last resort defense.

- New weapons technologies may allow reductions in total expenditures for conventional forces. This might occur because they render obsolete the most expensive conventional force elements, because they make possible manpower reductions and technologically advanced weapons can carry out a given mission using less munitions.

Contrary to the hopeful prospects for increased stability in the great power competition, advanced weapons technologies are assumed to be destabilizing in the third world context.

- The transfer of advanced weaponry is peculiarly dangerous because it produces exaggerated fears by threatening a greatly increased level of damage and aggressive nations may feel particularly emboldened by the possession of advanced weapons.[1]

- The transfer of technologically sophisticated weaponry is destabilizing because it inspires more vigorous arms races and increases the chances of exploitable arms imbalances.[2] In the extreme, the transfer of advanced systems may encourage nuclear proliferation as a hedge against the increased uncertainties regarding effective conventional deterrence and defense.

- The transfer of technologically sophisticated and, therefore, more expensive weaponry imposes an even greater economic burden on less developed countries.

These contradictory assessments – that the new conventional weapons are stabilizing in the European context but destabilizing in the third world – are perhaps best illustrated by Burt.[3] Specifically, with regard to the third world he argues that:

> Some analysts have speculated that such arms transfers are stabilizing because smaller states will become better able to defend themselves. But it is highly unlikely that the proliferation of these weapons will proceed in a balanced manner, and the sudden acquisition by some states of greatly increased military firepower could upset existing balances.[4]

However, such opposing conclusions appear difficult to rationalize. If precision guided munitions (PGMs) and other new weapons systems do indeed favor the defender, because they are basically defensive systems, it is not clear why an imbalance of such capabilities would give advantages to an aggressor or for that matter, increase the incentives for aggression as Burt argues. If such imbalances are potentially destabilizing, then Burt must envisage the balanced development and deployment of those capabilities in Europe if the favorable outcomes he projects there are to be possible.

It is not at all clear from the arguments raised in assessments of advanced weaponry why that weaponry should be stabilizing in the great power competition but destabilizing in the third world, or why it should favor the defense in one context but encourage aggression in another. One might ask why such weapons are seen to encourage arms control and less reliance on nuclear weapons in Europe, while inspiring arms races and nuclear proliferation in the third world. Whatever the merits of assessments of the military effectiveness of advanced weapons are as a general matter, inferences about their implications, based on a simple distinction between developed and underdeveloped countries, ignore important differences among nations within each of those general categories. It is unlikely that the implications of advanced weapons will be the same for nations with very different levels of military power at their disposal and different national security interests. In light of these considerations, the following analysis will distinguish between four types of national actors: (a) great powers: nations capable of projecting military power on a significant scale worldwide; (b) regional powers: nations capable of projecting significant military power only within a particular geographic region; (c) small powers: nations capable of posing a significant military threat only against their immediate neighbors and capable of an effective defense, except against a coalition of neighboring states or against a great power; and (d) others: nations who are incapable of posing a significant military threat or of ensuring their own defense.

Using this framework as a basis for critically examining the propositions noted above, the following questions will be addressed:

− Will the development and diffusion of advanced weapons effect revolutionary changes in conventional military capabilities or in the nature of conventional warfare?

− How will advanced weapons affect the conventional arms competition between the great powers, particulary in Europe?

− Do transfers of advanced weapons pose problems that are inherently different from arms transfers in general?

− Do transfers of advanced weapons pose different or more difficult problems for the supplier-recipient relationship?

− Are the potential costs and benefits associated with the diffusion of advanced weapons different for great powers, middle powers, small powers, and others?

THE REVOLUTION IN ARMAMENTS: FACT OR FANCY?

The first question to be considered is whether current technological developments in conventional weaponry are likely to produce rapid and fundamental changes in conventional capabilities and in the nature of warfare. Those who believe they will do so tend to focus on battlefield precision guided munitions, emphasizing the following attributes of PGMs:

− The "one-shot-one-kill" potential of PGMs, many of which are relatively small, light and mobile, and capable of being operated by one or a very few men, will greatly increase the effectiveness of even relatively small dispersed units against the main offensive striking systems – the tank and the tactical aircraft. Because of this increased vulnerability of offensive striking forces, the attacker will be forced to disperse rather than to concentrate forces in an attempt to gain a quick breakthrough.(5)

– This condition not only reverses the previous advantage of the offense against the defense, but also allows for a small defensive force and one which requires reduced and less sophisticated support and logistics backup. This latter condition holds because the defensive units can operate independently and fewer munitions will be necessary to destroy an equivalent amount of enemy hardware.(6)

– Because fewer men and less equipment and munition are necessary and the tank and tactical aircraft can be effectively neutralized, less advantage will accrue to the side with a superior manpower production, mobilization, and logistics base. As one PGM advocate concludes, "precision weapons (are) tailor-made for any nation with adequate technology but limited resources, desperately seeking a shortcut to combat power."(7)

If these propositions were valid and if PGMs were to be widely proliferated, then a revolution in conventional warfare would indeed be upon us. However, there are many reasons for doubting their validity. First, the "one-shot-for-one-kill" expectation is constrained by the facts that PGMs are dependent upon the ability to see and follow the object of attact and that battlefield PGMs are effective only at relatively long ranges. Thus, the opponent has many possible forms of protection: smoke, dust, camouflage, dummy units, terrain cover, jamming of PGM guidance systems, artillery fire to drive PGM units under cover, and rapid movement, high-firepower attacks to close quickly with units armed with PGMs. In addition, improved armor may significantly reduce the effectiveness of shaped-charge warheads which most antitank PGMs employ. Improvements in both electronic countermeasures and antiradiation weapons may significantly reduce the threat of antiaircraft missile systems.

Second, the argument that PGMs, by greatly increasing the effectiveness of the individual soldier, provide advantages not only for the defense but for a defense that can be inferior in manpower and hardware, rests on the assumption that these weapons either are possessed only by the smaller defensive forces or are purely defensive weapons. Contrary to these assumptions, in the 1973 War the Arabs demonstrated the usefulness of PGMs to cover an offensive operation where the defending forces – as would also be the case, say in the event of war in Europe – were heavily reliant on tanks and tactical aircraft. In the case of two-sided possession of PGMs, any increase in the efficiency of manpower should serve only to exacerbate the existing differentials in manpower levels rather than favor the weaker side. The question becomes one of which side most effectively exploits its greater efficiencies.

While PGM advocates may grant the above argument, they contend that PGMs at least provide the defender with both the advantage of preventing the attacker from massing its forces and the capability of doing so with relatively small and dispersed defensive forces armed with

PGMs. However, while a PGM may be effective against armor, it is not effective against infantry. Second, a defensive unit employing PGMs is itself vulnerable to attack. Because antitank weapons tend to be mounted on armored vehicles, they are as vulnerable to attack as the armored units of the opponent. Given these limitations on antitank and antiaircraft PGMs and the inherent vulnerability of a small, dispersed defense, it is not at all clear why the offensive force should not concentrate its strength for a breakthrough. attrition may be high on both sides, but if the attacker is willing and able to absorb high rates of attrition, then its superior numbers may still prevail.

These arguments are not intended to suggest that PGMs are unimportant, but rather that they have not radically changed the nature of conventional warfare. The tank and the tactical aircraft are not obsolete; they are simply vulnerable to a wider variety of weapons of improved effectiveness. The likely response to the threat of greater attrition of those systems is to add countermeasures, alter tactics, and increase their number. In the case of the tank and related ground forces, the reaction of the United States Army has not been to substitute PGMs and other advanced weapons for manpower or to reduce reliance on tanks. Though prolonged experimentation with a new divisional structure is about to begin, it will be a division employing more men, more tanks, and more artillery but with more emphasis on smaller, specialized units operating independently.(8)

Thus, rather than revolutionizing conventional warfare, PGMs have served primarily to reinforce and accelerate historic trends in the characteristics of conventional warfare. Those historic trends have included three factors in particular. First, the mechanization of armies has meant that increases in firepower have resulted from capital inputs rather than manpower inputs and that the fraction of military personnel directly involved in combat operations has steadily decreased. Second, there has been an increasing emphasis on force mobility, especially with tanks and tactical aircraft, to concentrate forces with high firepower capabilities. Finally, the combination of the first two conditions has led to high rates of munitions and hardware consumption. These have placed a high premium on substantial mobilization, production, and logistics capabilities for replacing losses quickly and on a substantial basis. The basic dimensions of these trends are depicted in Table 7.1.

The limited evidence available suggests that PGMs will underline these trends. PGMs are the latest means of increasing effective firepower through capital inputs, while also placing a premium on both offensive and defensive force mobility. That PGMs will primarily increase the rate of attrition on both sides rather than change the basic characteristics of conventional warfare is supported by the experience of the 1973 Middle East War. Tanks and tactical aircraft maintained their predominant role, but the rate and levels of destruction of these systems were much higher than previously experienced. Of course, the 1973 War may not be a good case to support these general conclusions. The fact that the vast majority of tank kills in that war were accomplished by other tanks rather than PGMs may be less of an observation about the potential effectiveness of tanks versus PGMs than

Table 7.1. Trends in United States Battle Inputs and
Manpower versus Firepower

	World War II	Korea	Southeast Asia 1966-1971
Scale of war effort (million man/years)	31.40	6.00	9.70
Combat exposure (million man/years)	6.20	0.40	0.50
Munitions expended (million tons)	6.96	3.13	12.93
Rates of munitions expenditure (tons per man/year of war effort)	0.20	0.50	1.30
Ratio of battle imputs (tons of munitions to man/ years of combat exposure)	1:1	8:1	26:1

Source: William D. White, U.S. Tactical Airpower (Washington, D.C.: The Brookings Institution, 1974), p. 5.

a reflection of the fact that PGMs may not have been employed in sufficient numbers or as effectively as they might, or that the generation of PGMs available at the time will be vastly improved upon in the future. However, battlefield line-of-sight PGMs are inherently limited by visibility constraints and by low rates of fire and are best employed at substantial ranges. At short ranges with concentrated forces, the more rapid rate of fire of tanks makes them a superior antitank system. The much lower cost of gun ammunition compared with PGM rounds make guns more cost effective in a high firepower context.(9) In 1973, the rapid mobilization, deployment, and concentration of highly mobile and armored forced were decisive elements in a combat environment of very high munitions consumption, which placed a premium on the capacity to resupply forces. Not only did the 1973 War find the role of ranks still predominant, but there were significant extensions of the role of armored vehicles. Given the need for ground force mobility and protection against improved direct and indirect fire systems, new armored personnel carriers that allowed mounted infantry to fight from a protected and mobile platform – as opposed to carriers intended simply to transport troops – proved particularly effective.(10) In addition, rapid-fire rocket systems mounted on armored vehicles were introduced, and precision-guided antiarmor weapons themselves were mounted on armored vehicles.

While the current generation of PGMs and those likely to be available in the near future may not revolutionize conventional warfare, technological advances on the horizon suggest the possibility of new systems which may have more significant impacts on the nature of conventional warfare. To achieve those effects the principle characteristics of future systems will be the fusion of precision guidance with long-range delivery systems. There are already available a variety of long-range systems including terminally guided glide bombs, remotely piloted vehicles, and cruise missiles. However, these systems suffer from a number of limitations that circumscribe their impact on conventional warfare. First, they are relatively expensive, and this limits the degree to which they can be proliferated on the battlefield or economically employed against a large number of targets whose individual value may be low. Second, while they may be effective against fixed targets, they are of limited effectiveness against mobile targets, given the current limits on the ability to acquire, designate, track, and allocate weapons to mobile targets, especially weapons with a long flight time. This latter point suggests that a major constraint on the utilization of advanced weapons lies not in the weapons technologies themselves, but in the supporting command-control-communications technologies necessary for effective use of these weapons.

If effective, long-range, precision weapons do become available, they will negate many of the problems posed by current line-of-sight battlefield PGMs which have limited protection, mobility, and range. While the expense of these long-range weapons would be prohibitive in many cases if one round could attack only one target, the development of a variety of clustered submunitions may eventually provide the capability for attacking many targets with each round. These new capabilities suggest not only a great capacity for battlefield units to call in a potentially large amount of effective firepower from remote launch platforms, but also a greater capacity for long-range rear attacks, including attacks against economic, political, communications, and other targets in the enemy homeland. These weapons could be used to disrupt significantly the adversary's rear area mobilization, deployment, and logistics capabilities, suggesting also increased incentives for preemptive attack. This would be true especially where a significant fraction of military assets are stockpiled in a few, large base areas, as in the case of NATO, and if command and control capabilities are concentrated and vulnerable. Insofar as the capabilities for rapid and sustained mobilization, resupply, and concentration of mobile or long-range assets are made even more critical in the context of new weapons technologies, the ability to disrupt these capabilities at the outset of conflict may provide a decisive advantage when other factors are more or less equal.

It is important to remember that technological constraints on the development or utilization of weapons systems of these types may not be the critical factor in determining the ultimate impact of advanced weapons on conventional warfare. Rather the central problem may be the ability to absorb and exploit technological advances as they become available. Military organizations, not unlike any large professional organization with a long and hallowed tradition, historically have not be particularly enthusiastic about or vigorous in accepting efforts to alter organizational structures, doctrines, or procedures in the face of changing conditions. The pace and extent of change in the nature of conventional warfare brought about by new technologies will depend on the willingness and ability of military organizations to undertake dramatic transformations. To use advanced weapons effectively will require not only dramatic alterations in the organization of forces and in military tactics, but also in the ability to deal with an enormously more complicated set of command and control logistics and other problems. The nation(s) which benefit most from technological advances in weaponry may not necessarily have the most sophisticated or the greatest number of weapons. Instead, those which benefit most will be the ones that have most effectively undertaken the organizational and other steps necessary to exploit the capabilities available to them.

In conclusion, the recent technological advances in weaponry have been significant, but they have not yet produced revolutionary changes. Furthermore, it is not likely that a revolution in conventional warfare capabilities will be realized soon. The current generation of new systems suffers from many inherent limitations. The debate about the implications of those systems and newer systems still in development indicates a lack of agreements about appropriate means of exploiting them and lack of relevant data with which to assess alternative arguments. Furthermore, incorporating those systems into the organizational structures and doctrine of the military will be slow. The currently planned experiment with a new American divisional structure mentioned previously will last several years. Even an early decision to reorganize along the lines of the experimental division will take a number of years more to complete, by which time it may be obsolete.

IMPLICATIONS FOR THE GREAT POWER COMPETITION

One might ask if advanced conventional weapons will benefit the United States, in particular to serve to redress the current force imbalances in Europe, and if those weapons will be a stabilizing factor in the American-Soviet military relationship. The preceding discussion suggested a number of reasons for doubting the predictions that advanced weapons will benefit the United States in particular or will be a stabilizing factor in American-Soviet competition.

First, hopes for substituting advanced weapons for manpower and for relying on smaller but more effective defensive forces are probably illusory. Precision weapons, in particular, not only increase the value of forces-in-being, logistics systems, and command-control facilities, but also increase the capability for destroying those assets, especially if they represent fixed targets. This fact suggests that the potential for and the benefits of surprise attack may increase as precision weapons proliferate. In any case, because NATO's forces, logistics, and command-control assets tend to be highly concentrated and vulnerable, it may be that precision systems will underline any numerical inferiority NATO suffers rather than offset such inferiority.

Furthermore, because advanced weapons portend significant increases in the rates of attrition on both sides, the Warsaw Pact's current advantages in quantities of men and equipment coupled with less constraining resupply conditions should be accentuated. Rather than requiring smaller forward-based forces, NATO may have to increase such forces. On the other hand, the Soviet preference for large quantities of relatively inexpensive hardware, for highly mobile blitz-krieg attack, and for whole unit replacement seems reasonably well suited to the world of advanced weaponry.

Even if advanced weapons in time reduce requirements for combat forces, more sophisticated technological weapons may well require more skilled and highly trained specialists to command, operate, and maintain those weapons. That manpower is likely to be expensive, and training and other costs are likely to rise in a manner that offsets cost savings from reduced manpower levels. Specialized manpower, larger forces-in-being, expanded logistics, and command-control capabilities coupled with ever more sophisticated weaponry suggest that the total costs of conventional defense will increase rather than decrease. Such a forecast runs contrary to the arguments of many advocates of advanced weapons.(11)

Some advocates of advanced weaponry find hope even in this pessimistic view of the implications of technological advances in weaponry. One advocate of PGMs has concluded that these and other new systems offer the possibility of posing clear thresholds in the escalation of conventional conflict that can facilitate deescalation or termination.(12) The argument is made that because of the increased rates of attrition associated with this new technology, it is likely that both sides in a conflict will exhaust their capabilities relatively quickly and a natural pause in the fighting will result. This pause could allow for negotiations and provide the basis for a deescalation or termination of further fighting. Furthermore, precision munitions are said to provide the opportunity for more carefully limiting damage to military targets while avoiding civilian damage. This will be true, it is argued, not only because precision guidance allows pinpoint aiming, but also because the explosive power of warheads can be lessened while inflicting the desired destruction to military targets. Furthermore, higher rates of attrition of forces mean that military targets will have greater value while general economic targets will have less. The latter can, therefore, be avoided at little or no military cost.

There are a number of problems with this formulation. First, it assumes that both sides exhaust their capabilities more or less simultaneously. If one side is better able to absorb attrition to outlast its opponent, that side is not likely to give up the battle unless surrender terms or its equivalent are forthcoming. Second, even if only conventional weapons are considered, this argument seems to overlook the implications of new weapons other than battlefield PGMs. The possession of long-range systems ot put the population or other valued assets of the adversary in jeopardy may be an attractive option for a nation facing imminent defeat. In the context of a NATO-Warsaw Pact conflict, where nuclear weapons are present, it is not clear why NATO, for example, would be less likely to resort to nuclear weapons in a rapidly paced, high attrition conflict. Indeed, higher attrition for a numerically inferior conflict participant would seem at least as likely to result in an earlier resort to nuclear weapons.

TRANSFERS OF ADVANCED WEAPONS:
PROSPECTS AND PROBLEMS

This section will deal with the pace and extent of the diffusion of advanced weapons and the degree to which transfers of these weapons pose peculiar problems for suppliers and/or recipients.

In order to assess the military implications of new conventional weapons for the particular conditions of third world conflict contingencies, it is necessary to make some judgments about the kinds and levels of those weapons that third world countries can acquire and can effectively use. Also of insterest are the considerations that might influence their choices of what to acquire and how to use their acquisitions. The demand for new technologies will obviously be affected by their cost, a nation's ability to pay, and its ability to provide the necessary supporting systems.   An equally important consideration will be the relevance of particular systems for the type of warfare the nation is most likely to confront, given geographic and terrain conditions and the size and nature of potential enemy capabilities.

The most evident constraint on third world acquisition of new weapons technologies is the limited capacity to finance arms transfers. Many advocates of PGMs consider their primary importance to lie in their relative cheapness, compared to other systems designed to perform the same mission and in particular, compared to the costs of the systems they can effectively attack. In this view, resource-constrained nations should find PGMs both attractive and acceptable on cost grounds.   However, even the smallest, least sophisticated of the new PGM and other weapons systems is expensive in an absolute sense. A TOW antitank missile launcher/guidance unit costs about $20,000, and the missile costs about $3,000. Such systems can be effective additions to infantry units covering wide defensive positions only if they are widely proliferated; the total cost implications of this fact can be very great indeed. For more sophisticated surface-to-air and air-to-surface missile systems, the costs are much greater, even when the costs of the launching platform are not considered.

Beyond these simple facts, cost considerations involving new weapons for third world countries suggest a number of reasons why such weapons may be of limited interest. First, calculations of the cost effectiveness of PGMs mean little unless the nation in questtion is faced with a threat that emphasizes systems that PGMs effectively counter. Because those threatening systems, particularly tanks and tactical aircraft, are, indeed, very expensive to buy, maintain, and operate, relatively few third world nations will be able to accumulate large quantities of them. Consequently, PGMs may be of little use or interest. Second, those nations which will be able to accumulate large quantities of these systems, whether by purchase or gift, will also very likely be able to acquire new capabilities that pose effective counters to PGMs. This suggests that "have not" countries, instead of improving their position by using their scarce resources to acquire PGMs rather than other weapons, may wind up worsening their situation because their PGM-heavy defenses may be more vulnerable. "Have" countries, on the other hand, will have little interest in expensive new weaponry that provides little advantage against the limited threats of "have not" country adversaries. In those cases where third world countries possess the ability to purchase large quantities of sophisticated arms, they face the added costs of acquiring technicians and military advisers from supplier countries to compensate for the lack of properly skilled manpower. Such considerations will severely limit the acquisition of new weapons systems in large numbers by all but the wealthiest of the nonindustrialized states.

In addition to cost constraints, third world countries confront other conditions that limit the attractiveness and accessibility of new weapons technology. The diversion of trained manpower to military service will reduce the skilled manpower available for economic developmental purposes. A further consideration is the uncertainty about the willingness or ability of arms suppliers to prove the necessary resupply of arms in the case of a conflict. To hedge against this potential problem, third world countries have several alternatives, all of which have their limitations. One is to rely entirely on one supplier and try to reach firm commitments about resupply, an option that leaves the recipient country extremely dependent. A second possibility is to purchase arms from multiple suppliers. If, however, the country in question is to maintain many forms of the same general type of equipment, this suggests that the stockpile of arms must be larger, logistics and maintenance requirements will be greater and more complicated, and the limited skilled manpower will be even more taxed by the need to learn to operate several different systems. A third option is simply to stockpile much larger quantities of arms and minimize the need for external resupply, but this, of course, will come at much greater cost. A final alternative is to develop indigenous production capabilities. This will not become a plausible option for many countries, and the number of systems produced will necessarily not be great for any one country.

Given these considerations, it is worth asking that weapons systems third world countries will want to acquire. Concern about transfers of new weapons systems to the third world has, of course, focused on the Middle East where terrain favors armored warfare, geography allows the use of tactical aircraft from homeland bases, and financial conditions and alliance arrangements allow the transfer of large amounts of the most sophisticated weaponry. However, for many third world regions, a wide range of these new classes of weapons will simply not be relevant for the most likely kinds of conflict contingencies. In many areas, geographic factors (long distances, large bodies of water, and mountains that constrain force deployments to potential battle areas) and battlefield terrains limit the likelihood of large-scale, armored operations; in other cases, financial and manpower – especially skilled manpower – resource limitations of local adversaries make the opposition of forces emphasizing tanks and tactical aircraft unlikely. In such cases, precision-guided munitions and other systems, primarily intended to attack tanks and aircraft, are likely to be of little relevance. In these situations, more traditional means of providing mobility for troops, i.e., helicopters, transports, trucks, and the like, will remain more attractive along with more traditional infantry weapons. In addition, where infantry is the central element, the non-PGM, antipersonnel area weapons and high-firepower, barrage systems may be attractive. Light, mobile rocket launchers, for example, can be relatively cheap and easy to operate and maintain. Therefore, they do not require a substantial skilled manpower input and do not impose special logistics, target acquisition, or command-control requirements.

A partial exception to the limited relevance of PGMs in most third world areas is the usefulness of some forms of antiaircraft systems. A larger number of nations are threatened by significant tactical air capabilities than by significant armor threats. In many cases, there is a potentially significant asymmetry in tactical air capabilities. Antiaircraft systems like the American Redeye and the Soviet Grail are relatively inexpensive and easy to use, do not require special support or maintenance, and can be very effective. In spite of the fact that larger surface-to-air missile systems impose greater demands on resources, require skilled manpower, and are less mobile, at least small numbers of them may be attractive to even the most resource- and skilled manpower-constrained nations. This would remain true even if those systems cannot assure effective defense of valuable assets. The reasons for this are suggested by examining the implications of Jordan's order of fourteen Hawk batteries from the United States.

This limited number of antiaircraft missile batteries could, without question, be overwhelmed by the Israeli airforce, but at a cost. In the past, the Jordanians were exposed to the threat of a free ride for Israeli aircraft, either in the context of a full-scale Arab-Israeli War or in the case of, say, limited Israeli reprisal attacks against Palestinian camps. Possessing the Hawks, the Jordanians change the calculation for the Israelis by making the decision to attack, for whatever reason, more difficult by being able to impose a cost on that action. Israeli attacks would have to be larger in scale than previously, with all of the diplomatic and military implications of committing larger forces, and there would be losses.

From the arms supplier's point of view, advanced weapons present a number of possible benefits as well as possible dangers. Because many have special requirements for operations and maintenance, command-control, and so on, which recipient countries often cannot satisfy, advanced weapons add a new source of recipient dependence on supplier nations. The potential cost for the supplier in providing these services directly to the recipient is, of course, the threat that the supplier is more directly and deeply involved if conflict should occur. On the other hand, the threat of withdrawing these services and of denying resupply can be a source of leverage to restrain the external policies of the recipient; this is discussed in Chapter 4.

For recipient nations, the resupply problem in time of war will be greatly exacerbated by the diffusion of advanced arms into the region of conflict. The problem will not be so much the need to acquire more advanced arms, but rather, general force replenishment in a high attrition conflict. If the arms supplier is a great power, there are many regions of the globe where neither great power may be capable of large-scale resupply on a timely or sustained basis. However, the closer proximity of the Soviet Union to many of the most important potential conflict areas may make it a more reliable supplier and may offer advantages to Soviet clients.

In response to the increased magnitude of the resupply problem, recipient nations may undertake one or both of two policies that could be destabilizing. One is to build up large stockpiles which may fuel local arms races. Another possibility is that the definition of arms supplier nations may change in time of war. If peacetime suppliers are unwilling or unable to resupply their clients, resupply may come from local nations which have acquired their arms through transfers. Indeed, a major source of influence for middle powers may be their ability to stockpile arms and offer resupply to regional small powers in conflict. Middle powers may also exploit the resupply dependence of small powers by denying militarily the efforts of outside suppliers to resupply their small power clients in the region. In this manner, middle powers may encourage, support, and protect the aggressive actions of an allied small power against a neighboring small power.

ADVANCED WEAPONS AND THE "STABILITY" ON MILITARY CONDITIONS

The focus here will be on whether there are fundamentally different implications of advanced weaponry for the stability of political-military relations in the developed, as opposed to the developing world. In addressing this question, the notion of stability will be operationally defined as those conditions which reduce the incentives for: arms races, initiation of conflict, escalation of conflict, and nuclear proliferation. As indicated in prior sections, the Middle East is presently, and will likely remain for the foreseeable future, the main third world arena for the proliferation of advanced weaponry. Consequently, the implications of those weapons for that region will be significantly different than for other regions. Nonetheless, the remainder of the third world will be affected as well. The question is how much and how soon.

It was argued above that the acquisition of advanced weaponry by the great powers, especially in the European context, may be destabilizing in a number of respects. Given the current and anticipated rapid technological changes in weaponry, there will be strong incentives for more rapid weapons modernization programs as new weapons and countermeasures for them emerge. In addition, advanced weapons will present strong incentives for an arms competition to possess the largest forces-in-being, to pose a preemptive threat to rear-area mobilization and logistics systems, and to possess an asymmetrical mobilization and resupply base. All of these become important primarily because of the implications of higher attrition rates portended by the new weaponry.

The conditions in the Middle East are very similar to those except that the Middle Eastern countries must rely on external sources of supply. The nations of this region are unique in their ability to pay for substantial arms purchases, or in their ability to exploit relationships with supplier countries. The terrain is particularly suitable for armored warfare and for the use of antiarmor systems. The potential conflict area is sufficiently small and compact to make the advent of long-range, conventional, precision, or area weapons an attractive capability. The objective would be to put large parts of adversary rear areas in jeopardy. The emergence of advanced weaponry has created strong incentives for Middle Eastern countries to compete not only for advantages in possessing that weaponry, but also for much larger numbers of those systems that have been traditionally dominant in the region but which are now more vulnerable to attrition, particularly tanks and tactical aircraft.

Advanced weaponry has clearly had an impact on the rate of arms acquisitions in this region and is likely to provide additional incentives as new systems are developed, which effectively counter the capabilities of the current generation of PGMs and other weapon innovations. It is important to consider if this will increase the incentives to initiate a conflict. Viewed independently of obviously crucial political considerations, the consequences of advanced weapons cut both ways. The very high rates of attrition and the possibility of greater threats to civilians than in the past may serve as a restraint. The costs of war, in terms of men and money, will be sufficiently high to make the choice of war a difficult one. Furthermore, the initiator would have to be assured of a rapid and plentiful resupply from arms supplier countries before making such a decision. On the other hand, the greatly increased costs of peacetime forces may make the continued avoidance of war, especially if war appears inevitable at some point, come at a very high political as well as economic price. For Israel in particular, maintaining large peacetime forces poses an extreme cost on an economy, which is severely constrained by manpower and financial limitation. Israel, however, is particularly vulnerable to high attrition warfare given its inferiority in men and machines. This may be a powerful restraining influence on its decisions, while providing a potential incentive for an Arab decision to initiate a conflict.

Outside the Middle East, the implications of advanced weaponry are even less clear-cut. One widely accepted view is that in the non-Middle East areas of the third world, regional powers,

. . . especially if they do not move toward nuclear status, will feel impelled to acquire new generation conventional capabilities.   Thus, regional military powers possessing advanced conventional capabilities will be in an unprecedented position either to deter attack upon themselves or to launch an attack against opponents.(13)

This argument is based, presumably, on the judgment that relatively few third world countries possess the resources to acquire, man, and support large quantities of advanced technology weapons. On the other hand, if the weaker states in a region cannot acquire or employ significant quantities of these new weapons, it is unclear why the regional power would want to buy systems that are both more expensive and more difficult to operate and maintain than more traditional systems. In other words, regional powers may be impelled to buy expensive, sophisticated equipment to offset similar purchases by regional competitors; but, if those competitors cannot or will not acquire those capabilities, the regional power's most cost-effective means to maximize military power is to acquire greater quantities of less technological sophisticated and less costly systems for the same budgetary expenditure.

Of course, this projection of behavior assumes a degree of rationality on the part of third world countries that would be considerably greater than they have demonstrated in past arms acquisition choices and incidentally, greater than has been demonstrated by developed countries. The fact remains, however, that even if third world countries acquire advanced weapons for prestige value or for other motives, this will not have particularly significant implications in many cases and will come at the price of less effective forces for the resources expended.

There are other reasons for concluding that the concern about asymmetrical acquisition of advanced technology is overdrawn. First, many of these weapons are not relevant to the form of conflict likely in much of the third world. Second, for those weapons systems that may be relevant, their acquisition, even in limited amounts, may favor the weaker states in a regional, adversarial relation more than the stronger states. This in turn may prove to be more destabilizing than the acquisition of asymmetrically greater forces by the stronger states.

Suggestive evidence for this hypothesis is provided by the case of Jordan and its acquisition of Hawk and other antiaircraft systems. It has been argued above that the acquisition of these capabilities might decrease the chances that Jordan's more powerful neighbors would conduct punitive attacks or would intrude on Jordanian territory in the event of another war because the price of doing so would be much higher than before. However, this new capability may also alter Jordan's previous policy of trying to remain outside of any local conflict. By reducing Israel's capability to retaliate against Jordan "on the cheap," Jordan may be willing to play a more aggressive role in concert with its Arab neighbors. In explaining to Congress Jordan's motives for buying the Hawk, Assistant Secretary of State Alfred Atherton reluctantly responded to congressional assertions that Jordan's noninvolvement in the 1973 War was related to the lack of effective air defenses. He stated that, ". . . it has been cited, as a matter of fact, as one of the reasons why they did not feel they were in a position to enter those hostilities . . . I have to say I think it was an inhibiting factor."(14) The evident implication is that the weaker parties to a regional arms race may feel emboldened by the acquisition of certain defensive capabilities to join forces and to confront the stronger party, which now may require considerably greater capabilities to subdue its individually weaker but collectively more secure opponents.

In the Middle East context, the recognition of likely high attrition rates, the proven benefits of surprise attack with rapid, hard-hitting follow-up offensives, and the possession of improved long-range systems provide both the incentives and the capabilities for maximal efforts from the outset of battle. In the past, the principal escalatory restraint was the avoidance of major population areas. If there is a next round, this restraint may be breached. If one side finds itself in a dangerously disadvantageous position, unable to absorb continued high force attrition it may find the option of threatening or attacking population areas too attractive to ignore. With respect to the possible resort to nuclear weapons in this role, there have been many reports not only of Israeli possession of nuclear weapons, but also of Israeli contingency preparations to use those weapons in the 1973 War, at a point when attrition of its forces threatened defeat. Whether or not these reports are accurate, the very rapid pace of high-technology warfare will have the consequences of shortening the time available for diplomacy to operate to limit the conflict and for considered judgments about military options. Simultaneously, it would greatly increase the incentives for escalation. The likelihood and various scenarios for the nuclearizaiton of the Middle East are found in Chapter 3; the role played by the great powers in nuclear proliferation is discussed in Chapter 2.

Aside from the political considerations of affecting decisions about acquiring nuclear weapons, the conditions of modern conventional warfare would seem to create strong incentives for proliferation. Uncertainties play a large role in the calculation of the benefits of and greater capabilities for suprise attack with advanced weaponry. Because of uncertainty over the outcome of a rapidly paced, attrition war, neither side in an adversarial relationship can be sure of its relative power position. Thus, while the weaker side might logically have a greater incentive for nuclear weapons, all potential parties to a conflict may reasonably view themselves as very insecure. Furthermore, they no longer can be sure that the other side does not have nuclear weapons, and the advent of long-range, dual purpose delivery systems raises the possibility of rapid acquisition of nuclear attack capabilities. In these circumstances, there is a strong incentive for all parties to acquire nuclear capabilities, both as a hedge against the possibility of adversary possession of nuclear capabilities and as a hedge against the possibility of disasterous, and possibly rapid, defeat of one's conventional forces.

CONCLUSIONS

For the foreseeable future, there are relatively few third world nations that are likely to acquire significant quantities of advanced conventional weaponry. In the Middle East, where such weaponry will abound, the military implications will be similar to those faced in conflict contingencies involving developed countries. The increased vulnerability of armor and aircraft will compel larger arsenals of these systems. The development of systems to counter the current generation of advanced technology systems will inspire continued, large transfers of advanced systems. The increased threat of surprise attack and of rapid attrition will compel larger forces-in-being in peacetime. Rapid attrition, improved long-range systems, and the uncertainties surrounding the outcome of battle create incentives for rapid escalation of conflict and acquisition of nuclear weapons.

In the remainder of the third world, the proliferation of many types of sophisticated new weaponry will be limited by one or a combination of constraints. These would particularly include terrain not favorable to mobile, armored warfare and the lack of financial and skilled manpower reosurces. For third world countries facing these constraints, the class of new or improved weaponry that may be very attractive includes a range of area or high-firepower barrage weapons that are relatively cheap, highly mobile, easy to operate and maintain, and most effective against manpower-intensive forces. Otherwise, the most likely capabilities for these countries to acquire will be more traditional and relatively unsophisticated systems for increasing force mobility and the firepower potential of ground forces.

Superior quantities of men and equipment will predominate in a battle against weaker forces, with or without advanced weapons. Thus, there will be disincentives to expend limited resources on expensive systems that increase demands for skilled manpower and more expensive maintenance and support requirements, and that will mean greater dependence on supplier countries. On the other hand, while the weaker states of a region will not be able to correct force imbalances by the acquisition of advanced weaponry, they may be able to raise the cost of attack by a stronger adversary sufficiently so that a decision to attack will be approached with greater caution. However, the general conclusion suggested by the arguments raised here is that the transfer of advanced technology weaponry is unlikely to have significant implications for the third world outside of the Middle East. Insofar as arms transfers will be destabilizing, that consequence will be linked to the total levels and distribution of arms transfers in general and not to the transfers of advanced weaponry.

NOTES AND REFERENCES

(1) Exactly why transfers of advanced weapons should be inherently more dangerous is seldom clearly explained by advocates of limiting these transfers. For example, the blue ribbon panel on conventional arms control of the United Nations Association reported, "The rapid proliferation of highly sophisticated weapons to the Third World may foster militaristic tendencies and encourage national leaders to think of military, rather than political means for resolving their international disputes," in National Panel on Conventional Arms Control, Controlling the Conventional Arms Race (New York: United States United Nations Association, 1976), p. 6.

(2) Ibid.

(3) Richard Burt, "New Conventional Weapons Technologies," Arms Control Today 5 (January 1975): 2.

(4) Ibid.

(5) This argument is made in James F. Digby, Precision-Guided Munitions: New Chances to Deal with Old Dangers, P-5384 (Santa Monica, California: The Rand Corporation, March 1975).

(6) Ibid.

(7) Colonel John T. Burke, "Precision Weaponry: The Changing Nature of Modern warfare," Army 24 (March 1974): 12-17.

(8) This new divisional structure is described in New York Times (February 27, 1977).

(9) This line of argument is well developed by Richard Ogorkiewicz, "The Future of the Battle Tank," The Other Arms Race, eds. Geoffrey Kemp et al. (Lexington, Massachusetts: Lexington Books, 1975), pp. 43-56.

(10) For a good, brief description of these systems and their effectiveness in the war, see Jac Weller, "Mideast Infantry Weapons," National Defense (March-April 1975): 403-6.

(11) See Digby (note 5 supra) for a particularly strong argument about the cost savings benefits of advanced weapons.

(12) James Digby, Precision-Guided Weapons, Adelphi Papers (London: International Institute for Strategic Studies, 1975), pp. 11-12.

(13) Amos Jordan, "Introduction: New Technologies and U.S. Defense: Planning for Non-nuclear Conflict," in Kemp p. xiv (note 9 supra).

(14) US Congress, House, Committee on International Relations, Hearings: Proposed Sale to Jordan of the HAWK and VULCAN Air Defense Systems, July 16-17, 1975 (Washington, D.C.: US Government Printing Office, 1975), pp. 8-9.

8 Economic Aspects of Arms Supply Policies to the Middle East

Mary Kaldor

The recent explosion in arms exports is generally attributed to a growing demand from Middle Eastern countries. This is explained by the Arab-Israeli conflict, increased competition from the Soviet Union, and the political vacuum in the Persian Gulf after the withdrawal of the British, coupled with the greater availability of resources due to the rise in oil prices. The benefits to supplying countries in recycling petrodollars and supporting defense companies tend to be considered fortuitous.

Yet this explanation fails to take account of certain related phenomena. First of all, the increase in arms exports to the Middle East over the last five years represents only half the increase in arms exports to all developing countries.(1) In 1976, the entire increase in American military sales agreements concerned non-OPEC developing countries.(2) In 1977, the increase in arms sales went mainly to NATO countries. Second, as is well known, the increase in worldwide arms exports has involved a shift from military assistance, i.e. gratis arms exports, to arms sales. This is true for the Soviet Union as well as the United States and has little to do with the political situation in the Middle East. Third, there is growing evidence, particularly in Iran, that recipient countries cannot absorb all the military equipment they have bought and that the quantity, sophistication, and complexity of such equipment actually hinders the development of military and hence political potential.(3) Unless one attributes a high degree of irrationality to recipient military planners, it is reasonable to suppose that they have been unduly influenced by the advice of their suppliers.

One might put forward an alternative explanation of the explosion in arms exports, including arms sales to the Middle East, which focuses on a different major feature of recent history, namely the economic recession in Western industrialized countries and the oil crisis. It is possible to argue that the growing importance of short-term economic benefits has lessened the restraint on arms exports imposed by supplying countries and that, in certain ways, this has affected the Soviet Union as well as Western suppliers.

This paper is about the short-term economic benefits from arms sales to the Middle East and the connection between arms exports, arms costs, and economic recession. The first part describes the various types of economic benefits conferred on Western suppliers by arms exports and how these have changed recently. The second part links the changes in the West to certain developments in the Soviet Union. The last part sketches some policy implications of the analysis: the kind of military and economic planning that would need to accompany an agreement to restrain arms supplies to the Middle East.

WESTERN COUNTRIES

The economic benefits of arms exports are benefits to the government. Benefits to the arms industry or other subnational groups are only relevant to an analysis of arms supply policies insofar as they affect the relationship between industry and government. The different types of economic benefits fall roughly into three categories. The first might be termed industrial. This is the relief of pressure on the defense budget through finding alternative outlets for defense industrial capacity, recovering expenditure on research and development, and reducing costs by lengthening production runs. The employment of excess industrial capacity can be said to be by far the most important of these factors.

The second type of benefit is the commercial benefit: the contribution to the balance-of-payments and other directly related commercial interests, for which the government has some responsibility. This would apply to arms sales directly exchanged for hard currency or some tangible commercial advantage, e.g. arms for oil, and so on. There are, of course, other economic benefits, such as increased employment or increased revenue for the Treasury; these can be discussed together with the commercial benefits.

The industrial and commercial benefits are immediate or short-term in nature. There is another, less tangible, more long-term benefit to be gained from arms exports and that is the necessary political influence and stability for the creation of favorable conditions for general investment and trading relations.(4) This long-term economic benefit can be called political because within the context of a study of the arms trade, it is indistinguishable from broader political objectives. To categorize these would be a task for a student of the international system as a whole, involving the issue of the primacy of economics and politics. As argued below, the industrial and commercial objectives of arms exports may well run counter to political objectives. A policy which concentrates on the former may prove, from the long-term standpoint of the economy, to have been myopic.

It is worth stressing the ambiguities in the distinction between economic and political benefits. Just as a policy which aims to extend political influence may be motivated by economic interests, so a set of short-term industrial objectives may be founded on a more fundamental political premise: the need to maintain a self-sufficient defense industrial base to preserve an independent role in world affairs.

Industrial Benefits

The industrial advantages of arms exports that are most often cited are the reduction in unit costs through lengthening production runs and the recovery of R&D expenditure. These advantages are much smaller than is generally supposed. The reduction in unit production costs results from learning − the improved efficiency that goes with experience − and from the spread of overhead costs. Most learning occurs in the early stages of production so that significant cost reductions can only be expected on the newest types of equipment. Furthermore, learning does not apply on "once-off" types of equipment, such as warships.(5) As production becomes more automated, learning becomes less important. The advantages of spreading overhead costs depend on the way in which these are computed on domestic orders. In Britain, a fixed overhead rate is applied to direct costs, i.e., labor, materials and bought-out components, so only that part of overheads used up in production of a particular product is attributed to the price of that production. This means that the cost of excess capacity is borne by the company and that the cost to the government depends on the government commitment to the company, which will be discussed subsequently. In the United States, overhead rates are negotiated each year and vary according to the projected total sales volume. To the extent that these projections are accurate, the government bears a part of the cost of excess capacity.

R&D recovery is greatest on the newest types of equipment because the levy charged is generally higher for new equipment. Nevertheless, the fact that governments experience difficulty in recovering the levy and they are prepared to waive the levy for important sales suggests that they do not attach great importance to this aspect of arms exports.(6) Of course, there are examples in which foreign customers pay for the development of a particular item of military equipment. In Britain, Iran has paid for the development of the improved Rapier missile, using the latest blindfire radar,(7) and for the improved Chieftain tank, using the new Chobham armor.(8) In the United States, Iran has paid for the development of the Bell 214 helicopter(9) and has offered to contribute to the development of the F-18L, the land-based version of the United States Navy's strike-fighter.(10) Both South Africa and Israel have contributed to French missile development.(11) These are exceptions, although they have become more common. In his statement to Congress on conventional arms transfer policy, President Carter said that, "Development or significant modification of advanced weapons systems solely for export will not be permitted,"(12) thus ruling out this form of cost savings in the future.

Two staff studies undertaken by the Congressional Budget Office came to a similar conclusion about the domestic defense savings generated by arms exports.(13) They conclude that R&D recoveries and lower production costs are mainly associated with the purchase of new aircraft and missiles. Since aircraft and missiles account for less than half of American foreign military sales, since only a portion of these are new, and since NATO countries tend to buy the most advanced equipment and account for one-third of total sales, the overall savings are likely to be small. Furthermore, such savings must be offset against additional costs resulting form the strain on resources from meeting foreign and American demands simultaneously.

More serious has been the impact of the Foreign Military Sales Program on army procurement. A November 1976 General Accounting Office report attributes a serious breakdown in the army's financial management system, which includes substantive over-obligations, to the rapid growth of the customer order program. Customer orders rose from $1.3 billion in fiscal year 1972 to $3.1 billion in fiscal year 1975. "The major part of this increase was in foreign military sales, which rose from $0.5 billion to $2.2 billion".(14) A further report in September 1977 concluded that United States capabilities have occasionally been adversely affected by the deferral of American inventory objectives, competition for spare parts, and the failure to program all Foreign Military Sales (FMS) support requirements.(15)

The Congressional Budget Office studies found that the most significant component of overall savings to the DOD was overhead costs. Yet these can be treated as part of a much wider problem, long since recognized in Western Europe and only recently given emphasis in the United States. The problem of employing excess defense industrial capacity is not simply the rent of idle facilities or the salaries of underoccupied overhead workers. It is the problem of keeping design teams together, maintaining so-called "warm" production lines on equipment not immediately required, and keeping defense companies in business. The slowdown in economic growth, which constrains the growth of public expenditure, and the growing cost of technical change in the defense sector have intensified the problem.

The capacity to develop and produce military equipment may be defined in general terms as the amount of plant, machinery, and labor available for development and production in a given time period. It may be measured in abstract monetary terms or as maximum output in value terms in a given time period. In particular terms, however, it represents a particular infrastructure of skills and techniques, a set of relationships with the services and subcontractors needed to manufacture a particular type of equipment. Defined in this sense, the capacity to develop and produce particular types of weapons systems is not the same as the capacity of particular firms, although the survival of capacity may be bound up with the survival of the prime contractor. The distinction is important, for the growing cost of weapons systems represents a real increase in overall defense industrial capacity even though employment among the prime contractors may have fallen.

In Western countries, for the most part, the developers and producers of military equipment are private firms. With the exception of traditional government arsenals, like the Royal Ordnance Factories in Britain, even those firms that are wholly or partially nationalized operate on the same principle as private firms – independent viability.

This means that companies must finance this capacity, in the sense defined above, and cannot afford long periods of idleness.

With the increase in the sophistication of military equipment, military technology has become increasingly divorced from civilian technology, and consequently, military industrial capacity has become increasingly specialized. Since the government is the main customer for military equipment, this means constant pressure on the government to order equipment in such a way as to avoid excess capacity.(16) In the United States, this phenomenon is observed in the follow-on system. Kurth has convincingly described how the follow-on system is determined by the need to keep production lines open.(17)

Avoiding surplus capacity is not simply a problem of employment. Every new order tends to entail an expansion of capacity so that solutions recreate the problem. The principle of independent viability entails the principle of profit maximization and the constant striving after technical change. In a competitive situation – competition being defined in its broadest sense as rivalry – firms must innovate; they must introduce new ideas, designs, and products in order to maintain their markets. This applies as much in the military as in the civilian sphere. Firms must keep up with wider national and international developments in military technology if they are to continue to receive orders and if the armed forces, in turn, are to justify those orders. In this way, of course, they contribute to the strategic developments they are trying to match.

Invariably, technical advance in the defense industry has taken the form of increased sophistication and complexity, improvements in performance characteristics that cost more. Some examples include variable geometry aircraft designed to improve aircraft flexibility, gas turbine propulsion for warships designed to improve speed, and improvements in navigation, communication, and other electronic systems. It has taken this form rather than the form of process innovation – finding cheaper solutions to military problems – presumably because of the current structure of the defense industry and the armed forces. Process innovation of this kind might undermine existing markets, causing the government to reduce military spending and abandon the current inventory of sophisticated and complex equipment as well as the raison d'etre of the specialized defense firm. This would be one interpretation of the current debate about PGMs.

The new technological developments must be paid for, and this means an increase in the value of orders and hence an expansion of capacity. The striving for technical change becomes more extreme the more limited the market is. The more that governments have tried to relieve the pressure on the budget by reducing the number or types of weapons, the greater has been the compensating cost increase. It is estimated, for example, that the real cost of producing 385 Multi-Role Combat Aircraft (MRCA), the current Anglo-German-Italian collaborative effort, is considerably greater than the entire wartime production of 21,000 Spitfires. The same phenomenon is to be found in shipbuilding. In the period 1965-74, the main British shipbuilders launched about half as much warship tonnage as they launched during the period 1945-54.

Yet real costs per ton have increased by factors ranging from ten to fifteen, resulting in a substantial overall increase in warship building capacity.

In the United States, a well-known extrapolation of current trends estimated that by the year 2036, the entire American defense budget would be devoted to the development and production of one plane.(18) The explanation for this tendency need not be viewed simply in terms of the need for profit. It is also a matter of redeployment following numerical reductions in orders. Designers who are shifted from one project to another bring with them pet ideas that can always find supporters in the services. The alternative to a rigorous elimination of unnecessary ideas and the choice between competing ideas is the compromise of doing everything. This would explain, for example, the cost and elaboration of an F-111 or a MRCA.

As the cost of military procurement has increased and economic growth has slowed, the problem of employing surplus industrial capacity has become more acute. Historically, the role of exports in preserving an industrial capacity which could be mobilized in time of war has always been considered important. When Liebknecht uncovered a bribery scandal in Germany in 1913, the War Minister pointed out that:

> The Government was dependent on private industry in order to ensure the great quantities of weapons that might be needed in a war for the state factory could not provide the necessary expansion, whereas a private company could obtain foreign orders in the meantime, to maintain its full production.(19)

While the same argument has been used in the United States,(20) the expansion of the United States military after World War II and the advent of nuclear weapons reduced its importance. In Western Europe, however, exports came to mean the difference between having and not having an independent arms industry, and this has been explicitly recognized. In France, arms exports rose as a share of total military production from 24 percent to 34 percent between 1965 and 1975, as indicated in Table 8.1. A similar increase can be observed in Britain. However, it should be noted that 1965 was a very low year for British arms exports, which declined by two-thirds between 1958 and 1965.

For particular types of equipment, e.g. aircraft, and for particular firms, exports are even more important. This is shown for Britain in Table 8.2. In France, the share of exports in total output in 1974 was 43 percent for Marcel Dassault, the manufacturer of Mirage; 92 percent for Panhard, the manufacturer of armored cars; 54 percent for the aeroengine company, Turbomeca; 92 percent for the naval constructor, CMN; and 46 percent for the electronics company, EMD.(21) In other words, many production lines are literally kept open by exports.

This function of arms exports is now becoming important in the United States as well. Formerly exports represented only a small part of total military production and were, in any case, mostly financed by the United States government. From 1970, the defense industries, especially aerospace companies, have experienced a severe recession resulting

Table 8.7. Exports, Military Production, and Military Exports: 1965 and 1975

Country	Year	Military Spending (US $mn)	Military Exports[a] (US $mm)	Estimated Military Hardware Production[b]	Total Exports (US $mn)	Military Share of Exports[c] (percent)	Share of Military Production Exported[d] (percent)
United	1965	51,800	1,490	16,940	27,000	6	9
States	1975	91,000	4,850	32,150	106,160	5	15
United	1965	5,190	120	1,840	13,830	1	7
Kingdom			(350)	(2,070)		(3)	(17)
	1975	10,200	380	3,440	43,760	(1)	11
			(1,040)	(4,100)		(2)	(25)
France	1965	6,100	100	1,860	10,040	1	6
			(560)	(2,320)		(6)	(24)
	1975	11,400	500	3,920	52,210	1	13
			(1,780)			(3)	(34)
West	1965	7,690	102	2,230	17,880	1	5
Germany	1975	14,700	260	4,670	90,020	–	6
Italy	1965	2,210	17	630	7,200	–	3
	1975	4,440	100	1,430	34,820	–	7
Japan	1965	1,250	11	360	8,440	–	3
	1975	4,780	10	1,440	55,840	–	–
Canada	1965	1,700	59	510	8,120	1	12
	1975	3,160	70	1,020	31,880	–	7
Soviet	1965	52,400	1,310	16,800	8,175	16	8
Union	1975	120,000	2,610	38,310	33,310	8	7

[a]There is some doubt as to the accuracy of these figures, which come from the United States Arms Control and Disarmament Agency. The British and French figures are very low when compared with official figures, which are shown in parentheses, or with those of other countries, for example, West Germany and China. Nor is it clear whether the figures for Soviet military spending and exports have been computed by the same method and are comparable. The Canadian figures appear to exclude exports to the United States since these are known to be of a comparable order to domestic Canadian procurement.

[b]This estimate is reached by assuming hardware costs to be 30 percent of military budgets. In fact, of course, hardware costs vary widely from country to

country and from year to year; to compute a comparable series of hardware costs would be a major and important research task. The 30 percent assumption was reached by a rough calculation of British and American hardware costs. For the United States, hardware costs were taken to be Procurement plus Operations and Maintenance, minus a certain proportion of civilian manpower costs. For the United Kingdom, hardware costs were taken to be Procurement minus Research, Development, and Headquarters Salaries, etc. British and American definitions of Procurement are, of course, quite different. United States hardware costs, as a proportion of the total military budget, were much larger than British hardware costs. Another estimate for American hardware costs was taken from census data on shipments of defense products, which can be found in Defense Indicators, February 1977, US Department of Commerce, Bureau of Economic Analysis. For 1975, the total value of defense shipments was $23,724 million, which is somewhat lower than the other estimates. This is presumably because it does not include some nondefense items like construction equipment that are included in Foreign Military Sales. To obtain a total military production estimate, imports were subtracted and exports added.

cMilitary exports as a proportion of total exports: B/D.

dMilitary exports as a proportion of estimated military production: B/C.

Sources: US Arms Control and Disarmament Agency, World Military Expenditures and Arms Transfers 1965-1974 (Washington, D.C.: US Government Printing Office, 1976) and World Military Expenditures and Arms Transfers 1966-1975 (Washington, D.C.: US Government Printing Office, 1977); United Nations Statistical Office, Statistical Yearbook 1976 (New York: United Nations, 1977) and Statistical Yearbook 1972 (New York: United Nations, 1973); Jean Klein, "Commerce des armes et politique: le cas francais," Politique Étrangère no. 5 (1976): 586; Guardian Weekly, Le Monde Section (October 17, 1976); Great Britain, House of Commons, Official Report of Debates (Hansard, March 10, 1977), written answers to questions.

from the cutback in military spending after the Vietnam War, the reduction in space expenditures, and the recession in the civilian economy. It was widely believed that the United States government could no longer support six major aerospace companies. There was a rapid reduction in the number of small arms supply companies acting as subcontractors, and there was considerable speculation about the imminent collapse of at least one major company. Such collapse was probably avoided by the increase in arms sales. A case in point, of course, was Iran's $200 million loan to Grumman Corporation. As a share of total United States production, exports increased from 9 percent in 1965 to 15 percent in 1975, as seen in Table 8.1, while the proportion of exports that were sold rather than given away increased from 14 percent to over 90 percent, as seen in Table 8.3. The shift was even more striking in the Middle East. A recent Pentagon study shows that capacity utilization in the aircraft industry is less than 50 percent and would be much lower were it not for foreign military sales.(22)

Interestingly, there has been a revival of the traditional argument

Table 8.2 Domestic Procurement and Exports in Britain
1972-73 and 1974-75
(million current pounds sterling)

| | 1972-1973 | | 1974-75 | | Exports as a Share of Total Production % | |
	Domestic Procure-ment	Exports	Domestic Procure-ment	Exports	1972-73	1974-75
Military Aircraft Aeroengines and Spares	275	136	424	241	33	36
Warships and Refits	68	35	94	44	34	32
Weapons, including Guided Weapons, Ammunition, AFVs, Electronics	369	86	439	183	19	29
TOTAL	712	257	957	468	27	33

Sources: Great Britain, Parliament, Defence Accounts, 1972/3 and 1974/5, (Commons) Sessions 1973/4 and 1975/6; Ministry of Defence.

about the need for excess capacity for mobilization in time of war. The Pentagon has come up with a new version which avoids the pitfalls of envisaging arms production on a large scale in the event of an all-out nuclear war. This is the notion of a surge capability i.e., the maintenance of a sufficient peacetime capacity to ensure a rapid increase in military output when necessary.(23) The role of arms sales in maintaining a surge capacity has received increasing emphasis. A Treasury report which accompanied President Carter's report to the Congress on arms transfer policy, emphasized this largely immeasurable benefit from arms exports.(24)

There have been a number of similar statements over the last two years. They represent explicit recognition, as in Western Europe, of the need "to institutionalize the concept that the defense industrial base is a national resource."(25) Essentially, this means that insofar as exports contribute to the survival of defense industrial capacity, the government is committed in the absence of alternatives to promote them. It also means that insofar as technical innovation needed to maintain a competitive position entails an expansion of capacity, this is going to become an ever increasing burden.

The role of exports in maintaining capacity can take many forms. They may simply smooth out fluctuations in the production rate and hence avoid the costly and often technically problematic turbulence in employment. They may help to keep particular production lines open. In the last resort, they may save a prime contractor in the way that Iran saved Grumman, or that exports are said to have saved Northrop,

Table 8.3. United States Foreign Military Sales (FMS) and Military Assistance
(MAP) to the Middle East, 1950-74
(thousand dollars)

		1950-64	1969	1974
Iran	FMS	1,285	235,839	3,794,369
	MAP	653,939	22,206	—
Israel	FMS	7,121	312,944	2,117,623
	MAP	—	—	—
Saudi Arabia	FMS	87,026	4,220	587,698
	MAP	30,400	620	184
Big 3 Subtotal	FMS	95,432	553,003	6,499,690
	MAP	684,339	22,826	184
Middle East	FMS	100,961	568,151	6,581,113
	MAP	779,307	23,448	358,969
Arab-Israeli Participants	FMS	10,044	326,418	2,178,239
	MAP	40,774	272	358,785
Oil (OPEC) Countries	FMS	90,917	241,733	4,400,240
Middle East	MAP	738,533	23,176	184
World Total	FMS	5,162,667	1,557,597	8,262,579
	MAP	30,528,327	454,154	788,614
FMS as a Share of FMS plus MAP (percent)	World	14	77	91
	Arab-Israeli	24	100	86
	Arab OPEC Countries	11	91	100
	Middle East	11	96	95
Share of Middle East FMS (percent)	Big 3	95	97	99
	Arab-Israeli	10	57	33
	Oil Countries	90	42	67
Share of Middle East MAP (percent)	Big 3	88	97	—

Table 8.3 Continued

		1950-64	1969	1974
	Arab-Israeli	5	1	100
	Oil Countries	95	99	—
Middle East	FMS	2	36	80
Share of World				
(percent)	MAP	3	5	46

Source: US Senate, Committee on Foreign Relations, Subcommittee on Foreign Assistance, Hearings: Foreign Assistance Authorization, Arms Sales Issues (Washington, D.C.: US Government Printing Office, 1975).

General Dynamics, and Vought. The Pentagon has mentioned the role of exports in keeping production lines open in a number of cases. Indeed, this was a component of the DOD cost savings in twelve of the thirty-five systems about which DOD provided information to the Congressional Budget Office. Particularly significant in this respect were the M-113 Al armored personnel carrier, the Lance missile system, and the F-4E combat aircraft.(26)

Another example is the recent sale of seven AWAC planes to Iran. The sale was agreed upon after President Carter's statement on arms transfer policy and does seem to violate one of the Carter guidelines, namely, that the United States will not:

> . . . introduce into a region newly developed advanced weapons systems which would create a new or significantly higher combat capability. Also any commitment for sale or co-production of such weapons is prohibited until they are operationally deployed with US forces, thus removing the incentive to promote foreign sales in an effort to lower unit costs for Defense Department procurement.(27)

It might be argued that as a surveillance system, AWAC does not represent a higher combat capability, but since it is supposed to increase combat capability through improved intelligence, this would seem to be hair splitting. The sale follows the decision by some European NATO countries not to buy the German Leopard tank, and it will involve a recoupment charge of $24 million per plane, as well as lower production costs. The role played by the Iran sale in smoothing the production rate is shown in Table 8.4.

Although DOD "insists that this consideration did not influence the decision to sell,"(28) it is very difficult to see how such an important industrial benefit did not affect the energies of political protagonists for the deal.

Table 8.4. AWACs Delivery Schedule

	1977	1978	1979	1980	1981	1982	1983	1984	Total
United States	7	8	5	3	3	3	3	2	34
Iran	0	0	0	0	2	4	1	0	7
Total	7	8	5	3	5	7	4	2	41

Source: Figures from Boeing Aerospace Company, quoted in US Library of Congress, Congressional Research Service, Foreign Affairs and National Defense Division, Implications of President Carter's Conventional Arms Transfer Policy, Report to the Committee on Foreign Relations, US Senate (Washington, D.C.: December 1977), p. 39.

Commercial Benefits

The commercial objectives of arms exports do not necessarily conflict with industrial objectives. On the contrary, both are likely to become more important in a situation of slow economic growth. Nevertheless, the evidence seems to suggest that commercial objectives are much less significant than industrial objectives.

A number of recent studies have suggested that since World War II, high military spending as a proportion of GNP has been associated with slow rates of economic growth in Western industrialized nations. The argument is that military spending is directly competitive with investment, as indicated in Table 8.5. The inverse correlation between military spending and investment has also been shown to hold historically in the case of Britain. Since slow rates of economic growth are also associated with slow rates of export growth, high rates of military spending are indirectly linked to balance-of-payments problems. It has been suggested that since the defense industries are also the export-intensive industries, e.g. machinery and transportation, high military spending absorbs export capacity; the consequent restraint on exports operates as a constraint on economic growth as a whole.(30)

It is not necessary to understand the nature and the direction of the relationship between high military spending and low economic growth in order to understand the implications for arms supply policies. My own interpretation is that the relationship between high military spending and low growth is a feedback or vicious circle. Slow economic growth involves the decline of certain important, generally defense-related industries, e.g. shipbuilding and heavy engineering in Britain in the 1880s and automobiles and aircraft in postwar America. For various reasons, including the need to keep production lines open, the government increases defense contracts to stem the decline. Defense industrial capacity then acquires its own momentum, as described previously, absorbing resources, particularly those suitable for R&D and

Table 8.5. Investment and Military Expenditure, Western Countries, 1974

Country	Military Expenditure[a] (US $ mn)	Military Expenditure as Percentage of GNP[a]	Investment as Percentage of GDP[b]	Average Annual Growth Rate in GNP, 1963-73[c] (percent)
United States	85,900	6.15	18	3.9
United Kingdom	10,100	5.24	20	2.7
France	10,600	3.63	25	5.7
West Germany	13,800	3.58	22	4.7
Netherlands	2,320	3.45	22	5.4
Sweden	1,780	3.10	22	3.4
Norway	671	3.13	32	4.7
Italy	4,630	2.93	23	4.8
Belgium	1,460	2.77	22	4.8
Denmark	728	2.37	22	4.5
Canada	2,790	2.05	23	5.2
Switzerland	856	1.91	27	4.0
New Zealand	237	1.75	26	3.4
Finland	255	1.31	29	4.9
Austria	292	0.91	28	5.2
Luxembourg	18	0.87	26	3.4
Japan	3,670	0.83	34	10.5

Sources: [a]US Arms Control and Disarmament Agency, World Military Expenditures and Arms Transfers 1965-1974 (Washington, D.C.: US Government Printing Office, 1976).

bUnited Nations, Department of Economic and Social Affairs, Statistical Office, Statistical Yearbook, 1975 (New York: United Nations, 1976).

cUS Arms Control and Disarmament Agency, World Military Expenditures and Arms Transfers 1963-1973 (Washington, D.C.: US Government Printing Office, 1974).

fixed investment which are needed elsewhere in the economy, leading to a further slowdown in economic growth.(31) First of all, slow economic growth and balance-of-payments difficulties . are likely to limit the growth of public spending, including the defense budget, hence the importance of industrial objectives. Second, the comparative advantage of military production and the comparative disadvantage of civilian production implies that arms exports are a suitable instrument for earning foreign exchange, hence the importance of commercial objectives. The relative importance, however, of commercial and industrial objectives depends not on the rate of economic growth but on the absolute size of the economy. The industrial importance of arms exports depends on the size of arms exports in relation to arms production, and the commercial importance of arms exports depends on their size in relation to total exports. In large economies, exports tend to represent a relatively small proportion of production, both civilian and military; hence arms exports are likely to be more important in relation to total exports and less important in relation to arms production. This is why commercial objectives are more important for the United States than for Britain or France.

The share of arms exports in total exports and in military production is shown in Table 8.1. In all countries, except Canada and Japan, the industrial importance of arms exports increased over the ten year period, 1965-75. The commercial importance of arms exports, interestingly enough, did not increase, and it is only significant in absolute terms in three countries: the United States, Britain, and France. In recent years, only American arms exports have been sufficiently large in relation to total exports to represent a policy option, albeit minor, in correcting a balance-of-payments problem. Since 1971, the increase in arms sales, together with the increased price of food, has been a reason for the improvement in the balance-of-payments. Prior to the trade deficit, the American balance-of-payment deficit was largely explained by the cost of overseas military spending. Today, with the increase in arms sales and the withdrawal of American troops from abroad, the military account has swung into surplus. The British balance-of-payments deficit up to the late 1960s was also explained by the cost of overseas military spending;   the increase in arms sales is expected to exceed these costs for the first time in 1978.

All the same, this argument should not be exaggerated. There are alternative options. The United States Treasury report, cited previously, concluded that an immediate reduction in arms sales of 40 percent would lead to a deterioration in the current account of $5 billion, or

$2.5 billion if the reduction were effected gradually over four years. However, it also suggests that this could easily be offset by depreciation of the exchange rate. Of course, it is argued that military sales frequently provide an entree into civilian markets. This argument has been particularly popular among the smaller European countries and has been made for the United States as well.(32) On the other hand, some recipient countries have a foreign exchange constraint, and income spent on arms might have been spent on civilian goods. The treasury report assumes that these two effects cancel each other out.

Other macroeconomic benefits of arms sales are also small. Although arms exports employ 350,000 people in the United States, 50,000 in Britain, and 70,000 in France, this represents a very tiny proportion of total employment. For example, a total ban on arms sales in the United States would increase the unemployment rate by only 0.3 percent.(33) Likewise, the effects on GNP or government revenue are also limited. Of course, the impact on particular sectors and particular regions is much greater. For example, a 40 percent cut in United States arms exports would displace 17.5 percent of all jobs in the professional technical categories.(34) The political significance of this depends to a large extent on the relative power of these groups, and this, in turn, is generally associated with the government-industry relationship.

The relatively small share of arms exports in total exports for all countries, except perhaps the United States, suggests that the function of arms exports in recycling petrodollars is less than is generally supposed. Naturally, after the 1973 oil crisis, several countries enthusiastically negotiated arms-for-oil agreements in the Middle East. Recently, with the introduction of the two-tier pricing system and the decline in Iranian oil revenues, these have taken the form of direct barter. In a recent British deal, for example, Shell will market Iranian crude oil and place the receipts in an interest bearing trust fund for the purchase of Rapier missiles. A similar three way deal has been negotiated with AGIP and EFIM-Agusta for the purchase of Chinook helicopters.(35) The enthusiasm, however, is to be explained by the opportunities for industrial benefits conferred by the increased oil revenues as much as the commercial opportunities for recycling petrodollars. This conclusion is supported by the fact that much of the recent increase in arms deliveries to the Middle East is the result of agreements concluded before the 1973 oil crisis.

Political Benefits

It can be argued that the growing importance of short-term economic objectives increasingly contradicts the pursuit of long-term economic objectives, i.e., the pursuit of favorable political conditions for long-term economic exchanges. For convenience, the former are termed economic and the latter political.

It should be noted that the economic motives by no means exclude political objectives. Both may be pursued together. It is evident that the political objectives for arms sales, for example as regards Israel, or the more general competition with the Soviet Union currently encapsulated in the new military aid program to Africa, are often very important. Furthermore, arms supply policies are pursued on different levels of government, and the debate about particular transfers will reflect a different configuration of considerations at each level. Hence, it is possible for a straightforward calculation of economic interest to be translated into a convincing political standpoint at the higher echelons of government. Equally, political guidelines enunciated by high level officials may prove ineffective in relation to the pressure, which is often economic in origin, from those involved in day-to-day activities concerning arms exports.

A political arms supply policy must involve restraint. President Carter's stated determination to restrain arms sales could be said to reflect less an attempt to reduce the arms trade for its own sake and more an attempt to politicize and control a policy which, under Nixon, had become prey to all sorts of special interests.(36) A political policy implies a willingness to withhold or interrupt supplies and the ability to influence the size and nature of the recipient's military potential. Yet an arms supply policy dominated by economic considerations cannot afford restraint. With the shift from grant to sales, the competition from alternative suppliers increases. Recipients can go elsewhere if arms sales are used to exert unwelcome political pressure. Further, the institutional structure governing the content of arms supplies, for example the American military assistance advisory groups, tends to break down giving rise to uncontrollable competing interests.

The Iranian example is a case in point. Prior to 1970, Iran received arms supplies on the basis of grant aid, and a certain amount of restraint was exercised by the United States government. For example, the quantity of Hawk missiles and F-5 aircraft supplied to Iran under an agreement in 1964 was less than demanded by Iran because it was considered too great a burden on the Iranian economy.(37) It is widely reported, however, that after the shift to sales, President Nixon on a visit to Iran in 1972 promised the Shah all the conventional weapons he wanted. This resulted in the Shah and the Iranian military being offered often conflicting advice by various members of the United States military establishment and American producers.(38)

A policy of unrestrained arms sales is self-defeating in the long run for both economic and political reasons. First of all, it encourages commercial competitors. Britain, France, and West Germany have all increased their share of the Middle East market recently. Further, the Soviet Union becomes a more attractive alternative. In addition, recipient countries are more likely to attempt a policy of self-sufficiency. This is evident in the growth of the Israeli defense industry and the decision to create the Arab Military Industrial Organization (AMIO) with European help. Further, the dissemination of military technology may undercut existing markets. There is considerable concern about Israeli exports of American technology, sometimes without even notifying the relevant authorities and in contradiction to the United States own supply policy.(39)

Second, increased commercial competition means increased political competition, i.e., the loss of monopoly power and the emergence of alternative blocs. It can be argued that the rise of new centers of power, like the OPEC countries, can be explained as much in terms of the openings provided by the increased competition between the major powers as by exogeneous factors such as the shortage of oil. This is, of course, a dynamic process in which the rise of new blocs further fuels political competition. One corollary of this argument is the proposition that the ability of the Soviet Union to penetrate new areas like Peru, Africa, or even Iran, is a consequence as much as a cause of the growing fragmentation of world power. The intensification of competition will be all the greater, the greater the dissemination of military power is as a result of the proliferation of arms.

Third, unrestrained arms supplies, whether or not they are mediated by increased competition, are not necessarily conducive to long-term political and economic benefits. Insofar as the idea of a stabilizing military capability is valid, it is only conceivable in the context of controlled supplies. Approval of arms purchases has to be assessed according to whether they contribute to an equilibrium based on a perceived military balance of power. In the absence of any control, the chances of being involved in local wars, unsympathetic coups, or revolutions multiply.

Finally, it can be argued that in the long term, industrial and commercial benefits will vanish. Arms exports do not stem from the growth of defense industrial capacity; they merely postpone the problem of matching government spending to industrial production and in so doing, help to magnify it. Likewise, arms exports do not improve the performance of civilian exports. On the contrary, insofar as they contribute to the growth of the defense industry and insofar as the size of the defense industry is a cause as much as a consequence of slow economic growth, increased arms exports may further slow down economic growth and the competitiveness of civilian exports, recreating the balance-of-payments problems they are supposed to solve.

The classic example of a country which shifted from political to economic objectives in its arms supply policy is Britain. That this was part of a process of declining power and slow economic growth hardly needs to be spelled out.

THE SOVIET UNION

Evidently, economic benefits are different in kind in a planned system. Where private costs are not the most relevant criterion for production, excess industrial capacity can be eliminated through planning or be utilized for other purposes. Likewise, the size of foreign trade is a matter of choice for the planners, rather than the consequence of numerous uncoordinated choices taken by individual enterprises. Insofar as the economic benefits of arms exports are considered important, this has to be explained in terms of specific bias in the bureaucratic structure responsible for planning.

The Defense Industry

The Soviet defense industry is a separate and privileged sector of the Soviet economy. It receives priority in the central planning system, for example, in receiving items in short supply, and it is considered to be more efficient and more capable of generating technical innovation than the rest of the economy. From the mid-1950s, Soviet planners decided to use idle capacity in the defense industry for the manufacture of civilian goods.(40)

In 1971, Brezhnev declared that, "42% of the entire volume of the defense industry's production is for civilian purposes."(41) Civilian products manufactured by the defense industry are reputed to be of much higher quality than those manufactured in the rest of the economy, even when identical models are compared.(42) Since prices are more or less arbitrarily determined in the Soviet Union and since part of the cost of civilian production, if indeed this is measurable, can be attributed to the cost of military production, the problem that so vexes Western defense companies, viz., the higher costs associated with producing civilian goods in military plants, can scarcely be said to exist. According to Checinski, attempts to introduce Western type, cost-benefit analyses into the defense industry have been thwarted by the immense difficulty of establishing a price for armaments which reflects the real cost to the Soviet economy as opposed to the relative bargaining power of the armed forces, the individual enterprise, and the relevant ministries.(43) In the last few years, Soviet planners have called on the defense industries to make use of their scientific and technical abilities to elevate the technological level of civilian production.

In these circumstances, the capacity problem for the Soviet Union is one of too little rather than too much, and arms exports can be treated as a burden rather than a benefit.(44) Table 8.1 suggests that this burden, i.e., the share of arms exports in total production, is about 7 percent. Ofer's figures for military assistance to the Middle East, based on the calculation of value burdens as well as physical burdens, are somewhat higher.

Foreign Trade

The Soviet economy has always been dependent on Western technology. In the first two five-year plans, 1928-37, imports from the West, paid for with raw materials and gold, played a key role, as did wartime lend-lease programs in later plans.(45) Since the late 1950s, the need for Western technology has received even greater emphasis. This is because the Soviet Union has been unable to achieve the rapid rates of growth of the early period of industrialization. This failure to grow cannot be explained by lack of investment; fixed capital formation as a percentage of GNP is about twice the proportion that prevails in most Western countries. Rather, it is due to low productivity growth apparently caused by waste and by failure to innovate. This, in turn, has been explained by the rigidities of the Soviet system, such as the lack of individual initiative, the emphasis on fulfillment of formal instructions, and the bureaucratic predilection for older, less dynamic sectors, viz., the heavy industries and the defense sector. In Western countries, crises provide the mechanism for eliminating inefficient enterprises; in the Soviet Union, they are planned away. The need to raise the level of consumption in the Soviet Union has caused Soviet planners to seek external aid for civilian innovation.(46) Military innovation also receives an external impulse indirectly, of course, via the arms race.

In the past, however, Western technology has been acquired without a substantial increase in dependence on foreign trade. Hanson has shown that up to 1971, the level of machinery imports to the Soviet Union was determined positively by the levels of exports to the West and negatively by the size of Western grain imports.(47) Moreover, there is evidence to suggest that the Soviet Union is prepared to tighten belts in order to reduce dependence on Western grain. In 1975, grain imports were reduced despite a shortfall in the Soviet harvest and the consequent slaughter of livestock. Nevertheless, most commentators consider that there has been a qualitative change in the Soviet attitude towards foreign trade since 1971. There are several reasons for this. First there are tangible indications that the Soviet Union is basing export policies on long-run considerations. These include investment in a large oil storage terminal in Antwerp; the buildup of foreign affiliates in banking and insurance; the marketing of automobiles, tractors, machine tools, and watches; and the growth of the tanker and merchant marine fleet. Second, it is argued that the complexity of modern technology means that unlike earlier periods, the Soviet Union needs to keep up a continuous flow of foreign imports.(48) Finally, of course, there is the willingness since 1971 to accept credit from Western countries. In consequence, Soviet hard currency indebtedness has increased substantially. In 1975, the Soviet deficit with the West was $6.4 billion, and in 1976 it was $5 billion.(49)

In this context, it seems reasonable to assume that there is an urgent and long-term need to increase Soviet hard currency earnings. The notion that such earnings can be achieved through increased output of raw materials, including oil, is belied by the experience of the last five years and in the case of oil, by the fact that the Soviet Union has had to divert exports from Eastern Europe to the West and to import oil and natural gas from Iran and Afghanistan for re-export to the West. Clearly, the production of arms is one area where the Soviet Union, like the United States, has a comparative advantage, and the sales of arms for hard currency is one obvious solution to Soviet debt problems. Indeed, a relatively large share of total exports, i.e. percent, consists of armaments as indicated in Table 8.1. This figure is considerably lower than the one in the CIA report, cited subsequently, which concludes that arms exports account for 10 percent of hard currency earnings.

The growing importance of this aspect of arms exports may have been one element in the breakdown of relations with Egypt, which according to President Sadat, was due to the refusal of the Soviet Union to cancel or reschedule Egyptian debts. At the time of the break, military debts amounted to $7 billion, some of which were payable in hard currency.(50) Given the heavy burden of military assistance, and during the early 1970s, Egypt accounted for 40 percent of the burden, as well as the need for hard currency; this rigid policy towards repayment may not be viewed entirely as a rationale. Ofer suggests that during 1973-75, hard currency sales of arms may have reached a couple of billion dollars or so:

> First, there is evidence that a considerable part of the arms supplied to Egypt and Syria since 1973 was paid for in hard cash by other Arab countries (Algeria, Libya, Saudi Arabia, Kuwait and other countries). Secondly, it is quite clear that arms deals with oil countries, Iraq, Libya, and possibly Algeria and Iran are also payable in hard currency or in oil and gas — which are equivalent to it since they are re-exported to the West. The increased proportion of arms sales also explains, I believe, the shift in recent years in the distribution of Soviet Military Assistance to the region — towards higher proportions of such "aid" going to oil countries — Libya, Iraq and Iran.(51)

This conclusion is supported by a recent CIA study of Soviet hard currency problems which suggests that Soviet arms sales will net $1.5-2 billion this year.(52)

The growing commercial importance of Soviet arms exports is not independent of developments in the West. Quite apart from the existence of increased oil revenues, it is hard to accept that the combination of Soviet willingness to accept Western credits, Western interest in Soviet markets, and détente is no more than coincidence. It would seem more appropriate to argue that Soviet interest in Western credit and increased economic exchange was fairly longstanding and that only the formal conclusion of détente made possible by other internal Western preoccupations enabled this interest to be translated into policy. If this analysis is correct, it suggests that changes in Soviet economic and foreign policy are responsive to Western developments.

CONCLUSION

In this paper it was argued that short-term economic considerations have increasingly come to dominate arms supply policies to the Middle East. In Western countries, especially Britain and France, arms exports play an essential role in maintaining a capacity for the development and production of military equipment. In addition, arms sales are a source of foreign currency, although this is probably only significant for the United States. Economic considerations affect Soviet arms exports as well, since arms sales may help to reduce the Soviet hard currency debt. It was also suggested that the emphasis on short-term economic benefits can be self-defeating in the long run, reducing long-term political and economic stability. Few would deny the case for a more political approach to arms exports, involving some measure of restraint.

If the above analysis is correct, then certain important policy implications can be drawn. Any effective attempt to restrain arms supplies to the Middle East, on a unilateral or multilateral basis, should be accompanied by measures which would minimize the economic pressures to export arms. Proposals for measures of this kind that ought to be considered include:

Alternative Solutions to the Problem of Excess Military Industrial Capacity in Western Countries. An obvious suggestion is subsidized civilian buffer production, and Senator McGovern's Defense Economic Adjustment Act is a move in this direction. A long-term solution, however, would have involved restructuring and probably nationalization of the arms industry.(53)

Alternative solutions to the balance-of-payments problems in Western countries. Again, an obvious proposal is intensive promotion of civilian exports, using perhaps the resources and experience involved in the export of arms. However, a long-term solution would have to be part of the wider efforts currently under way to create a new international economic order.

Alternative solutions to Soviet balance-of-payments problems. This might include, for example, increased willingness to accept Soviet imports.

Any of these proposals warrant independent investigation and study far beyond the scope of this paper. All would be part of wider proposals designed to cope with current military and economic problems. What they suggest, depressingly perhaps, is that the problem of arms exports is an indissoluble link between the problems of armament versus the problems of the world economy.

NOTES AND REFERENCES

(1) US Arms Control and Disarmament Agency, World Military Expenditures and Arms Transfers 1965-1974 (Washington, D.C.: 1976).

(2) US Department of Defense, Foreign Military Sales Agreements (Washington, D.C.: November 30, 1976).

(3) For the Iranian case see US Congress, Senate, Committee on Foreign Relations, Subcommittee on Foreign Assistance, Staff Report: US Military Sales to Iran 94th Cong., 2nd Sess. (Washington, D.C.: US Government Printing Office, July 1976).

(4) See, for example Michel Debré, La France Trafiquant d'Armes (Paris: Francois Maspero, 1974), p. 44.

(5) This argument is contained in Chapter 14 of Stockholm International Peace Research Institute, The Arms Trade with the Third World

(Stockholm: Almqvist and Wiksell, 1976), pp. 377-97.

(6) Great Britain, Parliament, Appropriation Accounts, 1975-76 (Commons). Session 1976-77, "Report of the Controller and Auditor-General."

(7) Stockholm International Peace Research Institute, World Armaments and Disarmament, SIPRI Yearbook 1976 (Stockholm: Almqvist and Wiksell, 1976), p. 256.

(8) Great Britain, Parliament, Statement on Defence Estimates, 1977, Cmnd. 6735 (London, February 1977), p. 37.

(9) Stockholm, p. 256 (note 7 supra).

(10) Aviation Advisory Services, Ltd., Milavnews (Essex, UK) NL 180 (October 1976).

(11) See Chapter 6, Stockholm, pp. 249-70 (note 7 supra).

(12) US Congress, Senate, Committee on Foreign Relations, "Text of the Statement on Conventional Arms Trade Policy," Report: Arms Transfer Policy, 95th Cong., 1st Sess. (Washington, D.C.: US Government Printing Office, July 1977), p. 2.

(13) US, Congressional Budget Office, Foreign Military Sales and US Weapons Costs, Staff Working Paper (Washington, D.C.: May 5, 1976); US, Congressional Budget Office, Budgetary Costs Savings to the Department of Defense Resulting from Foreign Military Sales, Staff Working Paper (Washington, D.C.: May 14, 1976).

(14) US, General Accounting Office, Serious Breakdown in the Army's Financial Management System, FGMSD-76, Report to US House, Committee on Appropriations (Washington, D.C.: November 5, 1976), p. 2.

(15) US, General Accounting Office, Foreign Military Sales – A Potential Drain on the US Defense Posture, LCD-77-440 (Washington, D.C.: September 2, 1977), p. ii.

(16) See, for example, Great Britain, Parliament, Fifth Report from the Committee on Public Accounts (Commons), Session 1975-76, Evidence before the Committee on Public accounts, HCP 556 (London: Her Majesty's Stationery Office, June 28, 1976).

(17) See Mary Kaldor, "Defence Cuts and the Defence Industry," Military Spending and Arms Cuts: Economic and Industrial Implications. Alternative Work for Military Industries, ed. Dan Smith (London: Richardson Institute for Peace and Conflict Research, 1977).

(18) Norman R. Augustine, "One Plane, One Tank, One Ship: Trend for the Future," Defence Management Journal (April 1975): 34-40.

(19) Anthony Sampson, The Arms Bazaar: From Lebanon to Lockheed (New York: Viking Press, 1977), p. 43.

(20) Ibid., pp. 78-9.

(21) France, Assemblée Nationale, Rapport, Commission des Finances, No. 1916, Défense, Annexe No. 49, Session 1975-76.

(22) US Department of Defense and Office of Management and Budget, Aircraft Industry Capacity Study (Washington, D.C.: January 1977), p. 6.

(23) US Congress, Joint Committee on Defense Production, Hearings: Defense Industrial Base: Industrial Preparedness and Nuclear War Survival, 94th Cong., 2nd Sess., November 17, 1976, p. 16.

(24) US, Department of the Treasury, "Study of the Economic Effects of Restraint in Arms Transfers," Arms Transfer Policy, US Congress, Annex 2, p. 50 (note 12 supra).

(25) Jacques S. Gansler, "Let's Change the Way the Pentagon Does Business," Harvard Business Review 55 (May-June 1977): 109-18.

(26) US Congress, House, Committee on International Relations, Hearings: International Security Assistance Act of 1976, 94th Cong., November 11, 1975, p. 172.

(27) US Congress, pp. 1-2 (note 12 supra).

(28) Quoted in US, Library of Congress, Congressional Research Service, Foreign Affairs and National Defense Division, Implications of President Carter's Conventional Arms Transfer Policy, Report to the Committee on Foreign Relations, US Senate (Washington, D.C.: December 1977), p. 30.

(29) Ron Smith, "Military Expenditure and Capitalism," Cambridge Journal of Economics no. 1 (March 1977): 61-76.

(30) Kurt Rothschild, "Military Expenditure, exports and Growth," Kyklos 26 (1973): 804-15.

(31) This is described in Mary Kaldor, "The Role of Arms in Capitalist Economies: The Process of Overdevelopment and Underdevelopment," in Arms Control and Technological Innovation, eds. David Carlton and Carlo Schaerf (London: Croom Helm, 1977), pp. 322-41.

(32) US, Department of the Treasury, p. 41 (note 12 supra).

(33) US, Congressional Budget Office, The Effect of US Military Sales on the US Economy (Washington, D.C.: July 23, 1976), p. 1.

(34) US Department of the Treasury, p. 38 (note 12 supra).

(35) See Aviation Advisory Services, Ltd., Milavnews (Essex, UK) NL-178 (August 1976) for information on the Rapier deal. See Aviation Advisory Services, Ltd., Milavnews (Essex, UK) NL-184 (February 1977) for information on the Chinook deal.

(36) For an elaboration of this argument, see Emma Rothschild, "Carter and Arms: No sale," New York Review of Books 24 (Sepbember 15, 1977): 10-14.

(37) See Stockholm, p. 577 (note 7 supra).

(38) US Congress, (note 3 supra).

(39) Aviation Advisory Services, Ltd., Milavnews (Essex, UK) NL-183 (January 1977), discusses an Israeli-Greek deal.

(40) Michael Checinski, The Cost of Armament Production and the Profitability of Armament Exports in Comecon Countries, Research Paper No. 10 (Jerusalem: Soviet and East European Research Centre, Hebrew University of Jerusalem, November 1974), p. 12.

(41) Quoted in David Holloway, "Science, Technology and Soviet Armed Forces" (Paper prepared for the Workshop on Soviet Science and Technology, Airlie House, Warrenton, Virginia, November 18-21, 1976).

(42) Checinski, pp. 13-14 (note 40 supra).

(43) Ibid.

(44) Gur Ofer, "Soviet Military Aid to the Middle — An Economic Balance Sheet," US Congress, Joint Economic Committee, Compendium: Soviet Economy in a New Perspective 94 Cong., 2nd Sess. (Washington, D.C.: US Government Printing Office, October 14, 1976), p. 233.

(45) See the seminal work of A.C. Sutton, Western Technology and Soviet Economic Development (Stanford, California: Stanford University Press, 1973).

(46) See Kosygin's comments in Samuel Pisar, Coexistence and Commerce. Guidelines for Transactions Between East and West (London: Allen Lane, 1971).

(47) See Philip Hanson, "International Technology Transfer from the West to the USSR" (Paper prepared for Workshop on Soviet Science and Technology, Airlie House, Warrenton, Virginia, November 18-21, 1976).

(48) Marshall I. Goldman, "Autarchy or Integration – The USSR and the World Economy," Soviet Economy pp. 93-4 (note 44 supra).

(49) US, Central Intelligence Agency, "USSR: Hard Currency Trade and Payments, 1977-78," CIA Research Aid, March 1977, quoted in Eugene Kozicharow, "Hard Currency Problems Spur Soviet Export Push," Aviation Week and Space Technology (April 11, 1977): 17-18.

(50) Keesings Contemporary Archives, (July 2, 1976): 27808A-27810B.

(51) Ofer, p. 237 (note 44 supra).

(52) Reported in Kozicharow (note 49 supra).

(53) Proposals of this kind are contained in Labour Party Defence Study Group, Sense About Defence (London: Quartet Books, 1977).

9 The Vulnerable Condition of Middle East Economies
Fred Gottheil

The Middle East region represents a highly differentiated set of nations. Among those properties that seem to bear most directly upon the issues of national economic vulnerability are a nation's oil endowment, the level and origin of GNP, the intensity of participation in the Arab-Israel confrontation. Each generates a particular form of vulnerability.

Middle East nations seem to polarize sharply on these differentiating properties. For example, they appear either to be well-endowed with oil reserves or to possess none at all. They have been either habitually involved in the Arab-Israel conflict or not at all. They either have high per capital incomes or chronically low ones. Moreover, when these properties are arranged in sets, as illustred in Table 9.1, these sets appear to be nonintersecting. Saudi Arabia, Iran, Iraq, Algeria, and Libya, for example, share relatively high per capital incomes and nonactive participation in the conflict. Syria, Egypt, and Jordan, on the other hand, are not only active confrontation states but also poor and oil-less. At the same time, they are the states that border Israel.

Table 9.1. Characteristics of Middle Eastern Economies

		Active Confrontation	Nonactive Confrontation
High Per Capital Income	Oil		Saudi Arabia, Iran, Algeria, Libya, Iraq, Kuwait, UAE.
	Nonoil	Israel	
Low Per Capital Income	Oil		
	Nonoil	Syria, Egypt, Jordan	

231

These sets of economies are subject to different forms of economic dependencies. The high income nonconfrontation set is dominated by oil economics, and the dependencies are thus oil derivatives. The oil poor confrontation set, on the other hand, is dominated by military events. This circumstance, more than any other factor, dictates not only the pace and direction of its economic performance, but also the character of its dependencies. Israel, in a set by itself, is more aligned with the latter simply because like members of that set, its economic performance cannot be understood outside the framework of the military conflict.

The links between these sets remain weak and essentially disconnected: large transfers of wealth from the rich to the poor Arab economies have not been forthcoming; nor have the oil-rich Arab economies become actively engaged in the direct confrontation with Israel. Even the events of 1973 and their aftermath have done little to alter these circumstances.

The following two sections will explore the relationships between the economic performance within these sets and the nature of the dependencies they generate.

LANDLORD ECONOMICS: THE OIL RICH
NONCONFRONTATION SET

The Theoretical Origins of the Oil-Based Vulnerability Argument

Discussion concerning Middle East oil and economic vulnerability is almost a déja vu of the late eighteenth and nineteenth century controversy among economists over the nature and causes of economic development.

One of the most revolutionary ideas in economic thinking is still found in Adam Smith's Wealth of Nations. It is that an exchange economy makes feasible the use of division of labor in the production process, and that this division of labor augments the quantity of product that can be produced with a given set of inputs. This notion undercut once and for all the dominant mercantilist thinking which saw the acquisition of wealth and power as strictly an additive process. Only more labor or land would yield more wealth. Since both of these wealth-yielding resources were scarce, it seemed reasonable to conclude that nations must view each other as adversaries. Smith's discovery that wealth can be created by extending the market changed the manner by which people and nations viewed each other. Now, both parties to an exchange could benefit. The idea of acquiring superior power with respect to other nations, therefore, no longer was a prerequisite to economic well-being.

David Ricardo carried Smith's argument further. Using the English and Portuguese trade of cloth and wine as his model, he showed that even in the circumstance where one nation was more efficient in producing both wine and cloth, it would still pay the efficient producer to give up the production of one and concentrate completely on the production of that commodity whose <u>relative</u> efficiency was the greater. Through such an international specialization of production, he argued, each of the nations would end up with a greater total produce than they would have acquired otherwise. In other words, trade under any circumstance is <u>always</u> beneficial.

Classical and neoclassical writers, like variations on a theme, developed and garnished this new wisdom. So impressed were they with the idea of economic gains through specialization that little attention was placed on the negative attributes associated with division of labor.

In retrospect, they overlooked precisely those things that most troubled the mercantilists. For while the latter may have erred in identifying the causes of the wealth of nations, they did nonetheless identify a legitimate fear arising out of international trade: <u>the vulnerability of nations whose economies become dependent for essential commodities on other nations</u>. That is to say, if England produced only cloth and Portugal only wine, then England's thirst is satisfied only if Portugal supplies the wine. Were Portugal to close the tap, England would not drink. While England can probably do without wine, it would be quite another matter if imports were grain or oil. In addition, if England were the only consumer of Portugal's wine, then Portugal's consumption of cloth depends entirely upon England's inclination to purchase wine. In other words, the dependency cuts both ways in a world of commodity specialization and trade.

The vulnerability qualification to Ricardo's ingenious theory of comparative advantage was not simply a theoretical commentary. The Corn Laws were, at the time of his writing, a very live and controversial issue. These laws fixed a surcharge on imported corn in order to make the much higher priced English corn competitive. Without the surcharge, English farmers felt that they could not successfully compete with European imports. Ricardo correctly viewed the political support by landlords for the Corn Laws as a means by which they were able to secure their rent incomes. The argument advanced in defense of the Corn Laws, however, was based on the national vulnerability issue. The landlords argued that unfettered trade in corn would ruin English production, make England dependent on other nations for food stuffs, and by so doing, undermine national independence.

The Middle East and Market Vulnerability

It may be instructive to apply these nineteenth century ideas of production, trade, and vulnerability to some of the economic issues current in the Middle East. A rather reasonable fit emerges between models economists construct today on exhaustive resources and the old mercantilist and classical theories. Moreover, the economic policies generated from the modern models appear to be no more sophisticated than the policies advanced over 150 years ago.

Until recently, the Middle East was virtually ignored by the industrially advanced economies. Although oil has been a strategic commodity for the twentieth century industrial world, the network of international economic relations that grew out of the oil business centered principally around intra-European and American transactions. Prices, output, and market shares were determined by Western decision makers for Western interests. Consideration of Middle East interests was, if it occurred at all, parenthetical. The conventional wisdom of the Smith-Ricardo thesis was sufficient to assure the oil rich Middle East that although not a participant in decision making, its interests were nonetheless being served.

The evidence, too, appeared to support the Smith-Ricardo thesis. After all, it was entirely Western enterprise that discovered, extracted, transported, refined, and consumed the oil. The Middle East income from oil was strictly in the form of economic rent. The before and after Western intervention comparison of Middle East welfare appeared obvious. If there was an issue of economic justice, it was not that the Middle East economy was shortchanged in its transactions with the West. In the pure classical sense of the term, the Middle East oil income recipients were unproductive landlords. No people better fitted John Stuart Mill's description of this landlord class:

> If the land derived its productive power wholly from nature, and not at all from industry . . . it not only would not be necessary, but it would be the height of injustice, to let the gift of nature be engrossed by individuals.(1)

Setting aside equity distribution, this newly discovered source of Middle East income, far from providing national economic security to the oil rich Middle East, as income is generally thought to do, produced instead a dependence relation between itself and the external world.

The economic forces generating this dependency, or vulnerability, are, to some extent, the familiar ones associated with a landlord class dependent upon the price of one commodity. However, the Middle East condition broadens the focus from the purely internal question of income distribution normally associated with landlords to the question of economic national security. This shift in focus has to do with the relative weights attached to the landlord's share within the economy and to the direction of trade in the commodity market. In the case of the nineteenth century Corn Laws, it was clear that although the English landlords raised the issue of national vulnerability in defense of the Corn Laws, the controversy centered on real income shifts within the English economy.

In the case of the Middle East today, the locus of the income shifts is different. While higher oil prices produce higher money rents for the landlord class, a significant segment of the national economy is the landlord class. Moreover, the Middle East oil market is not internal. Production has always been export oriented as indicated in Table 9.2. Changes in oil prices, then, do not affect internal, as much as global, income redistribution. When oil prices rise, the national income of the oil rich Middle East itself increases. Conversely, when oil prices fall, national income declines.

What OPEC has produced for these oil rich landlord economies in

Table 9.2. Middle East Oil, Oil Exports, GNP
1960-75
(in percentages)

	1975 Oil Exports/ GNP	1975 Oil Exports/ Total Exports	1960 Oil Exports/ Oil Production
Iran	25.6	97.0	87.0
Libya	56.0	99.0	—
Saudi Arabia	86.0	99.0	99.0
Iraq	60.0	98.0	96.0
Algeria	23.9	91.0	—
Kuwait	84.3	94.0	98.0

Source: International Monetary Fund, Financial Statistics 30 (March 1977), and A.A. Kabbah, OPEC, Past-Present (Vienna: Petro-Economic Research Center, 1974), p. 169.

the 1970s is not only substantial income as indicated in Table 9.3, but also a lock on the determination of oil prices. It is this lock that has given them an appearance of economic power and security. However, in spite of their new found wealth and their impressive foreign reserve accumulations, they are anything but secure. In fact, they may be among the most vulnerable of the world's rich economies; they are now, as they were before, still dependent upon one commodity and one locked price. Only now, the weight of this dependence has increased. If economic history teaches us anything, it is that all locks on resources and prices are time locks.

Thus, while the good fortune of the oil producers is abundantly apparent, the durability of the fortune is not. Unless they are successful in transforming oil income into internal economic development – no matter how unattractive the prospects may appear in comparison with the lucrative investment opportunities elsewhere – they will remain a set of landlord nations. Landlords' incomes, dependent as they are on one resource, are subject to the most corrosive of all economic agents – modern technology. The application of the sciences to all economic activity has produced a never-ending stream of declining and replacement industries; that is to say, in the long run, everything becomes obsolete. A national economy survives and can thrive on this process if it is sufficiently diversified to adjust internally to superior replacement. The problem with the oil rich Middle East is that oil revenue is not just a windfall. It is the economy of these countries. If oil goes the way of all prior energy industries, the Middle East oil fields of today become tomorrow's Appalachia.

Table 9.3. OPEC Exporting Countries' Revenues: Middle East and North Africa,
1960-74
(million US dollars)

Country	1960	1970	1973	1974
Saudi Arabia	355	1,200	5,100	20,000
Kuwait	465	895	1,900	7,000
Iran	285	1,136	4,100	17,400
Iraq	266	521	1,500	6,800
United Arab Emirates	a	233	900	4,100
Qatar	54	122	400	1,600
Libya	a	1,295	2,300	7,600
Algeria	b	325	900	3,700
TOTAL	1,500	5,727	17,100	68,200

[a]Libya and Abu Dhabi (United Arab Emirates) began production in 1961
and 1962 respectively.
[b]Not available.

Source: "The Middle East U.S. Policy, Israel, Oil and the Arabs: 2nd Edition",
Congressional Quarterly (October 1975): 30.

The King Midas Condition — Gold Versus Real Vulnerability

It is, therefore, necessary to ask how the real economic conditions in
the oil rich Middle East would be affected if oil were replaced by a new
energy source or if OPEC were weakened so that the money reserves
generated in the 1970s were no longer forthcoming in the 1980s. Posing
this question introduces the distinction between money and real national
wealth.

Table 9.4 shows the disproportionality between Middle East wealth
and well-being. Ranked among 132 nations, the oil rich Middle East
economies place above the median on per capita income (Saudi Arabia =
43rd, etc.) However, on such items as literacy (Saudi Arabia = 108th,
etc.) or infant mortality (Saudi Arabia = 104th, etc.) or even calories
per capita (Saudi Arabia = 83rd, etc.), their ranking falls well below the
median.

Unlike other sets of economies in Table 9.4, wealth in the oil rich
Middle East is derived essentially from one economic activity. In this

Table 9.4. Per Capita Ranking, GNP, Military and Social Indicators
(132 countries, 1973)

	Per Capita GNP	Rank	Literacy Rank	Infant Mortality Rank	Life Expectancy Rank	Calories Per Capita	Military Per Capita
Kuwait	8178	1	72	41	45	37	9
Libya	2747	23	96	87	45	57	34
Saudi Arabia	1037	43	108	104	74	83	12
Iran	781	50	80	95	81	80	22
Algeria	519	63	88	85	71	130	69
Iraq	598	56	88	99	71	100	21
Egypt	258	87	88	103	78	57	33
Jordan	345	79	84	68	71	61	28
Syria	359	78	86	68	54	44	27
Israel	3023	21	42	21	20	29	1
Argentina	1287	37	27	50	39	27	48
Turkey	542	60	73	76	66	25	52
Greece	1804	32	42	24	10	19	22

Source: Ruth L. Sivard, World Military and Social Expenditures (Leesburg, Va.: WMSE Publications, 1976), pp. 24-8.

sense, it reflects a King Midas syndrome. The oil rich Middle East economies are blessed with oil, but cursed with the inability to employ their surpluses internally. As a result, they go elsewhere to place their financial accumulations in profitable investment. Although the post-1973 condition clearly represents a quantum leap in dollar surpluses, in terms of dependence on the West, the structural relationships remain unaffected.

MILITARY PAUPER ECONOMIES:
THE NONOIL CONFRONTATION SET

Egypt, Syria, and Jordan have been the major Arab participants in the Arab-Israeli wars and near wars over the course of the past thirty years. More so than any other set of Middle East nations, this series of confrontations has dictated the pace and direction of their internal development. Algeria, Iraq, Saudi Arabia, and Libya form a second line confrontation set. Their participation in the Arab-Israeli conflict has been predominantly diplomatic. Their commitments of manpower and military hardware to the confrontation have been more symbolic than real. They do not start wars; they do not end them; and they have had little influence on their outcomes.

Saudi Arabia's participation may appear to be more than second line, but even as the major Arab financial contributor to the confrontation states' military budgets, it is questionable whether its influence is more than marginal in governing decisions concerning war. Moreover, there is little evidence to tie Saudi Arabia's basic oil policy to the confrontation issue. Of course, confrontation in the region is not wholly described by the Arab-Israeli conflict. There is a history of war among Arab states, civil wars within Arab states, and a multiplicity of attempted coups which may outlast the Arab-Israeli conflict altogether, as also discussed in Chapter 13. It may be in these areas that real Saudi interest is to be found. Thus, while the Arab-Israeli conflict represents the single most identifiable confrontation in the Middle East, it is by no means the only source of confrontation or the only confrontation determining the level of military expenditures in the region.

The Theoretical Origins of the Military Burden Vulnerability Argument

The relationship between levels of military expenditures and rates of economic growth is not a noncontroversial one. The dominant thinking on the issue is that military expenditures represent to the nation a straightforward loss of civilian product. The significance of this loss depends, of course, upon the parameters of the national output and the military expenditure. To the extent that the military deflects resources from civilian investment, it can be described as having a negative impact on the nation's rate of economic growth.

The issue of national vulnerability arises when military expenditures absorb so much of the national output that investment approaches zero.

The prospect of sliding into such an economically vulnerable condition is particularly real for low income developing economies whose invest- ment – GNP ratios are already critically low.

At the same time, it has been argued that military expenditures simulate the economy so that on balance, higher levels of civilian consumption and investment obtain with increases in military expendi- tures. Benoit's study of forty-four developing countries, for example, showed positive correlations between military expenditure – GNP ratios, civilian rates of economic growth, and investment rates.(2) Although Benoit's findings tend to contradict the view that military expenditures represent a burden on the economy, the contradiction can be resolved by differentiating among the specific values of the military expenditure – GNP ratio. Such a differentiation is shown in Figure 9.1.

The Benoit view is represented by the OA range of M – GNP values. Here, military expenditures are positively correlated with rate of civilian economic growth. Beyond A, increases in M – GNP come only at the expense of growth. At B, the positive attributes of the military expenditure are entirely dissipated and further increases in M – GNP produce negative rates of growth.

The Middle East and Economic Vulnerability

Whether ascribing to a simple burden model (The OC curve) or the more elaborate Benoit model for the oil poor Middle East, the military expenditure – GNP ratios in Table 9.5 would seem to represent a condition to the right of OB in Figure 9.1.

Nothing else seems to dominate these oil poor economies as much as war production and consumption. For Israel, Syria, Egypt, and Jordan, the military sectors are the most rapidly expanding and the most technically advanced. They enjoy the highest national priority. The Arab-Israeli Wars of 1967 and 1973 and their aftermaths continue to be the dominant factor shaping the prospects for economic development in the region.

The percentages shown in Table 9.5 would represent an over- whelming display of military activity even if they were not associated with countries of especially low per capita income. The 1974 Middle East military expenditure – GNP ratios, for example, exceed those of the United States (6.0) percent, the Soviet Union (10.7 percent), France (3.7 percent), and England (4.9 percent). Middle East military expendi- tures – GNP ratios are particularly striking when compared to the 1.8 percent Latin American average, the 2.6 percent African average, or the 4.3 percent average for all developing nations.

Military expenditures in the Middle East, by any reading of the numbers, are no ordinary expenditures. For the four principals in the Arab-Israeli conflict, they represent levels of critical importance. The burden imposed upon Egypt, Syria, Jordan, and Israel by these abnormally high military expenditures can be measured by comparing the conditions that would obtain for these economies under alternative military profiles. Suppose, for example, that military expenditures were reduced in these economies to levels comparable to those in other developing economies, e.g., 2.5 percent of GNP. Suppose further that the human and material resources released by the decline in military

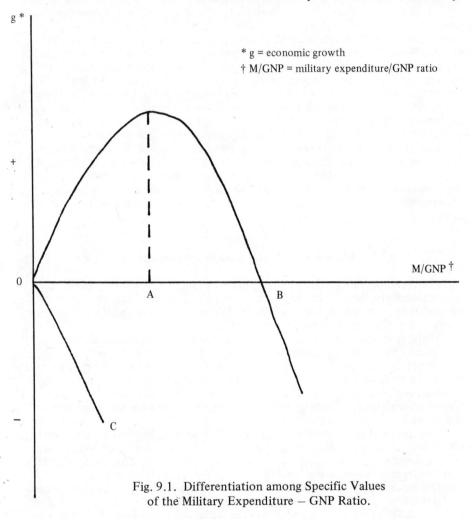

* g = economic growth

† M/GNP = military expenditure/GNP ratio

Fig. 9.1. Differentiation among Specific Values
of the Military Expenditure — GNP Ratio.

expenditures were converted to civilian investments. Under such conditions, the levels of national product generated for Egypt, Syria, Jordan, and Israel would be higher than those obtained under conditions of actual military expenditures.

In other words, the military burden represents the costs to these economies of forfeited national product.(3) Such cost estimates can be made by employing a simple variant of the Harrod-Domar Model in the form:

Table 9.5. Military Expenditures as a Percent of GNP for
Israel, Egypt, Syria, and Jordan
1960-74 as Compared with Averages for
Latin America, Africa, and Developing Countries, 1974

	1960	1969	1974
Israel	8.6	25.1	37.3
Egypt	6.0	13.3	19.8
Syria	9.8	14.4	16.5
Jordan	18.1	18.0	12.9
Latin America (average)			1.8
Africa (average)			2.6
Developing countries (average)			4.3

Source: Nadav Safran, From War to War (New York: Pegasus, 1969), pp. 150, 159, 177, 181; and US Arms Control and Disarmament Agency, World Military Expenditures and Arms Transfers 1965-1974 (Washington, D.C.: US Government Printing Office, 1976).

$$GNP_t = GNP_{t-1} \left(1 + r_t + \frac{(a_t - n_t)}{k}\right)$$

GNP_t = gross national product in period t,

r_t = rate of growth of GNP at constant prices in period i,

a_t = actual military expenditures as a percent of GNP in period t,

n_t = normalized military expenditures as a percent of GNP in period t, and

k = incremental capital output ratio.

If the actual military expenditure – GNP ratios for these economies were normal so that $a_t = n_t$, then the equation above becomes $GNP_t = GNP_{t-1}(1 + r_t)$. This simply says that the GNP in period t is equal to the GNP of the previous period plus the increase in GNP produced by a rate of growth r_t. If, on the other hand, the military expenditure – GNP ratios are abnormal, i.e., $a_t > n_t$, then the possibility of reducing a_t to n_t would make resources available for productive investment. The significance of this normalization or investment and the rate of growth depends upon the value of k, i.e., the amount of capital required to generate a unit of output. If, for example, k = 3 and a_t-n_t = 12, then the rate of growth in the economy could be augmented by 4 percent. That is, if the prevailing rate of growth of national product were 8 percent, the normalization of military expenditure – GNP ratios could produce a 50 percent increase in this rate.

Table 9.6 records a set of military burdens generated over the period 1975-85. These estimates are based on alternative values for the normalized military expenditures - GNP ratios, n, and the percent of the resources released by the military that is actually converted to civilian investment.

Table 9.6. 1985 GNP Estimates for Israel, Egypt, Syria, and Jordan
(million US dollars)

	100 percent conversion			30 percent conversion		
	n=a	n=2.5	n=5	n=a	n=2.5	n=5
Israel	18,902	35,052	32,574	18,802	22,841	22,324
Egypt	13,171	16,735	15,461	13,171	14,161	13,824
Syria	4,876	6,346	5,877	4,876	5,281	5,159
Jordan	1,432	1,815	1,678	1,432	1,538	1,502

Source: Author's estimates

Israel, for example, with n=2.5 and 100 percent conversion from military to civilian investment, obtains a 1985 GNP of $35,052 million (Table 9.6, column 2). This GNP compares to the $18,902 million that would accrue in 1985 were Israel required to maintain the 1974 37.3 percent military expenditure – GNP ratio from 1975 through 1985. In other words, the GNP forfeited in 1985 by Israel is $15,150 million ($35,052-$18,902), or as much as 85 percent of the expected 1985 GNP that would accrue under the persisting conditions of abnormal military expenditures.

The burdens imposed by the military expenditures for Egypt, Syria, and Jordan under the same comparative conditions are also quite substantial. In the Egyptian case, the GNP forfeited in 1985 is $3,564 million or 27 percent of its 1985 GNP. The loss to Syria is $1,470 million or 30 percent of its 1985 GNP. In the case of Jordan, the loss is $393 million or 26 percent of the 1985 GNP.

The military burden, then, to the four oil poor confrontation states totals $21,567 million or 56 percent of their combined 1985 GNPs. Even relaxing the 100 percent conversion assumption to 30 percent, the 1985 GNP levels are significant for these economies, as indicated in Table 9.6, columns 4, 5, and 6.

The severity of these military burdens is aggravated further by the economic environment upon which they are imposed. Consider, for example, the Egyptian situation. Per capita agriculture actually declined in Egypt during the 1961-65 to 1975 period as seen in Table 9.7. As a result, Egypt was forced to increase its agricultural imports. In the 1973-75 period alone, these imports rose from $310 million to $1,500 million. Thus, in 1975, over 90 percent of the urban bread supply in Egypt was made from imported wheat or flour. Approximately 27 percent of the 2,700 calories consumed by the average Egyptian came in the form of imported products. These imports are expected to provide as much as 40 percent of Egypt's 1980 food supply and to reach 50 percent by 1985.(4) Such imports are paid in foreign currencies which Egypt must borrow on the private, governmental, and international agency financial markets.

Table 9.7. Index of Per Capita Agriculture and Food for
Egypt, Jordan, Syria, and Israel
1961-65 to 1975

	Per Capital Agriculture		Per Capita Food	
	1961-65	1975	1961-65	1975
Egypt	100	93	100	101
Jordan	100	57	100	57
Syria	100	83	100	90
Israel	100	122	100	118

Source: US Department of Agriculture, Indices of Agricultural Production in Africa and the Near East, 1956-1975, Statistical Bulletin no. 556 (Washington, D.C.: July 1976), pp. 23, 91, 93, 97.

In other words, the Egyptian economy is highly vulnerable. Table 9.8 illustrates the extent of its foreign indebtedness. Thirty-two percent of 1974 Egyptian export income was required simply to cover the cost of servicing its external public debt. By 1976, Egypt's balance-of-payment deficit rose to $807 million, further committing the Egyptian economy to external dependency.(5)

It is difficult to consider this state of economic vulnerability outside the context of the military burden discussed previously. Under any reasonable set of parameter values for Table 9.6, it appears obvious that Egypt's vulnerability is strongly connected to the Arab-Israeli confrontation. In Egypt's case, the GNP forfeiture produced by the confrontation is paramount in explaining Egyptian economic stagnation and the consequential deepening dependency on foreign grants and credit.

Table 9.8. External Public Debt and Service Payments
on External Public Debt as Percent of Exports
(million US dollars)

	External Public Debt		Service Payments on External Public Debt as Percentage of Exports			
	1973	1974	1967	1970	1973	1974
Israel	4,519.5	5,562.0	15.7	18.6	20.8	18.7
Egypt	1,746.0	1,811.0	19.5	26.2	34.6	32.0
Jordan	222.7	286.0	1.8	3.6	3.7	4.9
Syria	180.6	291.0	11.6	9.2	7.3	4.9

Source: International Bank for Reconstruction and Development, World Bank Annual Report 1976 (Washington, D.C.: 1976), pp. 104-5.

Israel's vulnerability is no less severe. Although the Israeli economy is a high performer, its sustained military burden is debilitating. Like Egypt, it is burdened with an abnormally high debt service payment-export ratio and for 1975, a balance-of-payment deficit of $1,030 million.(6) No less than Egypt, confrontation has made Israel an externally dependent economy. Syria and Jordan are by comparison to Israel and Egypt minor debtor nations. However, with Syria and Jordan as well, the difference between a dependent or solvent condition is explained by the confrontation.

It is, therefore, not at all inaccurate to describe these oil poor confrontation economies as military paupers. Moreover, it appears that such a condition and the consequent vulnerability it produces will persist as long as the confrontation.

CONCLUDING REMARKS

No country is immune either from dependencies created by international specializations of production or from expenditures on military preparedness. What is unique about the Middle East, however, is the extent to which these conditions dictate the pace and direction of the region's economic development.

In the case of the oil rich, their vulnerability to the capricious behavior of one price can be overcome only by channeling their economies into a more diversified network of production activities. Such a transformation, however, requires both considerable time and modification of national character. It depends not upon the supply of investment funds, which have been readily available to the oil rich since the 1930s, but upon changes in the quality of their working population. This, in turn, requires modification in almost all of their social institutions. However, unless such a process of change occurs, the oil rich remain vulnerable to one commodity price regardless of their vast oil derived financial accumulations.

In the case of the oil poor, the military based vulnerability prospect is quite different. Here, vulnerability of the critically low income economies is a byproduct of the resource leak caused by pathological expenditures on the military. In the event of a political accommodation in the region, the leakage and the vulnerability it creates can be reduced by simple discretionary policy.

NOTES AND REFERENCES

(1) John Stuart Mill, Principles of Political Economy (1848; reprint ed., London: Longmans, Green and Co., 1909), Section 7.

(2) Emile Benoit, "Growth Effects of Defense in Developing Economies," International Development Review 14 (January 1972): 2-15.

(3) Fred Gottheil, "An Economic Assessment of the Military Burden in the Middle East," Journal of Conflict Resolution 18 (September 1974): 502-13.

(4) US Department of Agriculture, The Agricultural Situation in Africa and West Asia, Review of 1975 and Outlook for 1976, Foreign Agricultural Economic Report no. 125 (Washington, D.C.: August 1976).

(5) International Monetary Fund, Financial Statistics (Washington, D.C.) 30 (October 1977): 128.

(6) Ibid., p. 192.

10 Arms Transfer, Great Power Intervention, and Settlement of the Arab-Israeli Conflict
Abraham S. Becker

The mandate of these comments is to attempt to link the discussion of great power intervention in and arms transfer to the Middle East with the concluding consideration of settlement of the Arab-Israeli conflict. For the author of such a piece, the indicated scope is dangerously broad; it invites dabbling and sweeping generalizations, where his conference colleagues have probed this very large topic carefully in more manageable portions. In addition, it risks the charge of distortion of the conference contributions by selective summarization.

Let it, therefore, be made clear that the purpose of this paper is not to attempt to summarize the preceding papers and surely not to critique them in the formal conference style. Instead, what is presented subsequently are personal reflections on the three major themes of the conference – great power intervention, arms transfers, and settlement of the Arab-Israeli conflict – stimulated by the conference presentations. The first set of issues considered is the significance of arms transfers as a focus of policy concern. This leads to examination of the relationship between arms transfers and great power intervention in the Middle East, and then to assessment of the effect of great power interaction on regional stability. The last section discusses the connection of these factors to settlement of the Arab-Israeli conflict.

DO ARMS TRANSFERS MATTER?

By the usual volume measurements, arms transfers to the Middle East are currently of very significant proportions. The estimates compiled by the United States Arms Control and Disarmament Agency cited by Pajak in Chapter 5 provide an indication of the growing aggregate size, as well as of the concentration in origin and destination of the arms trade.(1) At least since 1972, the arms transfer problem is preeminently one of sales to the Middle East.(2) Valued in 1974 United

States prices, imports of arms into the Middle East jumped from about $1.5 billion in 1972 to almost $4.5 billion in 1973. They then declined to about $3 billion in 1975. Behind these dollar figures lie large numbers of military machines. Moreover, these annual flows represent merely the increments to inventories which despite the destructiveness of periodic fighting, had reached sizable proportions even before the 1973 War. Considering only the major equipment categories, by mid-1975 the holdings of Israel and four Arab antagonists (Egypt, Syria, Iraq, and Jordan) reached some 8,500 tanks, 12,800 armored vehicles, 4,800 field artillery pieces (excluding mortars and rocket launchers), and some 1,700 tactical aircraft.(3)

A second characteristic of global arms transfers, as well as those to the Middle East in particular, is that the flow is generated primarily by the Soviet Union and the United States. Together they provide four-fifths or more of the total transfers from all suppliers. Behind them Britain and France are scrambling to obtain and retain their places in the arms transfer sun, as they adapt government and private sector mechanisms to aid their arms sales efforts. Reluctantly, the Germans are gearing themselves up for a similar campaign. While somewhat behind Britain and France now, their potential is probably high. This suggests predominantly economic motivations for the three West European powers as arms suppliers. Soviet motivations are presumed to be somewhat different and American involvement also has a somewhat more complex character. This is a question of larger proportions returned to subsequently.

The concerns aroused by arms traffic of such magnitude relate to their significance in affecting the fate of the region. The kind of quantitative measures cited suggest a first level analytical question relating to the economic impact on the recipients, one of the themes in Chapter 9. The size of these flows could be expected to pose a serious burden on governments struggling to meet consumer needs and to modernize their economies. As we know from other evidence, the economic burden of arms imports is a major factor in accelerating or even triggering internal political, economic, and social dislocations for two of the major regional antagonists, Israel and Egypt. The effect of such internal stresses on external policy may be marked, but it appears to be difficult to specify. Quester suggests that even the direction of change is uncertain; the imposition of heavy economic burdens may be either stabilizing or destabilizing in regional conflict terms, as discussed in Chapter 11. One might ask if a severe economic constraint induces aversion to risk in the relations with antagonists. It might instead produce greater militancy to divert internal strains in external involvement, perhaps also with the hope of solving the external problem so that the military burden can be reduced. Both rationalizations are being applied to the current Middle Eastern situation. As for the evidence of the past, there are few good parallels, but Sadat has stated that Egypt's desperate economic situation in 1973 did not deter him from going to war. On the eve of the October War, Sadat told the Egyptian National Council, "I would like to make something clear to you. Our economy is less than zero. I do not have a loaf of bread for 1974 . . . Nevertheless, may God do what is best."(4)

Liberal arms supply has been linked directly, i.e., not just through the effect of economic burdens, with increases in the probability of war between the recipients. It might be supposed that each regional antagonist thinks of itself as satisfied with a defensive posture when the military balance is favorable to itself and sees aggressive intent when the other side reaches for additional weapons. The description fits Israel reasonably well. For example, Ben-Gurion's government took alarm at the "Czechoslovakian"-Egyptian arms deal in 1955 and, therefore, went to war in 1956. In contrast, after June 1967, the Labor government generally felt able to cope with the military threat because of the amplitude of American arms supply. However, the hypothesis fits Arab behavior far less well. This is true largely for a simple reason: Israel has been a status quo power, with the exception of 1956 and the brief six-week period just before the June 1967 War, and the Arabs have been revisionists. Arabs have looked to arms as a means to compel the satisfaction of their conflict demand; directly through various forms of warfare, or indirectly as leverage on the great powers and the international community. Nevertheless, it was not a belief that the balance had turned favorable which pushed Nasser on May 15, 1967 into the first of the series of moves that brought on the Six Day War. One wonders, too, whether Sadat would not have been as determined on war in 1973 without the Scud missiles. The connections between arms supply and the likelihood of war are not easily drawn.

It is probably fruitless, too, to attempt to develop any causal link between types of weaponry supplied and the likelihood of renewed war in the Middle East. Whether a weapon system is strategic or tactical, offensive or defensive, is a function of objective and context. For example, in the 1973 War, surface-to-air missiles served as the shield to protect offensive operations, despite the apparent defensive character of the weapon system itself. Perhaps there has been a secular trend in destructiveness of weapons supplied to the Middle East. Certainly this is true with respect to the effect on opposing weapons. The rates of attrition of military hardware in 1973 were on a far higher scale than the area had ever known before.

ARMS TRANSFER AND ARMS CONTROL

The distant observer, uninvolved in third world conflicts, may regard arms sales to the Middle East as only adding fuel to the flames. However, there are at least three arguments that have been advanced to suggest that arms transfers in some limited quantity and perhaps of particular types may play a stabilizing role in the region.

A recent and novel argument for continued arms transfers rests on a particular view of the future of military technology. It is suggested that the so-called "revolution" in conventional military technology, which many identify with the development of precision-guided munitions (PGMs), has strengthened the defensive side of the military equation and has put into question the continued mass use of the more traditional weapons of offensive and preemptive combat — the fighter bomber and the medium tank. Increasingly, it is the recipient who determines the weapon mix of arms transfers; supplier notions of offensive and defensive weapon technology will not necessarily be the guiding criteria. However, Foster doubts that the promise of future technology is for less complicated regional military balances; it may be, in fact, for greater difficulty in maintaining or regulating military balances, as discussed in Chapter 7. Because PGMs may mean high rates of attrition in battle, there could be an inducement to increase peacetime forces and stocks of material. Moreover, military survival may come to depend on speed and surprise in battle, thus raising the risk of surprise attack and preemptive war. The consequence is likely to be greater third world demand for arms transfers from the suppliers, leading to higher military budgets for the recipients. In short, this particular perception of technological change may lead to the conclusion that the new technology is likely to accelerate regional arms races. If these are, in fact, the current directions of technology, one must wonder if Israel or the Arabs will benefit more on balance. It seems hard to say. Perhaps Israel has a greater ability to use and to adapt rapidly changing military technology, but the requirements for large and increasing quantities of sophisticated weaponry may increase the strains on its economy as well as its relations with the United States, its principal supplier. Such difficulties are less likely to be a serious problem for any Arab state that continues to enjoy the financial support of oil rich patrons in the Persian Gulf.

A second and more orthodox argument for arms transfers is that they provide the supplier with a degree of control over client policies that wold not otherwise be available. It is not self-evident that increased supplier control would necessarily be stabilizing, but achievement of such control has proved difficult for both sides. Harkavy argues that the maintenance by the great powers of strategic assets all over the world is becoming heavily dependent on continued arms supplies and often on extension of a general security commitment to regional clients, indicated in Chapter 6. These assets are being purchased or maintained at sharply increasing economic and political costs and demanded by hosts who were once considerably more pliable. As arms have become available from several sources, the recipients have discovered the leverage inherent in supplier competition. Paradoxically, it was the Soviet Union in Egypt which came closest to developing a position of real control but also suffered the most humiliating crisis of lack of control. For the Soviet Union, military assistance has proved an uncertain way to attempt to secure influence over recipient countries; the degree of influence attained thereby has proved to be tenuous, fleeting, and subject to astonishingly rapid reversals.

Cahn's heuristic matrix, relating arms transfers and supplier influence, suggests that the United States should have more success than the Soviet Union in attempting to control client behavior, as discussed in Chapter 4. Israel's lack of alternative sources of supply and its quasi-pariah status should, in theory, make it more susceptible to attempts at influence than the Soviet Union's clients. Moreover, recognizable control should be attainable even with significant limitations on the flow of arms. Out of this could be fashioned an argument for doling out arms to Israel on a very short string. This would be inconsistent with another rationale for arms transfer to the Middle East, that of helping participants in a bitter regional conflict feel more secure so they can take the risks necessary for settlement. Since one side's security is likely to be perceived as the other's insecurity, it is difficult to achieve a balance in arms transfers to the two sides, particularly with competing sources of supply. However, even if the balance could be struck, tight restrictions on supply to Israel are likely to be counterproductive in maintaining or extending American influence over Jerusalem's policy. As Quester suggests, there is a strength of the weak: a client that feels pushed into a corner of high insecurity may become more doggedly determined to defend what it regards as vital interests. Some observers believe that this factor partly explains the rightwing victory in the recent Israeli parliamentary election.

This raises the issue of the introduction of nuclear weapons into the region. No transfer of nuclear arms or nuclear weapons technology has yet taken place in the Middle East, though Baker would ascribe that to the desire of the powers to "make the world safe for superpower intervention. Such intervention would, however, be a likely consequence of the appearance of nuclear arms in an Arab or Israeli arsenal. The contingency most frequently discussed is that of an Israeli nuclear capability. Israel has used the veiled threat of acquiring a nuclear option as a basis for maintaining its deterrent power vis-a-vis its Arab foes. Quester argues in Chapter 11 that this is responsible for moderating the tone of Arab statements. Baker and Jabber see Israel's policy on the nuclear option as a device for maintaining a high rate of flow of conventional weapons from the United States, as discussed in Chapters 2 and 3. The latter two are concerned that the example is bound to be infectious on the Arab side. Since a fear of military confrontation with the Soviet Union has been one of the major influences on United States policy and behavior in the region, it may be presumed that the threat of nuclearization of the Middle East is an element that deepens the commitment of the United States to the search for an early and stable settlement of the Arab-Israeli conflict. This would also enable Washington to escape the dilemma of attempting to effect control through arms transfer and yet prevent a dangerous increase in Israel's sense of isolation.

The obvious resolution to the conflict between the need to satisfy legitimate aspirations for security on the part of the regional actors and the dangers of large-scale arms transfers is regional arms control. Different forms have been suggested. Some involve a before-the-solution set of arrangements, for example, limiting the supply of long-range PGMs to avoid destabilizing threats to either side's vulnerable population centers. Other formulations deal with arrangements that are intended to be part of the conflict's resolution: demilitarization, buffer zones, joint patrols, and the like. Continued injections of increasingly sophisticated technology into the Middle East could dim prospects for any control arrangements, particularly because of difficulties in verification. The problem of third world arms control is essentially a problem of supplier agreement. Baker cites the London Group as a possible precedent for future agreements in the area of nuclear proliferation. Whatever modest success the London Group has achieved has been the result of the development of a common interest among its members. Control over the supply of conventional arms to the Middle East will similarly depend on a reconciliation of divergent supplier motivations.

Evidently, one cannot rely on self-constraint by the suppliers operating in a vigorous buyers' market. However, the nature and strength of the economic factor with regard to Western suppliers is viewed differently by Cahn and Kaldor, in Chapters 4 and 8. Cahn evidently attributes little real force to the economic arguments, while Kaldor thinks them increasingly important. The latter emphasizes industrial benefits, i.e., keeping production lines open. However, she agrees with Cahn that recovery of R&D costs and lowering production costs are secondary. Both of them recognize that rationalizations may, in fact, be disguises for political motives. Kaldor carries this a step further by arguing that short-uneconomic benefits sacrifice long-term political benefits in terms of control over supply and influence on the recipient. She believes that achievement of a supplier agreement to control arms flows to the Middle East would require considerable changes in the international economic order.

Military assistance has been the most important instrument of Soviet penetration into the Middle East, and for most of the two decades since the first major Soviet arms deal, the economics of arms transfers has been distinctly secondary in Soviet policy considerations. However, the Soviet Union has been seeking increasingly to sell arms for hard currency. Kaldor suggests, therefore, that securing Soviet adherence to a supplier arms control agreement would entail provision of relief for the balance-of-payments problems that the Soviet Union has experienced with the developed industrial countries in recent years. This observer doubts that economics takes priority over politics in Soviet policy in this sphere.

ARMS TRANSFERS AND GREAT POWER INTERVENTION

The relationship between arms transfer and scale of great power involvement is many-sided. The level of arms transfer to a client country may itself be a major index of involvement. To a very considerable extent, at least since the mid-1960s, the ebb and flow of Soviet supply to Egypt has been an important indicator of the scope and range, perhaps also the depth of Moscow's involvement with Cairo. However, there are a number of other factors to be taken into account. First, the absolute size of the arms transfer does not necessarily reflect the importance of the great power position in the particular country or the power's degree of commitment. The United States commitment to Israel in the mid-1960s was considerably greater than could be inferred from the direct American arms transfer. Soviet supply to countries in East Africa and in the Red Sea region has been small in absolute terms, but it is directed at achieving or protecting strategic positions of considerable significance. Second, monopoly of supply and dependence on the recipient generate different client patron relationships than active supplier competition. So too, there is a distinction between sales in hard rather than soft currency. The sense of commitment may be considerably lessened when the arms are being transferred in hard cash-on-the-barrelhead deals. Of course, deepening involvement has almost automatically meant a greater volume of arms transfer.

Involvement, which may feature such policy instruments as economic aid and diplomatic support, is not the same as intervention. In accordance with his mandate, Evron has confined his discussion to the subject of military intervention in Chapter 1, and fifteen cases are discussed on pages 40-62. He defines military intervention as the use by a great power of military force or the threat to use military force that is backed up by troop movements in the intervening power's territory or in the vicinity of the target state, either to oppose a Middle East country or another great power in the region, or to affect a Middle East country's internal development. Evron's fifteen cases fall into two major post-World War II periods. The first, which he views as the final phase of colonialism, saw interventions to maintain a colonial or imperial role. The Suez War was the largest and last example of that type. It is noteworthy that the role of arms transfers in this category was small. Interventions of the second period came within "a framework of global competition as projected into the Middle East." These involved efforts by a great power to increase its own influence or to deny increases in influence to another great power. The Suez War marked not only the end of the phase of colonialist intervention in the Middle East; significantly, it was also the point at which arms transfers began to assume a major role in regional affairs generally and became an aspect of military intervention particularly.

Soviet policy has not been content with strategic denial, although admittedly it is not always easy to distinguish the negative impulses of denial from the positive ones of expansion. In any case, while in a previous era great power competition under either set of goals was performed largely by the forces of the powers themselves, in the second post-World War II decade two major factors combined to vastly enhance the military role of the clients. The first was the great powers' fear of military confrontation that might escalate out of control to nuclear war; the second was the growing assertiveness of third world countries in regional and international politics. The first factor made it desirable and preferable to exert pressure against the other great power, either directly through the action of one's clients, or indirectly against the power's clients in the area. Long before the Nixon Doctrine was conceived, this basic rationale of great power relationships in a nuclear world was in itself conducive to creating a major role for arms transfers to third countries. That role was accentuated by the second factor, which brought third world countries into the arms market almost as soon as they achieved the formal symbols of sovereignty.

The Soviet Union became a major actor in the region through association with the radical elites that had come to power in several

Arab states in the 1950s. Soviet penetration of a part of the Middle East, south of the area of traditional Russian and Soviet interest, was made possible largely by arms transfers. The 1955 "Czechoslovakian"-Egyptian arms deal was the major break that enabled the Soviet Union to vault over the barrier of bases and alliances which Britain and the United States were in the process of constructing along the northern tier of the Middle East. From then on, arms supply was perhaps the chief pillar of Arab-Soviet amity, along with Soviet political support and economic aid. It also proved to be a prime factor in several fallings-out between patron and clients.

Accordingly, it was not surprising that Evron's ten post-Suez interventions were all heavily affected by sharply increased arms flows to the region. The relationship works in both directions. The perceived threats that triggered the interventions arose from a regional political-military environment in which arms transfer raised the offensive potential of one or another of the antagonists – United States and British interventions within a context of Egyptian and Syrian arms buildups and Soviet intervention directed against Israeli power. A few of the interventions cited by Evron clearly led directly to new or further arms proliferation. The clearest example is the 1967 War which was followed by intensification of the involvement of both powers in the region. Moreover, the war marked a major change in the American arms transfer role in the region. Washington now became the main, indeed sole, supplier of Jerusalem's military needs. Nothing in the chain of events was inevitable. Still, due to Israeli fears of an alteration in the strategic balance, the Soviet arms transfer breakthrough in 1955 was connected to the Suez War, threats of Soviet intervention, American alarm at the prospect of growing Soviet influence, and thus to the bifurcation of arms transfer flows – Western to Israel and the conservative Arab monarchies, and Soviet to the radical Arab military republics. Only the October 1973 War began to alter that basic pattern.

GREAT POWER INTERVENTION AND REGIONAL STABILITY

Evron suggests that great power intervention or threats to intervene may have helped diminish instability in the Middle East. Within the framework of cold war in the region, the great powers have developed modes of conflict that incorporate safety catches. Attention is given subsequently to efforts by the powers to control crises rather than to inflame them. It should also be recognized, however, that the Soviet reentrance into the Middle East scene in the mid-1950s marked a final rupture of the relative restraints on arms competition that had been embodied in the Western tripartite monopoly. The initial acts of Soviet involvement represented the start of what was to be a two-decade long arms race, which brought modern military technology into the region and had as one result sharply accelerating levels of intensity in the successive wars. Perhaps most disturbing is the introduction of strategic weapons with their implicit threat of devastating attacks on populated areas. Moreover, as Harkavy has noted, the Soviet Union has been the arms supplier of radical and revisionist forces in the Middle East as in the third world generally, with the Libyan and Palestinian cases being the latest examples. The west, first Britain and France, then the United States, was intent on maintaining regional stability as part of a policy of strategic denial vis-a-vis the Soviet Union. The latter was concerned with strategic access, especially after its initial efforts to thwart the erection of Western barriers along the northern tier. Almost by definition, Moscow's struggle for strategic access was inconsistent with an effort to maintain regional stability.

Nevertheless, largely because of the very real danger of military confrontation, the great powers seem to have developed forms of accommodation to each other's presence and activity in the region that may be said to constitute rules of the game governing their interaction in the region. Five of the rules proposed by Evron and Horowitz are discussed in Chapter 1 and include:

- The United States and the Soviet Union recognize each other's presence, as well as the legitimacy of their opposing interests and of the efforts each makes to advance its national interests.

- The powers agree explicitly or tacitly on rules of behavior that limit the means they may use to advanced their particular national interests. They thereby abandon goals that can only be achieved by violating these rules.

- Communications mechanisms of a tacit or explicit sort are established to ensure the viability of their mutual expectations.

- They explicitly or tacitly maintain "a system of tolerance thresholds" which serves to control the process of escalation.

- The powers exert a degree of control over their bilateral relations in the region that is greater than the control they exert over their clients. This, in turn, is greater than the degree of control the powers can exert over relations among the regional local actors. A sixth rule, each great power attempts to increase its own political and military influence, is also discussed in Chapter 1.

Elsewhere, I have suggested that between 1967 and 1973 the great powers pursued the politics of confrontation avoidance. This may be inferred from the policy they recommended to their clients and their circumspect behavior in relations with clients as well as with each other. The great powers' actions in this period thus may be viewed as observance of a set of rules of the game.(5) Nevertheless, the model of Evron and Horowitz seems somewhat mechanistic, for there is more play in the system than their rules suggest. The fifth rule indicates the major reason why this is so. Considerably greater control over their own relations than over relations with their clients, and certainly than over relations among the regional states, is the major factor that limits the degree to which the competition between the great powers can be regularized. The regional problem is more dynamic than seems implied by the Evron-Horowitz rules because tolerance thresholds do not remain unchanged. The rules are not a static given or an independent variable in decision making. It is difficult to believe, for example, that the buildup of Soviet forces in Egypt during the first half of 1970, reaching 15-20,000 Soviet troops, would have been tolerated by the United States five to ten years earlier. Now, after their expulsion, it is doubtful that the United States would react with equanimity to a return of Soviet forces to Egypt in anything like the strength of 1970. The rules of the game are significantly affected by the attitudes, policies, and power of the clients and other regional actors.

The first Evron-Horowitz rule raises the issue of the ease with which opposing interests can be established and legitimized. The principle seems clearly applicable to the reactions of the United States to the growing Soviet buildup in Egypt during the first half of 1970 and the soviet Union to American efforts in the Jordanian civil war to deter and then to neutralize the Syrian intervention.(6) However, the process of defining legitimate opposing interests is a highly chancy affair. There is no mechanism for the powers to define their relative interests to each other, much less to establish the legitimacy of such interests. In each crisis, the legitimization is heavily dependent on the success of one or the other power in establishing credibility through forceful action. Where interest legitimization must depend upon a process that contains such a large element of chance bluff, the risks of misunderstanding and of accidental confrontation are high.

Nor is it apparent that the powers are able to establish definite and stable boundaries around the means they may use to advance their unilateral interests. Soviet encouragement of the measures of economic warfare undertaken by the Arab states in the aftermath of the October 1973 War contributed importantly to the souring of the détente atmosphere in the United States. Evidently, it had not been at all clear in the United States that encouragement of economic warfare belonged within the means that might be legitimately used to advance great power interest in the Middle East. To many Americans, this and other Soviet actions in the region indicated that total displacement of American influence has not been rejected as an ultimate Soviet goal. If Evron and Horowitz's second rule applies to ultimate goals, it may be difficult to identify goals which either power has in fact agreed to abandon. It has been argued that objectives that are indefinitely deferred are de facto abandoned and that this is characteristic of Soviet policy in the Middle East. However, Soviet crisis behavior suggests that when the opportunity presents itself Moscow is prepared to resurrect its more ambitious goals. Indeed, informal, tacit means of limiting the danger of great power confrontation in the region have come to be established. In a number of senses, these may be said to have the characteristics of rules of the game. However, while they probably do contribute to moderating the competition, there remains considerable scope for destabilizing action by great powers themselves. In addition, there is room for maneuver by the regional actors as they atempt to use the great powers for their own particular interests.

THE GREAT POWERS AND SETTLEMENT
OF THE MIDDLE EAST CONFLICT

Beyond the concern aroused by the interactions of the great powers in the Middle East is the ultimate issue of their contribution to settlement of the festering Arab-Israeli conflict. In the interests of avoiding military confrontation between themselves, the powers have from time to time enforced some controls on their clients. However, by the nature of their competition and the relationships with their clients, they cannot jointly bring peace to the area. Only if great power competition is severely restricted or entirely removed from the Arab-Israeli arena is any settlement likely to endure.

Whether looked at from one side of the wall of hostility or the other, the fundamental issue of the Arab-Israeli conflict is the legitimation of Israel. The Palestinian question is, in large part, the obverse of this coin. The issue arose long before the creation of the state, and it is not self-evident that it is significantly closer to resolution now. That its resolution has been avoided so long is due to several factors. The first of these might be called the hope of Arab numbers. The Arab world has believed that eventually the imbalance between Israelis and Arabs in population, natural resources, and financial strength must result in the defeat of Israel. Arab disunity and Israeli qualitative superiority have helped to neutralize the effect of Arab numbers. In consequence, the Arab world has looked to external assistance for the augmentation of its as yet inadequate power. Thus, the involvement of the Soviet Union in the conflict has been a major additional factor helping to postpone resoluton. In turn, this has brought about the development of Israeli military power based on military assistance from the West, predominantly from the United States. From Jerusalem's point of view, indeed, Washington's as well, the historic importance of the American commitment to long-term arms assistance to Israel lies not in its immediate contribution to deterrence of Arab attack, but in the capability of such a commitment to force the abandonment of Arab hopes that superior numbers would eventually prevail.

Paradoxically, the October 1973 War may be viewed as an indication that the Israeli-American strategy was, at least in part, succeeding. Egypt and Syria were finally convinced that the Soviet Union would not directly involve itself in the effort to recover the lost territories and were fearful that the status quo would be frozen. Thus, they began a war with the limited aims of unfreezing the deadlock and forcing the powers to intervene. At the same time, however, the war triggered an oil embargo and helped accelerate the oil price revolution. These events underscored the vulnerability of the West and signaled the vast increase in the wealth of the Arab oil producers. They resurrected the hopes that the latent potential of Arab numbers could be translated into effective military and political power.

The calculations that led Egypt into the October War have also helped bring on heightened strains in its relationship with the Soviet Union. Soviet power has been relegated to a secondary role, and Sadat has placed primary emphasis on securing Washington's cooperation, with the threat of Arab oil power maintained discreetly in the background. The relative eclipse of the Soviet role may be only temporary. The exigencies of maintaining Egyptian military power, complicated now by internal economic crisis and the technical difficulties of incorporating radically different military systems, may force reconsideration of the value of the Soviet connection. This may also be the effect of a collapse of current American efforts to secure a speedy settlement.

These factors in combination may reinforce the view, which already has many adherents in the United States and Western Europe, that the Soviet Union must be brought as a full partner into the negotiation and implementation of a settlement. In particular, Soviet involvement in guaranteeing the settlement is often regarded as necessary and sufficient to insure regional stability. I have elsewhere expressed my skepticism regarding the alleged indispensability of Soviet participation in a Middle East settlement.(7) Soviet co-sponsorship of a guarantee to Israel would be incredible and dangerous. A Soviet guarantee to the Arab side complementing an American guarantee to Israel would help maintain or sharpen Soviet-American tensions in the Middle East. The disparity in the objectives of the great powers acts to perpetuate the abyss separating the regional antagonists. Even under more formalized rules of the game, controlled competition, Evron's term, is a dubious path to conflict resolution. That can only be achieved, if at all, by turning the Middle East into a buffer zone, the classical instrument of power politics under which the great powers agree to keep their hands off a region that neither can attempt to dominate without inviting unacceptable conflict with the other.

At present, there is little prospect of such an outcome. Moscow continues to see opportunity for a major Soviet role in the area, and perhaps this is correct. Nevertheless, it would be a step forward if Washington came to recognize that maintenance of the great power role, especially in a guarantee-centered settlement, promises only to formalize the Soviet opportunity and validate Moscow's hunting license.

NOTES AND REFERENCES

(1) US Arms Control and Disarmament Agency, World Military Expenditures and Arms Transfers 1966-1975 (Washington, D.C.: US Government Printing Office, 1976).

(2) Leslie H. Gelb, "Arms Sales," Foreign Policy no. 25 (Winter 1976-77): 4.

(3) International Institute of Strategic Studies, Strategic Survey 1975 (London: 1976), p. 81.

(4) Interview for al-Hilal (Cairo), as transmitted by the Middle East News Agency and translated by the Foreign Broadcst Information Service, Daily Report: Middle East and North Africa (October 1, 1976): D-15.

(5) A.S. Becker, "The Superpowers in the Arab-Israeli Conflict, 1970-1973," in A.S. Becker, The Economics and Politics of the Middle East, B. Hansen, M.H. Kerr, (New York: American Elsevier, 1975), pp. 99ff.

(6) Ibid., pp. 81-3.

(7) A.S. Becker, "The USSR and Middle East Settlement," in <u>Military Aspects of the Israeli-Arab Conflict</u> (Tel Aviv: University Publishing Projects, 1975), p. 100-8; reprinted as "Moscow and the Middle East Settlement: A Role for Soviet Guarantees?" <u>Middle East Review</u> no. 8 (Spring/Summer 1976): 52-7.

III

Prospects for Political Resolution

11 The Middle East: Imposed Solutions or Imposed Problems?

George H. Quester

The intent of this paper is to sort out and attempt to evaluate the military and strategic factors, as compared with the political and cultural aspects, of the possibilities of an imposed solution to the Middle East conflict.

The discussion will begin with an inquiry into the motives which might drive outside powers into wanting to impose a settlement. The paper will then attempt to assess blame for the conflict in terms of the political and cultural issues indigenous to the Middle East, as compared with stabilizing or destabilizing influences of military technology brought in from outside. The analysis will then close with a sorting out of kinds of intervention from the outside and a net assessment of the prospects of an imposed solution.

THE REAL MOTIVES FOR INTERVENTION

The first question to be considered about an imposed solution for the Middle East conflict is why an outside state would want to impose a solution. As a start, the American stake in the Middle East must be defined. Given a wave of sentiment opposing intervention in general, the reason for outside intervention may have to be coded in selfish terms in order to pass muster as rational. Various kinds of instrumental or selfish explanations can be offered quickly enough. The United States must fear war in the Middle East because such a war can spill over to damage the American economy, as with the 1973 oil embargo, or because it can spill over in terms of fighting itself, particularly if one combatant acquired and used nuclear weapons.(1)

Supporters of Israel in the United States, moreover, like to sell the idea that the United States obtains some de facto alliance benefits from Israel's position, that Israel is thus an asset rather than a burden. Perhaps Israel's advance position somehow contributes to shielding the NATO states in Europe, in the same manner that South Korea's position shields Japan. Perhaps part of the American involvement in the area could be explained by the fact that Israel is the "only democracy in the Middle East" and the state most friendly to the United States in the region.

A different argument is that of precedent. Israel may not offer much in the way of an advance base. On a practical basis, it may complicate and poison American relations with the Arab states more than it provides a lever. Nonetheless, the United States could not stand idly by to see a democracy pushed into the sea, indeed by military forces armed by the Soviet Union, and thus would have to intervene. Like West Berlin, Israel is not valuable for any position it offers – the exposed geographic position is indeed an embarrassing nuisance nor is the United States able to abandon the position, because of the bad example such an abandonment would pose for the future. The United States thus must seek to impose a solution precisely because the absence of a solution poses too many risks for an American-Soviet war.

A third interpretation of the American commitment and of the United States' compulsion for a solution is considerably different, however, and must be phrased in terms that many observers will greet with premature skepticism. It may be that the United States cares about Israel mostly for its own sake. It might be that a significant portion of American foreign policy has indeed all along treated the outside world as an end in itself, rather than as a realpolitik means to some domestic end. The United States may defend England just because England is England; the United States may want to defend Israel because it is Israel.

The arguments for Israel as a practical advance base for military or political ventures, and as buffer shielding the United States or its other allies, are not persuasive. The arguments on precedent are not so strong either. The Arab-Israeli conflict in many respects is sui generis, posing few neo-cold war precedents for the fate of other disputed territories. It may thus rather be that the real explanation of American attachment to Israel is that it is indeed a burden. Israel, like England, "the mother of Parliaments," is a consumption-good in American foreign policy rather than an investment-good. It is something the United States wants for its own sake and hence, a burden, rather than the means to carrying some other burden.

The more committed supporters of Israel in the United States will tend to reject this interpretation. In part, this is because they see their case would be stronger if they could state it in more practical and selfish terms for all Americans. In part, their rejection will be based on a certain uneasiness and distrust about relying on anything that even looks like altruism. Yet the hardheadedness of realpolitik can miss some important aspects of the motivation of American foreign policy, and the Israeli-Arab conflict may illustrate this particularly well.

Some of the same points need to be made on the motivation of the other superpower, the Soviet Union. It is necessary to understand why the Soviet Union seeks to influence Middle Eastern events, either in the direction of an imposed settlement or in the direction of an exacerbation of the conflict.(2)

Perhaps the Russians have been using the Egyptians and other Arab clients instrumentally, with a view to various geopolitical considerations. This is a view most commonly held in the West. Perhaps there are tensions here about precedent as well, such that the Russians cannot allow a "made in USA" Israeli triumph to settle into place. At the same time, they must also fear that any renewed conflict will have high risks of pulling Washington and Moscow into war. The third possibility above must be addressed too. The chance should not be ruled out that Moscow seriously cares about the merits of the case in the Middle East and wants to intervene quite apart from considerations of military position and psychological precedent. Perhaps the Soviet Union feels, from a Marxist ideological point of view, that the Arab case is just and that the existence of Israel indeed amounts to a success of European colonialism or bourgeois capitalism.

For both superpowers, therefore, the motivations will overlap, with a possibility of some serious positive identifications between patrons and clients. If the two superpowers are more altruistic and less opportunistic, however, the question of whether this makes any kind of solution easier has hardly been addressed yet.

Returning to American foreign policy motivations for a moment, the altruistic identification which exists for Israel is not without some counterpart for the Arab states.(3) Part of the Israeli distrust of American motives arises because an outsider's sense of justice and rightness, with regard to the geographical region of Palestine, can tip back and forth fairly rapidly, with the Carter Administration's policies being only a most visible example. If Americans were in a position to dictate political outcomes in the Middle East, they would not do so simply in terms of the material well-being and military security of the North American continent. They would instead dictate the continued survival of Israel. However, they would also dictate a more just treatment of the Palestinian Arabs, the handling of Jerusalem more in sympathy with Muslim religious sensibilities, self-government for the people of Nablus and Gaza, and so on.

The Soviet altruistic involvement in the Middle East is probably not two-sided. Russia, to its credit, has never gone as far as the Arab states and in particular the Palestinians in calling for the elimination of Israel. Moscow indeed recognizes Israel, although there have been no diplomatic relations since 1967. It recognizes, however, the boundaries of the 1948 United Nations partition proposal. It should be noted that the United States in some sense also limits its recognition to these boundaries, thereby steadfastly declining to move its embassy to Jerusalem from Tel Aviv.

Soviet declarations of intent and deliveries of military goods have more recently been much more one-sided, however. While the United States sells or gives some arms to the Arab side, the Soviet Union does not transfer any to Israel. One guesses that if the Soviet Union could dictate political outcomes in the Middle East, it would guarantee the right of some kind of Israel to exist. It might, however, also be tempted by the prospect of a secular Palestine as proposed by the Palestine Liberation Organization (PLO), presumably a "socialist secular Palestine. In terms of pure identification with the parties involved, one suspects that the Moscow Marxists identify <u>more</u> with the justice claims of the poverty-stricken Arabs and less with the bourgeois Israelis, while the identification of Americans leans in the opposite direction. Yet there are limits to the totality of the identification in either case.

Cynics about superpower diplomatic goals may respond that the Russians have much more Machiavellian reasons to want Israel to continue to exist, for it serves as a permanent barrier to cooperation between the Arabs and the United States.(4) There is undoubtedly something to this, but to assume that such instrumental explanations of foreign policy always outweigh the more substantive or altruistic explanations discussed above is "to throw the baby out with the bathwater." The Soviet Union in any event has some other frictions between the Arabs and the United States to exploit besides the existence of Israel, the price of oil now being an obvious example. The Soviet Union also does not want a nuclear war to emerge from the Middle East, and thus it cannot be reveling endlessly in the frictions the region is producing.

IS THE PROBLEM THE MIDDLE EAST?

The obverse of the question posed above might be as follows: do outside nations, in particular the two superpowers, offer the greater prospect of providing a solution to the Middle Eastern conflict, or do they instead impose a large part of the problem? If there were no Soviet Union and no United States, or if these two states were oblivious to the Middle Eastern conflict, would that conflict today have become perhaps much less virulent?

It would not be difficult to paint a picture of the Middle Eastern conflict which placed most of the blame within the region.(5) Few conflicts have come as close to seeming zero-sum as has the Arab-Israeli struggle for the possession of Palestine, especially as described by Palestinian organizations such as the PLO, but also as sometimes candidly described by Israeli spokesmen. Without discussing the morality of the conflicting claims, or who was the first aggressor, it seems entirely fair to characterize Palestine as the "twice promised land". It is a piece of territory which is altogether too attractive for both Jews and Arabs and so does not condition the region to peace.

If Zionism had perhaps been differently conceptualized, it would not have placed so much stress on a reliance on Jewish labor. Perhaps then it would have been possible to buy land for Jewish settlements without dispossessing the Arab tenant farmers who had worked the land previously. At the least, this might have postponed the Arab reaction and violence which erupted in the 1930s and which constitutes the core of the Arab grievance and yearning for revenge/justice, still stoking the conflict today.

Yet one is very tempted to agree with the Zionist founders that a Palestinian society comprised of a Jewish middle class and an Arab proletariat would in time have been a breeding ground for just the kind of anti-Jewish prejudice that the Zionists wanted to leave behind. Whether the reaction came simply in social alienation, pograms, or terrorism, the price of not achieving a predominantly Jewish political state seemed quite serious to Herzl and his colleagues. In choosing to seek to return to Palestine, the Zionists thus put themselves into a position of "damned if you do and damned if you don't." To separate themselves from the Arabs would be, and was, to deny the Arabs a higher standard of living. To have merged economically with the Arabs would have been to improve their standard of living, but only at the price of much greater and more direct resentment of the "exploitation" involved. The relative deprivation of a class society would have predictably produced an increase in unhappiness, even as there was an increase in objective well-being.(6)

Some would of course say that this paints the Israeli choices all too pessimistically. With more responsible Arab leadership, and with slightly better luck and better Zionist leadership, a well-functioning and happy economic interchange could have been achieved between separate Israeli and Arab political units. Whatever Arabs were dispossessed, in this view, would have been more than taken care of. Significant Arab economic growth would have been induced by having a prosperous Jewish state as an active and immediately adjacent trading partner.

Good leadership can indeed often make a difference, but tight political and economic constraints will tire and wear down even the best of leaderships. If the proof of the situation comes at all in the outcomes, the result has been clear enough. Arabs hate Israel for what they feel was the unjust takeover of Palestine and for what they felt was a selfish intention to rely on Jewish labor in a Jewish state which had very recently been predominantly Arab land.

IS THE PROBLEM WEAPONS AVAILABILITY?

Whether or not the Arab masses have been misled by demagogic leaders, they have thus been involved in a real and major conflict of interest with Jewish Zionists. Yet it is hard to tell how hopeless this conflict is, for it has never quite precluded all possibilities of a non-war-like resolution.

One must, therefore, give a careful hearing also to the possibility that the conflict has been worsened by technology and politics brought in from outside. If the Middle East were as short of weapons as it was in 1949, one can legitimately ask if peace would not be more likely. Similarly, there could well be less encouragement for conflict if the United States and the Soviet Union were not simultaneously interested in the area. Many more weapons have been delivered from abroad than anyone would have dreamed possible in 1949.(7) The tank battles of the 1967 and 1973 Wars surpassed virtually every battle of World War II in numbers of vehicles involved. The Sinai Desert tank battles of the 1967 War may have engaged five times as much total armor as the decisive North African battle of El Alamein in 1942. Enormous quantities of airborne firepower have been delivered to the scene to complement that of the armored forces.

Deserts are natural theaters for armored warfare and for the use of tactical airpower. There are few obstructions to block the free flow of tank battles, during which the jockeying for position often resemble war at sea, or to prevent targets on the ground from being spotted from the air.

Offense and Defense

The proper focus is not the quantity of weapons supplied, but their offensive or defensive impact.(8) Offensive weapons might be defined as those which offer advantages to whomever has moved against enemy positions, rather than waiting in their own prepared positions. Defensive weapons might be defined as those which instead reward the forces sitting still. The record is a little mixed, but the net impact may unfortunately have been to favor the offensive and hence to encourage war.

Long-range tactical aircraft favor the offensive, in that they offer the option of preempting the enemy's air and ground forces by arriving suddenly in the airspace above them. Shorter-range fighter aircraft tend to have a reverse impact, since they are more effective when the battle has been brought to them and less capable of taking the battle to the enemy. The aircraft which the United States has supplied Israel are like those used to equip its own forces. They have larger payloads, longer ranges, and greater capabilities than most observers would have expected for a tactical fighter-bomber. Thus, the United States has wound up offering an offensive capability to its ally. The Soviet Union, by contrast, tended to offer shorter-range fighter-incepter aircraft to Egypt and Syria. This may be simply because the Soviet Union tends to purchase such aircraft in large numbers also for its own services, perhaps because of the vagaries of the Soviet economic production process. Yet, deliberatley or inadvertantly, the net impact of the Russian sales in the aircraft category has been a little more stabilizing, suggesting a discouragement of preemptive air attacks by the Arab air forces.

On the ground, however, the impact of Soviet arms supplies may be the reverse, with its heavy stress on the tank. This may again reflect an abundance of such vehicles provided for Soviet armed forces. The tank, by and large, must be seen as an offensive-favoring weapon. The mobility it supplies allows huge concentrations of force to be applied suddenly and unexpectedly at one point along the front. The United States provides tanks for Israel as well. This, however, does not correct the imbalance; rather, it compouds some of the temptations toward a preemptive strike in a crisis.

The deployment and sale of tanks is easy enough to explain in the Middle East, of course, for this desert area is assuredly "tank country." There will even be justifications of tank deployments as intended to be "defensive in the aggregate." The aggressed-against side will be able to roll with the punch and then to marshall its counterattack, as the Russians indeed found themselves doing in their World War II defeat of the Germans.

Yet there are military technologies imaginable that might yet make offensive war less attractive, even in a desert. If the two superpowers had more in the way of antitank weapons to offer their clients and fewer tanks, this might have made the Wars of 1967 and 1973 less likely. In such an event, the two sides might have been more readily disposed to a settlement, imposed or natural. It is of course difficult to predict what weapons' developers of the superpowers will produce. They are probably not guilty of pursuing offensive technologies anymore than of pursuing defensive ones; rather, they chase whatever nature seems to offer as a superior weapons system. There will thus be times when the pursuit of technological battlefield superiority will pull these outputs in the offensive direction and other times when it pulls in the defensive.

A very recent bend towards the defensive may have appeared with the new precision-guided (PGM) antitank missiles, discussed in Chapter 7, which were utilized with significant impact towards the end of 1973 War.(9) A possible lesson derived from the use of these new missiles was that the tank might now be fairly easy to destroy in future wars, as any target might now be destructible once it has been identified. Since the identification of a military target is made considerably easier when it moves, this promises to impose real costs in the future upon the side that sends its military units forward, while the side that sits still in positions of concealment will be rewarded.

A similar defensive impact is provided in the new wave of surface-to-air missiles (SAM) that the Russian have supplied to their Arab allies. These SAM systems promise to crimp the utility of tactical aircraft severely in the future. Some of these missiles can be fired by a single infantryman carrying the launcher on his back. Having remarkably high kill probabilities for the entire zone around a battlefield, such weapons offer a net defensive impact. They remove the incentive and opportunity to carry the battle preemptively into the other side's airspace.

In all such assessments of offensive or defensive impact, however, one must be very careful to watch the confrontation to see whether the situation is stabilized or destabilized along a particular front. If the Arab side were ready to attack with tanks because it felt it had a preponderant number of them, it may have been dissuaded by an Israeli superiority in the air. If that air superiority were now to be made irrelevant because the new surface-to-air missile forces of the two sides generally cancel out tactical airpower, then the immediate impact of SAM would be to make the Arab forces feel free to attack. This, however, preloads the set of equations to give a defensive addition an offensive impact. Where a tremendous Arab tank advantage is not presupposed to exist — and there are new defensive additions, as noted in the tank versus tank realm, too — then the advent of such impressively effective SAM systems will instead probably still be a net contribution to the defense. If the Russians have been in the forefront of equipping their clients with SAM, Israel will eventually have air defenses to match those of the Arab side, or even to exceed them. Yet, for both sides to acquire such systems does not restore the situation to what it was before, far from it. Rather, preemptive air attacks and new military offensives are made to appear less inviting all around.

It is altogether too early to assess the full implications of the new precision-guided technology in the Middle East. Yet the bizarre possibility has at last appeared that the outside supply of weapons will now have an impact of discouraging war, rather than encouraging it. Weapons may get costlier and costlier, imposing enormous economic burdens on Israel and the Arab states as they continue their armed confrontations. Yet the tendencies of such desert confrontations lead to use of weapons might now at length diminish.

The Costs of War

A second aspect of the external supply of arms to the Middle East, its impact on the destructive cost of war, may have to be evaluated substantially differently; a discussion of cost is found in Chapter 9. The track record here is somewhat bizarre. The Wars of 1956 and 1967 were preemptive in nature and hence were very short. As a result, they were not very expensive in terms of lives lost in the armies involved, and particularly not in damage to civilian domiciles on either side. The 1973 War began with some similarly preemptive aspects, but then was slowed, at least compared to the earlier Middle East wars. The costs, on the Israeli side at least, were thereby made to seem suddenly more serious.

Two observations need to be noted. The parties to the Middle Eastern wars, while allegedly locked in close to a zero-sum political conflict, have thus been exceedingly careful to avoid slashing at each other's civilian centers, playing by what may be the textbook rules for limited wars. When Cairo and Tel Aviv practically never get bombed, one must take with a grain of salt the statements that the Arab and Zionist positions are diametrically at odds.

Second, however, one must remember to compare the casualty and destruction costs of any limited-to-the-battlefield war with the small size of the Israeli population base, perhaps now about three million people, or with that of Syria, about seven million. For Israel to lose twenty men in a day's battle is thus equivalent ot the United States Army losing 1,600; memories of the American reluctance to accept the attrition costs of the Vietnam War thus will show how severe the Israeli burden here can be.

If the costs of wars go up enough and the prospects of successful preemption of an enemy go down, wars will be much less likely. The upgrading of conventional firepower on each side has apparently not yet had this impact. In part, this is because the two sides have managed to fight by carefully circumscribed limited war rules. If one ceases to limit discussion to conventional military hardware, however, and introduces the possibility of nuclear weapons into the Middle East, then the impact on a settlement may be much more powerful and interesting.

The argument will be made here that a heavy portion of whatever settlement can be imposed on the Middle East, including very probably President Sadat's opening to Israel, will stem from the fact that Israel may have learned how to manufacture nuclear weapons which are comparable to those introduced into the American and Soviet arsenals in 1945 and 1949. The Israelis will have done this with no deliberate American help and indeed, very much against American wishes. The outside source was, of course, France, which supplied the Dimona reactor. The Israelis will also be careful never to state their possession of such weapons explicitly or to detonate such a bomb just as a test. Rather the course is likely to be, as it has been for the past decade, to allow rumors and hints to appear that "Israel probably has a stockpile of so and so many bombs," and then to watch for the impact of this in the Arab world.

The impact is not difficult to find. Since 1973 Arab leaders had already been increasingly inclined to make statements that they "of course" recognized the right of Israel to exist. The "of course" was gratuitous, even if it was welcome, since Arab leaders were not making such concessions of coexistence ten years ago. Given the improved Arab military performance in 1973 and the enormous economic leverage demonstrated thereafter by the Arab oil exporters, such a shift towards conciliatory formulations would be a little surprising. The causal explanation might only be found now in the fact that the years of rumors of Israeli nuclear weaponry have done their work. The Arabs have at last let the fact slip into their consciousness that a great tank battle victory in the Sinai Desert could not be exploited by a follow-up thrust into Tel Aviv to push the Israelis into the Mediterranean Sea. The nuclear revenue imposed thereafter on Cairo, Damascus, Aswan, and Mecca would be unbearable.

The Economic Cost of Arms

The third impact of arms availability on the Middle East is that these arms impose substantial drains on the living standards of the nations of the region.

Yet, in terms of policy preferences, it is hardly clear whether the choice here would be to couple or to decouple this impact of the arms race; i.e., the fact that the arms race robs citizens of these nations of their material wealth. If one reduces the costs of the arms race, it is possible that the Arab states and Israel might feel all the freer to try to procure the very latest in weapons. Furthermore, if Arabs are made poorer because their governments must consign funds to military uses, one must evaluate whether this makes Arabs less or more disposed to compromise. The erosion of the Israeli living standard could lead to peace in making Israelis less militant, or it could discourage peace by giving the Arabs hopes that a final victory may yet be won.

One naive hope must almost certainly be abandoned. There is little evidence anywhere of a clear positive correlation between greater prosperity and a will to peace. If one were to find ways to eliminate poverty among Egyptians, Syrians, and Palestinians, it is entirely possible that this would not conduce to peace at all, but simply nourish a greater lust for revenge as part once again of a "revolution of rising expectations." Americans may favor peace in the Middle East, even as they favor prosperity, but the two goals may not be easily merged into one. Prosperity in the Middle East could be encouraged easily enough by giving out weapons free.

The Exchange of Hostile Signals

Even where the supply of weapons makes the military offensive less attractive, the acceptance of such weapons by Middle Eastern states inevitably constitutes something of an insult to other nations in the region. It suggests distrust and leads to distrust, serving as precisely the kind of misleading mutual suspicion signal that keeps conflicts alive. The signals here are of course not symmetrical. Israeli arms procurements are indeed virtually totally anti-Arab. By contrast, the arms procurements of the Arab states may turn out to be anti-Israel, but they can also be viewed as directed by one Arab regime against another or as directed at non-Arab regimes, such as Iran, Ethiopia, or some sub-Saharan African states.

In discussing a settlement of the Middle Eastern conflict, reference has repeatedly been made to the Israeli-Arab conflict. Arms that renew this suspicion are surely bad for prospects of a settlement, but arms which renew suspicions among Arab states, or between Saudi Arabia and Iran, may indeed give Israel more of the leverage it so much needs and may tend to deemphasize the Arab-Israeli conflict.

While the acceptance of military hardware from the outside may thus be a somewhat upsetting mutual signal among the states of the Middle Eastern region, one must ask what it amounts to as a signal by and among the donor states. At least one side to the dispute has chosen not to make use of formal alliances; the supply of weapons could possibly serve in part as a surrogate for this formal link.

We have already discussed the extent to which the United States and the Soviet Union are committed to the region for various reasons. Geopolitical position may make less of a difference here than sometimes assumed, while a normal concern for issues of precedent and genuine concern for the substance of the case may play a larger role. For either of these latter motives, of course, the use of signals is most important. If Moscow or Washington really care about something like the closing of the Straits of Tiran, it will be important to let others know about this. If they care only about the precedents involved, it will similarly be important to make this known. Moscow and Washington might thus be tempted "to put carts before horses," as has been done elsewhere in the world on the role of deployments and sales of military force.(10) Rather than distributing weapons because they are militarily useful, the superpowers may have been giving them out at times as pledges that more aid would be provided when needed.

There are thus two distinct kinds of signals being transmitted in the arms transfers of the Middle East, signals of hostility and signals of commitment. The signals of hostility between Israelis and Arabs are a nuisance in every way. The signals of commitment between Washington and Moscow may be a more mixed commodity. One might perhaps welcome such signals when they reflect real identifications with the welfare of the people in the region and when they head off misunderstandings about superpower intentions. One would welcome them much less when they merely amount to escalations in a contest of precedent establishment, a contest where each side has to worry lest it seem pushed around by the other.

In the former case, the posturings of the superpowers merely identify responses which were already bound to come. They amount to reminders of what the adversary power should have been able to see itself: that there is an identification between patron and client which could indeed pull the patron into major intervention. In the latter case, the expressions of posture are less purely of a clarifying message role and more in the nature of the threat that may or may not be a bluff, but which would have had no reality until it was enunciated. A superpower may sometimes intervene merely because it swore it would and because to fail to do so would cast all future threats into question. In such cases, the signals of commitment may create new problems rather than solving old ones.

IS THE PROBLEM LACK OF VERIFICATION?

Turning to notions of the cause of the problem, one must ask if the tendency to supply arms to the Middle East is somehow just the result of inadequate mutual surveillance. In analyses of other arms races, this particular aspect is sometimes cited as the source of the problem. When nations can watch each other, as in the London and Washington treaties on naval arms limitations, the limitations tend to be adhered to. When they cannot watch each other this well, widespread cheating and failures to disarm are equally expected.

The lack of mutual surveillance argument would, of course, have two aspects. First, there could be a prisoner's dilemma situation in effect between the Israelis and the Arabs. Neither side would be able to trust the other to pass up such arms when offered. Second, a similar problem of mutual trust could exist between the arms suppliers. Neither could trust the other to withhold arms.

The facts do not tend to support either of these analyses of the problem, for weapons sales in the Middle East have not tended to be well-kept secrets. In part, this is because the landscape of the region lends itself to aerial reconnaisance. In part, it is also because the Arab societies have not really converged on anything as totalitarian as the Soviet Union. Information leaks through the region and the world press can speedily enough get the facts on the shipments of arms involved. The openness of the Middle East arms race may indeed also reflect the demonstration and declaration intent discussed above. If the Russians want to negotiate a Czechoslovakian arms deal as a gesture, it cannot be a secret gesture.

For any of the above explanations, therefore, the model of Middle Eastern arms acquisitions as the product of simple mutual lack of information is not so convincing. Wars may break out in the region because the nature of the weapons in place lends itself to preemptive sneak attacks, but the arrival and deployment of the weapons in the first place are not likely to occur in such a sneaky fashion. Arabs and Israelis may indeed have better reasons for conflict than simple mistaken mistrust.

IS THE PROBLEM BUREAUCRATIC POLITICS?

An entirely different kind of hunt for pathology in these arms transfers would turn not to the international secrecy of the case but to domestic flaws in social, economic, or bureaucratic practice. One such possibility would be that powerful vested interests in the United States military-industrial complex have an incentive to influence the Israelis and the rest of the Middle East by supplying arms. Another would be that there are similar special interests within the Soviet decision making process. Other possibilities would include an analysis of Israeli and Arab decision making systems, focusing on the special interests and bureaucratic pathologies of these societies.

There is not much point in going deeply into such theories here. Zionist spokesmen will argue that Arab hostility toward Israel is merely a reflection of bureaucratic incompetence in the Arab states. The Israeli scapegoat is used to divert the masses from domestic problems. Marxist analysts may come up with a complicated explanation of how Israel amounts to a colonialist, imperialist venture necessitated by the defects of capitalist economies.

Looking more narrowly at the bureaucratic motives of American or Soviet military officers, there is little evidence that they have been strong promoters of a Middle East involvement. There may even be less outspoken General Brown-equivalents in the Soviet military, who also see the Middle East as a burden rather than an asset and who are not particularly anxious to hitch their career wagons to ventures in such a troubled and unpredictable region.

One might discover an important problem of electoral politics rather than of bureaucratic politics on the Israeli side. The proportional representation system used to elect Parliaments and Cabinets in Israel has often given crucial leverage to small and determined factions, making Israeli governments less free to make concessions than they could be. The overwhelming bulk of the Arab regimes, of course, do not depend on anything that could pass muster as elections by Western standards. Yet many of these regimes are also electorally weak because the head of the regime does not govern by absolute violent power or by total charisma, but also by appeasement of determined factions who might stage a violent coup.

GENERAL FORMS OF INTERVENTION

Leaving aside the particular problems or solutions produced by military hardware brought into the Middle East, there should now be some consideration of broader questions concerning the impact of an outside power presence. Israelis would be quick to claim that the Soviet entry into the area has been entirely bad, for the Russians supply arms, without which the Arabs would pose no threat to the Israeli position. Yet there is another effect of the Russian presence that Israelis might welcome, for it has tended to pit Arab states against each other. Fear of Communist subversion remains real in the more traditional Arab regimes, Saudi Arabia and Jordan in particular, and this has produced disapproval and distrust of any Arab states willing to cooperate with Moscow. Even among the more radical regimes in the Arab world, the issue of cooperation with Moscow, and of what kind of cooperation, has produced deep divisions and disagreements.

One might wonder whether there is any analog, in the American presence in the Middle East, to the impact produced by this fear of Soviet subversion. If American arms are necessary for Israel, fear of the CIA and of the other embodiments of American imperialism could nonetheless have kept Israelis from uniting around their cause. It could also have kept the "natural" friends of Israel in the area from asserting themselves. There was, of course, a time long ago when Israelis were somewhat divided about what role to assume in the cold war, with some indeed favoring identification with Stalin's Soviet Union and many favoring neutralism. Those were also years in which Moscow showed great sympathy for Israel. The anti-Semitism of Stalin's last years and the subsequent Soviet material commitment to Egypt changed all this. In effect, it unified Israel behind a foreign policy that has little choice but to be very friendly to the United States.

As for the possible links between Israel and moderate Arabs, few commentators could argue that these have somehow become impossible because "the cold war has been brought to the Middle East," or because Israel has become suspect of being a base for the CIA and the American military. Arab moderates are immobilized, and Arab extremists are stirred to fury, not because they see Israel as doing America's bidding, but rather because they see America as doing Israel's bidding.

The Middle East is indeed remarkable for the lack of any formal alliance links between the United States and Israel, even when the device of a mutual security pact has been used extensively elsewhere as a means of signaling and making credible the American intention to intervene. This absence of American treaties, bases, and servicement was earlier a product of the aforementioned Israeli reluctance to take sides in the cold war. More recently, it has in larger part reflected the American desire to maintain links with some Arab states, links which might become impossible if the United States had chosen to become an open alliance partner of the Zionists.

In attempting a net assessment of the impact of outside influence on the Arab-Israeli conflict, one might contemplate some alternative cases in which neither superpower intervenes, or where only the United States or the Soviet Union intervenes.

First, consider the impact if only the Soviet Union were to intervene. Almost all commentators in Israel and elsewhere tend to agree that this would be disasterous for Israel since the Arabs with modern Soviet arms would sooner or later be able to overwhelm the outnumbered Israeli forces. The divisive impact on the Arab world of the Soviet subversion issue mentioned previously would in this view not outweigh the advantage of Soviet arms. An analogy might be found with the course of events in Angola. The issue of Soviet intervention clearly divided sub-Saharan Africa, but the sheer firepower of Soviet arms and the expertise of Cuban troops more than made up for this by enabling the MPLA to sweep the FNLA off the battlefield.

Then, one should consider the impact if only the United States were to intervene. By comparison, most Israelis do not see this as the obverse of the case of Russian intervention. They suspect quite rightly that the American government would be more even handed, doling out arms in rationed supply while doling them out also to Arab states and trying to force concessions on Israel with regard to Arab refugees, Arab lands, and so on. If there were no Soviet intervention, the Arab states might even be more unified in their opposition to Israel. By cold war arguments, the United States would be far less biased toward Israel if there were no such Soviet intervention on the Arab side, although what was initially said about American foreign policy attitudes might contradict this.

From the point of view of Israel, therefore, the ideal might be no outside power intervention at all and after that, some balanced intervention. To have one or the other superpower intervening by itself would seem less attractive than either of the above. From the point of view of the Arab states, the ideal might be intervention by either one, and only one, of the superpowers by itself. The worst outcome would perhaps be no intervention at all. The next worst would be the current state, where Soviet intervention on the Arab side is balanced by intervention by the United States, and where the impact of Soviet activities is that American intervention is made increasingly one-sided in favor of Israel, as discussed in Chapter 12.

In making an assessment, one might also discriminate between superpower interventions coming only in the form of arms transfers, and interventions actively seeking to shape the resolution of the conflict. A crucial question is how these will be compared and seen by the parties to the conflict in the region. Much of the previous discussion of the possible worsening of the conflict due to superpower influence is related to the direct impact of weapons transfers. At first glance, each Middle Eastern party might be tempted to summarize its preferences as "more arms aid for our side and less arms aid for theirs", a formula that is straightforward enough. On reflection, each might be persuaded to revise this in light of the tendency of arms races to produce action and reaction effects, with damage to the civilian economies of both sides, and the above-mentioned tendency of some kinds of arms to produce stampedes into wars which neither side might want.

When the issue turns to the spread of nuclear weapons, the problem becomes much more asymmetrical. The possibility of Israel acquiring nuclear weapons is clearly more significant for the political future than are the chances of Egypt or any other Arab state acquiring them. The atomic bomb, as the ultimate veto, is primarily significant as a deterrent against pushes into the sea. No one is threatening to push Egypt or Iraq into the sea, but the Arabs have until recently been proposing to do just that to Israel. Proliferation to any and all of these countries poses problems relating to further proliferation, irresponsible use, and the threats of nuclear terrorism. In terms of direct strategic considerations, however, the presence of an atomic bomb force in Israel would have an impact that would neither be matched nor undone by the presence of any similar force on the Arab side.

How do the two regional parties to the conflict assess the desirability of more active superpower participation in the political management of the conflict, beyond arms supply? When hopes have fleetingly appeared that some kind of mutually acceptable solution might be found and that possibilities of compromises have somehow been missed, then some Israelis as well as some Arabs have welcomed more active superpower intervention. The United States for various reasons may be more suited to this role, but Israelis have not written off the possibility of the Soviet Union. They have at times been ready to talk to a Soviet Ambassador when there has been one, or to Victor Louis as a substitute. When such hopes diminish, the attitudes of the two sides have tended to fluctuate with their immediate satisfaction with the situation. Israel, after all, is basically a status quo power, while the Arab states are consistently the revisionists. Between 1967 and 1973, therefore, Israelis were prone to suggest that the region would be better off without political inputs from the outside, since the situation in their view was working toward resolving itself. The pessimism of the period since 1973 correspondingly made Israelis more receptive to an imposed solution, but certainly not yet as receptive as the Arabs.

SPECIFIC FORMS OF INTERVENTION

How then would one propose to impose a solution on the Middle Eastern conflict, rather than imposing a worsening of the problem?

One approach, which would these days win wide approval in any poll of American opinion, is simply staying out of the conflict.(11) Much of this, of course, reflects bad memories of Vietnam, memories which have been expanded to a general pessimism that the United States somehow messes up whatever it touches. At least a few commentators have taken this to mint up a general principle that the United States should not intervene anywhere. One can, of course, quickly rebut the alleged moral purity of this kind of isolation by responding that "to do nothing is to do something." One could cite the bad consequences of an uncontrolled war in the Middle East. Staying out of the Middle East might, of course, loom more attractive if one knew that the other superpower and all the other arms suppliers were also likely to stay out, but there is no real evidence that they want to stay out. The Soviet Union may not desire conflict and war in the Middle East, but it does not want a guarantee of peace so badly that it would relax its support of the irredentist position in the area, the Arab position.

Public opinion polls for the moment thus show a great reluctance to see the United States intervene in virtually any fashion in the Middle East; they also generally show low endorsements for military support for Israel.(12) Regrettably, there are no matching polls for public opinion in the Soviet Union. Yet the exact significance of such polls has always been difficult to determine. Some of such swings between isolation and intervention seem simply to be governed by fashion and cycles. There is reason, moreover, to guess that poll respondents show an unwillingness to endorse military responses on behalf of a foreign country while the threat to that country is not at the immediate stage. When the threat becomes more real, conversely, there is frequently an endorsement of military assistance and even of the dispatch of troops. If there are distortions in the readings produced by opinion polls, however, it is at least probable that Americans are currently less willing to intervene than they have been in the recent past. All of the other solutions to the Middle East crisis will thus be a little more difficult to implement because a substantial number of Americans will favor the lowest effort solution of all, simply to stay out of the Middle East.

A second kind of solution would see the outside powers on both sides screening the conventional weapons they deliver with a view to reducing offensive temptations. This would not always mean holding back weapons. It would, however, mean paying more careful attention to what is sold, rather than simply sending whatever one has in surplus or whatever Israeli or Arab governments are requesting. At a minimum, selling the right kinds of weapons will be better than selling the wrong kinds; at some points, it may even be better than selling none at all. Yet the power of this approach is clearly limited, because political tensions might still spill over into war even if arms supply were more regulated and because the natural flow of military technology may not so consistently cooperate with an effort to deemphasize offense. As mentioned, PGMs may reduce the punch of the tank if they work as predicted; if they do not work so well, however, the tank may remain the offensive meace that it has been. Since few would suggest that the superpowers should be content only with emphasizing defensive instead of offensive weaponry, it may never be learned whether such an emphasis alone could make peace more likely.

Another role that the superpowers can play in imposing a solution is to have one or both of them interpose itself between the belligerents. Simple-minded solutions often work in the politics. There is no denying that war between Arabs and Israelis will be a little less likely if the armies of the two sides cannot get at each other. Some of the logic of this, of course, accounts for the stationing of American technicians as part of the listening posts at the crucial passes in the Sinai desert. The technicians are allegedly in place because they are needed to maintain various sensing devices which would give the Israelis early earning of an Egyptian tank attack, or vice versa. A more important unstated value of having them there, however, is to commit the United States more probably to intervene if an Egyptian attack came. The United Nations forces used for interposition between Arab and Israeli forces in the past have played the same role. However, the vagaries of the United Nations General Assembly now have made this seem a much less reliable bulwark from an Israeli point of view.

Yet the pitfalls here are also obvious since the American public does not want to risk having its young men embroiled once again in a shooting war. Also, as was demonstrated by the Turks on Cyprus, an aggressive force can sometimes devise ways to get around an interposing force, without killing its personnel or drawing outside world condemnation and interference. Moreover, even if the American technicians could not be bypassed but had to be killed in the process of an Egyptian attack, there is the risk that this would not suffice to deter such an attack.

Yet another kind of imposed solution is for one or the other of the superpowers to move itself into a plausible role of "honest broker," trusted enough by both sides to let this be of value in finding consensus when all had despaired of finding it. This is much the role that Secretary of State Henry Kissinger tried to establish for himself after the 1973 War. While his initial successes were impressive, most would agree that the momentum was not maintained. Perhaps Kissinger had some success because of the sheer novelty of the situation after the partial Arab victory of 1973 and the new power of the Arab oil embargo. Perhaps it was instead the novelty of Kissinger as a Jewish Secretary of State, seen to be bending over backwards to balance between American pro-Israeli and pro-Arab sympathies. Some would then charge that the momentum has been lost because Israelis were unable to perceive its possibilities; the honest broker role depends heavily on the views and illusions held by the adversaries needing such a broker, but illusions may fade when they are not renewed.

Skeptics would argue, of course, that there was not really any consensus to find, and that outsiders trying to be "honest brokers" run the risk of being duped by a side which has only masked its belligerence but has not given it up. Sadat's alleged fondness for "his friend, Henry" in this view was merely a ploy to win concessions that might facilitate a later military attack on Israel. If the game is close to zero-sum, nothing that one side would agree to could possibly be of any value to the other. One's assessment of this interpretation obviously depends heavily again on one's core analysis of the Middle East conflict.

The world will probably not cease to have candidates ready to try to search for consensus where others have failed. At an earlier time, the backing of the United Nations seemed to be a sufficient makeweight to launch such a search. With the disappearance of any tone of impartiality in that body, the backing of a superpower may now be the prerequisite.

Is there an as yet unfound crucial link? Would compensation for the refugees, or the establishment of diplomatic normalcy be the icebreaker which would free the peaceful instincts of all the rest of the Middle East? There will be at least a few peace theorists — one wonders whether to call them optimists or pessimists — who will argue that only through such a basic move can the conflict be settled and peace really be achieved.

If one stressed the impose as much as the solution, one could imagine the United States or the Soviet Union backing up their discovery of a new peace formula with very strong pressures and threats. American financial and military assistance to Israel, or Soviet arms aid to the Arab states surely are sources of leverage which can be twisted to effect.

Yet much depends on the solution nonetheless. Israel for certain, and perhaps the Arab states also in their relationship with the Soviet Union, displays some of the classic "strength of weakness" which has appeared numerous times in client-patron dealings since World War II. Since its very existence is threatened, Israel can get away with rejecting American proposals that do not take the prerequisites of that existence sufficiently into account.

A fifth kind of solution is drastically different, viz., to allow Israel to move closer and closer to the status of a nuclear weapons state, trusting that some unmistakable acquisition of massive retaliatory instruments will suffice to reinsure Israel's existence and will force the Arab states to come to terms with it. There are at least a few problems with this.

First, the United States will have to be concerned with the precedent set for proliferation. Even if the presence of nuclear weapons served to stabilize peace, a failure of nuclear deterrence would have the most horrendous consequences. If the United States is in part being pulled into the Middle East conflict by the fear of nuclear war, it cannot then so easily reconcile itself to nuclear proliferation.

Second, the fear would also remain that nuclear deterrence on behalf of Israel would not work, mostly because the Palestinians and their supporters would not cease to use terrorist methods. The threat of an Israeli nuclear retaliatory strike against Arab cities is entirely credible for the contingency of an Arab battlefield victory where there was a real prospect of a follow-up massacre of the Israelis as they were pushed into the sea. It is far less credible as a response to Arab terrorist attacks, attacks which are intended to war down the Israelis' resolve and make them consider packing their bags and leaving for Europe or America. No one could plausibly threaten a nuclear response to the terrorist attacks of the PLO. Such a threat would leave itself open to the inherent nickel and diming of such attacks, which always make it difficult to define a threshold. Such a threat would, moreover, give some of the less sane elements of the Palestinian leadership a leverage over world events far beyond their wildest dreams.

As in the case of the superpowers' use of their nuclear weapons stockpiles, nuclear deterrence can thus not work well against pinprick attacks. The analogy with superpower deterrence does not stop here, however, for one also must cite the continuing concern about force survivability. As a far more grizzly scenario by which nuclear deterrence would not work, one would have to worry lest Arab air forces contemplate some kind of desperate grand preemptive strike, somehow hoping to catch all the Israeli nuclear forces to keep them from carrying through the retaliatory mission. The inevitable result would, of course, be that the Middle East would be plunged into a nuclear war. If the Arab attack succeeded, it would be bad for Israel and the world; if the Arab preemptive attack failed, it would still be bad for Israel and the world.

These objections hardly mean that no use at all will be made of the nuclear proliferation solution; Israel, as noted, is getting some results from it, and the United States as Israel's patron is either unwilling or unable to prevent this. Israel, under American pressure, will limit itself to rumor and background preparations that give some reality to the rumors. There will be no detonations and no public declarations. The rumors will affect Egyptian, or perhaps Saudi or Syrian opinion, even if they do less to dissuade the Palestinians. It will not turn off all serious Arab hostility, but will tend to channel it into new paths and approaches. Quasi-proliferation, in short, is now a fact of life in the Middle East, generating some embarassment for the United States for the precedent it sets and producing part of a solution, but leaving other parts to come.

One may never be able to prove or know whether the possibility of Israeli nuclear weapons played a crucial role in the decision of Egyptian President Sadat to go to address the Israeli Knesset in Jerusalem and thus, thereby to accord Israel a legitimacy and recognition which all the Arabs had worked so hard to deny. Yet, whatever the role of nuclear weapons possibilities in winning Arab recognition of Israel's right to exist, the events since Sadat's visit also are substantial testimony to the limitations of nuclear proliferation as a peace-imposer in the Middle East. Issues of exact frontiers, Jewish settlements, and the future of the West Bank remain unsettled even if the existence of Israel is now somehow settled. Peace is not yet at hand.

A PESSIMISTIC SUMMARY

To summarize the imposed solutions that one might expect from the superpowers may simply thus entail some averaging and addition of the possibilities listed. Those favoring American noninterference will in effect be tolerating, abetting, and relying more upon the solution of nuclear proliferation. Those disquieted by nuclear proliferation and/or those feeling a greater moral or practical involvement with the Middle East will hunt for the other avenues of approach. There is limited mileage in the techniques of qualitative arms control and in the possibilities of interposition. Depending upon one's world view, there is either greater or lesser mileage than this in the role of the consensus finder or honest broker.

One may thus argue about which of these approaches has the most pitfalls. If one is really pessimistic, of course, one might conclude that there is no solution, imposed or nonimposed, and that nonpeace for the Middle East will simply be a fact with which the world must live.

NOTES AND REFERENCES

(1) For a discussion of the impact of the possibility of Israeli nuclear weapons, see Fuad Jabber, Israel and Nuclear Weapons: Present Option and Future Strategies (London: Chatto and Windus, 1971).

(2) See Avigdor Dagan, Moscow and Jerusalem (New York: Abelard-Schuman, 1970) for a discussion of Soviet motivations in the Middle East.

(3) The United States identification with Arab, as well as Israeli, concerns is discussed in George Lenczowski, "Evolution of American Policy in the Middle East," in U.S. Foreign Policy: Perspectives and Proposals for the 1970s, eds. Paul Seabury and Aaron Wildavsky (New York: McGraw Hill, 1969).

(4) For an example of such a cynical analysis of Soviet interest in maintaining Israel's existence, see Adam Ulam, The Rivals (New York: Viking Press, 1971), pp. 251-4.

(5) For such a pessimistic analysis of the historical record, see Christopher Sykes, Cross Roads to Israel (London: Collins, 1965).

(6) The relative deprivation model is, of course, adapted from the work of Ted Gurr, Why Men Rebel (Princeton, New Jersey; Princeton University Press, 1970).

(7) For an overall picture of arms deliveries to the Middle East, see Arms Trade with the Third World (New York: Humanities Press, 1971). Also see subsequent volumes of the yearbook series, Stockholm International Peace Research Institute, World Armaments and Disarmament (New York: Humanities Press; or Cambridge: MIT Press. Annual publication).

(8) For this author's more general views on the analytical value of this distinction, see George H. Quester, Offense and Defense in the International System (New York: Wiley, 1977).

(9) Details on the possibilities and prospects of precision-guided missiles (PGM) can be found in James F. Digby, Precision Guided Weapons, Adelphi Papers no. 118 (London: International Institute for Strategic Studies, 1975).

(10) A fuller version of the idea that the Russians "put the cart before the horse" in using arms sales as an entering wedge in the establishment of political and economic relations with third world countries is to be found in Gabriel Sheffer and Gerald Steinberg, Patron-Client Relations and Political Crises in the Middle East, Peace studies Program Monograph.   (Ithaca, New York: Center for International Studies, Cornell University, in press).

(11) For an explicit nonintervention position, see Robert W. Tucker, A New Isolationism (New York: Universe Books, 1972).

(12) See, for example, Current Opinion 3 (January 1975): 12.

12 Critique of "The Middle East: Imposed Solutions or Imposed Problems?"
Walid Khalidi

The paper by Quester in Chapter 11 falls into three principal sections. The first deals with the motivations of superpower intervention in the Middle East. Current hardheaded interpretations are scrutinized, and the suggestion is offered that these may have been held at the expense of a more meaningful one, i.e., the altruistic motivation. The second section explores the extent to which indigenous political or cultural factors, as opposed to exogenous ones, such as superpower arms transfers, are responsible for the conflict. To the extent the latter is the case, Quester discusses in sequence the impact on the conflict of seven factors: the availablility of weapons according to sheer quantity, the offensive/defensive capabilities of the weapons supplied, the cost in human lives, the economic cost, the signals implicit in the arms transfers from the perspectives of donor and recipient, the presence or absence of an adequate mutual surveillance problem, and the bureaucratic pathologies of donors and recipients. In the third section Quester discusses the preferences of the regional protagonists with regard to superpower intervention and specific modalities of superpower intervention and specific modalities of superpower intervention, or nonintervention, for the resolution of the conflict.

Quester reaches no overall conclusion as to where all these variables point in terms of the theme of his paper: the feasibility/desirability of an imposed solution. He ends on a note of diffuse skepticism, if not pessimism, in which quasi-proliferation by Israel, i.e., a continued nondeclaratory but ambivalent Israeli nuclear posture, supplies part of a fatalistically unpropounded solution.

THE REAL MOTIVES FOR INTERVENTION

Quester suggests that perhaps it is not realpolitik considerations but altruism that really explains the United States attachment to Israel and Soviet support of the Arabs. Because Israel is a burden and not an asset,

281

it, like England, "the mother of Parliaments," is a "consumption-good
. . . rather than an investment-good . . . something the United States
wants for its own sake," pages 261-2.

Refreshing as it is to be reminded of the non-realpolitik dimension
of foreign policy making and without quibbling about the relevance, for
example, of the Berlin analogy of Israel — the paramount power in the
eastern Mediterranean, thanks to American support — two immediate
remarks are perhaps in order about this line of reasoning. First, the
proposition that Israel might be a consumption good teeters rather
precariously close to considering American support of Israel as a matter
of taste. In this way, the psychocultural and the domestic-political
dimensions of this support are bypassed. The ineluctable love-hate
intimacy of the Judaeo-Christian relationship and the "gentilism" of the
worlds of Islam and Arabdom from the Western perspective are but two
of the elements which will have to be subsumed under the psychocultural dimension. Others include the collective Western-Christian guilt
at the barbarities of the Third Reich, American fascination with the
pioneering image of Israeli society, and the persuasiveness of the pro-
Zionist opinion-makers in the United States. Under the domestic-
political dimension will have tc be subsumed the structures of the
electoral processes in the United States, the organized skills and reach
of the pro-Israeli lobby, and the cumulative commitment to Zionism of
American presidents beginning with Woodrow Willson's endorsement of
the Balfour Declaration in 1917. Second, while it is important to keep
the non-realpolitik dimension constantly in mind, some overall balance
between it and the realpolitik dimension is probably called for to
optimize the maintenance of contact with realities.

Applying the altruistic consideration to Soviet support of the Arabs,
Quester wonders whether the Soviet Union does not identify with its
Arab clients because it perceives their cause in the light of Marxist
ideology as inherently more just than that of bourgeois Israel. This is a
moot point. Even more moot is Quester's extension of this argument to
the speculation that the Soviet Union, although having maintained
diplomatic relations with Israel until 1967, might, if it could dictate the
outcome, be tempted not to guarantee its existence and might indeed go
for a Palestinian secular democratic state.

It is difficult to go along with this speculation given the historical
record. It was, after all, the Soviet Union which in April 1947 was the
first great power after World War II to openly suggest the partition of
Palestine. It was likewise ardent Soviet support of partition in the
General Assembly, no less than American support, which ensured the
passage of the partition resolution in November 1947. Subsequently, it
was the first Czechoslovakian arms deal in March-April of 1948(1)
which gave the Zionist forces in Palestine the additional clout needed to
smash Palestinian resistance before the end of the Mandate and prior to
the entry of the regular Arab forces. This is, by the way, an instance of
great power intervention in the Middle East that escapes the finely
meshed net of Evron's catalogue in Chapter 1. The Soviet Union was
also the first great power to give de-jure recognition to Israel; the
United States preceded with only de facto recognition. Throughout
1948, Soviet broadcasts maintained an unabated barrage of abuse

against Arab interventionism in Palestine, and it was the Russians, well ahead of Truman, who helped to shoot down Bernadotte's revised partition plan. It is fatuous to describe all this, as is done by Wlater Laqueur, as being due to "a fit of absent-mindedness" on the part of Stalin.(2) Likewise, it is oversimplistic to attribute Soviet actions solely to a desire to eliminate the British presence from Palestine.

Similarly, PLO-Soviet relations were very late in developing, and Nasser virtually had to dump Arafat onto the lap of the Kremlin. To say that the Soviet Union recognizes only the 1948 frontiers of Israel is inaccurate if by that one means the frontiers of the 1947 partition. What the Soviet Union does recognize are the pre-June 1967 frontiers, which are substantially the frontiers of the 1948-49 armistice agreements. There is no evidence that Russian recognition is confined to the 1947 frontiers just as there is no evidence of serious, or for that matter flippant, support of the Palestinian secular democratic state.

The irony of Quester's speculation is that it is precisely on the issue of Russian supprt of a Jewish state in Palestine that the Arab Communist parties have split vertically since 1947-48. It is precisely because of this issue that Arab nationalist parties, the Arab Nationalist Movement (ANM) and the Baath, have traditionally maintained their guarded stance vis-a-vis Moscow. It is also primarily on this issue that Habash's Popular Front for the Liberation of Palestine (PFLP) feels alienated from the Soviet Union as opposed to Arafat's Fath. Indeed, Arab positive neutrality and nonalignment under Nasser, however unneutral and aligned they may have been, derived their principal rationale as much from the perceived Western as from the perceived Soviet support of the Jewish state.

Ironically, too, in the intra-Palestinian and inter-Arab dialogues, the argument that the Soviet Union would not endorse anything beyond the pre-June 1967 frontiers has been the major consideration in the Palestinian leadership's shift from the objective of a Palestinian democratic state to that of a state on the West Bank, Gaza Strip, and East Jerusalem. Yet, this same perception of limited Soviet support on boundaries has been a principal factor in inducing the contemporary mood of Arab pragmatism. In fairness to Quester, however, he does observe that the Soviet Union is anxious to avoid a nuclear war in the Middle East and "thus it cannot be reveling endlessly in the frictions the region is producing," page 264.

A more general comment on Quester's discussion of motivation is that it shies away from the cardinal question. Given their motivations, one can ask what are the perceived objectives of each superpower as such and vis-a-vis each other within the region. Given these objectives, whatever they are, one must then ask what are the chances of a solution, imposed or otherwise. In brief, one has the feeling that Quester's discussion takes place in vacuo.

However, it is not only Quester who is guilty of this, if guilty is the word. The most striking common denominator between all the papers submitted at this conference is this self-same coyness about addressing the questions just posed. To be sure, the modalities of intervention are analyzed, categorized, and pigeonholed, often brilliantly, but one still does not know where to go from there. Are the objectives of the superpowers mutually exclusive or reconcilable, and is this immediate-, medium-, or long-term? No attempt is made to project scenarios of possible solutions along a cooperation/conflict spectrum, postulating varying assumptions about the concrete objectives or sequences of concrete objectives perceived to be pursued by the superpowers toward each other in the region and/or toward the region itself. The whole linkage issue is bypassed. One must explore the linkages between the Middle East and SALT or between the Middle East and the leapfrogging Russian offensive in Africa. The possibilities of horse trading between these theaters and the likely outcomes of the presence, absence, and extent of such horse trading on the solutions in each theater all need to be examined.

Thus, for example, Cahn's analysis in Chapter 4 of the rationales of obtaining influence through arms transfers avoids the issue of the direction of this influence, i.e., whether it is towards or away from a settlement. Nor does Evron in Chapter 1 in his typology of the objectives of intervention encompass the objective or otherwise of such a settlement. Harkavy's discussion of Russian strategic access in Chapter 6 does not question the purposes for which access might be sought.

INDIGENOUS-EXOGENOUS FACTORS

Is the Problem the Middle East?

Of course, one can agree with Quester that it is not difficult to paint a picture of the Middle East conflict which places most of the blame for its continuation on forces within the region. It is debatable, however, whether this picture is necessarily closer to historical reality than others, assuming that such a reality exists. To be sure, it cannot be gainsaid that both Arabs and Israelis have massively miscalculated since the establishment of the state of Israel in 1948, just as Jewish and Arab leaders did before that date. The process, however, by which the Jewish state was established can hardly be described as purely indigenous in character. Some distinction needs to be made between the genesis of the problem, i.e., the process begun by the Zionist colonizers in the early 1880s and culminating in 1948, and the period after 1948.

After all, the Zionist movement was of European provenance and constituted a reaction to European intellectual stimuli and to the European societal environment in which the early Zionists had lived for centuries. The central Zionist organizations were initially and for a long time afterwards European based, funded, and powered; many of them still are. In a sense, the Zionist movement anachronistically represents the last great European "white" wave of colonization of a third world territory in the twentieth century on the eve of the demise of European colonialism. The great watershed of Zionism was 1917 when the paramount Western imperial power in the world, Great Britain, took Zionism under its wing. The imposition of the British Mandate on

Palestine in 1922 was not in consonance, to say the least, with the wishes of the vast majority of its inhabitants, the Palestinan Arabs. Whatever the subsequent differences between the British government and the Zionist leadership over immigration quotas and land settlement, it was within the administrative, political, economic, and legislative womb of the British Mandate, under the aegis of the British imperial flag, and at the point of the British bayonet that the infrastructre of the Jewish state was laid. In desperation, the Palestinian Arabs rose in the 1930s in revolt against the pro-Zionist British policy. It was the might of Britain, no indigenous phenomenon, that crushed their resistance, disarmed their peasantry, arrested or exiled their leaders, dismantled their political and military organizations, and obliterated or scattered their guerrilla forces.

Quester speculates whether there would have been a different outcome if Zionism had been conceptualized differently. He sees the reliance on Jewish labor, resulting as it did in the dispossession of Arabs from lands purchased or otherwise acquired by the Zionists, as symptomatic of a Zionist policy of economic separatism. (However, at least 15 percent of Zionist landholdings before the establishment of Israel had been transferred into Zionist hands by the British Mandatory as state domain.) This policy, by denying the Arabs a higher standard of living, significantly exacerbated the relations between the two peoples and compounded their confrontation. That the Zionists followed a policy of economic separatism is, of course, true, and that this was a continual irritant in interracial relations is also true. However, the inference – that if somehow the Zionists had shared economic benefits with the Palestinians,who already were nationalistically aroused even before World War I, they would have deflected them from the pursuit of their national aspirations on what, rightly or wrongly, the Palestinians believed to be their ancestral homeland – is to fly in the face of all the evidence of extra-European colonial experience. Quester is nearer the mark when he observes that ". . . the price of not achieving a predominantly Jewish political state seemed quite serious to Herzl and his colleagues," page 265. This is a monumental platitude, and I say this in breathless admiration, which can comfortably take its place of honor atop the mountainous literature on the Arab-Israeli conflict.

Incidentally, a maximum of 15 percent of the total Jewish community lived on the land up to 1948, while total Zionist land acquisition, by purchase or transfer of state domain, in the period 1880-1948 amounted to no more than 6.5 percent of the total area of the country. The balance of land held by Israel within its 1967 frontiers, some 75 percent of the total area of Palestine was acquired by conquest, albeit under the umbrella of implementing the United Nations General Assembly Partition Resolution, which technically was nonbinding on the Palestinians. Ostensibly this was done in reaction to the opposition of the Palestinians to this resolution, which gave 55 percent of their country to the Jewish state, and also in reaction to the subsequent entry of units of the regular Arab forces at the end of the Mandate after the collapse of Palestinian resistance.

An interesting point raised by Quester in this part of his paper is the perception of the conflict by Arabs and Israelis as a zero-sum game. He is rightly suspicious about the extent to which the protagonists do in fact see it this way.

As far as the Arabs are concerned, one of the most remarkable developments of recent years has been the evolution of Arab, including Palestinian, perceptions in the direction of greater pragmatism. This is not due to the impact of Israel's percieved or feared acquisition of nuclear power, as Quester suggests in another part of his paper. After all, if October 1973 has a moral, it is precisely the failure of Israel's strategy of deterrence, a strategy that Israel had been building up, refining, and driving home since 1948. Some observers, though not Quester, claim that the Syrian and Egyptian objectives in 1973 were unlimited. In this case, it would be even more difficult to square such an assessment with Arab perception of a credible Israeli nuclear threat.

The cumulative operation of six principal factors accounts for the trend towards pragmatism in the Arab world. The first is the collapse of the union between Syria and Egypt in 1961, involving as it did the falling-out between the vanguard Pan-Arab party, the Baath, and the charismatic Pan-Arab leader, Nasser. The second element is the falling-out between Syrian and Iraqi factions of the Baath party itself in the period 1963-70. Third is the growing perception of the limits of Russian support. The fourth factor is the growing perception of the "organic" link between the United States and Israel. For Arab radicals, the stress is on the systemic link; for conservatives, the stress is on the American domestic factor. The fith factor is the new self-confidence deriving from oil wealth and Arab military performance during the first phases of the 1973 October War. Sixth and last is the efficacy of the Israeli conventional fighting military doctrine in the prevailing environmental conditions. The essence of this doctrine is the marriage of qualitative air superiority and reach to the utter nakedness of the tank in the open desert. The Israelis, although understandably euphoric about their crushing victory in June 1967, have, paradoxically and with all evidence to the contrary, been unaware that they won their Waterloo ten years ago. For after all, while the moral of 1973 may be the failure of Israeli deterrence, a concurrent moral is the continued efficacy of Israel's conventional fighting military doctrine in the unchangeable environment, Arab surprise notwithstanding.

Returning to the impact of Israel's nuclear posture, the ambiguous signals from Washington and Israel concerning Israel's nuclear capacity and status have, rightly or wrongly, reinforced in Arab eyes the impression of bluff. However, in my opinion, it is the Arab perception of an "organic" link between Washington and Tel Aviv that fundamentally erodes the credibility of Israel's nuclear posture. This does not mean that in the continued absence of a settlement, and particularly if Israel moves towards a declaratory nuclear policy, no momentum would gather towards the horrendous scenarios envisaged by Jabber in Chapter 3. In this connection it might be a useful exercise to investigate Soviet perceptions of and reactions to a heightened Israeli nuclear profile, particularly in the light of hints that Israel's nuclear posture is directed as much at Moscow as at the Arabs.

The Availability of Arms

Quester asks if peace would not be much more likely were the Middle East as short of arms as it was in 1949. The sheer availability of arms is, of course, staggering.(3) Yet, the obvious answer to Quester's question is that one does not fight because one has weapons. Rather, one acquires weapons because one wants or has to fight. It is sometimes forgotten that in spite of the low level of armament, the 1948 War was the most costly of all four Arab-Israeli wars, not only in terms of lives, both military and civilian, but also in terms of its devastating socioeconomic impact, particularly on the Palestinians.

Many comparisons have been made since the October 1973 War between the levels of Arab and Israeli armaments during this war and those of the principal combatants in World War II. Perhaps more to the point is a comparison between regional armament in 1973 and in 1948. The Syrians, for example, deployed a total of nine tanks in 1948, whereas according to Dayan, they threw some 3,000 tanks at Israel in 1973.(4) A clue for understanding the nature of the conflict as it has developed should be found in this extraordinary disparity. One wonders if it is only the intensity of the Palestinian irredentism in Damascus that accounts for the acquisition of all these tanks, or whether it is not equally that a proud and authoritarian regime like Syria finds it simply intolerable to acquiesce in the annexation and settlement of the Golan. If it is argued that the Syrians brought this on themselves by shelling the settlements in the Jordan Valley from the Golan Heights, such an argument needs at least to be set against a not entirely implausible version of Syrian-Israeli conduct vis-a-vis the armistice arrangements in the period 1949-67. There, the blame for disturbing the status quo, e.g., settlement in the DMZs and diversion of the Jordan waters, does not unmistakably lie with the Syrians.

The Israeli government argues for the retention of the Golan in the name of the security of the Jordan Valley settlements, a development of the Syrian Golan shelling argument. Against this, it is possible to query why, if the security of Israeli civilian life is the issue, Israel is pushing its civilian line forward across the Golan and nearer the Syrian military lines. In other words, the incentive for the acquisition of arms is a function of one's perception of what the other side is planning. It is difficult to believe that the October 1973 War would have occurred if there had been no June 1967 War. Similarly, it is difficult to believe that Nasser's opening moves in May 1967 would have taken place without the 1956 War. It is intellectually fascinating, if also disturbing, that Western observers by and large refrain almost a priori from at least theoretically debunking declared Israeli motives and objectives. Perhaps the Israelis are simply "bloody-minded" about the Golan because they get a kick out of humiliating the heart of Arabdom, Damascus. Perhaps they have an atavistic European nostalgia for the Alpine snows of Mt. Hermon and its skiing possibilities, not to be found anywhere else in Israel. Perhaps Zionism is still in its revisionist phase. None of these considerations is likely to endear itself to the Syrians.

Offense and Defense

Quester wonders whether the arms supply policies of the super-powers have favored offense over defense or vice versa. He rightly points out that the aircraft which the United States has supplied Israel "wound up offering an offensive capability to its ally." On the other hand, Soviet sales of aircraft to the Arabs have "been a little more stabilzing, suggesting a discouragement of (Arab) preemptive air attacks." At the same time, Soviet largesse in tanks to the Arabs, though unmatched by American suplies of tanks to Israel, may conceivably be justified as intended to "be defensive in the aggregate". This would reflect Russian World War II experience, though the tank must be seen by and large as an "offensive-favoring weapon."Irrespective of Soviet motivations concerning the quantity of tanks supplied to the Arabs, the tanks provided for Israel by the United States while not equalizing the imbalance, "compound some of the temptations toward a preemptive strike in a crisis, page 266-7.

This analysis is evenhanded enough as far as it goes, but it does not go far enough for the hardware aspect is only part of the picture. To this must be added four additional factors. The first is Israeli military excellence, reminisscent of the edge the Germans had in World War II in their field performance over the Russians and Western Allies.(5) The second factor to be considered is the desert environment in which the Israeli military doctrine, alluded to previously, operates. Here Quester's lyrical endorsement of the desert as ideal tank country must be qualified. In the absence of either air parity or superiority, it is an ideal burial ground for even the most menacing tank formations. Third, one must not forget the logistical realities. They include Israel's superb network of interior lines of communication and the distances to be traversed across open desert, not only by the front-line Arab states, e.g., Egypt, but by potential allies such as Iraq. Equally important here are the problems of coordination along an extended perimeter faced by the Arab coalition partners who have no land contact with one another. Fourth, there are the political realities of the Arab world in terms of its divisions and the different priorities of the various Arab countries.

It is against this background that the American emphasis on aircraft to Israel and the Soviet emphasis on tanks to the Arabs become particularly relevant. Equally important is the implicit axiom in Washington's arms supplies policy to Israel, which is not referred to by Quester: Israel should at any point of time be able to withstand any combination of Arab countries. The snag is that Israel is literally empowered to take on any single Arab country or any combination of Arab countries it chooses to take on. Thus in 1956, it took on Egypt in the name of prevention, and in 1967, Egypt, Syria, and Jordan in the name of preemption.

Of course, the linchpin of American supply policy is the assumption that Israel is fundamentally a status quo power, and as Quester puts it, "the Arab states are consistently the revisionists," page 273. The assumption is also that Israel is fighting for survival. It is, of course, difficult to say what the Almighty Omniscient Observer might say in this regard, but this rather spontaneous adoption by Western observers of Israel's ostensible perception must be considered as the most formidable item in the entire arsenal of Israel. Sacreligious as this may sound, perhaps as Kant would say, the thought should be occasionally added that arguments of survival and security might have, even if only unwittingly, an alibi function. This point was partly foreshadowed in the remarks on the Golan above.

Part of the problem, of course, is the choice of the cutoff point. Zionism was hardly pro-status quo at the time of the first Zionist Congress in 1897. The pro-Zionist Balfour Declaration and the whole Zionist colonial venture up to the United Nations partition resolution in 1947 was hardly pro-status quo either; nor was the partition resolution itself pro-status quo.

Israel fought the 1948 War not to preserve an existing situation but to create a new one. In the period 1948-56, its movement into and its annexation of the DMZs on the Egyptian and Syrian frontiers and of No Man's Land on the Jordanian frontier were not pro-status quo. Its invasion of Sinai in 1956 and its renaming of Arab geographical localities during the occupation were not pro-status quo. The Israeli diversion of the Jordan waters in 1964 was not pro-status quo; neither was its annexation in 1967 of East Jerusalem and the extension of its municipal frontiers. Finally, it is, at the least, problematic to describe the occupation of Egyptian, Jordanian, and Syrian territory during the 1967 War as pro-status quo. Of course, Israel with its present post-1967 frontiers is pro-status quo. Like the balance of power, status quo is a relative concept. Perhaps more specifically, a meaningful distinction could be made between the new status quo created by the 1948 war, i.e., the frontiers of pre-June 1967, and the still newer status quo created by the June War.

By and large, pro-Zionist spokesmen tend to look at the map of the entire Arab world and, contemplating its several million square kilometers, to expostulate that after all even the current frontiers of Israel embrace only 60,000 of these millions of square kilometers. Conversely, the Arabs tend to look at the pre-Zionist colonization map of Palestine (c. 1880). Contemplating the total absence of Zionist settlement at the time, they tend to infer (paranoically?) that Zionist encroachment on Arab land progressed from zero square kilometers to 1,755 square kilometers in the period from 1880 to the United Nations partition resolution in November 1947, to 18,900 square kilometers during the Palestine War of 1947-49, to some 60,000 square kilometers in the aftermath of the 1967 War.

Returning to the question of qualitative arms policies, Quester wonders whether the acquisition of precision-guided missiles (PGMs) by both protagonists, with their mutual devastating impact amply demonstrated by the October 1973 War, might not open "the bizarre possibility" that the outside supply of arms "will now have an impact of discouraging war," page 268. It is tempting to clutch at this straw in the wind particularly if the advanced antiaircraft systems, constraining as they do the Israeli air superiority, which Quester fails to mention, are taken into account. However, considering the historical pendulum in weaponry between offense and defense, one tends to agree with Foster's grimly plausible prognosis: "Rapid attrition, improved long-range systems, and the uncertainties surrounding the outcome of battle create incentives for rapid escalation of conflict and acquisition of nuclear weapons, page 204.

The Costs of War

It is true that the cost in human lives for Israel in 1973 was greater than in 1967 and 1956, but it was less than in 1948. Given the intensity of firepower available to both sides, the dead-to-hardware casualty ratio of the October War is mercifully lower than one would have expected. In calculating the losses of either side, one tends to oppose the population of the entire Arab world to the Israeli population of approximately three million. The Arab countries constitute distinctive societies, Pan-Arab slogans notwithstanding, and the Quester's poignant projection of Israeli casualties on an American scale, 20:1600, could just as easily be applied to some Arab countries. Syria, for example, has a population that is just above twice that of Israel, and Syrian casualties in the October War were larger by roughly the same factor.

Perhaps some comfort can be derived from Quester's observation that the two sides seem to abide by limited rules. This is evidenced by the fact that they do not slash at each others' capitals. Perhaps one can even infer from this that the conflict may, after all, not be perceived in quite the zero-sum terms in which statements from both sides tend to depict it. On the other hand, these limited rules, if they exist, have tended to get somewhat frayed. Practically the entire Golan has been depopulated, creating some 100,000 Syrian refugees.   The war of attrition on the Suez Canal in 1969-70 devastated the Egyptian towns along its banks, creating about one million refugees; this is the equivalent of some 5.5 million refugees in American terms. No one surveying the human and material debris of Palestinian refugee camps in the Jordan Valley or Lebanon in the wake of Israeli "retaliatory" raids would be particularly struck by the constraints of the limited rules of warfare.

The Economic Cost of War

Surely Quester is right in observing that "There is little evidence anywhere of a clear positive correlation between greater prosperity and a will to peace," page 269. This is, incidentally, an observation which is at some variance with his emphasis on the failure of the previously mentioned economic policy of the early Zionist colonizers towards the Palestinians.

The Exchange of Hostile Signals

One brief comment on this section: in the analysis of signals of commitment between Washington and Moscow in their Middle East arms supply policies, it is difficult to follow Quester's distinction between signals that "head off misunderstandings about superpower intentions," welcome signals, and others that "merely amount to . . . a contest where each side has to worry lest it seem pushed around by the other," less welcome signals, page 271. It is not clear if the latter, when properly conveyed and decoded, necessarily preclude the avoidance of misunderstandings.

Moreover, the whole concept of commitment raises the issue discussed at the beginning of these remarks: commitment to what?

Is the Problem Lack of Verification?

It is also difficult to follow Quester's discussion of the possible lack of mutual surveillance as a cause of the tendency to supply arms to the Middle East. Of course, it is agreed that "the model of Middle Eastern arms acquisitions as the product of simple mutual lack of information is not so convincing." Simultaneously, however, he seems to link the mutual mistrust between the recipients and donors almost exclusively to an at least theoretical lack of mutual surveillance, page 270-1. In reality, these feelings of mistrust are both autonomous in derivation and compounded by the openness of the Middle East arms transfers. Quester is, of course, well aware of the latter point.

If a lack of mutual surveillance has not been an exacerbating factor on the conventional level, it could well assume increasing significance on the nuclear level. Given the number of eggs that Quester puts in the Israeli nuclear basket, it is somewhat surprising that he does not probe into this aspect of the problem.

Is the Problem Bureaucratic Politics?

Quester refreshing calls for an analysis of the link between the United States and the Soviet military-industrial complexes and their Middle East supply policies. Equally refreshingly, he calls for a somewhat more widely based analysis of Israeli and Arab "decision making systems, focusing on the special interests and bureaucratic pathologies of these societies," page 272.

It is indeed possible that if these lines of investigation were pursued with American and Russian decision making analyzed, not only with reference to their military-industrial complexes but, especially with regard to the United States, with reference to the total web of public and special interest interactions that go into the making of Middle East policy, important new insights could be gained. As a consequence, it may be possible, for example, to see Israeli arguments based on security and survival against the wider vista of interparty dynamics. It would, in short, enable these arguments to be seen as a function of Israeli domestic politics, at least as much as the embodiment of concepts standing in their own right and with their own rationales.

This approach will now be briefly applied to the Arab-Palestinian side. Perhaps the first point to make is that the impact of the Palestine problem at the interstate level and within each Arab state is not essentially a function of the military strength or political organization of the Palestinians. It rather derives from the value system which predominates in the Arab world. The Palestine problem encapsulates the major subthemes of Pan-Arabism and Pan-Islamism: unity of Arab territory, integrity of Arab territory, the oneness of the Arab Nation, and the spiritual kinship between fellow Moslems.

Although there has been no successful institutionalization of Pan-Arabism, but rather evidence of Arab divisiveness and factionalism — Gottheil, in Chapter 9, has exaggerated these divisions — Pan-Arab ideology has so far remained frontally unchallenged and is seemingly frontally unchallengeable. It finds an area of ready resonance through-out the Arab world among the intelligentsia, the urban masses, and in its Pan-Islamist variant, among the peasantry. This makes it a powerful tool in the hands of revolutionary and radical incumbents for interstate interventionism in the name of the super/supralegitimacy of the mythical, One Arab Nation. It is equally powerful in the hands of the revolutionary and radical counterelites as a means of delegitimizing the so-called reactionary or conservative incumbents. It is this manipulative function of Pan-Arabism and Pan-Islamism and by derivation of the Palestine problem that gives the latter the role it plays in inter-Arab political dynamics. It is likewise responsible for investing the visible champion or leader of Palestine, be he a Nasser or an Arafat, with the symbolic halo in popular eyes.

Paradoxically, the most relevant feature of Palestinian potential with regard to a successful overall settlement is the one to which the least attention is paid by the West or Israel, i.e., its potentially stabilizing "fig leaf" role necessary to the incumbents exploring an overall settlement. But if the leaf is to stick, it must be a genuine one. Arafat, not a quisling, has to give his nihil obstat. The Arab incumbents understand this. The Arab counterelite waiting in the wings understand this. Arafat himself and the PLO understand this. The Soviet Union over the last decade, unlike Israel or the West, acquired an acute understanding of these dynamics.

INTERVENTION

General Form of Intervention

Quester rightly distinguishes between superpower interventions in the form of arms transfers and interventions actively seeking a resolution of the conflict. Perhaps another form of intervention is relevant particularly for Israel, i.e., the enormous support that Israel gets from abroad, both moral and diplomatic but also financial. This comes not only in the form of official aid from the United States, but also as annual, mostly tax-exempt, contributions from Zionist and Jewish constituencies and organizations in the United States and other Western countries.

Because Quester ignores this dimension of intervention, his discussion of the preferences of the regional protagonists with regard to superpower intervention is somewhat unrealistic. Nevertheless and even with this qualification, one cannot altogether agree with the preferences he attributes to the regional protagonists. Thus, for example, the preferences he discerns for the Israelis are, in descending order: no outside power intervention, balanced intervention by both superpowers, and either power intervening by itself. The preferences for the Arabs are, in the same order: either superpower intervening by itself, no intervention, and the current state of affairs. It is at least arguable that a second set of preferences for the Israelis might be: American intervention alone, the current state of affairs, and balanced intervention. For the Arabs, the second set might be: no intervention, balanced intervention, and the current state of affairs. Another dimension lacking in the Quester discussion on intervention is, if one is talking about intervention for conflict resolution, intervention on behalf of what solution?

The Israeli Labour Alignment's formula for a solution involved two principal features: direct retention of larger or smaller chunks of Egyptian and Syrian territory, and ostracism of the PLO. In the light of the previous discussion about the function of the Palestine problem in inter-Arab politics, it is not difficult to see how this formula would not only perpetuate Palestinian irredentism but would also compound it with Egyptian and Syrian irredentism. It is the surest recipe for fueling the engine of Pan-Arabism and is a solution that paradoxically, the Soviet Union would be wary of endorsing. If this analysis is substantially correct, a solution along these lines – even if Arab incumbent signatories were found for it, which is doubtful – would maximize the likelihood of instability.

It seems incomprehensible that a Middle East settlement could be envisaged without full Soviet participation. Imposition has become an obscene word in the Middle East vocabulary; but worse things can happen in the Middle East, however, as the two superpowers know well enough, than the muttering of obscenities.

I agree with Becker's remark during discussions that the core issue is that of legitimization. Where I perhaps disagree with him is that it does not involve the Israelis alone; it also involves the Palestinians. Not only that, but given the dynamics mentioned earlier, one cannot have a settlement without the legitimization of the Palestinians in a state on the West Bank, the Gaza Strip, and East Jerusalem within the pre-June 1967 frontiers. At worst, Palestinian legitimization is required, not for the inherent justice of their cause which in Arab and many non-Arab eyes is self-evident, but for its crucial functional utility.

Specific Forms of Intervention

Quester lists and discusses the following four forms of intervention.

A hands-off policy for the United States

I don't see how this would keep the Soviet Union out of the region or reduce the level of conflict, particularly since Quester sees its supporters as simultaneously favoring a more articulated Israeli nuclear policy. Since both official and private American financial aid would presumably continue even under this policy, the Soviet Union and the Arabs would probably not be convinced of American disengagement.

Screening the weapons supplies

Given the size of the Middle East market and the lengthening queue of potential suppliers as indicated by Kaldor's conclusive evidence on this point in Chapter 8, this is doomed to be a nonstarter unless both superpowers are seriously committed to it. If it were part of a package settlement, then clearly its effect on nonsuperpower suppliers would be optimized. Quester gives it limited mileage, partly it appears because he does not explicitly envisage it as part of a package settlement.

Imposition by a superpower

Again Quester gives this notion limited mileage, and again it seems he does so at least partly because he does not envisage it as part of a package settlement to which both superpowers would be committed. It is difficult to accept his pessimistic Cyprus analogy when United Nations forces were bypassed. To be sure, United Nations forces in the Middle East itself have been pushed around before: by the Israelis in the period 1949-67 along all four armistice lines, and by Nasser in May 1967. But what is being discussed here presumably are token elements, or personnel from both superpowers. Quester fears the Egyptians might not be deterred by the prospect of killing American technicians. Why the Egyptians only? It is not clear either why the Egyptians would attack if the interposition of both superpowers is part of a package, involving a return to the 1967 frontiers and the legitimization of Israel and the PLO.

The consensus finder or honest broker role by one or both superpowers

The fact that Kissinger's efforts along these lines petered out need not, as Quester interlinearly seems to imply, preclude the possible success of such efforts in the future. Kissinger ran out of steam partly because he was mesmerized by his concentration on the step-by-step approach into believing that the best chance of reaching one's rendezvous is by not knowing where it is.

The cooperation of the superpowers in the Middle East is a sine qua non for a settlement. The roles that they can perform under the general rubric of honest broker are many and varied. There is the sheepdog role to herd and nudge the client and ally towards the conference table. There is the wine-tasting role while the negotiaitons are ongoing, not only to sniff the bouquet of the various formulas and propositions but to attest to the client-ally the absence of poison. There is the umpire-referee role in the transitional phase before final settlement to declare fouls and pinpoint defaulters. There is the co-guarantor role in situ after settlement is reached to make it stick.

Daydreams? Utopian visions? Perhaps. That is why the master key is the considered evaluation of what the objectives of the two superpowers are towards each other in the Middle East and towards the region itself. In any event, Quester's fifth solution, the path of Israeli nuclearization, can only lead into the Chamber of Horrors depicted by Jabber in Chapter 3. Perhaps an investment in naiveté might not, after all, be such a bad bargain.

NOTES AND REFERENCES

(1) For the Soviet-sponsored Czechoslovakian arms deal to the Jewish community in Palestine in March-April 1948 see Arnold Krammer, "Arms for Independence: When the Soviet Bloc Supported Israel," The Wiener Library Bulletin 22:3 (1968): 19-23.

(2) W.Z. Laqueur, The Soviet Union and the Middle East (New York: Praeger Publishers, 1959), p. 147.

(3) Moshe Dayan, Story of My Life (London: Weidenfeld and Nicholson, 1976), p. 511.

(4) The 1948 figures are from the private papers of Jamil Mardam Bey, Prime Minister and Defense Minister of Syria, 1948, in the author's possession; the 1973 figures are from Dayan, p. 511 (note 3 supra).

(5) T.N. Dupuy, "The Current Implications of German Military Excellence," Strategic Review 4 (Fall 1976): 87ff.

13 Critique of "The Middle East: Imposed Solutions or Imposed Problems?"

Don Peretz

Implicit in the theme of this panel is the assumption that the Middle East conflict is synonymous with the Arab-Israeli conflict. This conflict is seen as the primary cause of upheaval in the region, and it is assumed that a solution to the Arab-Israeli conflict will eliminate or diminish considerably the unrest and turbulence in the Middle East. It is true that, for a variety of reasons, the struggle between Israeli and Arab nationalisms has captured the world's attention, especially the attention of the West. Though it has, therefore, been given high priority in the list of international involvements and concerns of the United States, the Soviet Union, and the United Nations, the Middle East would be far from tranquil if there were no dispute between Arabs and Israelis.

There are a number of problems affecting the region which would be as acute and as crisis-provoking as they are elsewhere in the world even if there were no Israel and no opposing Arab nationalist movement. Included here are tensions among Arab states, such as the ideological disputes between the Ba'ath socialist parties of Syria and Iraq, and territorial quarrels like those between Morocco and Algeria. There are also questions of unresolved national identity still being fought out in the Lebanese civil war, as well as the struggle for political hegemony between Saudi Arabia and Iran in the Gulf area. More significantly, there is the emerging social and political unrest which cuts across and through all the above-mentioned problems, including the Arab-Israeli dispute.

Perhaps the Arab-Israeli conflict even distorts our perception of Middle East realities by distracting us from many of the emerging deeply rooted social tensions. Since 1948, some of these diverse conflicts have converged with the Arab-Israeli struggle. More recently, they have surfaced in the Lebanese civil war. In both the Arab-Israeli conflict and the civil war in Lebanon, there are obvious reflections of inter-Arab disputes over territory, competing ideological commitments, and tactical differences, as well as personality clashes. Increasingly, the underlying social conflicts of the region have surfaced in the Arab-

296

Israeli and Lebanese situations. Although the latter reflect most tensions in the region, they do not cause them. In the Palestine dispute, labeled by most Westerners as the Middle East conflict, radical Palestinian organizations with ideologies influenced by Marx, Mao, and Che Guevara have emerged. They have extended their goals beyond replacement of Israel by an Arab state to revolutionary change in all Arab nations. Their aspirations indicate how the Palestine problem converges with some of the more fundamental social unrest pervading the whole region. Understanding the linkage between what is called the Middle East conflict and the array of other problems in the Middle East is essential if discussion of an imposed, or any kind of, solution of the Arab-Israeli conflict is to be meaningful.

To give validity to this discussion, it is necessary to examine the question of solutions, imposed or other, in some historical depth and perspective. Neither imposed solutions nor imposed problems are novel in the Middle East. Indeed, the region has acquired both its distinctive identity and many of the problems, for which solutions are now being sought, through imposition by those powers whose intervention is discussed in this volume.

Not only Israel and Palestine, but the regimes of nearly every other state in the region can be traced to outside intervention, and in many instances, to outside imposition. Iraq, Syria, Lebanon, Jordan – none of these nations have ancient historical pedigrees. All are relatively recent creations superimposed on the old map of the Ottoman Empire by statesmen in London and Paris. While each state in the region, including Israel, may have acquired its own distinctive identity in the last generation or two or three, and the national leadership, the state apparatus, and even the national consciousness might have acquired a momentum of their own. Nevertheless, in each instance these factors developed, if not because of, then certainly with the catalytic action of outside intervention.

Since World War I, major political developments in both domestic and foreign affairs of the Middle Eastern countries have been much influenced by outside intervention, at first British and French, then American and Russian. Examples of outside interventions, which might be perceived as imposed and have set the course of events in specific countries, include the post-World War I partition by the Allied powers of the Ottoman Empire into states whose boundaries remain essentially the same today. American involvement in the trasition of Egypt from a monarchy to a republic, which began the Egyptian revolution with its ripplelike impact throughout the Arab East, had far-reaching effects. The role of the CIA in the overthrow of the Mossadeq government in Iran and the perpetuation of the monarchy there had a regional impact. Before departure from the Gulf, Great Britain shaped the boundaries and the regimes of Gulf states, both of which still remain intact. Additionally, the original United Nations partition plan, which divided Palestine into the Jewish state of Israel and an Arab state, gave not only identity but international credibility to the existence of Israel.

Intervention by the West and Russia through the imposition of both problems and solutions in the Middle East has been a fact of life there for a century and half. Such intervention and imposition did not begin de novo in the post-World War II era as part of the Soviet-American cold war. There has been and will probably continue to be such intervention and imposition as long as the region remains of such crucial importance to those world powers which have the means to intervene and to impose.

There have been and continue to be changes in both the degree and the extent to which interventions and impositions occur. Increasingly, the extent of intervention by any single power is limited by the countervailing influence of competitive powers. Unlike the situation over a century ago or after World War I, the countries of the region no longer face a monolithic international consortium that has predetermined the kind and shape of a Middle East its members desire. Differences between the two superpowers have been an obstacle to imposition of an internationally-agreed-on solution. Increased popular awareness of the larger world scene and growing mass participation in the political processes become restraining factors in the implementation of imported solutions. At present, the power generated by oil finances, temporary as it may be, is a factor that must be given serious consideration by the West in its dealings with Middle Eastern states. Thus, checks and balances have been and are now developing to offset outside interventions.

A few words about the role of Russia in the region are also in order. Contrary to much of the rhetoric concerning the international relations of this region, Russia is not a newcomer. The Russians did not suddenly burst upon the scene in 1955 with the Egyptian arms deal. Russia has been in the region since the expanding Tsarist empire absorbed large slices of the Middle East in the nineteenth century. As a result of Tsarist acquisitions of Ottoman and Persian provinces, there are today more Muslims in the Soviet Union than in any Arab country. Nearly as many Soviet citizens speak Turkish and Persian tongues as there are speakers of these languages in modern Turkey and Iran. Russian Central Asia is an integral part of the cultural, historical, and geopolitical Middle East. Throughout the nineteenth century, Russian troops and navies were active in the Levant; as recently as World War I, Great Britain and France promised the Turkish Straits to Russia in the secret Constantinople Agreement.

The aberration in Russian activity was during the era between World War I and World War II, the so-called idealistic or withdrawal phase of Soviet foreign policy, when Moscow played a relatively inactive role. By the end of World War II with Russia's ascent once again to world power status, its diplomacy in the Middle East was reactivated, especially in Turkey and Iran. By 1955, the Soviet Union was no longer content with regional power. It began to assert its global role in the Middle East, a most logical arena for such an exercise in power from a geopolitical perspective.

Soviet policy in the Arab-Israeli dispute has been both consistent and clear: where possible, it has sought to diminish Western, especially American, influence without jeopardizing overall patterns of relationships based on parity and coexistence with the West. The image of Egypt and Syria as Soviet satellites, colored red on the global map, which was widely diffused in the late 1950s, was simply inaccurate. When Russia and the Arabs found mutual interests, their policies converged but not their political systems, ideologies, or loyalties. When their interests conflicted, their policies have also conflicted.

Soviet policy on Israel is quite explicit and is also discussed briefly in Chapter 12. It differs distinctly from that of the PLO and is one of the causes of continued tensions with the Arabs. In comments by Soviet theoreticians on the draft program of the Syrian Communist Party in May 1971, the Russians observed:

> Israel is a fact . . . the slogan of the elimination of Israel is unsound not only tactically but also as a matter of principle. . . . It is permissible to struggle against the racialism of the State of Israel, its reactionary qualities, its colonialist character, but it is not permissible to talk about eliminating the State of Israel.(1)

Since 1967, Soviet policy in the Arab-Israeli dispute has been based on United Nations Resolution 242. The Soviet Union calls for withdrawal by Israel to the prewar frontiers, not to those of the 1948 partition plan. According to Mezhdunarodnaya zhizn of October 1974:

> Recognition of the lines of demarcation existing prior to the June 1967 conflict as the final borders between Israel and the Arab countries constitutes the only reasonable basis on which a settlement in the Middle East can be reached. If one considers that, from the point of view of international law, there are no recognized borders between Israel and Arab countries at all so far, then their establishment along the lines defined would signify great progress in Arab-Israeli relations, and would considerably improve the entire political situation in the Middle East.(2)

Where then does one go from here in light of the following considerations: a) The Arab-Israeli conflict is part of a much larger pattern of social and political upheaval in the region; b) the superpowers, including the Soviet Union, are in and are part of the Middle East for the foreseeable future; and c) although they are code terms that have acquired pejorative meaning and that fan emotional sensitivities, "intervention" and "imposition" are facts of life in the contemporary Middle East.

True, an ideal solution would envisage withdrawal of the great powers from the Arab-Israeli conflict, if not from the region altogether. It would be a full peace settlement in which the Begin and Sadat families could periodically exchange visits in Tel Aviv and Alexandria and in which tourists, trade, and commerce would freely cross frontiers, as they did before partition in 1948. More realistically, what is likely to occur is some variation of the pattern of settlement that has already been imposed by the great powers in Resolution 242. Nearly every credible proposal for settlement, whether Arab, Israeli, Soviet, or American, has been some version of Resolution 242 with modest alterations or supplements. The plan proposed by United States Secretary of State William Rogers in 1970-71, the much maligned plan of the American Friends Service Committee (Quakers) proposed in Search for Peace, the Jarring proposals, the various Egyptian and Russian plans, the plan proposed by the Mapam party in Israel, and even the plan proposed by Israeli Foreign Minister Yigal Allon have been based on Resolution 242. Unfortunately, more often than not, rather than substantive differences in content, it is who makes proposals, the time of proposals, or the tone of the proposals which determines their success or failure.

In the Middle East, psychology rather than rationality is the determining factor in resolving contentious issues. The success of United Nations mediator Ralph Bunche in negotiating the 1949 armistice agreements and the early success of United States Secretary of State Henry Kissinger were more the result of their ability to manipulate psychological factors than a consequence of a rational plan.

It will take considerable prodding to move the issues toward solution again, and President Carter seems to be on the right track. If asked to anticipate what might result from a Geneva Middle East peace conference, I would envisage some version of the Allon plan as a first step toward implementation of Resolution 242. This would include substantial withdrawal by Israel from areas occupied in 1967, especially from those with large Arab populations, and from most of Sinai and the Golan Heights. Through some form of demilitarization, and also as a participant in those forces which would guarantee demilitarization, Israel could retain control over its own security frontiers. In exchange, this initial process would include formal adoption of nonbelligerency, softening if not actually opening frontiers, and continued relaxation of restrictions on shipments through the Suez Canal to Israel. After attainment of these first steps, which could perhaps involve months or a year and a half of negotiations, they would be tested in an experimental period, which would determine what next steps might be taken toward that ultimate goal in which the chiefs of state and their families would exchange frequent visits of amity.

NOTES AND REFERENCES

(1) "The Soviet Attitude to the Palestine Problem: From the Records of the Syrian Communist Party, 1971-72," Journal of Palestine Studies 2 (Autumn 1972): 191-3.

(2) V. Vladimirov, "A Peaceful Settlement for the Middle East," Mezhdunarodnaya zhizn no. 10 (October 1974): 109, cited in Galia Golan, The Soviet Union and the PLO, Adelphi Papers no. 131 (London: International Institute for Strategic Studies, 1977), p. 7.

14 The Year of Sadat's Initiative
Mattityahu Peled

FLEXIBILITY UNDER BEGIN

Many people wonder whether a government led by the Labour Alignment in Israel could have brought about the dramatic visit of President Sadat to Israel in November 1977. It seems clear now that this unique step signifying a complete volte face on Egypt's part regarding its position toward Israel came only after the Egyptian president was satisfied that Israel's position on the question of the peace process had undergone fundamental changes. Those changes were severely criticized by the Labour opposition as exposing Israel to the worst kind of diplomatic isolation which would necessarily force it to appear intransigent and obstructive.

That Begin could bring himself to adopt positions of greater flexibility than those of the preceding government seemed inconceivable in the first few days after he became head of the largest Parliamentary faction on May 17, 1977. Two statements made by Begin at that time were sufficient to send a chill down the spines of many Israelis. On the night that the election results became known, Begin stated that this was the most important event for the Jewish people since Jabotinsky had proposed that the Zionist movement adopt the establishment of a Jewish state as its defined goal. This was a reference to a rather obscure episode in the history of the Zionist movement, going back to the early 1930s, which resulted in the secession of Jabotinsky's followers from the Zionist organization and the establishment of the Revisionist Zionist organization from which Begin and his underground group, Etzel, subsequently emerged. In terms of the history of the Jewish people and Israel between the early 1930s and the year 1977, that particular episode could have been considered of such importance only by someone whose political thinking had the symptoms of ossification.

The second statement, made by Begin on the day following the general election, was that from then on there would be many

301

settlements like Kadum, an illegal settlement established by Gush Emunim after violent clashes with law enforcement forces. By proximising many Kadums, Begin indicated his determination to proceeed with a comprehensive program for establishing Jewish settlements in the thickly populated West Bank despite the objection of many Israelis and the outspoken criticism of the United States. The impression, then, was that Begin was on the verge of launching Israel into open conflict with the United States as well as creating severe internal discord.

Begin was soon invited to meet President Carter in Washington, and after his talks with American leaders, he began to speak in an entirely different style, enunciating some startling new principles as guidelines for Israel's policy. In the first place, Begin announced that Israel was committed to the idea of a comprehensive peace conference in which all Arab adversaries of Israel would participate. Second, he announced that there were no issues which had to be barred from the agenda of such a conference, except that of the destruction of Israel. Third, he made it quite clear that settlements in the occupied territories would be allowed only in accordance with the government's policy of the moment.

The third point, of course, merely reinstated the preceding government's policy. As it turned out, Begin proved much more resolute than his predecessor in enforcing this policy, and he allowed no illegal settlements. The issue was brought to a head in September 1977, when Gush Emunim planned to establish ten new settlements in conjunction with the Sukkot holiday but was stopped by the prime minister who was firmly backed by his defense minister. This was something which Israel had not seen for some three years.

The first two principles, however, that of supporting a comprehensive peace conference, which in fact meant a Geneva Peace Conference as envisaged by Security Council Resolution 338, and that of allowing every issue to be brought up for discussion, marked a clear departure from previous policies and a willingness to adopt a more flexible posture at least insofar as procedural matters were concerned. There is no doubt that for a number of months in mid-1977 Begin succeeded in creating the impression that Israel was moving toward moderation. This was certainly the impression obtained by the President of Rumania when Begin visited that country. This change was further substantiated when Israel agreed with the United States on a way of allowing the Palestinians to participate in the Geneva Peace Conference.

With the publication of this agreement on October 13, 1977 in the form of a "working paper on suggestion(s) for the resumption of the Geneva Peace Conference," it became clear that very little indeed remained of the principles which had guided the Labor Alignment government regarding the peacemaking process. Prior to these changes, the Israeli government had been dedicated to the policy of achieving only partial and temporary agreements with its Arab antagonists. These were modeled on the three interim agreements made with Syria after the October 1973 War and the so-called Sinai I and Sinai II agreements, all of which had been reached through the mediation of United States

Secretary of State Kissinger. The reasons for this preference were basically two in number. One was that a comprehensive peace conference to be terminated with a comprehensive peace would necessarily isolate Israel since both the United States and the Soviet Union could be expected to favor Arab positions rather than Israeli ones. The other reason was that through the slow process of partial agreements Israel could test the sincerity of Arab commitments to peaceful coexistence without Israel having to commit itself to any definite peace plan. Until the Carter Administration came to power, it was firmly believed in Israel that this was also the preferred policy of the United States.

When it became clear that the Carter Administration had developed a preference for a comprehensive peace treaty to be negotiated at a peace conference, Israel indicated great uneasiness with this course of action. The Israeli government was determined not to allow a peace conference to be convened by raising insurmountable problems of procedure. The most effective contention on Israel's part was that Resolution 338, like its predecessor Resolution 242, left no room for the participation of a Palestinian component in the conference. In 1977, this was an obstacle which could, to all intents and purposes, prevent the conference. The Arab governments were by that time obligated by the Rabat resolutions of the Arab Summit to take the position that no one could represent the Palestinians in any forum except the Palestine Liberation Organization (PLO) and that no peace could be achieved without a just solution to the Palestine problem. Thus, it became clear that without finding a formula for Palestinian participation, acceptable to both Israel and the Arab governments, there could be no peace conference. Begin enabled that obstacle to be overcome when he agreed to the formulations of the working paper.

SADAT IN THE ISRAELI KNESSET

Ever since the Security council passed Resolution 242, the Palestinians have consistently objected to it primarily because it has completely neglected to recognize the political nature of their problem. The only reference that the resolution makes to the Palestinians is found in the section calling for a solution to the refugee problem. Thus, the issue is characterized as a humanitarian one, devoid of any overtly political significance; at any rate, this is how Israel and the Palestinians have interpreted it. It took the Palestinians many years to persuade the Arab governments to recognize the need for an identifiable Palestinian component as part of whatever process was initiated to bring about the resolution of the Arab-Israeli conflict. Only in November 1974, some seven years after the PLO had reconstituted itself in its present form, did the Arab Summit finally recognize the legitimacy of the Palestinian contention. This was not only too late for Resolution 242, it was also too late for Resolution 338 which was adopted after the 1973 War. Under these circumstances, it is quite clear that by refusing to allow a Palestinian component to participate in the peace conference, Israel was firmly backed by the language and spirit of the relevant Security Council resolutions, while the Arab governments which were expected to attend the conference were committed to the position that no peace could be negotiated without the Palestinians taking part in the process.

The nature of this difficulty must be grasped in order to understand the historic significance of the working paper. For the first time, Israel agreed that the Palestinian issue had to be discussed primarily as a political one and that there should be a Palestinian component at the conference. Furthermore, Israel agreed that the future of the West Bank and Gaza would be discussed in a special working group to be formed at the peace conference. This group would have a Palestinian component in addition to Israeli, Egyptian, and Jordanian representatives. There is no doubt that this fundamental change in Israel's position came about as a result of very definite United States pressure, described by Dayan as "brutal." The working paper was approved by the Israeli Cabinet with Begin arguing vehemently for its acceptance.

Under these circumstances, the road to Geneva seemed open although the PLO showed an astonishing lack of appreciation of the significance of this breakthrough. It appeared quite possible that a Palestinian delegation nominated by the PLO would participate in the conference, and that subsequently, provided the conference made some progress, the PLO itself might be able to participate under its own name. It was possible to anticipate such a development because the Geneva Peace Conference was to be guided by the principles enunciated in the American-Soviet statement on the Middle East of October 1, 1977. The two superpowers are the cochairmen of the conference, and their joint statement specifically mentioned that among the questions to be resolved during the conference was that "of the Palestinian question including insuring the legitimate rights of the Palestinian people." The Palestinians were never closer to obtaining their goal of being accepted as a party to an overall settlement of the Middle East conflict. The PLO failed to react positively to the new situation. They refused to recognize that even though the accepted formulas were far from what would be considered by them as fully satisfactory, they nevertheless marked significant progress in the right direction from the Palestinians' point of view. Even so, the PLO position was not viewed with undue concern since there was no doubt that the working paper had indeed brought the parties much closer to the conference table.

At this point, Egypt could well have considered that the time was ripe for a demonstrative act showing that some kind of direct communication with Israel was in order. But as was learned at a much later stage, another far-reaching move had been made to facilitate such an Egyptian step. A meeting between Dayan and Touhami, the Egyptian Deputy Prime Minister, resulted in the understanding that Israel would be willing to relinquish the whole of the Sinai peninsula to Egypt if peace between these two countries could be achieved. The significance of this position must not be underrated.

In February 1971, President Sadat, upon offering to conclude a peace treaty with Israel, had mentioned only the return of the Sinai to Egyptian control as a condition to be accepted by Israel prior to negotiations. At the time, Israel rejected it since its government, then under Golda Meir, believed that at least one-third of the Sinai should forever remain under Israeli control. The one-third was marked by a line leading from El-Arish to Sharem al-Shaykh and was commonly referred to as the line guaranteeing "a territorial link between Eliat and Sharem al-Shaykh." This position was noted in the official minutes of the Cabinet as a binding, nonnegotiable decision. Indeed, Sadat's offer of 1971 was rejected by Israel on the ground that its one precondition was unacceptable. Yet, in 1977, the Cabinet under Begin was prepared not only to offer the whole of Sinai to Egypt but also went as far as to abrogate the decision regarding the territorial link, thus giving itself the freedom to make that offer to Egypt.

At this point, it was clear that the stage was set for a dramatic move by Egypt to acknowledge that the circumstances were ripe for a more rapid movement toward a settlement. In his speech to the Knesset, President Sadat said that he had given a lot of thought to the idea of a personal visit to Israel. Nevertheless, his step took the whole world by surprise. It was certainly designed to force a change in traditional attitudes which would allow further communication between Israel and Egypt to proceed unhampered by the old refusalist Arab positions. In fact, Sadat explicitly made remarks to that effect in his speech to the Knesset.

Apart from the attempt to forge a new framework within which future relations could take shape, Sadat's speech outlined the principles upon which a stable peace could be achieved. Little was really new in that part of his address. Since, as Sadat pointed out, this was not the first time he had put forward his ideas about peace with Israel, although this was perhaps the first time Israel was paying attention to them, no great surprises awaited his listeners. The principles he proposed were: a) all territories occupied by Israel since 1967 should be returned to the Arabs; b) the rights of the Palestinian people must be recognized; c) Israel has a right to exist as a sovereign state in the Middle East, should be recognized officially by its Arab neighbors, and its legitimate security needs should be respected.

If there was little that could surprise in Sadat's address, Begin's reply was a complete letdown. His reasons for failing so miserably to rise to the occasion remain unclear. He could certainly have responded with an address that would have been considered a major contribution to the peace process and as magnanimous as that of Sadat. All that was necessary on Begin's part was to reiterate the concessions made by his government since it assumed power. He could have dramatized Israel's preference for a comprehensive peace treaty, as opposed to its former preference for limited, bilateral agreements. In doing so, he would have met one of Sadat's main points. Begin could have stressed that Israel was willing to discuss amicably every idea put forward with the intention of enhancing the chances for peace. He could have further stressed the new position Israel adopted in the working paper on the nature of the Palestinian issue and taken pride in agreeing to the presence of a Palestinian component at the peace conference. Finally, he could have announced Israel's willingness to hand over the Sinai to

Egypt by way of implementing a formal peace treaty, thus accepting what had long been Egypt's position regarding this territory. This would certainly have encouraged other Arab leaders to support Sadat openly at a time when opposition to his move was crystalizing in some important Arab countries.

Had Begin made this kind of response, no one could have criticized him for failing to respond to Sadat's gesture, and at the same time, he would have offered only what he had already agreed to offer. However, Begin preferred to delve into the past, ancient and recent, thus appearing to lend a deaf ear to Sadat's promise that policies of the past would be discarded and that Israel's long-standing grievances would be eliminated. This historic failure of Begin defies explanation. Could it be that he really meant not to stand by his new positions once Sadat seemed more forthcoming than anticipated? Is it conceivable that Begin was so incapable of realizing the greatness of the moment that all he could think of was to settle old scores with a traditional adversary?

Perhaps the true explanation lies in Begin's fear of his own party, which was by and large left out of the diplomatic process and was not aware of the extent of Begin's concessions. This explanation sounds plausible in view of Begin's behavior in January 1978 when he was indeed faced with an open rebellion within his party, Herut, and in other elements of the Likkud bloc upon which his coalition government is based.

BEGIN'S PEACE PLAN

This confrontation was first noticed when Begin presented his peace plan to President Carter in December 1977. The resignation of Begin's public relations assistant took most observers by surprise, since he was a member of the Prime Minister's innermost circle. When Begin returned to Israel, the Likkud bloc was in turmoil. After Begin submitted his plan to President Sadat at Ismailia, the revolt became public. Begin's peace plan was nevertheless approved by the Knesset and became the only binding plan which the government could negotiate. With the approval of the Knesset, Begin could very well have decided, de Gaulle-like, to turn his back on his party and to proceed according to his own convictions. This was not to happen. Faced with an open revolt, Begin gave in and began to modify his plan in a way that made a shambles of it.

The plan, as submitted to Sadat in Ismailia, consisted of two parts. One, regarding the Sinai, was fairly straightforward. Israel would return the Sinai to Egypt up to the pre-1967 borders. As revealed months later by Defence Minister Weizman, no reservations were made regarding Israeli airfields in the Sinai constructed by previous Israeli governments within the area then believed to be part of the territorial link to Sharem al-Shaykh. In addition, no reservations were made regarding the new settlements established since 1973 in the Rafiah basin on land owned for generations by thousands of Arab bedouins.

The second part of the plan concerned the Palestinian territories of the West Bank and the Gaza Strip. To be sure, Begin never meant to propose anything which could be considered satisfactory by the Palestinians or any Arab leaders, but the plan contained the following elements which made serious consideration possible. Begin proposed to leave the question of sovereignty over these areas open "because of other claims," a clear reference to Palestinian claims. The plan suggested a five-year period in which internal autonomy would be exercised by the people of these areas, and it is quite clear that the line dividing sovereign Israel and autonomous Palestine would be the pre-1967 line separating Israel from the West Bank and the Gaza Strip. Thus, that border regained a measure of legal validity after it had been declared null and void on numerous occasions by Begin himself.

Other parts of the plan guaranteed Israel effective control for the duration of the five-year period and generally indicated no willingness on Israel's part to relinquish control at the end of that period. On the contrary, the plan called for continued Israeli settlement, and by offering Palestinians living in the occupied territories the option of becoming Israeli citizens, it provided for eventual annexation of these areas. Yet, the plan left sufficient room for future maneuvering to have alarmed important parts of the Likkud bloc which claimed that the plan laid the foundations of a future Palestinian state.

In sum, the plan certainly had the merit of being sufficiently attractive to Sadat for him not to reject it, and for that reason it was distasteful to many in Begin's own camp. It must be assumed that Begin and Sadat saw the dangers and the promises offered by the plan and that they, therefore, agreed in Ismailia that the plan should be considered in detail by two parallel committees: a political one to consist of the foreign ministers, and a military one to consist of the defense ministers. The importance of creating these committees was to enable the parties to clarify and even to modify elements of the plan in the relatively secluded atmosphere of private diplomatic exchanges.

The opponents of the plan, in Begin's own party and inside his own Cabinet, were determined to torpedo it before it gained any currency. By a series of carefully planned acts, they forced Begin to reinterpret his proposals in a way that deprived them of any merit that they were believed to have had initially. To begin with, the condemnation of the plan as a complete sellout was energetically concerted in the press and in the Knesset. As Dayan complained several times, it became a government plan attacked by the opposition (which was natural) and rejected by the coalition, leaving open the question of who really did support it. More tangible measures were soon taken to force Begin to withdraw his plan. Under the leadership of the Minister of Agriculture, Sharon, a large-scale operation started in the Rafiah region with the declared purpose of establishing some ten new settlements. This was one of the most photographed and the most televised activities in Israel. Its purpose was to make sure that everyone clearly understood that Begin's plan had no political support in Israel.

At the same time, Gush Emunim, which had been kept under control since September 1977, reemerged, now with the support of important government agencies. They began to implement the plans which they had been forced to abandon earlier. The chaos was complete. Officials gave conflicting statements; Begin lost any vestige of control. Soon he came to the conclusion that he would have to mend his fences with the opposition within his own Likkud bloc. Through a series of statements he reneged on his plan without allowing this to be expressly stated. On the Sinai settlements, he stated that it was never his intention to allow them to come under Egyptian control. He suggested first that although they might live under Egyptian sovereignty, they would be protected by the Israeli police. Later, he had to retract that statement and claim that he had never promised to give the Rafiah region back to Egypt. Then, the question of the airfields came up, and he denied that he intended to give them away. Faced with the resurgent Gush Emunim, Begin declared that they were acting in accordance with the principles of his peace plan since it provided for continued settlement. Then, out of the blue, Begin came up with the new interpretation of Resolution 242, claiming that it did not apply to the West Bank and Gaza.

There can be little doubt that, practically speaking, there was no point in holding meetings of the two committees set up in Ismailia because Begin had preempted any conclusion they could conceivably have reached through negotiation. Sadat very sensibly put an end to the committees' work, first by recalling his foreign minister from Jerusalem and later by refusing to allow the military committee to convene in Cairo. By February 1978, it was clear that Sadat's initiative was nearing a point where its failure could not be concealed.

REGRESSION

Even before Sadat set out for Israel, it was known that his initiative aroused strong opposition in a number of Arab countries. His meeting with President Assad of Syria prior to the visit to Jerusalem was known to have ended in a stormy exchange, and the Saudi royal family was upset that their views had not been sought before the decision to go to Jerusalem was taken. After the visit to Jerusalem, the opposition in the Arab world to Sadat's move consolidated in a kind of rejection front which included Syria, Iraq, Libya, South Yemen, Algeria, and the PLO. Sadat, for his part, demonstrated his determination not to be intimidated by such a show of hostility. He cut off relations with the five governments which attacked his initiative and froze Egypt's relations with the PLO.

The Arab opposition to Sadat was varied. Syria had already committed itself to participation in the Geneva Peace Conference and had subscribed to Resolutions 242 and 338. Furthermore, President Assad has publicly stated that in the event of peace he would agree to a total demilitarization of the Golan Heights, thus meeting a significant Israeli security requirement. But now he suspected that Sadat favored the move toward Jerusalem to be free to strike a deal with Israel without being tied to any of the Arab participants. It is indeed possible that Sadat had hoped to come to some understanding with Israel before the Geneva conference met to avoid getting bogged down in unnecessary, time-consuming arguments. Other countries, like Iraq and Libya, objected to the very idea of dealing with Israel, regardless of how this was brought about.

The PLO's position was ambivalent. While taking part in the Arab summit convened to denounce Sadat, they allowed support for his move to be voiced within their camp. There were at the time clear indications that important elements in the PLO were considering a public statement suggesting the establishment of a Palestinian state alongside Israel, on the West Bank, and in the Gaza Strip. To ensure its future neutrality, this state would be limited in its alliance-making power by a provision in the peace treaty with Israel similar to the one found in the Austrian Agreement with the big powers. Likewise, it was contemplated that the new state would have very limited military capability, compatible with Israel's security sensitivity. In fact, these ideas were eventually put forward by Walid Khalidi in the Spring 1978 issue of <u>Foreign Affairs</u>. Although it is quite clear that his article is not an official PLO statement, it can be assumed that it is being supported by many in that organization. Thus, opposition to Sadat was very uneven and could have been weakened by allowing Sadat some immediate, tangible success in order to disprove the predictions of some Arab leaders that he would get nothing from Israel for what they saw as his humiliating conduct.

There is no sign that Israel was at all sensitive to Sadat's need for some fortifying evidence which he could use against his Arab detractors. Just before Sadat went to Israel, the Israeli Cabinet discussed the possibility of making a symbolic gesture such as placing the desert town of El-Arish under Egyptian control. Begin saw no need for that, and the idea was dropped. Months later, when Weizman, upon his return from a meeting with Sadat in Salzburg, suggested that Sadat might be able to resume direct talks with Israel if a gesture like returning El-Arish were to be offered him by Israel, Begin retorted that no one would get anything from Israel for nothing. He expressed confidence that the American people would have no difficulty in understanding the validity of this hardnosed bargaining position, thereby betraying an amazing lack of appreciation for the sometimes selfless American generosity toward Israel itself. In any case, this stiff position taken by Begin resulted in callousness when a little magnanimity could have alleviated the pressure on Sadat to call off his attempt to work directly with Israel.

When speaking to the Knesset, Sadat made a moving appeal to Israel to abandon its belief that power is the only language understood by the Arabs. This was a clear reference to an attitude adopted by Israel very soon after its establishment and manifested on various occasions where resort to brute force was considered the best way of reacting to Arab violence. However, in March 1978, Israel demonstrated that it would take more than an appeal from the Egyptian President to persuade Israel to give up the principle of retaliation. After the raid on the Israeli coast by a group of PLO terrorists which culminated in the death of a busload of vacationers, Israel invaded Lebanon and forced some 300,000 Lebanese to flee their homes. This massive operation directed against a population which was entirely innocent was justified by the argument that the south of Lebanon was being used by PLO units as a base of operation against Israel.

From a stricly military point of view, the operation was a fiasco. Very few of the PLO troops were hit, and the bulk of its forces withdrew into northern Lebanon. The connection between that massive military operation launched by Israel and the raid was very hard to see. The raiders came by boat from a point north of Sidon. As was later established, they could easily have been spotted and intercepted had the Israeli security forces been more diligent. As a matter of fact, the possibility of invading south Lebanon has been a subject of public debate in Israel since the region was evacuated by Israeli forces following the Armistice Agreement with Lebanon in 1949. Those Israelis demanding a reoccupation of that region have argued that Israel needs the water of the Litani River, most of which flows unused into the sea. The demand to annex the area between the Israeli border and that river has been renewed on several occasions. The most recent one was when the Syrian army entered Lebanon to bring about an end to the civil war in 1976. The Israeli government did not invade south Lebanon then, but demanded that the Syrian army keep out as well. The Syrians complied with this demand, thereby allowing south Lebanon to become a refuge for Palestinian organizations that wished to escape Syrian supervision. Thus, the wisdom of stopping the Syrian army on the so-called "red line" some twenty miles north of the Israeli-Lebanese border proved very questionable.

Now, faced with growing domestic dissatisfaction at letting the inpetus of Sadat's initiative peter out, outraged public clamoring for revenge or retaliation for the latest terrorist raid and persistent demands for moving to the Litani emanating mostly from circles close to Likkud, Begin approved a plan for invading south Lebanon.

From Sadat's point of view, the situation became desperate. Initially, he had hoped that the PLO would be willing to join the Cairo Conference which he had called after his visit to Jerusalem. Relying probably on the nature of Israel's new position as defined in the working paper and knowing the strong interest of the PLO in becoming a party to the negotiations with Israel on the basis of mutual recognition and acceptance, Sadat invited the PLO to Cairo with absolutely no prior conditions. This invitation was viewed with great concern in Israel, but Sadat could speculate that Israel would find it very difficult to reject it so soon after his epoch-making visit to Jerusalem. Indeed, the Israeli government was at a loss how to react were the PLO to accept Sadat's invitation, but the PLO, for reasons of its own, decided to reject the invitation. The raid on Israel in March signaled the PLO's reversion to violence against Israel after a period of some three years in which the mainstream of that organization, as distinguished from the rejectionist groups, studiously refrained from acts of violence.   One of the explanations offered by Arab observers to this change in PLO policy was that Sadat had shown that moderation toward Israel did not pay. Thus, a move meant to encourage moderation and compromise was used as an excuse for increased violence and intransigence. Clearly, with the two main antagonists in the Arab-Israeli conflict, Israel and the Palestinians, once more at each other's throats, Sadat was faced with an impasse.

Yet, rather than give up, Sadat decided on a new move in an attempt to salvage his initiative. It soon became clear that rather than allow the PLO to undermine his efforts, he would concentrate on a solution which did not immediately call for active Palestinian participation or contemplate the establishment of a Palestinian state for a number of years. The solution which came under consideration was that the interim period of five years suggested by Begin regarding the West Bank and Gaza would be allowed to serve as a period of transition during which Israeli control would be replaced by some kind of Jordanian-Palestinian sovereignty. This went against Begin's doctrine that the territories referred to by him as Judea and Samaria are to remain forever under Israeli control with some form of autonomy for the local population. However, Israel's claim to unlimited control over these territories is an innovation which the world has never accepted. The chances that Israel would have to relinquish total control over these territories in order not to bear the responsibility for a complete breakdown of the search for peace seemed reasonable. The United States government certainly felt that this new approach by Sadat had merit and asked Israel whether it would agree that at the end of the five-year period the status of the Palestinian territories should be altered and, if so, by what means this could be achieved.

It took Israel a long time to produce an answer. When it came, it made it clear that any consideration of the status of these territories was unacceptable. At the same time, it became evident that no unanimity existed even within the Cabinet on this issue. The United States was unable to allow this kind of intransigence to stand in the way of what seemed a possible compromise and succeeded eventually in persuading Israel to modify its reply. At the meeting of the three foreign ministers, Vance, Dayan, and Ibrahim in Leeds Castle, Israel finally agreed that the status of the territories could be reconsidered at the end of the five-year period. At the same time, it emphasized that any expectation that this would lead to territorial concessions was unwarranted.

The experience of the Leeds meeting is rather discouraging in the sense it proved that merely getting together does not in itself guarantee progress. An additional lesson is that the United States can contribute to progress more than it has to date by taking a more active part. When the Israeli Cabinet drafted its reply to the questions submitted by the United States, the Cabinet was divided. Later, Begin admitted that he preferred the more flexible formula allowing the status of the territories in question to be reconsidered, but that he gave in to pressure from the more intransigent elements in the Cabinet, partly because his illness made him more susceptible to such pressure. The Israeli reply to the United States was very damaging to the entire negotiating process, and the Americans decided to retrieve the situation by calling the Leeds meeting. Then, under some pressure from Vance, Dayan accepted a different formula with the approval of Begin. There is no doubt that the American intervention came too late to save the situation and that Sadat felt too discouraged to continue his attempts to prevent the complete breakdown of the dialogue with Israel. An earlier intervention by the United States might have spared the parties the agonizing experience of seeing Sadat practically admitting defeat after almost a year of patiently trying to avoid it.

As these lines are being written, the preparations for the Camp David Summit Meeting of President Carter, President Sadat, and Prime Minister Begin are underway. There is no doubt that Israel and Egypt know very well what stands in the way of settling the conflict. They know that the obstacles are not procedural but substantive. Perhaps one reason why they cannot agree on the principles which would govern the resolution of the differences is that both are hoping for American support of their own particular position. As long as the United States limits its role to that of offering procedural means for the continuation of the dialogue, there can be no real progress. Both Israel and Egypt are operating under a great deal of pressure from many quarters, and it may be necessary in order to enable the parties to resist some of that pressure to have a clear idea of United States policy on the substantive issues. If the United States is to help the parties overcome the obstacles they now face, President Carter will have to clarify which principles the United States feels should govern the resolution of the conflict. It would be very difficult for either Israel or Egypt to disregard a clearly stated American policy in these matters.

The Camp David Summit Meeting was being held as the book was sent to the publisher. A short Epilogue on the Summit and subsequent events starts on page 335.

15 Great Power Intervention in the Middle East: 1977-78

David Pollock

Since 1977, two events have dominated Arab-Israeli diplomacy and to a great extent, the entire international politics of the Middle East: the election of Menachem Begin as Prime Minister to Israel, and Egyptian President Sadat's dramatic visit to Jerusalem in November of that year. Taken together, these and subsequent events serve to illustrate both the continuing importance and the limits of great power intervention in the Middle East. This chapter will attempt briefly to analyze that series of events, relate them to different forms of outside intervention in the region, and assess the prospects for such intervention in the immediate future. The overall argument presented here is that recent diplomatic developments are part of a broader pattern of shifting alignments in which the involvement of the United States has become concentrated on the Egyptian-Israeli heartland of Arab-Israeli affairs and that of the Soviet Union on its periphery. In neither case has this occurred entirely by design. Consideration will be given to the regional policies of each of the two superpowers both before and after the Sadat initiative.

RECENT BACKGROUND OF AMERICAN POLICY IN THE MIDDLE EAST

The Carter Administration adopted its predecessor's goal of a compromise Arab-Israeli settlement for the sake of reconciling the American commitment to Israel with American political and economic-energy interests in the Arab world. However, the tactics involved in pursuing that goal changed.(1) It was felt Kissinger's step-by-step diplomacy had at first helped to forge a relatively moderate and pro-Western Arab axis composed principally of Cairo, Damascus, and Riyadh. Later, however, it had split that coalition by moving too fast on the Egyptian front (in the second-stage Sinai Disengagement Agreement of late 1975) for the Syrian government to follow. The latter, as a

313

result, moved closer to both the radical Arabs and the Soviet Union. Moreover, the exclusion of the Syrians from the American pursuit of an Arab-Israeli agreement left the Egyptians more vulnerable to charges of betrayal. This, in turn, endangered both the agreement itself and the American position as its sponsor. The new American policy was characterized by the pursuit of a comprehensive Arab-Israeli settlement, which could perhaps be implemented in stages but which had to cover all of the issues and all of the actors involved in the dispute. As additional insurance against disruption, the Soviet Union was to be included in future negotiations.

This reasoning explains many of the new features in early Mid-East policy statements from the Carter Administration, such as the suggestions for resumption of the Soviet-American sponsored multilateral Geneva Peace Conference to promote real peace. Similar reasoning explains the American insistence on addressing immediately in that forum the procedural and substantive demands of the Palestinians, whose participation in a comprehensive settlement could alone legitimize it throughout the Arab world.

It was on the Palestinian issue, indeed, that Carter Administration policy took its most original turn. Previous administrations had made overtures to the Palestinians, but the differences in emphasis, priority, and degree were sufficiently great to qualify as a difference in kind. Less than three months after taking office, President Carter himself surprised many people by revealing, almost casually, that the United States now favored the creation of a Palestinian homeland. In practice, the new American policy tended to make Arab-Israeli diplomacy a hostage of the Palestine Liberation Organization (PLO). Carter now publicly conceded that the PLO represented a "substantial part" of the constituents it claimed. Behind the scenes, an extraordinary amount of diplomatic effort was devoted to securing Palestinian participation in a revived Geneva conference; I had a brief opportunity to observe that effort at close hand during a week of conferences with senior American policy makers on the Middle East in the spring of 1977. A major obstacle in this connection was the explicit American commitment not to negotiate with the PLO until it accepted the well-known United Nations Resolution 242.(2) This implicitly recognized Israel's right to exist in peace but omitted any reference to the   Palestinians except as a "refugee problem." Considerable American energy was expended in an effort either to obtain PLO acceptance of that resolution or to come up with some ingenious alternative formula for Palestinian representation acceptable to both Israel and the PLO. PLO conferences in March and August 1977 did endorse the establishment of a Palestinian "state," as opposed to a "fighting national authority," in territories regained from Israel. They could not, however, agree on any further softening in the organization's position. American attempts to arrive at a compromise continued nonetheless.

Simultaneously, a new, unexpected obstacle to the American diplomatic strategy arose: the Israeli election in May 1977 resulted in a government pledged to uphold Israeli sovereignty, as opposed to territorial compromise, over the territories from which the new

Palestinian homeland was presumably intended to arise. The election ended the era of rule by the Labour Party, which had dominated Israel's coalition governments since independence, and brought the Likkud Party, headed by Menachem Begin, to power for the first time. Analysis of Israeli voting patterns suggests that the major underlying factor behind this upset was popular disenchantment and frustration born precisely of Labour's long period of uninterrupted rule. This was especially the case among the chronically underprivileged Sepharadim, or so-called "oriental Jews," who accounted for over half the Israeli electorate by 1977.(3) The immediate cause of the large-scale defections from Labour's voting strength, on the other hand, was probably the series of scandals that had shaken the party during the preceding months and which involved Housing Minister Ofer, Bank of Israel Governor Yadlin, and Prime Minister and Mrs. Rabin. Even though the election was decided largely on the basis of domestic Israeli issues, Likkud's foreign policy platform threatened to confound American plans. Moreover, Washington's diplomatic interventions on the Palestinian issue had, if anything, probably only added to the magnitude of the Labour Party's loss. Begin's victory thus exemplified some of the constraints occasionally imposed by the vagaries of Mid-East domestic politics on outside influence in the region.

The Likkud platform emphasized Israel's "eternal and inalienable right" to hold on to the entire West Bank.(4) Begin's personal position since the Six Day War has been that the West Bank was not occupied territory but the liberated areas of Judea and Samaria, part of the historical "Eretz Israel" (Land of Israel), which Jews alone could rightfully claim.

Both the party platform and other policy statements by Begin, during and after the electoral campaign, laid equal stress on the notion that Israeli retention of the West Bank was "also an integral part of the right to security and peace."(5) In 1967, of course, Israeli forces had quickly been able to advance and defeat the armies of three neighboring Arab states without the supposed advantages of control over the West Bank territorial salient. In part, subsequent security arguments reflected a disposition to hold on to gains already acquired, as well as Israeli concern over the increased quantity and quality of weapons available to both Arab governments and Palestinian guerrillas. More important, however, was the experience of the 1973 War, which suggested to many Israelis that they could not count on a repetition of 1967. In the face of an unexpected and coordinated Arab attack, Israel might need room for a strategic retreat. The October War, then, seemed to serve as a reminder of how dangerous hostile control of territories, like the West Bank and Gaza, fronting Israel's geographic and population center might be. The majority of Israeli public and professional military opinion, and not just convinced adherents of Begin, concurs that the ultimate disposition of those territories is of considerable importance for Israeli security in the future. From a short-term – some would say short-sighted – military perspective, the claim is made that the safest way of assuring a disposition satisfactory to Israel is to retain full physical control over the territories in question.

The problem, however, is that the strategic importance of those territories to Israel is at least matched by their political importance to their Arab inhabitants and to Israel's other Arab neighbors. It is precisely this point that the Begin government has been unwilling to concede. Soon after his election, Begin made a ceremonial visit to an Orthodox settlement on the West Bank. In July 1977, the government formally authorized three existing Jewish colonies there. Although these moves were largely symbolic, statements by individual government figures like former war hero and Agriculture Minister Arik Sharon indicated that many more such settlements would be forthcoming.(6)

Nevertheless, American-Israeli discussions on the Palestinian question continued as both countries made an effort to minimize their differences. Official American spokesmen were content to reiterate their conviction of the necessity for Israeli territorial withdrawals, while attempting to reassure the Israelis on the issue of arms supplies. On this latter issue, the Carter Administration's ostentatiously restrictive rhetoric had earlier caused some concern.(7) Begin himself was warmly received on an official visit to Washington in July 1977. The Israeli government, for its part, made only a few symbolic moves to implement its claim to the West Bank, although it demonstrated some flexibility on the format of proposed peace negotiations.

These American-Israeli discussions were, however, suddenly derailed by the parallel American project of coordinating Mid-East diplomacy with Moscow. Although the wording of the October 1977 American-Soviet statement on the issue of the Palestinian rights and representation at a Geneva conference did mark an erosion, from Israel's point of view, in the American position, it was still sufficiently vague to allow a variety of interpretations. The principle of Soviet participation in the formal negotiations had, of course, been conceded long before. More objectionable to the Israeli government was the highhanded manner in which the joint statement had been negotiated and presented, suggesting some private deal between the superpowers at Israel's expense. Israel's immediate and vociferous protests soon resulted in a partial American retreat. A prolonged, high-level American-Israeli negotiating session, described by Dayan as "brutal," yielded a new diplomatic working paper. This reinstated an earlier proposal for the inclusion of some unaffiliated Palestinians in a unified Arab delegation to Geneva.

In effect, the attempt by the two superpowers to intervene in Arab-Israeli diplomacy in a coordinated fashion had been thwarted by the American client. It was subsequently further compromised by the regional clients of the Soviet Union. It finally exploded altogether when Egypt and Israel launched a spectacular diplomatic initiative of their own. The roots of Sadat's surprise journey to Jerusalem can be traced in retrospect to the vicissitudes of Soviet-Egyptian relations since his assumption of power in 1970.

RECENT BACKGROUND OF SOVIET POLICY
IN THE MIDDLE EAST

The political legacy that Anwar Sadat unexpectedly inherited from his predecessor included a state of relations with Israel often described as the "crime of no peace, no war." Sadat, whose relatively shaky domestic position necessitated at least the illusion of movement in the international arena, promptly proclaimed 1971 to be the "year of decision." In this, he counted on the Soviet Union for assistance. Although they concluded a Treaty of Friendship in May 1971, the Soviet Union gave Sadat neither the military wherewithal nor the diplomatic endorsement necessary to convert his rhetoric into reality. Nor did the concomitant discovery and suppression of a pro-Soviet cabal led by his own Deputy Premier augur well for Sadat's relations with the Soviet Union. In retrospect, the decision of 1971 seems to have been for a showdown, not with Israel, but with the Kremlin, thousands of whose military advisors were ignominiously expelled in mid-1972. The expectation, no doubt, was that the rival superpower would oblige by pressing its own ally, Israel, to give Sadat the foreign policy success he so desperately required.

However, Sadat discovered that the United States was content at that time to let his problems simmer on a back burner of international affairs. The Egyptian President then evidently decided that he had little to lose by going to war. Preparations for battle included a temporary rapproachement with the Soviet Union, as insurance against the obvious risks of so daring a maneuver. This was a policy that was to serve Sadat well in October 1973.

It was not long, however, before Egypt again shifted to what one spokesman called a more even-handed policy toward the two super-powers. Only a few months after the war, Sadat had suggested that his armed forces might find a more reliable arms supplier than the Soviet Union. Domestically, the Egyptian government put increasing emphasis on economic development through foreign investment and began to take practical steps to make such investment more attractive to enterprising capitalists in the West. More immediately, Sadat's postwar turn to the United States was an attempt to revive his earlier gambit of inducing Washington to pressure Israel for a settlement agreeable to Egypt.

The initial Soviet reaction to this Egyptian turnaround served to escalate Moscow's public estrangement from Cairo in a sort of diplomatic vicious circle. Sadat flirted with the United States; the Soviet Union, in order to forestall a Mid-East Pax Americana, backed a hard line in Syria. Sadat began voicing disenchantment with the Soviet Union; Moscow responded by broadcasting charges that Egypt had sold out its brother Arabs, and so on. The circle was broken briefly in 1974. Sadat, with Kissinger's apparent blessing, restored harmonious relations with the Soviet Union, which in return helped to deliver the Syrian agreement to disengagement on Israel's volatile northern front.(8) Even though Soviet and American interests in the Middle East are generally defined by opposition, the two superpowers do have one interest in common: to avoid, if possible, an explosive confrontation that might get out of control.

Soviet-Egyptian relations, meanwhile, resumed their downward spiral. The Soviet Union gradually restricted arms supplies. The Egyptian government, for its part, renounced payment for past weapon deliveries and finally in 1976, the treaty with the Soviet Union. Domestically, the campaign of "de-Nasserization" continued. By that time, Soviet policy makers, thrice burned, might well have taken a certain grim satisfaction had Sadat's government collapsed. It was hardly likely any longer, barring a change of regime, that the Soviet presence in Egypt could be restored to full strength even as part of an arrangement with the United States for joint superpower sponsorship of a peace settlement in the region. Instead, the Soviet Union began to concentrate on reinforcing, with arms supplies and a limited military presence on the ground, its position among the radicals elsewhere in the Arab world. By 1976, Soviet weapons deliveries to the Middle East went primarily to Algeria, Syria, Libya – where nearly 1,000 Soviet and East European military technicians were stationed – and especially Iraq. Moscow had made a billion-dollar arms commitment to Iraq in exchange for use of a naval base on the Persian Gulf. A large naval facility and military advisory group were also maintained in the People's Democratic Republic of (Southern) Yemen at the entrance to the Red Sea. These Soviet activities seem to have been valued not only for their own sake, but also for the opportunities they provided to embarrass Sadat and the American sponsorship of a settlement that he envisaged.

Sadat himself lacks the pan-Arab pretensions of Nasser. Nevertheless, domestic political considerations given rise to some concern on his part about pan-Arab support. The Egyptian President can take some comfort in the knowledge that there is no other Arab leader strong enough to challenge him from without and few Palestinians who could create problems from within Egypt itself. Still, internal opposition among other disaffected elements would be mildly encouraged were charges of betrayal to be voiced against him abroad. The gravest dangers to his rule, however, would probably stem either from Egypt's economic difficulties or a prolonged deadlock in peace negotiations. For help with the former problem, Sadat depends largely on Saudi financial support. The Saudi government, in turn, has a vested interest in keeping Sadat in power. Sadat's conservative, pro-Western orientation precludes a repetition of the ideological and even military threat to the Saudi royal family that a radical, pro-Soviet regime under Nasser once posed. On the diplomatic front, Sadat's short-term desire for continual progress has tended to override his longer-term concern about maintaining a unified Arab front. Thus, Sadat has been prepared to tolerate, at least temporarily, the danger of alienation from the Soviet-backed radical Arab camp.

Of greater concern to Egypt by early 1977 were Soviet activities in Africa.(9) It was one thing for the Soviet Union to provide diplomatic, economic, and military support to Sadat's Arab ideological rivals. It was another, more unaccustomed, and ultimately more disconcerting thing for the Soviet Union to do as much for potentially hostile regimes among Egypt's closest neighbors who together controlled not only the southern approaches to the Suez Canal but also the Nile. In Sudan in

August 1976, local Communists with Libyan support had made their third coup attempt against Numeiri's staunchly pro-Egyptian regime. Soviet relations with Libya itself as well as with Uganda continued to improve. In mid-1977, Soviet and Cuban military advisors were still entrenched in Somalia, even as thousands of their compatriots began to supervise the deployment of a large-scale infusion of weapons across the border into America's erstwhile ally, Ethiopia. Egyptian alarm over these developments figured prominently in the discussions held during that period, both by Sadat in Washington(10) and his Foreign Minister in Moscow. Neither were of any immediate avail. The unrelieved tensions finally exploded in a short series of border skirmishes between Egypt and Libya in July 1977.

Nevertheless, in view of Egypt's military preponderance, the hostile encirclement on the periphery hardly posed an urgent danger to Sadat's position. In the near term, he must have suspected, the Soviet strategy was simply to obstruct further Arab-Israeli diplomatic progress by encouraging Syria and the PLO to maintain an unyielding position. This suspicion was seemingly confirmed by Syrian and PLO behavior in the wake of the Soviet-American joint statement on the Middle East in October 1977.

To Sadat, the call for adequate Palestinian representation at Geneva was actually an improvement over past Soviet positions. It neglected to mention the PLO by name and thereby promised to avoid controversy over its seating. However, having accomplished this much, the PLO was now determined, with Syrian backing, to hold out for an explicit invitation. At the same time, the Soviet Union, which may have been upset at the American diplomatic retreat from the joint statement in the face of Israeli objections, proved similarly unwilling or unable to bring its regional clients into line. The combination thus threatened to undo at a stroke, just on the verge of success, all the painstaking effort that had gone into the search for a compromise formula for Palestinian representation at the peace conference. This may well have been the proverbial last straw that led Sadat to announce, ironically with Arafat in attendance, that he was going to end the wrangling over procedures for getting to Geneva by going straight to Jerusalem instead. This unthinkable option was apparently one which he had agreed with the Israelis to hold in reserve.(11) A PLO spokesman hastily declared that the Soviet-American joint statement was in fact the "minimum basis" for the organization's attendance at Geneva. However, it was too late; Sadat refused to reconsider.

The circumvention of Soviet and American plans for Geneva by means of direct Egyptian-Israeli contacts at the highest level did not, however, mean the net decline of great power intervention in the region or even in Arab-Israeli affairs. Soviet diplomacy, it is true, was henceforth confined even more closely to the margins of that dispute, but the importance of American mediation actually increased in proportion.

AMERICAN POLICY SINCE THE SADAT INITIATIVE

From the view point of American policy makers, an initially wary reaction to the new Egyptian diplomatic offensive was dictated, not only by the mixture of caution and resentment normally occasioned by unanticipated complications, but also by concern over the broader implications of Sadat's bold unilateral move. His diplomacy now threatened to undermine one of the fundamental new assumptions of American policy in the Middle East; i.e., coordination among the most important Arab governments was necessary if the regional stability desired by the West were to be achieved. By breaking ranks, Sadat risked further alienating the Soviet Union, the Syrian government, and other radical Arabs, as well as polarizing inter-Arab politics, thereby compromising Saudi Arabia's precarious neutrality and, ultimately perhaps, the prospects for an overall Arab-Israeli peace. Some of these fears, as it turned out, were not unfounded, in spite of American efforts to moderate the diplomatic momentum of Sadat's initiative and divert it into multilateral channels.

There was, in addition, one other American fear that might at first have been occasioned by Sadat: that he would deprive the United States of a desirable share of credit for mediating difficult Arab-Israeli negotiations. There is little doubt that Kissinger occasionally reasoned this way during his shuttle diplomacy and that some of his former high-level Middle East assistants now working in the Carter Administration were aware of, if not actually sympathetic to, this line of reasoning.(12) At any rate, if this concern arose, it was premature. The negotiations did prove difficult, and American mediation was in fact sought by both sides: first Egypt, then Israel.

It is no detraction from the nobility of Sadat's unique gesture to point out that it was directed as much, or perhaps more, toward the United States as it was toward Israel. Sadat himself had long expressed the opinion that the key to a peaceful settlement was held by the American government, which alone could extract the necessary concessions from Israel. A gesture of the magnitude of his visit to Jerusalem, Sadat undoubtedly believed, would delight American and American-Jewish opinion and eventually generate an American government campaign of inducements and pressures for Israel to reciprocate in kind. Sadat's account of his original plan for a great power conference in Jerusalem, along with the three-sided Cairo conference convened after the trip to Jerusalem, testify to his early insistence that the United States be intimately involved in the Egyptian-Israeli discussions. Even a cursory perusal of Cairo's government-supervised press since then provides ample evidence of the continuing and well-nigh overriding significance attached to this factor in official Egyptian eyes.

To be sure, Sadat has also taken Israeli public opinion and domestic politics into account in conducting his new diplomacy. It is possible, in this connection, that Begin's election actually created a favorable climate for an Egyptian peace overture. Sadat might well have realized that the new Israeli government, unlike its predecessor, would be susceptible to dovish rather than to hawkish pressures, not only from the opposition but even from within the ruling coalition. Certainly Sadat has played on this theme from the start. First, there was his insistence on hearing and meeting with the opposition during his visit to the Knesset. Later, he had audiences with opposition leader, Shimon Peres, and with Likkud's own pragmatic defense minister, Ezer Weizman, while maintaining personal attacks on Begin.

Even here, however, the ultimate intended audience for these maneuvers may be none other than the United States. Sadat, to judge from some of his own statements, seems to hope that political divisions inside Israel might help to drive a wedge between the United States and the existing Israeli government, encouraging the formation of a more flexible Israeli leadership from afar. To date, in spite of all the rumors and of raucous internal debate, there is no evidence that the American government has in any way actively promoted Begin's resignation or that his government is otherwise in imminent danger of demise.

The direct discussions with Egypt were not very far advanced before the Israeli government, too, solicited the good offices of the United States. To the Israelis, Sadat's initiative had been doubly welcome. It not only provided the long-awaited signs of recognition and acceptance, it also promised, at first a potential Israeli bargaining advantage in strictly bilateral negotiations, to the exclusion, that is, of both other Arab governments and outside powers. Jerusalem, in fact, had for some time been enamored of the very prospect that now so discomfited the United States: a separate peace with Egypt. Nevertheless, once Sadat had invoked American intervention in the negotiations, the Israeli government was obviously disposed to do the same. Indeed, for all his nationalist rhetoric, the notion of a mutuality of interests and a close Israeli relationship with, not to say dependence on, the West is also vintage Begin. Since by that time the issues at stake in a broader comprehensive settlement had become unavoidable, Begin journeyed to Washington to seek endorsement of his plan for Palestinian self-rule in "Judea, Samaria, and the Gaza Strip".(13)

In the event, then, the course of negotiations reflected the interaction between American preferences and those of Egypt, on the one hand, and those of Israel on the other; the result has been a bit confusing, at least to outside observers. This is partly because official secrecy still shrouds some of the details of negotiations and partly because the participants themselves have been ambivalent about the major issues. They have alternated positions on some of the major points, either out of genuine changes of heart, or for bargaining purposes, temporary tactical advantage, or domestic and Pan-Arab political considerations. Somewhere in this latter category, for example, belong Israel's shifting interpretation of resolution 242 and its stop-and-go policy on new Jewish settlements in occupied territory, as well as Sadat's occasional vitriolic denunciations of Israeli leaders.

Still, the major contours of the negotiations and of the American role in their development can be more or less plausibly reconstructed. The central question has consistently been the connection between the fate of the Sinai and that of the West Bank. Sadat himself, both in his speech to the Knesset and afterward, rejected the notion of a separate Israeli-Egyptian peace. He might, however, have been content with a concrete agreement on the recovery of Sinai alone, provided that it was accompanied by an acceptable declaration of principles on the other issues. The Israelis, on the other hand, sought to entice Sadat away from even this commitment with an offer to restore Egyptian sovereignty over the entire Sinai Peninsula, excluding the Gaza Strip. This offer was, however, conditioned upon Israeli retention of civilian settlements under Israeli military protection along the Mediterranean and Red Sea coasts of Sinai. These would be designated buffer zones under the United Nations flag. At the same time, the Israeli government made no offer of any withdrawal from either the Gaza Strip or the West Bank.

When Sadat, encouraged perhaps by American and possibly also Saudi advice, held firm, the Israeli government appeared to have hardened its bargaining position on the precise terms of a deal with Egypt. It is quite possible that an Israeli offer in principle on the Sinai had been made in advance of Sadat's arrival in Jerusalem.(14) If so, this would contribute to an explanation of several seeming mysteries: why the Israeli government conceded total Egyptian sovereignty in Sinai almost at the very start of negotiations; why the negotiations broke down when the offer was subsequently qualified; and, last but not least, why Sadat took the chance of going to Israel in the first place.

At the start of 1978, just as a new round of negotiations was getting underway, the Israeli government announced an expansion of Jewish settlement in Sinai. The announcement may have been intended for Israeli domestic consumption. Alternatively, it may have been intended as a bargaining chip in the negotiations, to be traded, perhaps, for Arab concessions on the West Bank. The effect, in any case, was understandably to antagonize Sadat and thereby contribute to the rapid breakdown of negotiations, as discussed on pages 298-9.

At much the same time, another factor entered the picture as American diplomatic intervention underwent a subtle change. American policy makers finally decided to abandon Syria and the PLO to their own devices temporarily and to concentrate instead on Jordan, whose king was showing new signs of interest in joining the negotiations. Such a move had both benefits and drawbacks for Israel, which would have preferred to hold the entire West Bank issue in abeyance. However, it appeared to serve the interests of a number of other American friends in the region, including Saudi Arabia. If successful, it would have both pried Jordan away from Syria and precluded the creation of a new and potentially radical state in such a sensitive area. In early January 1978, Carter met with King Hussein in Teheran and then with Sadat at Aswan, where the new strategy was apparently agreed upon.(15)   It soon developed, however, that the Egyptian-Israeli declaration of principles which had been envisaged would not suffice to bring Jordan into the negotiations openly. Since the prospect of an acceptable Sinai settlement had already faded, Sadat evidently decided to suspend direct talks in the expectation that more vigorous American mediation would eventually produce a forthcoming Israeli position. This, presumably, is what Sadat meant when he said, a few days before he broke off the Jerusalem negotiations, that he had "absolutely no hope" for their success, and when he urged the United States soon afterward to become a "full partner" in any further talks. By mid-1978, in a further symbolic move along these lines, Sadat ended the last institutionalized direct contact with Israel by requesting the withdrawal of the Israeli military delegation from Cairo, as noted on pages 318-9.

After this rupture, American emissaries kept the two sides in contact while attempting, in a series of diplomatic exchanges, to elicit a definite Israeli commitment-in-principle to withdraw from at least some part of the West Bank. Progress in this area during the first half of 1978 was exceedingly slow. At first, the Israeli government refused to concede that the requirement of Israeli withdrawal in United Nations Resolution 242 even applied to the West Bank at all. Later, in response to American urgings, the Cabinet agreed to discuss "the nature of relations between the parties" involved in the future of that territory, but only after a five-year transition period during which Israeli control would be maintained. Still later, the Israeli government agreed to consider the question of sovereignty for the West Bank in the current round of negotiations. Finally, in August 1978, Dayan told the Knesset that Israel would discuss "partition" or "territorial compromise" in the West Bank, and other government spokesmen conceded that the application of Israel's "right" to that territory might have to be postponed for a while.(16) This fell short, however, of a specific commitment to Israeli withdrawal.

On a practical level, the Israeli policy of authorizing or creating new Jewish settlements in occupied territory remained in effect. Some changes were evident, however. In February, 1978, United States Secretary of State Vance had termed the Sinai settlements "illegal" and contended that they "should not exist." The Israeli government, while insisting that those settlements were legitimate, reportedly promised not to establish any new ones there.(17) This did not prevent Israel from proceeding to expand existing colonies in Sinai or to authorize new ones on the West Bank. In the case of Shiloh, this was done on the pretext of an archeological expedition.(18) The actual number of Jewish settlers involved was small. Still, the issue was a constant irritant in the peace negotiations, and partly for that reason, it became deeply entangled in Israeli domestic politics. In March 1978, Weizman threatened to resign unless settlement expansion in the Sinai was halted. It was. In August, the Cabinet announced plans for five new settlements in the West Bank and then abruptly reversed itself within a matter of days.(19) There was still no indication that this was more than a temporary postponement and certainly not that Israel contemplated giving up any of the settlements already in place.

The wide gap that remains between the Israeli and the American – let alone the Egyptian – positions should not be allowed to obscure the substantial shift that has occurred in the latter. Cairo has returned to an earlier preference for a West Bank linked to Jordan, at least for a transition period. The reversion to this option was formalized in a peace plan relayed by Egypt to Israel during the summer of 1978 at the behest of the United States.(20) In July, after a meeting with Weizman in Europe, Sadat observed for the first time in public that he would be willing to countenance border "rectifications" on the West Bank.(21) Since that time, however, Sadat has been reluctant, in view of his disappointment with Israeli reactions, to negotiate with Israel except under American auspices. A tripartite foreign ministers' converence was accordingly held at Leeds Castle in England, but with no apparent result. Afterward, in response to American prodding, Sadat agreed to attend a three-way summit with Begin and Carter at Camp David in early September 1978.

Altogether, the American role in Arab-Israeli diplomacy since the Sadat initiative has lain somewhere between that of mere intermediary and that of mediator. American influence of this sort has so far helped to move Egyptian policy toward American desires for a more explictly comprehensive settlement. Israeli concessions, while slow in coming, have also been substantial, especially considering the original platform of the Likkud, i.e., Israeli withdrawal from most of the Sinai, a greater measure of civil autonomy for the Palestinians under Israeli military occupation, and even the possibility of some Israeli withdrawal from the West Bank. In private, American officials reportedly credit Israeli determination with some of the movement already exhibited by Sadat; they are also reported to believe that he has gone about as far as he can for now. Egyptian political, popular, and especially, professional military sentiment has, with some isolated exceptions, generally been patient until now. Nevertheless, Sadat has recently taken some prophylactic measures against dissent. More will probably be necessary unless he can continue to show progress from time to time, either further toward peace or further away from it. One can, therefore, expect continued American pressure on behalf of additional Israeli concessions.

So far, the means of exerting American influence over Israel have been confined almost entirely to diplomatic remonstrance and persuasion, including the threat of a breakdown or unfavorable change of direction in the negotiating process. However, the implicit threat of more concrete and coercive instruments of influence has hovered in the background. A case in point, despite repeated American disavowals, is the perennial problem of arms transfers.

The issue of American arms supplies came briefly to the force in the spring of 1977, when an Administration proposal for jet fighter sales to Egypt and Saudi Arabia, as well as to Israel, was formally announced. It is a measure of the changes in American perceptions of Egypt's intentions wrought by Sadat's trip to Jerusalem that the sale of warplanes to Egypt caused scarcely any expressions of concern in Congress. The Saudi purchase, by contrast, was the object of a fierce lobbying campaign in which the methods and motives of both opponents and proponents of the sale were as much discussed as were the merits of the issue. The argument was complicated by the presentation of all three sales in a package, which occurred in anticipation of a Congressional effort to block the Saudi deal. Some members of Congress were unhappy about what looked like an attempt to get around the Nelson Amendment of the International Security Assistance Act of 1975, as subsequently modified, which specified that Congress had the right to block major individual arms sales. The Israeli government objected to the precedent set by the package both for indirect American pressure via arms transfers and for qualitative Arab-Israeli parity in arms. In the end, as might have been expected, a compromise of sorts was found. The Carter Administration essentially had its way in Congress, but not before it had altered the package aspect a little, agreed to sell Israel more planes, and had given private assurance that Saudi Arabia would deploy its new aircraft in a primarily defensive mode. Soon afterward, Vice President Mondale also repeated his earlier assurance that the United States would not use "crucial military assistance" as a form of pressure on Israel.(22)

The precise meaning of this commitment is, of course, subject to different interpretations. However, it is plain that American policy makers have grown extremely wary of schemes to manipulate arms supplies in order to impose a solution on Israel. Recently, on a few important occasions, American delay of new arms commitments has helped to extract Israeli concessions, such as the acceptance of the Rogers cease fire in 1970, the abortive cease-fire-in-place after the first week of the October War, and the second-stage Sinai disengagement of 1975. Nevertheless, American pressure on the arms supply issue does have certain drawbacks. For one thing, it arguably risks damage to the credibility of American security commitments not only in Israel but elsewhere in the world. American pressure, for example, might undermine the credibility of American guarantees to Israel that could potentially be traded for Israeli territorial concessions. Washington must also take American domestic politics into account. Nor can one overlook the stubbornness of the Israelis themselves, for which American policy makers have by now developed a healthy respect.(23) This last concern is especially problematic in view of current doubts about the acuteness of Israeli dependency on the United States in the absence of a perceived immediate threat. On the other hand, in situations of acute Israeli dependency, American pressure could conceivably produce an Israeli threat to use the nuclear option Israel is widely believed to possess; this option is discused in Chapters 2 and 3. Finally, quite apart from the propsects of an Israeli backlash, or desperate overreaction, is the problem of third-party reaction. Too much American pressure on Israel threatens to provoke, as it has in the past, the escalation of demands by Arab nations or by the Soviet Union. For this reason alone, an imposed solution is probably eternally elusive. It is indeed a basic and time-honored premise of American policy that a regional balance-of-power in Israel's favor is a precondition for Arab willingness to make peace. This view has left room for selective and limited American restraints on arms supplies to Israel. Still, on the whole, the constraints on great power manipulation of arms deliveries for political purposes are many and varied indeed; Chapter 4 discusses this issue as it relates to American arms sales to the Middle East.

In any case, it seems fairly clear from the context that the Carter Administration's aircraft sales package was not primarily intended as a form of direct American intervention in the current phase of Egyptian-Israeli negotiations. It was, rather, symptomatic of the broader pattern of recent American involvement in the Middle East. The United States is now heavily involved, sometimes in loose coordination with some of its allies, in military sales, construction, technical assistance, training, and/or trade in the major Mid-East oil-exporter nations and friendly neighboring countries. This program today encompasses the presence of tens of thousands of American advisors and technicians under military assignment or commercial contract servicing various military equipment or facilities. Furthermore, arms sales are part of overall relationships in which oil prices, production levels, and revenues have been important concerns. Iranian and Saudi arms purchases are one way of recycling petrodollars to the United States. Other Saudi petrodollars have been expended in the form of financial assistance to neighboring regimes of uncertain political coloration; North Yemen and Somalia are two recent converts to this more conservative, pro-Western cause.

The most important and successful example of this process is Egypt itself to which the United States has contributed about one billion dollars in loans and grants each year during the past three years. The conservative oil exporters have provided an even greater amount. Such foreign aid is supposed to help Sadat survive the social problems, like the food riots of early 1977, created by Egypt's debt-ridden and dilapidated economy. It is primarily in this role that the United States has tried to cast Saudi Arabia as a participant in Arab-Israeli affairs. This role is important enough for the Carter Administration to ignore Riyadh's failure to endorse Sadat's peace policy in public and to praise its "constructive support" of Egypt instead. The expectation is that such Saudi "Riyalpolitik" will continue to exercise a discreet influence for relative Arab moderation. Eventually, perhaps, Saudi influence and Syria's own embroilment in Lebanon might bring the Syrian government back into the moderate camp. However, so far since the break with Sadat, Syria has remained very much on the sidelines of American activity in the region. Instead, it is now numbered among the favored recipients of military and diplomatic support from the Soviet Union.

SOVIET MIDDLE EAST POLICY SINCE THE SADAT INITIATIVE

Much less is known about Soviet motivations or even behavior in the foreign policy arena. Like their counterparts in the United States, however, Soviet policy makers must have been taken aback by Sadat's trip to Jerusalem, which broke all the rules by which they had contrived to reenter Arab-Israeli diplomacy at Geneva on acceptable bargaining terms. When the radical Arab governments denounced Sadat's move, the Soviet government also refused his invitation to the conference convened in Cairo in December 1977. Since then the Soviet Union seems to have remained convinced that Sadat's initiative, and with it Sadat himself and a great deal of American prestige in the region, would eventually falter and that an Egyptian successor would then turn to Moscow for support. In the meantime, the Soviet Union has done what it could to make this a self-fulfilling prophecy by extending its blessing and support to the Arab rejection front. Moscow simultaneously consolidated its physical presence elsewhere on the region's periphery, a presence that had helped drive Sadat to undertake that initiative in the first place.

The Arab rejection front is neither united nor subject to Soviet control, and Russia has had as much trouble trying to organize it as the West has had with its own so-called sphere of influence in the region. Often, indeed, even the least extreme rejectionists have been too much so for Moscow's tastes, obstructing, as they did the revival of the Geneva Conference, not only American but also Soviet diplomacy. Yet the Soviet government has continued to supply arms and diplomatic support in exchange for varying degrees of political allegiance, access to military ports and airfields, and some hard currency. All this has been done despite the rejectionists' internecine quarrels and continued economic ties with the West. In general, then, Soviet diplomatic initiatives on their behalf advanced a strategy of competition for influence with the West and secured certain concrete dividends as well. At any rate, the Soviet Union has been loathe to forfeit the friendship of the rejectionists for the sake of concerted great power diplomacy in Arab-Israeli affairs.

Of all the parties in question, the ones closest to the front line are also, not surprisingly, the least extreme. The PLO and the Syrians, in particular, have been almost as anxious to keep open the option of a negotiated settlement, and thus their bridges to the West, as to maintain reasonably good relations with the Soviet Union and with each other. The PLO remains deeply divided on the question of peace with Israel. Underlying this political division, in large measure, is a demographic one. Palestinians with family origins in pre-1967 Israel demand to return to Israel, while those from the West Bank can more easily imagine a Palestinian homeland there. Sadat's initiative, like some other Arab-Israeli diplomatic breakthroughs, only exacerbated these divisions. Since then, behind an initial facade of unity, an intense and occasionally violent internal struggle has broken out.

Toward the outside, too, the PLO's predictable concrete response to the Sadat initiative was terror. The assassination in February 1978 of Yousef Al-Sebai, a well-known Egyptian editor and confidant of Sadat, only served to increase the latter's estrangement from the organized Palestinian movement. Still more serious consequences flowed from another terrorist raid one month later which provided the immediate occasion for a large-scale Israeli invasion of southern Lebanon. The PLO's main fighting forces escaped intact. However, their base of operations was further restricted and even more exposed to the mercies of their Syrian protectors, who stayed firmly entrenched to the north. Some PLO spokesmen, including Arafat himself, have reacted to these latest reverses with renewed signs of interest in a negotiated settlement leading to a truncated Palestinian state. However, Arafat's would-be interlocutors are no longer very interested; his movement is still bitterly split; and the moderate faction which he heads is more than ever dependent on Soviet weapons, protection, and diplomatic support.

The Syrians, for their part, have also attempted to follow an independent line in the face of the Pan-Arab and great power polarization set in motion by Sadat. Assad has thus resisted identification with the position not only of Egypt but also, by refusing to renounce United Nations peacemaking resolutions, of the extreme rejectionists and even, by rejecting a return to Geneva, of the Soviet Union.(24) Militarily, the Syrians are stretched quite thin by their partial occupation of Lebanon, an occupation which has enjoyed the support of the conservative Arabs and the apparent silent acquiescence of the United States. Assad has, therefore, found it useful to maintain good communications with Washington. In view of the higher stakes of

American Mid-East peacemaking diplomacy, the associated risk of internal unrest, and his own self-conceived role as champion of the Palestinians, however, Assad has so far elected to remain aloof from the current round of Arab-Israeli discussions. The choice has certainly been facilitated by Syria's reliance on the Soviet Union as arms supplier and defender of last resort. Soviet access to Syria's Mediterranean naval bases has been part of the price for this support.

Further afield in the rejectionist camp, loosely allied with the Soviet Union, are Libya and Iraq, both of which, as major oil-exporters, also have important economic links with the West. Libya must be the strangest Soviet bedfellow of all, but the two have managed to retain a cordial arms supply and diplomatic relationship in spite of the ideological abyss that separates them and of Qaddafi's penchant for international adventurism. The Soviet Union has also been the primary source of arms and diplomatic backing for Iraq, as well as the exclusive foreign beneficiary of the Iraqi military port at Umm Qasr on the Persian Gulf. This has remained the case notwithstanding numerous differences on internal and external matters, including Baghdad's intermittent suppression of local Communists, arms purchases from France, and greatly improved relations with Iran. Iraq also constantly feuds with other regional clients of the Soviet Union, like Syria, the moderate PLO factions, and Ethiopia, where Iraq has until recently supported the secessionist guerrilla struggle of the Eritreans.

The most active recent Soviet intervention in the region has been on the periphery of those Gulf oil-producing states most important to the West. Bordering Saudi Arabia is Aden, which, together with Ethiopia, controls access to the Red Sea through which oil tankers pass on their way to Israel, Jordan, and the Suez Canal. The Soviet Union has been transporting not only arms into this area but military advisors and Cuban combat forces as well. In July 1978, an attempted opening to the West in Aden ended in a pro-Soviet coup. Not long before, a similar sequence of events had taken place in Afghanistan, which is of special concern to neighboring Iran. Finally, the Soviet Union has also managed, on the whole, to improve official relations with the governments of Turkey and Iran, even though those two governments have blamed Marxist elements for the political violence that has plagued their countries in the past year.

Thus, the general pattern of recent Soviet initiatives in the Middle East seems to be one of seeking to contain the influence of the West and to threaten its oil supplies. For the time being, Soviet policy makers are probably reluctant to jeopardize their existing footholds in the region in the interests of an understanding with the United States. Even if overall Soviet-American relations improved to the point where an arrangement of this sort were conceivable, it is far from certain whether Soviet influence with its regional clients would suffice to bring them along. The immediate outlook, then, is for a continuation of the broad pattern of great power diplomatic, economic, and indirect military intervention in the Middle East that has crystallized over the preceding year. Active American involvement in mediating between Egypt and Israel, with the tacit endorsement of Saudi Arabia and Iran, is likely to be juxtaposed against Soviet support for the radical and rejectionist governments on their periphery.

CONCLUSION

What of the future? If recent events in the Middle East have taught us anything, it is that politics there are full of surprises and that the combination of internal upheaval and external intervention produces unexpected results. This being the case, it is probably wise to conclude without the customary venture into prediction and prescription. Nevertheless, the very complexity of the subject suggests one general piece of advice for those who would presume to undertake those tasks. The realities of international politics in the Middle East cannot be captured in simple dichotomies. This holds true for the global as well as for the regional powers. For Israel, the choice is not, as it has often been posed, simply one of territory or peace; rather, the question is which territory, under what conditions, for what kind of a settlement. Similarly, for Egypt, the real choice is not between a separate and comprehensive peace, or as it has sometimes been put, between Egyptian as opposed to Arab natonalism; here too it is a question of nuance and degree. It is, indeed, precisely because the alternatives are so ambiguous that both sides are trying so hard to keep their options open. Thus, dramatic events like Begin's election or Sadat's initiative notwithstanding, recent changes among the local powers do not lend themselves to analysis in absolutist categories.

The same holds true, in the last analysis, for the new pattern of great power intervention in the Middle East, connected with the recent changes within the region, which has been the theme of this discussion. The argument presented here has been that events have moved the center of gravity of Soviet intervention – not just with diplomacy but with men, money, and materiel – toward the fringes of the region, leaving the United States in the role of mediator of the Egyptian-Israeli dispute. However, the question is not then whether the American government can or cannot impose a solution on its friends; in reality, much more subtle kinds of influence are involved. More active American intervention on behalf of a settlement, for example, could take the form not of negative but of positive sanctions, such as an offer to assume greater formal or even physical responsibility for security arrangements in the area. The story of Sadat's initiative to date shows that Egypt and Israel actually joined forces, at first, to divert the course of American diplomacy in the Middle East, only to fall back on it separately in the end. In the Soviet case, too, it has been shown that influence between a great power and a regional actor is a mutual process in which each can affect but not necessarily control the other. This is as true of Soviet relations with the rejectionists today as it was of Soviet-Egyptian relations in the past.

Moreover, a similar caveat applies to the future prospects of the overall pattern of Soviet and American intervention that has been discerned in relation to the Middle East. The influence of the two superpowers is distributed, not in exclusive spheres, but in rather shadowy and overlapping zones whose exact boundaries are in constant flux. There can be little doubt of the significance of the new pattern of great power intervention in the region. Of its permanence, however, there can be no certainty, if only because regional domestic politics or indigenous initiatives may well again confound the plans of outside powers.

(The Camp David Summit meeting was being held as the book was sent to the publisher. A short Epilogue on the Summit and subsequent events appears on page 335-40.)

NOTES AND REFERENCES

(1) On the reasoning behind this change, see especially William B. Quandt, "Conclusion," Decade of Decisions (Los Angeles: University of California Press, 1977).

(2) See, for example, statements by Secretary of State Vance as reported in New York Times (January 12 and February 11, 15, 17, 1977).

(3) See, for example, analyses by Uri Ra'anan, Shlomo Avineri, and the Louis Harris polling organization as reported in New York Times (June 4, August 15, and September 6, 1977). Cf. an Israeli preelection poll reported in New York Times (February 21, 1977).

(4) Excerpt of text in Armed Forces Journal (October 1977): 32.

(5) Ibid. Begin statements in Jerusalem Post (May 17, 1977). (Interview and television debate)

(6) As reported in New York Times (September 3, 1977).

(7) See New York Times (February 8, 10, 16, and May 9-13, 1977).

(8) This reading is implicit in the account given by Quandt (note 1 supra) of Kissinger's shuttle diplomacy at that time.

(9) See, for example, the report in Le Monde (April 4, 1977).

(10) This impression was confirmed in discussions held with United States State Department Middle East officers during Sadat's 1977 visit to America.

(11) Among Sadat's original ideas were a preparatory conference with the PLO, a PLO-Jordanian delegation, or a plan to have Palestinian-American professors represent the PLO at Geneva. See Sadat statements as reported in New York Times (March 4 and November 4, 1977); cf. also New York Times (December 12, 1977). For reports of earlier,

private Egyptian-Israeli contacts via Rumania, see New York Times (August 26, and November 27, 1977). Other undocumented but generally convincing reports cite Morocco as the probable locus of advance arrangements for Sadat's trip. See, e.g., Jeune Afrique no. 904 (March 3, 1978); Walter Laqueur, "Is Peace Still Possible in the Middle East," Commentary (July 1978); and Time (August 7, 1978).

(12) On these points, see Quandt's account of Kissinger's reaction to the direct negotiations between Egyptian General Gamasy and Israeli General Yariv immediately after the October War (note 1 supra).

(13) Text in New York Times (December 29, 1977).

(14) On this point see especially Rabin interview in Ha'aretz (June 30, 1978).

(15) See on the Teheran discussions generally, Kayban International (January 3, 1978).

(16) Jerusalem Post Weekly (April 18, and July 25, 1978).

(17) Text of Israeli Cabinet statement in New York Times (February 13, 1978); see also Washington Post (February 11, 14, 21, 27; March 1, and April 20, 1978); and especially Jerusalem Post Weekly (February 26, 1978).

(18) Washington Post (February 6, 1978).

(19) Ha'aretz (August 14-17, 1978).

(20) Text in New York Times (July 6, 1978).

(21) Al-Ahram (July 15, 1978).

(22) Text of Mondale's first assurance in Department of State Bulletin, July 11, 1977, p. 45.

(23) Author's interviews with American officials, Washington, D.C., February and April 1977 and February 1978.

(24) See, for example, statements by Assad as reported in New York Times (November 23, 26, 1977).

IV
Epilogue

16 Epilogue
Milton Leitenberg
Gabriel Sheffer

The two final papers in the book were written before the American-Egyptian-Israeli Camp David Summit of September 1978 was held. The pace of the political events related to the subject matter of the book made the inclusion of some material on the outcome of the summit negotiations desirable.

The initial American reaction to Sadat's visit to Jerusalem had been one of caution mingled with unease. In the months preceding it, the United States Administration had become increasingly committed to a comprehensive solution, to a Geneva-like approach. At one stage, it even went quite far in searching for a Soviet-American joint policy on the Middle East situation. Sadat's initiative forced the United States Administration to change all that. As seen by American officials, another problem was that hopes engendered by the visit were so high that it seemed a failure would lead to a much worse situation compared with the one prevailing before Sadat's visit. However, the Administration soon realized that it must give its support to the new initiative. A failure would be intolerable, and besides, it was the first occasion on which an Arab leader, and one from the most important Arab country, was ready to alter completely the public Arab position towards Israel. Indeed, after a while, it became clear that the United States was an indispensable factor in the new initiative. In the weeks and months following Sadat's Jerusalem visit when the initiative did seem to be on the verge of collapse – precisely the situation that the United States Administration feared might develop – Washington had to intervene and try to save the negotiations. The Cairo-Jerusalem negotiations ended all too rapidly, and some measure of the peace process is to be found in the rapidity of that collapse, as well as in the difficulties which have followed the subsequent Camp David Summit. Four months after Sadat's visit to Jerusalem, Israeli firepower created a reported 300,000 refugees in South Lebanon in seven days. Though this operation did not interfere with Israeli-Egyptian relations, it certainly was indicative in other ways of the general Middle East situation. The Israeli action was apparently not something that the United States government had any ability to temper, despite the use of American military supplies in the operation. However, the Salzburg and Leeds negotiations followed, and these led to Camp David. In late November 1978, when the negotiations stalled again some weeks after Camp David, a similar situation developed. Efforts by the United States government were necessary to prevent an impasse.

The Camp David negotiations and agreements demonstrated that the role of the United States is central in the move to new levels of stability in the Middle East. Immediately after the visit to Jerusalem, there had been some talk in both Cairo and in Jerusalem about diminishing the role of both superpowers in the Middle East. It was suggested that Egypt and Israel by themselves should try, and were capable of, reaching an accord by direct negotiations and that they should turn the Middle East into a closed system, in the sense that the regional powers would control events in the region. Events proved that this was a mistaken assumption. Both Egypt and Israel needed heavy American involvement for many reasons. Continued American involvement in the post-Camp David-Washington negotiations on an Israeli-Egyptian peace treaty was yet a further demonstration of that. Moreover, it appears that Jordan's King Hussein will join negotiations only if and when he gets a firm American commitment both about the American role in future negotiations and about the nature of the American position in these negotiations on the future of the West Bank. In sum, as far as the great powers are concerned, the Camp David accords reinforced the role of the United States as sponsor of Egyptian-Israeli negotiations, along with the role of the Soviet Union as sponsor of the Arab rejection front opposed to Sadat's diplomacy. The Soviet Union was quick to join the Arab rejectionists in denouncing Egypt's unilateral action and to pledge additional concrete assistance for them on the occasion of Syrian President Assad's most recent visit to Moscow. However, the Camp David agreements underlined the diminishing power of the Soviet Union in the Middle East.

In retrospect, the past twenty years have seen a surprising turnabout in the positions of influence of the United States and the Soviet Union with the Middle Eastern nations, excluding Israel. In 1955, the West began organizing a formal defense organization of the northern tier of the Middle East. In reaction, and due to the convergence of interests of the Soviet Union and Egypt, the former jumped into the heart of the Middle East. Thus, a situation was created whereby the West was building its position in the outer ring of the Middle East and the Soviet Union began its push into the heart of the region. Now, twenty-odd years later, the heart of the Middle East seems to be moving back in the direction of the West. The Soviet Union, while still having strong positions of influence in Syria, is pursuing its interests and applying much influence on Iraq and the fringes of the Middle East: Yemen, the Horn of Africa, Afghanistan, Libya, and Algeria.

After the Salzburg and Leeds meetings, the Israeli government was left with several basic questions. Would it rule out further settlement and annexation of territory in the West Bank in return for a full peace with Egypt? Would it pursue negotiations of new borders with Jordan and West Bank Palestinians? What would be its definition of continuing security requirements beyond those borders? President Sadat had claimed that he would bring Jordan and the Palestinians to the negotiating table if that agenda were accepted by the Israeli governments. Both Jordan and others had found Begin's proposals on the West Bank inadequate. Under these, Israeli purchase and settlement of land in the West Bank could have continued. The Israeli government had to decide if it would continue to expand into the West Bank or if it would trade the occupied territory for security through negotiations. In the new political context after Sadat's visit to Jerusalem, if Israel would not stop the territorial expansion in the West Bank, it would have to reassess how Israeli security was defined.

The Camp David Summit produced a very strong feeling of movement, importance, and possibility. Israel and at least one of its Arab opponents had been negotiating directly and publicly on at least some of the major issues for a year. Major advances were made at the summit, and both sides were seen to have made compromises. At the same time, many basic elements of the Middle East conflict were left open: the West Bank, the ultimate boundaries of Israel, the nature of the autonomous Palestinian entity, the fate of Jerusalem, and the security arrangements for Israel. At the time of writing, the fraction that was dealt with cannot be said to have been settled; five months after Camp David, the negotiations face a virtual deadlock. Nevertheless, assuming that the talks would eventually succeed, the United States would be faced with major new obligations.

The Camp David negotiations produced two documents, signed by President Carter, President Sadat, and Prime Minister Begin. The first was a framework for an Egyptian-Israeli peace treaty which was to have been signed by the two countries within three months. All of the Sinai is returned to Egypt, in exchange for full Egyptian-Israeli peace. Both sides of this equation are to be implemented in stages. Egypt is to regain sovereignty throughout the Sinai. Israel abandons any claims to the settlements and air bases constructed in the Sinai since 1967. Israel is entitled to ask for security zones, and Egypt is limited to civilian use of the former Israeli military airfields in the Sinai. Additional points include partial demilitarization of the entire peninsula and stationing of United Nations forces in especially sensitive areas; and guarantees of free passage for Israeli shipping through the Suez Canal and the Straits of Tiran, and for Egypt and Jordan across a new Israeli highway above Eilat. Three to nine months after the treaty is signed, Israel must pull back its forces from a substantial portion of the Sinai. Thereafter, diplomatic relations are to be established. Final Israeli withdrawal from the Sinai is to take place two to three years after the treaty. The details of these arrangements were to be negotiated in the three months following the summit meeting.

The second agreement outlined a broad set of general principles, which would provide a framework for peace among Israel and all its neighbors, and for "the resolution of the Palestinian problem in all its aspects." Unfortunately, this document left the resolution of the most important issues to a prolonged period of future negotiations. These issues were the final political status of the present Israeli occupied West Bank of the Jordan River and the Gaza Strip; who would eventually hold sovereign authority over the area; whether Israeli troops would withdraw; questions of Palestinian refugee immigration and Israeli settlements in these territories; and the future status of Jerusalem. These questions were relegated to negotiations among Israel, Egypt, Jordan, and a prospective West Bank-Gaza elected, self-governing authority. However, some specific improvements over Begin's original self-rule proposals of December 1977 — from the Arab point of view — are evident in the Camp David text. Among these are the omission of certain Israeli claims, i.e., to sovereignity over these territories, or to an exclusive security role in them; acceptance of certain principles, e.g., "the legitimate rights of the Palestinian people;" and commitment to certain concrete steps, such as partial withdrawal and redeployment of Israeli troops and final agreement on the nature of the full autonomy to be accorded the West Bank and Gaza within five years. Israel would retain specific military bases, but its military government would come to an end. Israel was not to establish new settlements in the occupied areas during the five-year negotiating period. Also new and notable was the explicit provision for an Egyptian role in helping to establish a new, official spokesman for the Palestinians.

But it was in regard to this second agreement that problems developed within a day or two of the end of the summit meeting. The flexibility, or the ambiguities, of the initial agreements which enabled them to be signed in the first place, and which some even found praiseworthy, were   precisely what enabled each side to   present unilateral interpretations which rapidly moved the two parties apart. Prime Minister Begin immediately sought to disclaim any linkage between the two agreements. The Israeli government moved to expand its existing settlements on the West Bank and claimed to be surprised and irritated when everyone else found that move quite puzzling. For Israel, the major strategic implication of the agreements was in the first one, the prospective peace treaty with Egypt. The likelihood of war against Israel declined considerably. Admittedly, peace agreements can be revoked, but their abrogation requires much more effort and energy on the part of decision makers than going to war when they do not exist in the first place.

This, of course, was precisely what the other Arab parties who opposed the summit feared. It removed the Arab military option. However, if a peace treaty with Egypt should be calculated to ease pressure on Israel, it should also be calculated to alter Israel's own estimate of the risks it can then afford to take in coming to terms on the West Bank. President Sadat stated that Egypt would not sign a treaty that did not clearly spell out future negotiations dealing with the fate of Palestinians on the Israel-occupied West Bank of the Jordan River. The Egyptian President broadened the remark by stating that a comprehensive Middle East settlement "can never be agreed upon if the legal position of the Palestinians is ignored." None of this was settled, and in October and November 1978 the state of the negotiations seesawed daily for weeks. In December and January, and into the new year, the negotiations had lapsed into another – hopefully temporary-stalemate. As the months after the summit passed, it became more evident that Israel had in fact hoped to obtain a de facto separate peace with Egypt. The Begin government was no more prepared than previous Israeli governments to relinquish the West Bank, and certainly not to consider the establishment of Palestinian autonomy, despite the new context of the peace negotiations. During the negotiating period, the Israeli government became considerably disturbed on any occasion in which it interpreted United States suggestions or actions as seeking a comprehensive settlement, which would necessarily include those two issues. The Camp David negotiations had not mentioned Syria and the Golan, but at some time there would have to be an accommodation between Israel and Syria concerning this area as well.

Several aspects of the summit and postsummit negotiations directly concerned the themes of this book. Egypt proposed that both Israel and Egypt renounce nuclear weapons and also accept limits on conventional arms as part of their projected peace treaty. The proposal was rejected by Israel on the grounds that even after a peace treaty with Egypt had been signed, Israel would face continuing military threats from Syria, Iraq, and other Arab countries and would need to retain the strongest possible military force. Both sides sought additional arms. Israel already had a $10.5 billion, ten-year arms package on file with the United States. In addition, both Israel and Egypt had submitted long "wish-lists" of American weaponry to the Carter Administration before the summit meeting was held. Secretary of Defense Brown visited Cairo and Jerusalem in February 1979 to review these requests.

Both Egypt and Israel were also expecting large amounts of American economic aid, particularly Israel. Israel now receives a $1.8 billion American aid package annually. Prime Minister Begin indicated that Israel would need a special loan of $3.3 billion to finance the military expenses involved in withdrawing from the Sinai. The United States had also formally agreed to consider aiding Israel to build two new air bases in the Israeli Negev to replace the two it would give up in the Sinai. Under the present agreement, Israel would not leave the two bases until the new ones were operational. Cost estimates for constructing the two new bases range around $1 billion. However, Administration requests for these sums would have to be approved by Congress. President Sadat has also informed the United States that Egypt's present economic aid of $1 billion should be doubled or tripled. The oilfields in the Sinai have also been an issue. These were developed by Israel during its occupation of the Sinai. Israel would like to maintain control of them as long as possible and to obtain their oil at concessionary rates from Egypt afterward. Egypt does not agree to that and, in addition, seeks payment for the oil that Israel has extracted from these fields in the past years. These would seem to be minor issues but Israel's Foreign Minister Dayan stated that the two questions of American aid for rebuilding the airfields and the transfer of control of the Sinai oilfields had to be settled in some way before Israel agreed to the peace treaty with Egypt. It is difficult to know which of these many moves and claims are negotiating tactics aimed at squeezing every possible additional advantage out of one or the other of the parties concerned and which are essential requirements.

Finally, it has been very difficult to determine if anything that could be categorized as explicit American pressure took place during this entire 1977-78 period or to find evidence for it. One might argue that in the fact of a failure of the negotiations, neither Israel nor Egypt could expect additional United States aid and would find it increasingly difficult to purchase or obtain credits for arms. That may be so, but that is far from direct pressure. Though Foreign Minister Dayan complained of strong United States pressure in 1977, there is no indication that American officials suggested withdrawing any aid or threatened any change in its positions, as had taken place in 1975. When disagreements developed between Prime Minister Begin and the United States Administration over Israel's commitments to refrain from establishing any new settlements on the West Bank, a small incident took place involving the holding back from public release of Secretary of Defense Brown's letter to his Israeli counterpart concerning the proposed American collaboration with Israel in building the two new air bases in the Negev. The United States stated that Israel had committed itself not to set up any new settlements for five years; Prime Minister Begin suddenly said that the commitment was perhaps only for three months. In two days, President Carter ordered the letter on the bases released, although the difference of interpretation remained. The Israeli government certainly took United States Assistant Secretary of State Saunders' visit to the Middle East in late October, in which he met with Jordan's King Hussein and West Bank Palestinian leaders, as pressure. The Israeli government's reaction was to announce plans to further increase the number of Israeli settlements on the West Bank. Nevertheless, in none of these cases is there any evidence that the government of Israel was confronted by the United States Administration with the possible loss of United States support if Israel carried out or failed to carry out a particular policy.

Suggestions for United States forces on the West Bank have always been opposed by the Israeli government, but the United States will be more rather than less involved in the future, whether or not it exerts discernible pressure. It is possible that American surveillance facilities, similar to those presently in the Sinai, may still be part of subsequent Israeli-Arab accommodation in various parts of present Israeli-occupied territory.   But peace has not come to the Middle East yet.   The American and Soviet naval presence in the Mediterranean was active in 1970, 1973, and most recently, in the Lebanese crisis. Until there is peace, further American and Soviet intervention in the area is to be expected, and it may continue even if peace does come.

Index

About the Editors and Contributors

STEVEN J. BAKER is an Assistant Professor in the Government Department, University of Texas at Austin, where he is also Director of International Studies. He has held research appointments in the Peace Studies Program at Cornell University and in Harvard University's Program for Science and International Affairs.

ABRAHAM S. BECKER is a Senior Economist at the Rand Corporation. An honors graduate of Harvard in History and Literature, he received the Certificate of the Russian Institute and an M.A. and Ph.D. in Economics from Columbia. In addition to numerous works on the Soviet Union and its economy, Dr. Becker has also written extensively on Soviet involvement in the Middle East and on Soviet-American relations in that region. A consultant to several agencies of the United States government, he has also served as the American member on several United Nations disarmament expert groups.

ANNE HESSING CAHN has been Chief of the Social Impact Staff of the United States Arms Control and Disarmament Agency since 1977. She graduated from the University of California at Berkeley with a bachelor's degree in 1951 and received her Ph.D. in political science from Massachusetts Institute of Technology in 1971. Prior to joining the Administration, Dr. Cahn was affiliated with the Center for International Studies at Massachusetts Institute of Technology and the Program for Science and International Affairs at Harvard University. She directed the 1973 summer study on "New Directions in Arms Control." Her most recent publication is Controlling Future Arms Trade, and she has published widely on arms control. She also served as a consultant to the Department of Defense and the United States Senate Committee on the Budget.

YAIR EVRON is a Senior Lecturer in the Department of Political Science and Fellow of the Center for Strategic Studies at Tel Aviv University. In 1978, he was a Visiting Professor in the department of government at Cornell University. He has taught International Relations and Middle East International Politics at the London School of

Economics, Sussex University and the Hebrew University of Jerusalem. He has been a fellow of the Program for Science and International Affairs, Harvard University, and a Fellow of the Center for Arms Control and International Security at the University of Southern California. He is the author of The Middle East: Nations, Superpowers and War and the editor of International Violence: Terrorism, Surprise and Control.

JAMES FOSTER has been a member of The Rand Corporation's Social Science Department since 1973 and is currently the Program Director of Rand's Strategic Assessment Program. That program is concerned with the range of political, technical, and methodological issues related to assessments of force posture requirements and capabilities and assessment of arms control opportunities. His publications include assessments of conventional arms control opportunities, implications of alternative arms transfer policies, assessments of the strategic balance, and policymaking behavior in crisis and war. He received his B.A. degree in political science from Stanford University in 1965, did graduate work toward an M.A. at the School for Advanced International Studies at the Johns Hopkins University, and completed his Ph.D. in political science at the Massachusetts Institute of Technology in 1975.

FRED GOTTHEIL is currently a Professor in the department of economics at the University of Illinois. Dr. Gottheil is the author of many scholarly works on the Middle East. He has been a consultant to both Congress and the Administration on Middle Eastern issues. He is currently working on a book on nineteenth century Arab-peasant economy in Palestine.

ROBERT E. HARKAVY is an Associate Professor of political science at The Pennsylvania State University. He previously has taught at Kalamazoo College, has served with the United States Atomic Energy Commission and the United States Arms Control and Disarmament Agency, and was recently a research fellow at the Cornell University Peace Studies Program. He has authored works on arms transfers, the Israeli nuclear program, pariah states, and preemption, and is currently engaged in research on the major powers' competition for overseas strategic access.

PAUL JABBER is an Assistant Professor in the Department of political science, University of California at Los Angeles. He is the author of Israel and Nuclear Weapons, The Politics of Palestinian Nationalism with W.B. Quandt and A.M. Lesch, and other studies on Middle East security issues.

MARY KALDOR is a Fellow of the Science Policy Research Unit at Sussex University. She formerly worked for the Stockholm International Peace Research Institute where she was principal coauthor of The Arms Trade with the Third World. Currently, she is working on the role of arms industries in western economies.

WALID KHALIDI, who was born in Jerusalem, Palestine, is Professor of political studies at the American University of Beirut, Lebanon. He is currently a Research fellow at the Harvard Center for International Affairs, which is publishing his forthcoming book, Conflict and Violence in Lebanon: Confrontation in the Middle East. He is the editor of From Haven to Conquest and coeditor of The Palestine Problem and the Arab-Israeli Conflict: An Annotated Bibliography.

MILTON LEITENBERG has been a Research Associate with the Cornell University Center for International Studies, Peace Studies Program, since July 1974. Prior to that time he spent 1972-74 at the Swedish Institute of International Affairs in Stockholm, and 1968-72 at the Stockholm International Peace Research Institute (SIPRI). He has authored some seventy papers and monographs across the entire area of arms control and strategic studies since 1967, many of which have appeared in the Yearbooks and other volumes of SIPRI.

ROGER F. PAJAK, Senior Foreign Affairs Adviser with the United States Arms Control and Disarmament Agency, serves as the Agency's specialist on Soviet and Middle East affairs, the Arab-Israeli military situation, and international arms transfer issues. He spent two years, 1961-63, in the United States Army as a Military Intelligence Officer and has been with the United States Government as a Soviet Foreign Affairs Specialist since then. Besides speaking overseas on behalf of the International Communication Agency, Dr. Pajak has lectured widely in the United States and has contributed studies on Soviet Middle East policy and the international arms trade to numerous publications. His monograph, Soviet Arms Aid in the Middle East, was published by the Georgetown Center for Strategic and International studies in 1976.

MATTITYAHU PELED, born in Israel in 1923, is a Professor of Arabic literature at the University of Tel Aviv and Chairman of their Department of Arabic Studies. He received his Ph.D. at the University of Southern California in 1971, after retiring from twenty-two years of military service in Israel. He is a Major General in the reserve forces of the Israel defense forces, and writes regularly on questions of policy and military strategy.

DON PERETZ is Professor of political science at the State University of New York at Binghamton. A 1945 graduate of the University of Minnesota, he received his Ph.D. from Columbia University in 1955. He has been awarded a Fulbright Scholarship to Haifa University in Israel for 1979. His most recent publication is Government and Politics of Israel. He has written widely on topics pertaining to the Middle East, including Israel and the Palestine Arabs, The Middle East Today (3rd Edition), and Middle East Reader (2nd Edition).

DAVID POLLOCK is currently an Assistant Professor of political science at George Washington University, specializing in the domestic and international politics of the Middle East. In 1977, after having completed his undergraduate and graduate training in Middle Eastern studies and political science at Harvard University, he joined the Peace Studies Program at Cornell University as a Postdoctoral Research Associate. He speaks both Arabic and Hebrew and has lectured widely on Middle Eastern topics. He has also been awarded fellowships by the Institute for the Study of World Politics and the Center for Science and International Affairs, Harvard University, to pursue his research in this area.

GEORGE H. QUESTER is a Professor of Government at Cornell

University and has written extensively on problems of military strategy and arms control. He is the author of <u>The Politics of Nuclear Proliferation</u> and <u>Offense and Defense in the International System</u>.

GABRIEL SHEFFER obtained his Ph.D. from Oxford University in England. He teaches political science at the Hebrew University of Jerusalem. He has been head of the M.A. Program in Public Administration and Policy at the Hebrew University and a Visiting Professor at Cornell University. He has edited <u>Dynamics of a Conflict: A Reexamination of the Arab Israeli Conflict</u> and coauthored <u>Planning and Politics in Israel</u>. He has published a number of articles on the Palestine problem, the Middle Eastern system, and public policy.

Pergamon Policy Studies